Understanding and Teaching
Native American History

The Harvey Goldberg Series
for Understanding and Teaching History

The Harvey Goldberg Series for Understanding and Teaching History gives college and secondary history instructors a deeper understanding of the past as well as the tools to help them teach it creatively and effectively. Named for Harvey Goldberg, a professor renowned for his history teaching at Oberlin College, Ohio State University, and the University of Wisconsin from the 1960s to the 1980s, the series reflects Goldberg's commitment to helping students think critically about the past with the goal of creating a better future. For more information, please visit www.GoldbergSeries.org.

Series Editors

John Day Tully is a professor of history at Central Connecticut State University and was the founding director of the Harvey Goldberg Center for Excellence in Teaching at Ohio State University. He has coordinated many Teaching American History grants and has received the Connecticut State University System's Board of Trustees Teaching Award.

Matthew Masur is a professor of history at Saint Anselm College, where he has served as codirector of the Father Guerin Center for Teaching Excellence. He has also been a member of the Teaching Committee of the Society for Historians of American Foreign Relations.

Brad Austin is a professor of history at Salem State University. He has served as chair of the American Historical Association's Teaching Prize Committee and has worked with hundreds of secondary school teachers as the academic coordinator of many Teaching American History grants.

Advisory Board

Leslie Alexander Associate Professor of History, University of Oregon
Kevin Boyle William Smith Mason Professor of American History, Northwestern University
Ross Dunn Professor Emeritus, San Diego State University
Leon Fink UIC Distinguished Professor of History, University of Illinois at Chicago
Kimberly Ibach Principal, Fort Washakie High School, Wyoming
Alfred W. McCoy J.R.W. Smail Professor of History, Director, Harvey Goldberg Center for the Study of Contemporary History, University of Wisconsin–Madison
David J. Staley Associate Professor of History, Director, Center for the Humanities in Practice, Ohio State University
Maggie Tran Chair of Social Studies, McLean High School, Virginia
Sam Wineburg Margaret Jacks Professor of Education and (by courtesy) of History, Director, Stanford History Education Group, Stanford University

Understanding and Teaching Native American History

Edited by

KRISTOFER RAY AND
BRADY DESANTI

The University of Wisconsin Press

Publication of this book has been made possible, in part, through support from the Anonymous Fund of the College of Letters and Science at the University of Wisconsin–Madison.

The University of Wisconsin Press
728 State Street, Suite 443
Madison, Wisconsin 53706
uwpress.wisc.edu

Gray's Inn House, 127 Clerkenwell Road
London EC1R 5DB, United Kingdom
eurospanbookstore.com

Printed in the United States of America
This book may be available in a digital edition.

Library of Congress Cataloging-in-Publication Data

Names: Ray, Kristofer, editor. | DeSanti, Brady J., editor.
Title: Understanding and teaching Native American history / edited by Kristofer Ray and Brady DeSanti.
Other titles: Harvey Goldberg series for understanding and teaching history.
Description: Madison, Wisconsin : The University of Wisconsin Press, [2022] | Series: The Harvey Goldberg series for understanding and teaching history | Includes bibliographical references and index.
Identifiers: LCCN 2021055211 | ISBN 9780299338503 (hardcover)
Subjects: LCSH: Indians of North America—History—Study and teaching.
Classification: LCC E76.6 .U53 2022 | DDC 970.004/97—dc23/eng/20211129
LC record available at https://lccn.loc.gov/2021055211

Contents

Acknowledgments   IX

Introduction   3
  KRISTOFER RAY AND BRADY DESANTI

Part One: Essential Topics in
         Native American History

Before Columbus: Native American History, Archaeology,
  and Resources   11
  MAUREEN MEYERS

The "Virgin" Soil Thesis Cover-Up: Teaching Indigenous
  Demographic Collapse   29
  TAI S. EDWARDS

Understanding and Teaching Native American Slavery:
  From First Slaves to Early Abolitionists in Four Myths   44
  DENISE I. BOSSY

Teaching the Indian Wars   60
  MARK VAN DE LOGT

Teaching the Broad and Relevant History of American
  Indian Removal   78
  JOHN P. BOWES

Teaching the History of Allotment   93
  ROSE STREMLAU

Contents

Storied Lands; Storied Peoples: Teaching the History of
Federal Indian Law through Native American Literature   112
N. BRUCE DUTHU

Nation to Nation: Understanding Treaties and Sovereignty   129
MARGARET HUETTL

Teaching Indigenous Environmental Histories   145
PAUL KELTON AND JAMES D. RICE

Teaching and Understanding Genocide in Native America   160
GRAY H. WHALEY

**Part Two: Reflections on Identity and
Cultural Appropriation**

An Appropriate Past: Seminole Indians, Osceola, and
Florida State University   171
ANDREW K. FRANK

Looking Past the Racial Classification System: Teaching
Southeastern Native Survival Using the Peoplehood Model   185
MARVIN M. RICHARDSON

Teaching Native American Religions and Philosophies in the
Classroom   198
BRADY DESANTI

Sustenance as Culture and Tradition: Teaching about Indigenous
Foodways of North America   214
DEVON A. MIHESUAH

Native American Art 101   228
NANCY MARIE MITHLO

Land Acknowledgments in Higher Education: Moving beyond
the Empty Gesture   247
JOSHUA THUNDER LITTLE AND MIYE NADYA TOM

Contents

Part Three: Reflections on Teaching Native American History

How I Learned to Teach Indian History: A Memoir   261
    THEDA PERDUE

Teaching American Indian History Using the Medicine Way   274
    DONALD L. FIXICO

Transnational History and Deep Time: Reflections on Teaching
    Indigenous History from Australia   284
    ANN MCGRATH

Being There: Experiential Learning by Living Native
    American History   298
    BERNARD C. PERLEY

čʷèˑʔn neyękwaʔnawèˑrih: Reflections on Teaching Indigenous
    History from a Native Student   309
    TAYLOR HUMMEL

    Contributors   321
    Index   327

Acknowledgments

This project can be viewed as a kind of time capsule of the many changes that have occurred in my life the past few years. I began this undertaking with some amount of anxiety, as I never thought I would enjoy a career in academia, let alone experience the great fortune of working on a project of this scope. It has been an absolute honor working with the authors included in this volume. Their dedication, professionalism, and patience cannot be overstated. I am also grateful to my coeditor and brother-in-arms, Kris, for his steady hand, dedication, and camaraderie. Together, we persevered through the storms life sometimes threw at us to achieve a work we are both supremely proud of. Along the way, I was lucky to come to know Kris and his family as relatives.

In the introduction to his excellent volume of short stories, *Worlds Enough & Time: Five Tales of Speculative Fiction*, Dan Simmons noted that "time is generous to things but brutal as hell to us human beings. Perhaps we have worlds enough in our three-score-and-ten, but time denies us room to celebrate those worlds; time is the only gift that takes away everything and everyone we love if we get enough of it." Time can indeed be brutal, but putting together a project of this size reminded me as well of time's fleetingness. I am grateful that upon the completion of this volume I still have time enough to celebrate with my friends and loved ones. This book is dedicated specifically to my parents, Tony and Mary DeSanti, and my brothers, Tony and Joe. My parents raised me right and supported me throughout my journey to this point in my life. Their unwavering love has been an anchor that has helped me on my life's journey. I want to also thank my Anishinaabe (Ojibwe) biological mother, Mary, for the gift of life, my biological siblings, and many relatives on that side of my lineage who have been kind, generous, and welcoming toward me for many years. *Miigwech* to you all.

Brady DeSanti, Omaha, Nebraska

Acknowledgments

This book took far too long to complete, and that's entirely my fault. I sincerely thank the authors for their patience and confidence over the last few years. Thanks also to Brad Austin for offering me the project in the first place and for shepherding it to conclusion. Particular thanks to Robbie Ethridge for serving as a sounding board and for helping me through some very rough patches, and to Paul Kelton for introducing me to Brady and for going above and beyond the call of duty to help with this volume. You deserve a medal, Paul. Most importantly, thanks to Brady for being there when I needed it and for not allowing me to give up. I really do appreciate it and am proud that he's willing to call me a friend.

Kristofer Ray, Hampstead, North Carolina

*Understanding and Teaching
Native American History*

Introduction

KRISTOFER RAY AND BRADY DESANTI

Indigenous people are crucial to American history.

This sentence states the obvious, but it is nevertheless the case that Indigenous Americans are largely missing from the narrative. Their cultures, lifeways, spiritualities, processes of polity formation, economic activities, gender norms, legal customs, and environmental practices are the least taught elements of our shared history. While available resources have multiplied exponentially in recent decades, only a handful of teachers outside of formal Native American Studies (American Indian Studies) or university history programs make use of them. Furthermore, many sympathetic teachers ultimately steer clear of Indigenous history because they do not know how to portray Native peoples in an accurate and responsible way. *Understanding and Teaching Native American History* provides vital insights and concrete strategies for educators to employ to restore Natives to their rightful place in American historical consciousness. In the process, it will help to correct misrepresentations of the diversity and complex lived experiences of modern Indigenous communities.[1]

In our experience, teachers at all levels tend to follow a well-established but problematic manual of American history. They sweep through millennia of pre-Columbian life via "summer reading" or perhaps will cover the topic in a day or week at the start of term, before turning to the context for and process of the 1492 European invasion. They offer generalizations about Indigenous demography, the idea of Columbian exchange, disease epidemics, and (sometimes) the brutal exploitation of Indigenous peoples by Spanish conquistadors and encomenderos. They provide snapshots of the English encounter with the

3

Powhatan Chiefdom at Jamestown in 1607, of Puritan interactions with Algonquian polities between 1620 and 1636 (focusing particularly on myths stemming from "the First Thanksgiving"), and of King Philip's War of 1675–76. In each case teachers usually present the geospatial regions in European terms and Indigenous polities as foils—subject to external brutalities, incapable of stopping the inexorable forces of invasion, implicitly stepping aside as European civilization moves further west. After 1676 the standard narrative only sporadically returns to Native issues, most notably by contextualizing the Seven Years' War with events such as the 1754 skirmish at Jumonville's Glen and subsequent confrontation at Fort Necessity, or more likely by explaining the ways in which Native polities sided either with the French or the British in order to "play them off one another" and secure their diminishing autonomy. The greater focus, however, tends to be on turning student attention to local and imperial Anglo-American squabbles to explain the "inevitability" of the coming Revolution.

The narrative (usually) returns to American Indians in the nineteenth century, but it remains oversimplified at best. Perhaps teachers will contextualize the Creek Civil War of 1812–1815 with "America's Second War of Independence." More likely they will explore the injustice of removal by focusing on the constitutional issues raised by President Andrew Jackson's quarrel with John Marshall's Supreme Court. They may include some insight into the brutal mechanics of the "Trail of Tears" before metaphorically removing Indigenous people in favor of Black/ White binaries of race, slavery, and sectional crisis. After the Civil War, teachers typically discuss trans-Mississippi problems by way of the Railway Enabling Act, the Battle of Greasy Grass (more commonly called "the Battle of Little Bighorn"), 1880s confrontations between the American military, Apaches, and Sioux, and the 1890 genocide at Wounded Knee. In the twentieth century Indigenous people are all but forgotten, reduced to caricatures in cartoons, television shows, and films. If they appear in the classroom they do so as tragic members of a monolithic people utterly broken and reduced to the past tense (although one certainly does see occasional nods to "feel good" stories like the Navajo code talkers of World War II). Complex issues such as allotment, surviving boarding schools, termination policies, the protection of sacred spaces, the Native civil rights movement, national sacrifice areas, fracking and pipelines, water rights, and tribal sovereignty are reduced to one- or two-minute conversations regarding "current events" and framed as "celebrity activism" rather than organically Indigenous in origin.

The historical record powerfully upends this narrative, as do the last thirty years of scholarship. One wonders why so little of it has trickled into the classroom. This volume's authors offer more specific clarifications, but a general explanation is an entrenched (if implicit) sense that including Indigenous people would destroy the received contours of the nation's story. Native people alter the chronology of the American experience and distort perceived realities. Their lifeways and understandings of time are decidedly non-Western and at odds with prevailing Euro-American ideas of history. They represent sovereign polities that have actively shaped geopolitical and cultural dynamics in North America, a fact that interferes with the insistence that imperial Europeans fought to control the continent before 1763 and qualifies standard explanations for why an intrepid group of "patriots" created a new Republic thereafter.

The Indigenous lived experience also challenges the basic elements of some of the country's most controversial early legacies. Merely one example is the role of Native people in the birth and evolution of slavery in the Americas. In the sixteenth century an emergent Indian slave trade created networks of travel and commerce that shaped the continent for centuries to come. It contributed thousands of workers to the Atlantic world's evolving labor market, served as a blueprint for the African trade, and coexisted with the African system of slavery into the nineteenth century. At the least, this experience challenges commonly held assumptions that North American slavery began in 1619 or that slavery was African exclusive and South centered (New England was equally culpable in the extension of the Native slave trade, after all). It also qualifies the widespread belief that the American experience was formed through African labor exploitation and Indigenous land theft. This assertion is accurate as far as it goes, but it is limited by the implicit idea that America's formation hinged upon Native removal from its earliest moments.

If Native peoples drove the construction of the early American experience, they are crucial to more contemporary history as well. Greater understanding of migration patterns has transformed the nineteenth-century story of removal. Rather than a catastrophic ending, post-removal cultural persistence and innovation stretched eastern issues into trans-Mississippi geopolitics. Better insight into sexuality and allotment

5

policy have revealed the downside of progressivism and state growth at the turn of the twentieth century. Rethinking racial binaries as imposed in the late nineteenth and twentieth centuries has underscored how Native people—classified as Black in the law—sustained identity, culture, economy, and community in the face of Jim Crow. And applying a broader lens to the twentieth-century civil rights movement has shown how Native community leaders such as LaNada War Jack, Richard Oakes, and John Trudell helped rewrite the era's legal, media, and social norms.

Understanding and Teaching Native American History is designed to help educators more effectively integrate Indigenous people into their classrooms. By providing content and resources from across the time and landscape of the American narrative, the volume encourages teaching Natives as fundamental to the continent's experience. Through it they will have a better sense of how to approach Indigenous realities, and how to navigate sensitive issues surrounding Native lives and legacies. By outlining responsible ways of teaching the past the volume also demonstrates how Native peoples and tribal nations continue to shape both their own and the nation's destinies. Whether by challenging oil pipelines, protecting traditional homelands, reasserting their sovereign power, or taking active roles in shaping the country's urban landscapes, Indians "are still here."

Understanding and Teaching Native American History is composed of three sections. Part One offers insight into teaching essential historical topics such as archaeology, the pre-Columbian world, disease epidemics, slavery, removal, Euro-Indigenous warfare, allotment, federal Indian law and literature, the complexities of Native sovereignty, Native environmental history, and genocide. Part Two focuses on identity and cultural appropriation. Topics include mascots, art, foodways, spirituality, rethinking racial approaches to southeastern Native communities, and land acknowledgments. Part Three offers general advice and observations from Native and non-Native scholars who have had (or will have) a tremendous impact on the teaching of Native history.

Three final, interrelated thoughts. First, *Understanding and Teaching Native American History* is rooted in the belief that students should internalize that historical narratives describe real people and that studying history provides a medium through which to shed light upon their complex, contradictory, tragic, and triumphant lives. Our central hope is that by sharpening students' critical analysis skills they will both better understand their place on the continent and become more complete citizens of the twenty-first-century world. Second, we happily concede that this volume does not provide anywhere near an exhaustive list of topics or approaches to Native history. Such coverage, simply put, is impossible. Instead, we see it as an entryway for a broader conversation about challenging prevailing American historical curricula, and we encourage readers to consider other ways of illuminating the Native experience. Finally, we urge everyone reading this volume to contact Native communities in your area, attend powwows, and invite members to speak directly to your students. Nothing reveals the vibrancy of the Indigenous experience or encourages a process of cultural reconciliation and renewal as effectively as direct dialogue with those who are at the heart of this book.

A note on nomenclature is in order. Although it naturally is an issue to which we are sensitive, there is no universal agreement on so-called best practice—whether inside Native Country or outside. Whenever possible this volume's authors use a nation's or tribe's official title. Teachers should note that that can be complex, however, because tribal nations possess names in their languages that differ from English appellations. Merely a few examples: Anishinaabe (Ojibwe/ Chippewa, Odawa, and Potawatami), Diné (Navajo), Ho-Chunk (Winnebago), Ani-kituwah (Cherokee), or Haudenosaunee (Six Nations, or Iroquois). When speaking more generically things become murkier. In modern Canada common terms include "First Nations," "Indigènes," "Aboriginal," or "Autochtone." In the United States one tends to see "Native American," "Indian," and "American Indian." Readers will see all three in this volume. We have tried, however, to avoid overuse of both "Indian" (for obvious reasons) and "Native American." (That appellation cedes power and agency to the early sixteenth-century Europeans [and their descendants] who arbitrarily put a name on the continent rather than to the people at the heart of this volume.) Although imperfect in its uniformity, we most often will employ the terms Indigenous or Native.

NOTES

1. Very short sections of this introduction were inspired by Andrew K. Frank and Kristofer Ray, "Indians as Southerners; Southerners as Indians: Rethinking the History of a Region," *Native South* 10 (2017): vii–xiv.

PART ONE

Essential Topics in Native American History

Before Columbus

Native American History, Archaeology, and Resources

MAUREEN MEYERS

Every American first grader can tell you that Columbus sailed the ocean and came to America in 1492. What few can tell you is the name of the Native polities inhabiting that land in 1492. What should high school and undergraduate students know about the history of peoples in North America before European contact? The short answer is, the diversity of groups that existed here before contact and the time depth of their occupation. Most primary and secondary school students across America are presented with a trope about Native people that combines romanticism and false information. This trope suggests that only one type of Indian lived in North America, that he (often the Indian is portrayed as male) rode a horse and wore a headdress, was one with nature, and that he and his tribe were mostly gone before White people settled North America. As a result, our future citizens believe that the past before European settlement is unknowable and untraceable.

This chapter presents an overview of the over twelve thousand years that Native people have lived, and are still living, in North America as well as the diversity of groups, over five hundred, that were here at contact. This history is followed by a brief discussion of basic archaeological methods. That is, how do archaeologists know which groups were here and how long they were here? This is followed by a review of laws that guide archaeological research related to North Americans

11

in the United States. Finally, I present a list and description of resources for teachers for additional information and lesson plans and suggest ways teachers can actively engage their students in Native American history in their communities.

An Indigenous History of the Continent

Generally, there are four time periods of Native American history in North America. While the specific time varies by location, it is helpful to have a broad framework in which to understand this history.

Paleoindian Period, 25,000–10,000 years ago

Archaic Period, 10,000–2,500 years ago

Woodland Period, 2,500 years ago–AD 900/contact (varies by region across North America)

Mississippian Period, AD 900–1540

Below, each historic period is described in general terms.

Paleoindian Period

The Paleoindian period is marked by the first arrival of Natives in North America. This occurred via the Bering Strait over multiple periods around 20–25,000 years ago, or perhaps earlier based on recent data. Two primary theories attempt to explain the settlement of North and South America. First, groups of people likely wandered onto the Bering Strait when it was connected to Alaska because sea levels were so low that the land, now submerged, was exposed. Eventually, groups made their way into what is now California, the Great Plains and Midwest regions, and the East Coast by about 12,000 years ago. The second theory is that Natives used boats to move down the coast, settling along the way and eventually making it as far as South America fairly early, at least 25,000 years ago. Likely, Natives used a combination of migration routes and passages.

Paleoindian groups were organized as bands. All humans around the world were organized as band societies as recently as ten thousand years ago. Bands are mobile hunters and gatherers; that is, they do not grow any crops but move from place to place to get food. Settlement is on a short-term basis and over time usually follows a seasonal round. For example, people might settle along river shoals in the spring and summer and in the mountains in the fall, allowing them to obtain resources that are plentiful at those times. Bands are composed of extended family groups, usually thirty and no more than fifty individuals. They often congregate in larger "macrobands" on an annual basis to share information, find mates outside the smaller group, and reassert territorial boundaries. These macrobands are similar to extended family gatherings that we might be part of at holiday times. Bands practice reciprocity, where goods of equal value are exchanged. Because bands do not stay long in one area and have minimal material goods— for example, they did not make pottery at this time—archaeological traces of bands are often limited to stone tools and associated debitage and flakes and, occasionally, evidence of structures suggesting longer occupations.

Some of the earliest Paleoindian sites in North America include Meadowcroft Rockshelter in Pennsylvania, Cactus Hill in Virginia, and Folsom in New Mexico.

Archaic Period

The Archaic period represents a time when population expanded, and as a result territories became more constrained. People were still organized as bands, but because there were larger populations the areas exploited by these bands was circumscribed. Seasonal subsistence rounds were common. Over time, population grew steadily as resources were relatively abundant. People had intimate knowledge of their environment and made use of a range of foodstuffs. For example, along the Savannah River Valley in Georgia and South Carolina, archaeologists have been able to identify evidence of about eight Archaic bands whose seasonal round included exploitation of the upland and mountain areas in the fall and early winter for berries, nuts, and deer, movement to the Piedmont river shoals in the early spring for fish, and movement in the summer to the ocean for shellfish and macroband gatherings.

It is easy to consider Paleo and Archaic peoples as "simple"; however, no cultures are simple. Although their focus was on subsistence and their lifestyle was mobile, Archaic and Paleo bands had specific ways of life including complex religious beliefs. These are reflected at sites like the UNESCO World Heritage site of Poverty Point, Louisiana. There, archaeologist T. R. Kidder has uncovered the complex history of this multimound site, where he suggests Natives built earthen mounds in certain shapes to reenact a creation myth of a bird emerging from a muddy underworld into this world. Groups from across the Southeast came to Poverty Point to assist in this building effort, and the point of Poverty Point seems to have been the building of the mounds rather than the use of the mounds, similar in some ways to decorating a Christmas tree or burning fireworks. A larger example would be the Burning Man festival where individuals gather on an annual basis to build and then burn large wooden sculptures. Other important North American Archaic sites include Indian Knoll in Kentucky, where evidence of long-distance trade is present; the Head-Smashed-In Buffalo Jump World Heritage Site in Alberta, Canada, with evidence of group buffalo-hunting practices preserved; and shell rings in the Florida coast, suggestive of intensive subsistence exploitation tied to ritual meaning over time.

Woodland Period

During the Woodland period a large change occurred and became solidified in Native lifeways. Natives learned to cultivate food. This probably occurred slowly and was facilitated by women, the primary gatherers. It was probably known that seeds created foods, and that preserving seeds and intentionally burying them would create more food. As territories became more circumscribed, the ability to ensure food would have been attractive to Natives. At some point, it would have been more cost-effective to stay and protect the food than to continue on a seasonal round. This was a subtle yet significant change in the way the seasonal round was done, which involved either less time moving around and increasingly more time in one place, or the deepening of gendered tasks, where women stayed with plants and men returned to the women after completing the seasonal round. People in different areas experimented with different ways, resulting in a decrease in mobility over time and an increase in population. Eventually, the band organization changed into a tribal organization. Tribes lived in villages with permanent houses, and not everyone in a tribe was related to one another. Tribes had a leader; however, that leader usually earned their role through repeated actions, such as being a successful gardener or warrior. The types of food eaten changed as well. Seeds were favored, and these required long periods of cooking time to be more easily digested. As a result, pottery was invented, which allowed for long cooking of stew-like meals. Over time, the bow and arrow was invented as well, which not only led to more efficient hunting but in some cases resulted in increased warfare, further exacerbated by increased population competing for territory.

Woodland peoples also participated in the building of ceremonial centers. Some were otherwise vacant and used by multiple groups on an annual basis, much in the same way our churches and synagogues are full on a weekly basis but during the week could be viewed as vacant. Some of the mounds were used to bury people, which served a secondary purpose of marking territory. In the Ohio River Valley, the Adena culture emerged, which is known by its conical mortuary mounds and distinctive engraved artifacts. This was followed by the Hopewell culture, which was found over a wider geographic area across the Southeast at places such as the Garden Creek site in western North Carolina. Hopewell appears to have been a belief system that was expressed in burial mounds but also in earthen animal effigies, such as the Serpent Mound in Ohio, and elaborate items with distinctive forms made of material traded across North America, including mica from western North Carolina, shark teeth from the Florida coast, and even turquoise from the Southwest. When I teach Hopewell, I often liken it to an evangelistic movement. In the same way that Christianity has a set of shared core beliefs but each denomination emphasizes those beliefs differently, Hopewell could be viewed as a type of religion that, as it spread, resulted in different people identifying with and emphasizing some beliefs while ignoring others. By the end of the Woodland period, Natives were living in established villages, and some had begun to grow crops, resulting in a surplus of food.

Mississippian Period

In the southeastern region, the Mississippian period was present beginning around AD 900. First emerging in present-day St. Louis, at the site of Cahokia, the Mississippian culture encompassed a different way of life, one that merged old Woodland ways with new beliefs and practices. Mississippian cultures were different from those that came before because they were organized into chiefdoms, or societies with institutionalized hierarchy. That is, chiefs did not achieve their status; rather, they were born into it. Chiefly power emerged from a combination of factors. Increased crop production of maize resulted in surpluses. Chiefs managed those surpluses, keeping some in reserve for future crops or crop failures, and also using some surplus to exchange for elaborate trade goods, primarily made of copper and shell. Chiefs had retinues, which might consist of their family, but often also a war chief and sometimes a priest. Sometimes the chief encompassed all three roles. Commoners' roles included primarily tending crops and creating the surplus, although in larger chiefdoms some specialized artisans may have been employed to create goods for chiefly trade. These goods are present across the Southeast, using similar motifs that represent religious beliefs and related mythology.

Mississippian sites often contained a mound and a plaza, or open area in front of the mound, and both mound and plaza were encircled by rows of houses. Chiefdoms consisted of a few hundred people, although the largest chiefdom, Cahokia in east St. Louis, likely had at least twenty thousand inhabitants at its height. There are still many Mississippian sites that are open to the public. The largest of these is Cahokia, whose forty-story Monks Mound, made by hand out of basket loads of dirt, is the largest earthen monument in North America. Other sites include Moundville, in Tuscaloosa, Alabama; Etowah, north of Atlanta; Emerald, Winterville, and Lake George mounds, in the Mississippi Delta; Chucalissa, in Memphis, Tennessee, and Ocmulgee Mounds, in Macon, Georgia.

Contact Period

In the last thirty years our knowledge of the contact period and Native life during this period has grown tremendously. Much of this work in the Southeast was originally based in the reconstruction of the Hernando de Soto route, which began in 1539 in Tampa and wound its way through the Southeast, recording Native communities it encountered. Using a combination of archaeological and historic data, researchers have been able to reconstruct the route accurately. In so doing, they used the documents to better understand Mississippian chiefdoms De Soto encountered along the way. Other, later routes, such as that by Juan Pardo, have received additional attention. Most notably, the Berry site in Morganton, North Carolina, has found the remains of Pardo's camp in the Native village of Joara.

Post-settlement, Natives regrouped and re-formed, often as a result of what has been termed the shatter zone, a period of instability fueled by European incursions resulting in disease, enslavement of Indians, and the introduction of guns to the Southeast. The late sixteenth and seventeenth centuries were a time of movement, coalescence, enslavement of Natives by Europeans, and restructuring of Native groups as a result. What emerged were the so-called Five Civilized Tribes: Cherokee, Creek, Choctaw, Chickasaw, and Seminole, although other, smaller groups such as the Natchez also should be included in this group. These groups engaged in trade with English, French, and Spanish colonists, first Native trade that was supplanted by deerskin trade after the European settlers began enslaving Africans. By the time of removal around 1830, in which southeastern Native lands were forcibly taken and the Natives themselves were forcibly removed, many groups had adapted successfully. Chief Vann of the Cherokee had a plantation home in northwest Georgia that was comparable to homes of many Whites, for example. This home is preserved by the state of Georgia and can still be visited.

Activities for Classrooms

1. Find out what Native groups lived in your area. Are any descendants of these Native groups present now? If so, invite one to the class to discuss tribal history and how Native lifeways and culture are preserved.
2. Ask the class to discuss the meaning of the terms "civilization" and "primitive." Discuss how these words are used to create an imbalance of power in history. If Natives have been building houses for thousands of years, does this mean they are primitive? If modern human practices adversely affect the environment, does this mean they are civilized?
3. Watch videos on primitive technology and discuss the knowledge needed to make so-called primitive tools.
4. Bring students to a wooded area and discuss what they could survive on there. Are there stones to make stone tools? Sufficient flora and fauna? Wood for building houses or other shelters? Clay to make pots?

Archaeology Overview

The history presented above is very brief but provides an outline of the over twelve thousand years of Native history. But how do we know this? That is, how do archaeologists and historians find sites, excavate sites, and re-create Native history from those findings? The following section presents a brief overview of archaeological methods.

Excavation Methods and Importance of Provenience

The goal of archaeology is to reconstruct past culture. Archaeology is a subfield of the larger field of anthropology, which studies human culture. So, when archaeologists excavate, they do so with a research goal in mind: reconstructing the behavior of those who lived in the past based on the material remains they left behind. The key to reconstructing past behavior is using provenience in excavations. People visiting sites or watching archaeological excavations on television often remark that archaeologists dig neatly, or in square holes. This is because they are maintaining provenience.

One could consider an archaeological site similar to a crime scene: both attempt to reconstruct past behavior from clues left behind. Although to do this, a crime scene must be disturbed as little as possible, archaeologists, by contrast, have to disturb the ground in order to find the evidence of past behavior. Provenience means you can identify precisely where everything at a site came from. In order to reconstruct the behavior, all of the material remains must be recorded before removal. This is done in archaeology through a few methods that allow archaeologists to maintain vertical and horizontal control.

One classroom exercise that can be useful is to have students leave their material possessions at their desks and stand together as a group. Could they determine sex, age, height, weight, or other characteristics about the individuals from the materials left behind? What about the group as a whole?

First, vertical control is obtained through the use of a grid system. As with any grid, there must be a starting point, and this is known as the "site datum." Site datums are normally placed outside the site limits, or at least outside the known site limits. Site datums can be thought of as "Ground Zero" and are usually considered point zero on the imaginary X, Y grid that emanates from them across the site. Instead of X, Y, however, archaeologists use north and east coordinates to place the datum in real space. However, they rarely, if ever, label the datum as "0, 0." This is because the site might extend behind the datum, and if it did, the points on the site would be assigned negative numbers, creating confusion and error. Instead, site datum is normally labeled "N500, E500" or "N1000, E1000." These numbers are arbitrary designations. Archaeologists can later use mapping systems to find the exact location of the datum's longitude and latitude. Usually the grid is laid out in one-meter (approximately 3.3 feet) increments, and each increment, or test unit, is assigned a northing and easting coordinate that tells its location in relation to the datum. For example, Test Unit N1010 E 1050 is 10 meters north and 50 meters east of a datum arbitrarily labeled "N1000, E1000.

Once site remains are identified, which include non-artifact remains known as "features," such as posthole remains of a house, their distance from the datum can be measured. One posthole in and of itself does not reveal much information; however, it is the location of a pattern of postholes that indicate a structure was once there, and multiple structures across the site, all related in space to the datum, that allows a site settlement to be reconstructed.

When teaching elementary-aged children, I ask them to imagine coming upon their house in fifty years' time or more. How would an archaeologist know which rooms were the parents' and which belonged to the children? Could they tell the age or sex of the children or parents? How could they identify the kitchen from the bedroom, and why are most kitchens located far from bedrooms?

A second part of maintaining provenience is horizontal control. Archaeologists must be able to identify not only the X and Y axes of an artifact but also its depth in relation to the datum, that is, a Z coordinate. This is because many sites were occupied by people at different time periods, so you must be able to ascertain which artifact is from which time period. Also, though a site may have been occupied by one culture for over one hundred years, houses would have been rebuilt over that time. Recording which artifact types came from which occupation allows archaeologists to reconstruct change over time of a culture. This could include technological change, such as hunting with arrowheads replacing hunting with atlatls, that likely had long-standing changes in the larger culture. These other changes might be apparent in the way houses were constructed or the foods people ate.

In classrooms of high school students, one exercise that can illustrate this is a comparison of cell phones. Some students will have older phones, others newer phones, and they can identify the attributes that allow them to know the approximate age of the cell phone.

In order to maintain this horizontal control, archaeologists excavate usually in ten-centimeter levels. This is true for each test unit excavated. Based on our understanding of geological layering, that is, stratigraphy, we assume that layers of earth occupied at the same time are deposited at approximately the same rate. If a person later disturbs the natural stratigraphy, this should be relatively easy to see, but only if the layers of the strata are removed the same way they were laid down: uniformly. Therefore, archaeologists remove the ten-centimeter layer in a uniform manner across the test unit, using either trowels or flat shovels. This allows them to record where nonnatural disturbances, that is, cultural or natural changes, are present and identify if any stratigraphic changes, suggesting natural formation changes, are present.

The dirt from each level is put in buckets together and then screened to recover artifacts, allowing for the provenience of the artifacts to be recorded. These artifacts are then bagged together and labeled with the site name, the test unit north and east location, and the level. Each level is recorded by plan maps and field forms that require recording opening and closing depths of each corner and the center, ensuring that exactly ten centimeters were removed from that level. Each level is then photographed. Once excavation of the test unit ceases, a profile map and photograph of the test unit wall(s) are taken and drawn.

The provenience of the artifacts are maintained as they are taken to the lab, washed, and analyzed. In this way, archaeologists can compare type of pottery or frequency of stone tools from one area of the site to another, and ideally can identify food preparation areas versus sleeping areas within houses or special-use structures versus family structures. That is, they can reconstruct the behavior, at each time of the site occupation, and the change of that behavior over time to reach the goal of archaeology to reconstruct culture over time.

Dating: Culture History, Types, and Radiometric Methods

Once sites have been excavated, archaeologists can use the information recovered to reconstruct what happened there. A key building block in knowing what happened, and reconstructing change over time, is knowing when it happened. During the middle part of the twentieth century, archaeologists lacked modern radiometric dating methods, and the field itself was relatively new. As a result, much of the focus of archaeologists was on reconstructing change over time rather than asking why things changed over time. This was an important building block in archaeology, and understanding how archaeologists date artifacts and sites and ultimately, cultures and phases (such as Paleoindian, Archaic, Woodland, and Mississippian) is still a basic method.

As archaeologists excavated more sites, they began to recognize similarities in the types of artifacts they recovered. For example, early sites had distinctive spear points, while later-occupied sites had smaller, triangular projectile points (or arrowheads). Once the archaeological horizontal and vertical controls became widely used, this allowed archaeologists to provide stratigraphic control to these finds. That is, they now knew that spear points were excavated from earlier or lower levels and triangular points from upper levels. Although they recognized a general similarity in projectile point and, later, pottery styles across North America, there were also distinct regional differences. Archaeologists began to record characteristics, or attributes, of the different types of points and pottery, and by tying these attributes to stratigraphic control, they could recognize the changes over time by region. These became known as types for regions. For example, most Woodland pottery is grit tempered, with some variation across space. However, different types of designs, or surface decorations, were present in different areas, so one can differentiate between Woodland-period pottery recovered in north Georgia versus Woodland-period pottery from south Florida or central Virginia.

For archaeologists trained in the typology of artifacts of a certain region, this can become as easy as recognizing the decade a car was made or a fashion design was popular by looking at its characteristics. And like these examples, it is approximate: most people can't tell you the year that a particular car was made, but most can tell you the decade. If asked, they could identify a particular attribute. In class, another example is examining cars. I often show a slide of cars, each from a decade spanning the last fifty years, and ask students how they know which decade the cars date to, to specifically list the attributes (car lights, lack of seatbelts, radio) to identify the decade. I often note, though, that some attributes, like color, reflect idiosyncratic taste in our culture, so all attributes don't mean something.

In the 1950s radiocarbon dating was invented, which made dating sites much more precise. Radiocarbon dating is the primary type of radiometric dating method used in North America. It can date items between about five hundred to forty thousand years old, which nicely fits into the length of occupation of humans in North America. Radiocarbon dating can only be used on burned organic material. By measuring the amount of carbon left in the organism, scientists can determine how old the material is. When that burned material is found in context with artifacts—for example, a piece of pottery with soot on it—it dates the artifact by association.

Radiocarbon dating revolutionized archaeology in North America, because it allowed archaeologists to date the types they had created. It also, to their surprise, showed that humans had been in North America much longer than previously thought. Initial radiocarbon dates of Paleoindian sites were about ten thousand years old. Over time, as more sites and more precise excavation and radiocarbon dating has been used, these dates have been extended to about fourteen thousand years ago and, in some cases, possibly older.

The other thing radiocarbon dating allowed archaeologists to do was move beyond merely reconstructing culture history and begin to answer bigger questions, such as why did cultures change? What effect did technological changes have on the larger culture? For example, examining our cars across sixty years would show that car sizes got smaller over time during the late 1970s and early 1980s. When we ask why, we know one reason is the oil crisis of the late 1970s. Delving into this more deeply, we might be able to reconstruct economic, political, and, ultimately, social changes in our culture brought about by this crisis. In the same way, archaeologists can see the bigger cultural picture and truly begin to reconstruct past culture.

It is all of these methods—provenience, horizontal and vertical control, culture history, the creation of types, and radiocarbon dating—and the ensuing bigger questions archaeologists have asked and often answered in the last fifty years that allow for the full (though brief) overview of Indigenous cultures I present at the beginning of the chapter.

Archaeology and Native American Laws

National Historic Preservation Act, Sections 106 and 110;
State Historic Preservation Offices; Site Files

Archaeology has been assisted, and has assisted in, the creation of laws that protect our cultural resources. An overview of these laws is provided to understand not only the impact they have on archaeology but, more importantly, the vital role they play in preserving our past.

The American Antiquities Act of 1906 is the oldest law protecting cultural resources. Signed into law by Theodore Roosevelt, it allows for protection of archaeological sites on federal lands and imposes fines for looting sites. Arguably one of the most far-reaching laws for archaeologists is the National Historic Preservation Act (NHPA) of 1966. This law did a few things. First, it created the National Register of Historic Places (NRHP) for both historic structures and sites. These are nominated to the NRHP under one of four criteria: association with important places (Criterion A), such as Gettysburg; association with important people (Criterion B), such as Mount Vernon; association with important characteristics (Criterion C), such as a Frank Lloyd Wright building; and actual or potentially significant archaeological resources (Criterion D). Structures and sites have to be at least fifty years old to be considered for inclusion on the NRHP.

Second, the NHPA created a State Historic Preservation Office (SHPO) for each state, and this office is responsible for creating and maintaining an archaeological site registry for the state. Finally, Section 106 of the NHPA stipulates that any undertaking (such as road or bridge construction) that uses federal monies must take into account the archaeological resources that might be affected. What this means is that archaeological resources must be looked for first and then determined if they are eligible for listing in the NRHP. Initially, universities tried to answer this suddenly increased need for archaeology. By the 1980s a new professional arm of archaeology was born: cultural resource management, or CRM. This private multimillion-dollar industry employs 80 percent of archaeologists in North America and is responsible for the identification of thousands of sites. Our knowledge of Native American history has been substantially bolstered by CRM, which is a valuable and vital part of the field.

Native American Graves Protection and Repatriation Act

The other game-changing law is the Native American Graves Protection and Repatriation Act, or NAGPRA, passed in 1990. This law was brought into being in large part due to Native lobbying. It provides for protection of Native American graves and cultural materials uncovered on federal and tribal land. It also requires the inventory of skeletal, funerary, and other sacred items and, if requested, the return of these items to federally recognized Native tribes if links between the graves, remains, and items to those tribes can be substantiated. This is required of all federal or federally funded institutions.

The passage of NAGPRA speaks to archaeology's colonial legacy and its mistreatment of Native remains in the United States. The field began in the late nineteenth century as an antiquarian's hobby, done by rich men to acquire, or loot, Native remains, after Natives had been removed by the US government through war and genocide and placed on reservations. By the 1930s this changed drastically, especially in the eastern half of the country. Through the New Deal programs of the Roosevelt administration, primarily the Works Progress Administration (WPA) and the Civilian Conservation Corps (CCC), dozens of trained archaeologists and thousands of untrained mostly men were hired to excavate sites, primarily in the Southeast and Mid-Atlantic. This resulted in the largest excavations known to date in the United States, and a massive creation of artifact data, which also included skeletal remains. After the outbreak of World War II, these programs abruptly ended. Most of the artifacts and associated skeletal and funerary remains were stored in university archaeology labs, often basements, and, due to a lack of funding, were not properly cared for. NAGPRA was passed in recognition of this unethical treatment of human remains. Its passage created much division among archaeologists, who felt that potential future research data was being taken away. This is most explicitly seen in the case of the Kennewick Man, an ongoing twenty-year saga. Over time, though, many archaeologists have changed their mind. NAGPRA allowed universities to thoroughly inventory their remains before they were repatriated, and in so doing, data was recorded. Relations between Native people and archaeologists have improved over the last twenty-five-plus years since NAGPRA passed. For example, the Choctaw pay for their students to excavate sites in the Mississippi homeland with University of Mississippi archaeologists.

Some laws are specific to federal lands. Section 110 of the NHPA mandates that federal agencies, such as the National Park Service and the National Forest Service, must account for NRHP-eligible sites on their properties and must continually survey for sites on the properties and manage them properly. The Archaeological Resources Protection Act of 1979 imposes penalties for looting or damage of sites on federal and tribal lands. Although ignored or unknown by the court system at first, in the last twenty years some significant ARPA cases have been successfully brought to court and large fines levied against looters.

Resources for Teachers

In this section I outline federal, state, and local history sources for teachers. First, though, I want to emphasize the dangers of looting archaeological sites. Looting can range from picking up arrowheads to complete destruction of Native (and non-Native) sites. First, if you want to collect artifacts, work with archaeologists. Get permission of the landowner before going onto a site, for your own protection. Next, record what you find and where you find it. You can share this information with your SHPO. Just recording the data helps archaeologists fill in gaps about where and when Natives settled. Finally, don't ever attempt to excavate a site yourself, especially if you are untrained in archaeological methods. If you are interested in Native American history, US history, and archaeology, there are many volunteer opportunities across the United States and opportunities through your National Park Service, state parks, and National Forest Service, as well as private organizations such as The Archaeological Conservancy.

Federal Organizations

Federally funded national sources of information include the National Park Service, which oversees the National Register of Historic Places. Its website (https://www.nps.gov/archeology/) allows you to search their database for lists of NRHP-listed sites and structures by county and state. In addition, federal laws are explained in depth. Resources for teachers are also available, including newsletters such as *Common Ground*, which contain lesson plans for specific sites.

The National Museum of the American Indian, part of the Smithsonian Institution, is another resource. Its website, Native Knowledge 360° (https://americanindian.si.edu/nk360), provides a searchable database by subject, nation, language, region, and grade, many with digital lesson plans, but also including printable posters, PDFs, and some videos.

The Society for American Archaeology (SAA), the professional organization of archaeologists, has information on its website for teachers and lists of multiple resources for teachers about Native people and archaeology.

The American Institute of Archaeology (AIA) is another resource with local chapters across the United States. In addition, the organization publishes lists of volunteer opportunities for archaeology across the country.

State Organizations

In addition to the SHPOs, whose websites contain much information about each state's history, each state has an archaeology organization made up of mostly amateurs interested in history. Many states, such as Virginia, have certification programs for amateur archaeologists. Trained amateur archaeologists contribute a lot of labor to archaeology and increase our knowledge of Native America and US history. Finally, many of you are lucky to live near reservations. Many tribes/nations have their own websites with their own histories and culture described. These are valuable resources—inhabitants or their descendants telling their own history in their own words.

Some specific states, such as Florida and Arkansas, have more extensive programs. The Florida Public Archaeology Network has multiple offices across the state that actively educate the public about Florida's archaeological resources. The Arkansas Archaeological Survey is set up in a similar manner.

Ideas for Finding Local History

It is important to recognize that wherever you live in the United States, Native polities lived there too. There are Native sites in your county. Many of these have been identified. It is important to connect students to their local history, and this certainly includes the fourteen thousand years of Native history. You can research some of this local history or do it as a class project. Much of this information may be available through your state archaeology programs. Each state's SHPO often has online state histories that include Native American history. This is a good place to start and to find sources relevant to your area. Local universities may have archaeologists on their faculty who are knowledgeable about the Native history in your state. In addition, many have artifacts in their collection. At the University of Mississippi we have a VISTA (Volunteers in Service to America) coordinator whose job is to connect the history in our collections with the elementary and secondary school students in the north-central region of the state. Local history museums are also excellent sources of information.

Conclusions

As is clear from this chapter, it is difficult to learn about Indigenous America without learning about archaeology; the two are interlinked. Although it should be clear that archaeology has identified much of this Native American history, we have down a poor job of sharing this history with the larger public. Many of my students are shocked to learn that there are Native sites where they are from, and that Indigenous people are part of the myriad of active, vibrant cultures that make up our country today. Teaching students this history, and teaching them to respect the remains of that history, is crucial to helping them understand the meaning of "We the People."

FOR FURTHER READING

Archaeology for Teachers

National Park Service Archaeology Program, "For Teachers," https://www.nps .gov/archeology/public/teach.htm. Contains lesson plans for teachers about archaeology.

National Register for Historic Places, State Historic Preservation Offices List, https://www.nps.gov/subjects/nationalregister/state-historic-preservation -offices.htm. Provides a list by state and a link to each state's SHPO. Websites often have information particular to states about local history and archaeology.

Society for American Archaeology, Education and Outreach, "What Is Public Archaeology?" https://www.saa.org/education-outreach/public-outreach/ what-is-public-archaeology. Aimed more toward teaching archaeologists about teaching the public but provides some helpful resources.

Native American Lesson Plans

American Institute of Archaeology, "Interactive Digs," https://www.interac tivedigs.com. Offers visitors a chance to watch archaeologists excavate in real time at sites around the world, including Pompeii, Ireland, Crete, Suriname, and Ohio.

Archaeology in the Community, "Teacher Dig Program at Montpelier," http://www.archaeologyincommunity.com/educators/. A nonprofit program that works to partner with community and educators. Site contains four lesson plans on archaeology.

Florida Public Archaeology Network (FPAN), "Find Events in Your Area," https:www.fpan.us. Offers lesson plans, handouts, smartphone apps, and videos, more specific to Florida.

National Education Association, http://www.nea.org/tools/lessons/native-american-and-alaska-native-heritage-month-grades-k-5.html. Lessons, activities, and resources.

Teachnology, https://www.teach-nology.com/teachers/lesson_plans/history/native/. Lesson plans.

Scholastic, https://www.scholastic.com/teachers/collections/teaching-content/native-american-heritage-0/. Nonfiction books about Native Americans.

The "Virgin" Soil Thesis Cover-Up

Teaching Indigenous Demographic Collapse

Tai S. Edwards

In September 2015, a debate in a Sacramento State University classroom garnered national news coverage. Professor Maury Wiseman, in an introductory US history course, was teaching about early colonization when he said, "There were a large number of people on this continent when Europeans arrived. I don't like to use the term 'genocide' because 'genocide' is something that is done on purpose, but needless to say European diseases primarily . . . will wipe out Native American populations in the two continents." An Indigenous student in the class, Chiitaanibah Johnson (Navajo/Maidu), disagreed with the professor's dismissal of genocide, spent several days finding sources to back up her views, and presented them to the professor in the following class period. According to Johnson, a heated debate ensued, the professor accused her of "hijacking" the class, dismissed the other students, and told her she was expelled from the course. The university maintained that Johnson was never disenrolled, and an official investigation eventually concluded no wrongdoing on the part of the student or the professor.[1] There are many issues in this series of events that have and should continue to garner analysis and action. But at the heart of that class period seemed to be an examination of how diseases impacted Indigenous people and if diseases can be linked to intention, and thus genocide. Professor Wiseman taught his students what is often taught in classrooms around the nation: the "virgin" soil thesis.

29

The thesis goes like this: Old World populations had experience with a variety of diseases contracted from their domesticated livestock. New World populations, lacking domesticated animals, were thus "virgin" populations, and once they were exposed to these Old World diseases, widespread infection and mortality ensued. These epidemics supposedly spread rampantly after 1492, often ahead of colonizers, killing upward of 90 percent of Indigenous Americans. Not only were Natives immunologically defenseless, but they were also socially inept at treating these new diseases. Though massive Indigenous depopulation was certainly tragic, it was, in the end, deemed an unavoidable biological accident. Who or what was to blame? Old World germs.[2] Professor Wiseman, by teaching disease in this way, came to a predictable conclusion: germs lacked intention, and thus disease deaths could not constitute genocide.

This "virgin" soil thesis (VST) reached scholarly consensus in the mid-1970s and has prevailed ever since. However, as is common in historiography, the subsequent decades have witnessed a wealth of research on the experiences of Indigenous Americans with disease that either complicated or entirely refuted VST. Now it is clear, as the editors of *Beyond Germs* argued, that "no single depopulation model can explain all cases," and therefore, as several Canadian scholars have concluded, "the social history of each Aboriginal community must be evaluated to determine the extent to which infectious disease debilitated and depleted it." This chapter outlines how to teach Indigenous demographic collapse in light of this extensive scholarship. First, epidemics must be contextualized. As David Jones has shown, "epidemics among American Indians . . . were caused by the same forces of poverty, social stress, and environmental vulnerability that cause epidemics in all other times and places." European and neo-European colonization disrupted Native social systems, undermined subsistence, reduced fertility, inflicted violence, and literally displaced communities. This compromised mental and physical health that *then* made Native people vulnerable to disease. Second, Indigenous people used a variety of strategies (some old, some new) to limit mortality and maintain communities, which were in some cases successful. But, in many cases, sustained colonial disruptions inhibited population recovery. Finally, because "social forces and human agency" enabled epidemics to decimate Native communities, the question becomes, was this genocide?[3]

Central to VST was the assumption of relatively high precolonial Indigenous populations supposedly obliterated by European diseases that spread like "wildfire" ahead of colonizers and thus went undocumented. For years scholars have employed a variety of sources and methodologies (from archival research to spatial density models and beyond) to more accurately quantify precolonial Native North American populations, which today are estimated between two and seven million. Even so, there is much that is still unknown about precolonial demography; hence it is likely that future research will continue to revise these numbers.[4] Throughout the Western Hemisphere, research has demonstrated that European diseases did not strike immediately, nor did they spread quickly. In the Caribbean colonies, it took at least twenty-five years before smallpox epidemics emerged. Archaeological evidence has disproved the infamous stories of Hernando de Soto's expedition leaving massive disease deaths in its wake. Pueblo communities lived with Spanish colonizers for almost a century before they experienced major epidemics. And on the northern plains, there is no evidence of "virgin" soil epidemics in the sixteenth century, and if any occurred in the seventeenth century, the population recovered.[5] Hence, the mere presence of Europeans was not enough to ignite continent-wide epidemics and produce demographic collapse.

Instead, the colonial context was determinant. In Europe, smallpox was a childhood disease, and most adults had already acquired life-long immunity via contraction as children, meaning they were unlikely vectors in the Americas. A weeks-long voyage across the Atlantic, especially with a small European crew, would have also inhibited the spread of smallpox and possibly other diseases. Over time, though, the context of colonization changed. For example, as the Spanish colonized the Caribbean, they increasingly established large settlements with children and enslaved Africans, dramatically expanding potential human disease vectors. Beginning in 1518, smallpox spread along Caribbean shipping routes, including to Cuba in 1519, from which Cortés and five hundred men launched their effort to conquer Mesoamerica. The large Spanish force invaded a region that was home to sizable, densely populated Indigenous communities, producing significant disruption and facilitating the spread of disease in the 1520s. However, smallpox did not spread uniformly across the region or the hemisphere because the local and colonial contexts were different.[6]

In North America, numerous scholars have shown that some Indigenous populations were declining in the several centuries preceding European colonization due to climate change that compromised agriculture and wild-food yields resulting in malnutrition that then increased regional warfare as people competed over scarce food sources. To combat these environmental and social challenges, some communities moved, others created political alliances with neighboring groups, while still others formed entirely new communities from remnant populations that developed distinctive ethnic and cultural identities (a process known as *ethnogenesis*). These surviving North American communities increasingly dispersed, and large buffer zones separated communities from one another. Though people had contact and sometimes traded or warred with one another, so doing involved a relatively small group of individuals traveling potentially hundreds of miles. Such infrequent, long trips prevented the transmission of "virgin" soil epidemics. In fact, smallpox epidemics did not appear to plague Natives near English colonies until after 1630, when the tens of thousands of immigrating English colonists included many children.[7] Again, it was the context of colonialism, rather than Native "virginity," that determined disease deaths.

So how did the actions of colonizers endanger the health of Indigenous people? When Spain colonized the region they named "La Florida" in 1565, their goal was to exploit local Native labor for agricultural production via a food tribute system that would feed the local colonizers and hopefully produce a surplus for export. The Spanish missionaries, targeting the Guales, Timucuas, and Apalachees, implemented the *reducción* system that forcibly resettled people into "larger, more densely crowded mission centers" where they could be managed and controlled—and where disease could spread. This caused what Clark Spencer Larsen called the "regional homogenization of Native lifestyles and foodways." Overall, Native diets became less varied and involved less animal protein, producing iron deficiencies. As they farmed more corn, Indigenous people ate more corn. This had implications for oral health, weakening tooth enamel and increasing dental cavities, leading to gingivitis and periodontal disease, which in turn undermined general health, especially in adulthood. Spanish colonization imposed very hard labor on Native bodies, especially Native men who also had to transport food long distances on foot or leave families for extended periods to work in other Spanish communities. This compromised

Native health and simultaneously limited births. And, of course, missionization assaulted and subverted Native spirituality and culture. Hence, forced relocation, population concentration, dietary changes, labor exploitation, and coerced conversion all compromised physical and mental health, making Natives vulnerable to both old (nonvenereal syphilis, tuberculosis) and new diseases (smallpox, measles) that killed en masse. Larsen characterized colonization in La Florida as an example of "structural violence," where Spanish "social structures, institutions, and policies . . . suppress[ed] the ability of members of Native societies to reach their full potential," limiting their ability to "reproduce and recover from the colonial traumas." As a result, Guale, Timucua, and Apalachee populations were decimated. However, Spanish imperialism was not the only problem.[8]

The slave trade was another aspect of colonization that had far-reaching implications for Native populations. As has been well documented, Indigenous Americans (like most people around the globe) had a long history of warfare and captive-taking. Most captives were women and children, and they were often adopted into their captor's communities or traded to another community where they were then adopted. Captives, sometimes replacing those who had died due to war, famine, disease, and so forth, then enlarged the population—and thus power—of their new community. Women in particular also promised future population growth via their reproductivity. Catherine Cameron has argued European colonization changed everything. Native allies were important in maintaining a particular European empire's power relative to their imperial rivals. For example, English traders along the Atlantic coast provided guns to the Westos (who had already been displaced by French colonization in the Great Lakes), whom the English encouraged to attack mission Indians in Spain's La Florida. In so doing, the Westos acquired thousands of Apalachee captives they traded to the English, which simultaneously destroyed the Spanish labor source, the La Florida colony, and the region's Indigenous population. English traders profited from supplying Native captives to international slave markets, and enslaved Natives ended up in colonial mines, plantations, and homes.[9]

Not surprisingly, the slave trade significantly disrupted Native life. Incorporation into the Atlantic market economy provided access to goods that Natives found useful in daily life and that increased their power relative to Native rivals (either as "middlemen" in trade or as well-armed enemies). However, the goods European traders wanted in return were often slaves. Consequently, the region became embroiled in warfare, which itself led to population decline. In fear, some Indigenous communities did not hunt or farm normally; some moved into old buffer zones or concentrated in unsanitary, compact settlements, while others created confederacies in self-defense. The result for many was hunger and a rise in aboriginal diseases. Paul Kelton argued that these changes in the social landscape have often been erroneously interpreted by archaeologists as the result of "virgin" soil epidemics. Instead, Carolina and Virginia slave traders likely exported upward of thirty thousand Natives from the region. Because so many of these captives were women, future population growth was also hampered. Hence, English colonialism had produced "this highly vulnerable state of warfare, slaving, resettlement, and malnourishment" for Indigenous people. Enter smallpox. By the 1690s, Virginia finally had internal English population growth, meaning local children and adults were also smallpox "virgins." At the same time, the colony was importing a much higher number of enslaved Africans who were likewise unexposed. It was in this colonial context that a four-year-long smallpox epidemic commenced in 1696, inflicting "the most damage it would ever do to the region and its people."[10]

As Catherine Cameron has shown, the southeast was not particularly unique in its experience with European slave trading. The French slave trade exacted similar destruction in the Great Lakes region. In the Southwest, the Comanche empire in particular trafficked in a large number of captives traded to Spanish and French colonists. Some of these enslaved people ended up in far-away Mexican and Caribbean colonies. But many became domestic slaves in Spanish households, where they and their descendants were eventually incorporated into Hispanic society, obscuring their Native ancestry. The colonial European slave trade proved massively destructive to Indigenous populations across the continent. In addition to the loss of life from increased violence between Natives to obtain slaves, the final destination for many captives was no longer North America. And this led to a decline in Indigenous populations overall. For those enslaved locally, the result tended to be erasure of Indigenous identity. Hence, the non-epidemiological aspects of colonialism reduced Native populations without the help of "virgin" soil epidemics. In fact, as Kelton demonstrated, it was not until after this destruction that European disease ravaged Native communities.[11]

My own research has examined the experience of the Osage with disease. Osage towns, located in what is now central and western Missouri, had sporadic contact with French colonists beginning in the 1680s and then sustained contact with them after French trading posts were built nearby in the 1720s. But French colonization did not produce disruption or decline for the Osage. In fact, the outcome was the opposite — the rise of an Osage empire, where they dominated the hide and slave trade, expanded their territorial control, and served as "middlemen" between French traders and other Indigenous communities. For the Osage, the eighteenth century was a time of economic prosperity, regional power, and good health. Their first known colonial-era epidemic, believed to be smallpox, emerged after Zebulon Pike visited an Osage town in 1806. Though it would be fifteen years before another epidemic, Pike's visit was symbolic of the differing impact of French trading colonies compared to US settler colonialism. In a settler empire, Natives had to be eliminated in order for the empire's settlers to possess Native land. And much like the Spanish in La Florida discussed earlier, US colonization involved "structural violence" where American political, economic, and social constructions produced institutional policies that assaulted Indigenous mental, physical, spiritual, and community health.[12]

By the 1820s, US settler colonialism had led to refugee migration and forced expulsion of eastern Natives who congregated on the Osage homeland, closely followed by invading American settlers and government-funded missionaries. This compromised farming, hunting, and trade leading to malnutrition, while simultaneously increasing warfare between Native groups competing over increasingly scarce natural resources. The Osage were then eliminated from their Missouri homeland and confined to a reservation in present-day Kansas, where their towns were in unprecedentedly close proximity and the climate and soil were inhospitable to agriculture. This alienation from their homeland also prevented the Osage from fulfilling many spiritual responsibilities, which assaulted every aspect of their lives. All of this disruption made the Osage vulnerable to disease; subsequently smallpox, measles, influenza, and cholera (among others) began to strike them every few years. The deadliest disease outbreaks coincided predictably with the American settler invasion of Kansas that began in the 1850s. Settlers stole Osage crops, timber, horses, and homes, while mobilizing local militias with the governor's support to terrorize — and ultimately eliminate —

the Osage in Kansas. In the 1870s they were expelled again to present-day Oklahoma. Over a fifty-year period, their population declined by at least 70 percent. The Osage did not die from accidentally introduced "virgin" soil epidemics. They died because US settler colonialism and its associated structural violence severely and continuously undermined physical and spiritual health, food production, and fertility.[13]

Once colonization disrupted Native communities, facilitating epidemic death, how did they react? Scholars employing VST typically claimed Indigenous people had essentially no idea what to do in the face of epidemic disease; so their actions often made the situation more deadly because no one was left to nurse the sick or acquire food, and their spiritual foundation was shaken, if not entirely toppled. In contrast, Paul Kelton has argued, "Native Americans were capable of responding creatively to epidemics and avoiding complete physical and spiritual destruction." His examination of the eighteenth-century Cherokees, Creeks, Choctaws, and Chickasaws showed that new diseases were understood in the same spiritual context as all other illnesses, and religious faith was not undermined. These nations intentionally limited contact with colonial settlements during outbreaks, used ritualized quarantine to reduce the spread of disease, and relied on experienced healers to provide treatment. All of this "kept large numbers of people from getting sick at the same time and allowed normal social services, such as food gathering . . . to continue." As a result, during the last half of the eighteenth century, their response to disease was so effective it ensured "the Four Nations survived not only physically but also culturally and spiritually."[14]

Kathleen Hull has also disproven the assumption that new diseases led to "inevitable and unidirectional" cultural change. She documented how the varied Native responses to colonization and disease came from past experience that predated European arrival—often involving community migration and aggregation. Taking a long, often archaeologically based approach, she described how Native life changed in response to climate fluctuations (including the Little Ice Age, ca. 1450) and other factors in order to show continuity in adaptations before and after colonization. Disproving VST, she detailed how interior Indigenous communities spanning North America did not experience epidemics until they were directly or indirectly impacted by European colonization via the deerskin trade, fur trade, slaving, and other operations in adjoining regions. Native communities frequently relocated as a temporary solution to initial population loss. And in some cases, Native populations rebounded. In many instances, after epidemics reached interior communities, there was little or no cultural change. Often subsistence, settlement patterns, and technology remained stable. In other cases, cultural change can be attributed to nondisease factors, such as adoption of the horse and the influence of new Native neighbors. What she found significant was that epidemics typically preceded full-scale European invasion by, at most, decades. This relatively short "lag time," Hull concluded, was "the critical element in the case of colonial-era depopulation" because "insufficient time elapsed to reverse consequent, otherwise shorter-term, cultural adjustments prior to physical impingement by Europeans." And, most importantly, it was this permanent colonial presence, rather than initial disease exposure, that "ultimately undermined traditional lifeways." Hull repeatedly emphasized the need to contextualize the experience of each Indigenous community with colonization, not only to understand the impact of disease, but to understand "the ability of the native people to make decisions, chart their own course, and persist in the midst of colonial upheaval, often drawing on a dynamic long-term history and inherent cultural flexibility in order to do so."[15]

As is clear from the scholarship, "nothing was fundamentally unique about the disease experience of Native Americans: all human populations have experienced devastating epidemics. What was unique for Indians was European colonization. Had Indians simply experienced new pathogens, their populations would have declined and recovered."[16] It was "the phenomenon of European colonialism as conceived and implemented . . . that explains the delayed or failed recovery of indigenous American populations."[17] The decades-long focus on VST has obscured how "warfare, enslavement, land expropriation, removals, erasure of identity, and other non-disease factors . . . had a more detrimental impact . . . [on] the indigenous population as a whole."[18] By the time Native people started dying of epidemics, European and neo-European colonization had already weakened or killed them, meaning "disease was the secondary killer."[19] Consequently, VST "covers up more than it reveals."[20]

If, as the overwhelming weight of scholarship shows, "human agency, not microbes, was the key" in determining Indigenous population decline, then who or what was to blame for demographic collapse?[21] As Paul Kelton and I have argued, VST has unfortunately played a key role in debates over genocide in American history. VST framed epidemics as an unintended consequence of contact. For many this meant: no intent, no genocide. Even those who argued colonialism was inherently genocidal employed VST, in part because its high population estimates and 90 percent mortality seemed to increase the magnitude of death. But the issue of intent remained. The real problem in this debate was reliance on VST, which has been replaced by more specific and complex research on disease. In order to investigate genocide, the intent and impact of colonization must be determined for a given community, especially in terms of violence and disruption to Native life that then made people vulnerable to disease. Colonizers bear responsibility for their actions that undermined Native health, facilitated epidemic death, and inhibited recovery. VST has proved an intellectual barrier for many in accepting that genocide occurred in the Americas, but that stumbling block has been removed. Now scholars of disease and genocide need to connect their arguments.[22]

Another important question is why have scholars and the public been so easily seduced by the simplistic—and widely disproven—"virgin" soil thesis? David Jones claimed VST has a "powerful and promiscuous appeal" because it "provided an alternative to human-centric histories, something that . . . shifted blame off Europeans . . . and onto morally neutral biohistorical forces."[23] VST also relied heavily on other myths, such as the romanticized—and condescendingly paternalistic—image of an Edenic Western Hemisphere filled with Natives living in "harmony" with each other and the environment. Not only did these stereotypes "restrict the agency" of Native people, as Suzanne Alchon has argued, but they simultaneously framed Native people as childlike inferiors to Europeans—justifying colonization and marginalization.[24] It was this ideological purpose, rather than its historical accuracy, that Jones believed was central to VST's hegemony.[25]

But none of this is new. New England Puritans claimed Native depopulation was God's will. In the nineteenth century, Americans chose to believe their dominance on the continent was civilization triumphing over savagery. And by the twentieth century, the justification was Darwinian racial superiority. As Alan Swedlund described it, "indigenous bodies themselves have been colonized and scripted, [and] plagues and epidemics have been used as a means for blame and shame."[26] Unfortunately, scholars have been "complacently uncritical" of primary sources that even among eighteenth-century contemporaries deliberately advanced stories of powerful germs, Native incompetence, and exonerated colonizers. Paul Kelton has shown how discussions of the Indigenous experience with disease were not and are not morally neutral. "Narratives of disease thus continue to be told that obscure how colonialism—in all its manifold yet connected aspects—has negatively impacted indigenous health and well-being. Most troubling, and far from being morally neutral," Kelton concluded, is how all of this "silence[s] Native voices."[27] Kathleen Hull agreed: "It is a disservice to both descendant communities and our collective heritage and history to ignore the myriad factors that contributed to when and how Native peoples confronted such challenges to survival and how groups, if not many individuals, often endured."[28] VST remains an appealing story, Jones contended, because "Euroamericans are the beneficiaries of the deaths of tens of millions of American Indians; Africans were enslaved and brought to the Americas to provide labor as Indians died. Virgin soil theory attempts to isolate the present from the horrors of the past . . . [and] the theory makes it easier to ignore those same factors where they operate today."[29] And they do operate today. Jones has chronicled how "American Indians have always experienced higher rates of disease than their European and American contemporaries." Whether it was eighteenth-century smallpox and measles, nineteenth-century tuberculosis, or twentieth-century diabetes, disparities in health reflect the enduring "disparities in wealth and power."[30]

Does inaccurate scholarship and teaching on the role of disease in Indigenous depopulation constitute continued colonization? The very language employed is revealing: "virgin Indians were helpless before the thrust of European pathogens." Claims that Native people were weak, vulnerable, defenseless, and virginal in terms of disease furthers the feminizing and queering of Indigenous peoples in relation to colonial heteropatriarchy. In other words, Indigenous peoples are constructed as an inferior, dependent, sexualized, strange, and subordinate minority, which defines their position in non-Native-dominated society past and present. VST is construed as documenting history, but in reality, does it tell us more about the predominantly non-Native authors and teachers that propagate it?[31] As historian James H. Merrell has concluded, "we are all, in more ways than one, 'colonial historians.'" The words we use and the arguments we teach reflect the power of colonial hierarchies even today. For decades, VST has framed, and thus limited, our view. Therefore, is it another example of what Larsen called structural violence, where systemic and institutionalized inequalities have "suppress[ed] the ability of members of Native societies to reach their full potential," limiting their ability to "reproduce and recover from the colonial traumas?" Have we, as Merrell argued, "met the enemy and he is us?"[32] Chiitaanibah Johnson, based on her experience in her Sacramento State history class, certainly seemed to answer in the affirmative. In an op-ed in the student newspaper, she wrote: "The truth about the American Indian genocide has been covered up for far too long. For native students such as myself, this truth is not something we are used to hearing in a classroom. We are told horror stories of the days of the genocide, not from professors but from our parents and elders."[33]

VST is flawed and outdated, but it is also well known and entrenched. So, how should educators address these issues in their classrooms? Any of the sources referenced above could be used to craft lectures or assignments showing how diseases actually functioned in a diversity of contexts. Another method is using the classroom experiences of Johnson and Wiseman as a teaching tool. Again, there are many important themes in this series of events, but one of the major issues was historiography. Professor Wiseman—like many scholars, teachers, and the general public—did not seem aware that VST was no longer the standard in the field, and thus his dismissal of genocide easily followed. Once outbreaks of disease are contextualized, it is clear that the actions of colonizers disrupted Native life, and *then* diseases struck. If colonial disruptions continued, Native populations failed to recover. Individual case studies are useful in allowing students to define intention and apply genocide and other concepts to the Indigenous experience. Ask your students, ask yourself: Who's to blame?

NOTES

1. Maury Wiseman, "Sac State Professor Explains His Use of Word 'Genocide,'" *The State Hornet*, October 22, 2015, http://statehornet.com/2015/10/sac-state-professor-explains-his-use-of-word-genocide/ (accessed June 18, 2018); Chiitaanibah Johnson, "Native American Student at Sac State Shares Her Story," *The State Hornet*, October 22, 2015, http://statehornet.com/2015/10/native-american-student-at-sac-state-shares-her-story/ (accessed June 18, 2018); Vincent Schilling, "History Professor Denies Native Genocide: Native Student Disagreed, Then Says Professor Expelled Her from Course," *Indian Country Today Media Network*, September 6, 2015, https://indiancountrytoday.com/archive/

history-professor-denies-native-genocide-native-student-disagrees-gets-ex pelled-course (accessed June 18, 2018); Colleen Flaherty, "Academic Freedom and Compassion," *Inside Higher Ed,* October 9, 2015, https://www.insidehigh ered.com/news/2015/10/09/sacramento-state-ends-investigation-disagreement -over-what-professor-said-about?utm_source=Inside+Higher+Ed&utm_cam paign=49e358182c-DNU20151009&utm_medium=email&utm_term=0_1fcbc04 421-49e358182c-198405841 (accessed June 18, 2018).

2. Alfred W. Crosby, "Virgin Soil Epidemics as a Factor in the Aboriginal Depopulation in America," *William and Mary Quarterly* 33, no. 2 (April 1976), 289–90; David S. Jones, "Virgin Soils Revisited," *William and Mary Quarterly* 60, no. 4 (October 2003), 703–10, 712; David S. Jones, "Death, Uncertainty, and Rhetoric," in *Beyond Germs: Native Depopulation in North America,* ed. Catherine M. Cameron, Paul Kelton, and Alan C. Swedlund (Tucson: University of Arizona Press, 2015), 16–22. In both of his articles Jones provides a lengthy overview of popular and scholarly sources that utilize the "virgin" soil thesis.

3. Tai S. Edwards and Paul Kelton, "Germs, Genocides, and America's Indigenous Peoples," *Journal of American History* 107, no. 1 (June 2020): 54, 69, 75–76; Paul Kelton, Alan C. Swedlund, and Catherine M. Cameron, introduction to Cameron, Kelton, and Swedlund, *Beyond Germs,* 3, 6; Jones, "Virgin Soils Revisited," 705, 742; James B. Waldram, D. Ann Herring, and T. Kue Young, *Aboriginal Health in Canada,* 2nd ed. (Toronto: University of Toronto Press, 2006), 71.

4. Kelton, Swedlund, and Cameron, introduction to Cameron, Kelton, and Swedlund, *Beyond Germs,* 5; Jones, "Death, Uncertainty, and Rhetoric," 25–26; Crosby, "Virgin Soil Epidemics," 289–90.

5. Jones, "Death, Uncertainty, and Rhetoric," 26–27; Dean R. Snow and Kim M. Lanphear, "European Contact and Indian Depopulation in the Northeast: The Timing of the First Epidemics," *Ethnohistory* 35, no. 1 (Winter 1988): 17, 24–25; Kathleen L. Hull, *Pestilence and Persistence: Yosemite Indian Demography and Culture in Colonial California* (Berkeley: University of California Press, 2009), 270, 280.

6. Snow and Lanphear, "European Contact and Indian Depopulation," 17, 25–26; Paul Kelton, *Epidemics and Enslavement: Biological Catastrophe in the Native Southeast, 1492–1715* (Lincoln: University of Nebraska Press, 2007), 49–50.

7. Jones, "Death, Uncertainty, and Rhetoric," 26–27; Hull, *Pestilence and Persistence,* 226–27, 237, 243, 262, 268, 277, 281; Kelton, *Epidemics and Enslavement,* 48–50; Clark Spencer Larsen, "Colonialism and Decline in the American Southeast: The Remarkable Record of La Florida," in Cameron, Kelton, and Swedlund, *Beyond Germs,* 79; George R. Milner, "Population Decline and Culture Change in the American Midcontinent: Bridging the Prehistoric and Historic Divide," in Cameron, Kelton, and Swedlund, *Beyond Germs,* 57, 59–61, 63; Snow and Lanphear, "European Contact and Indian Depopulation," 26–28; Ann L. W. Stodder, "The History of Paleopathology in the American Southwest," in *The*

Global History of Paleopathology: Pioneers and Prospects, ed. Jane E. Buikstra and Charlotte A. Roberts (New York: Oxford University Press, 2012), 289, 291–92.

8. Larsen, "Colonialism and Decline," 75, 77, 79–86, 88, 93; Kelton, *Epidemics and Enslavement*, 82–87.

9. Catherine M. Cameron, "The Effects of Warfare and Captive-Taking on Indigenous Mortality in Postcontact North America," in Cameron, Kelton, and Swedlund, *Beyond Germs*, 175–81.

10. Kelton, *Epidemics and Enslavement*, 101–4, 119–20, 141–43.

11. Cameron, "The Effects of Warfare," 181–92; Kelton, *Epidemics and Enslavement*, 102.

12. Tai S. Edwards, "Disruption and Disease: The Osage Struggle to Survive in the Nineteenth-Century Trans-Missouri West," *Kansas History: A Journal of the Central Plains* 36, no. 4 (Winter 2013–2014): 219–24; Tai S. Edwards, *Osage Women and Empire: Gender and Power* (Lawrence: University Press of Kansas, 2018); Larsen, "Colonialism and Decline," 88.

13. Edwards, "Disruption and Disease," 224–33; Edwards, *Osage Women and Empire*, 96–97, 128.

14. Crosby," Virgin Soil Epidemics," 293–99; Paul Kelton, "Avoiding the Smallpox Spirits: Colonial Epidemics and Southeastern Indian Survival," *Ethnohistory* 51, no. 1 (Winter 2004): 46–47, 54–64.

15. Hull, *Pestilence and Persistence*, 20, 221, 243, 260, 265, 267, 273–74, 280–82.

16. Jones, "Death, Uncertainty, and Rhetoric," 23.

17. Suzanne Austin Alchon, *A Pest in the Land: New World Epidemics in a Global Perspective* (Albuquerque: University of New Mexico Press, 2003), 3.

18. Kelton, Swedlund, and Cameron, introduction to Cameron, Kelton, and Swedlund, *Beyond Germs*, 3.

19. Edwards, *Osage Women and Empire*, 97.

20. Paul Kelton, *Cherokee Medicine, Colonial Germs: An Indigenous Nation's Fight against Smallpox, 1518–1824* (Norman: University of Oklahoma Press, 2015), 215.

21. Jones, "Death, Uncertainty, and Rhetoric," 31.

22. Edwards and Kelton, "Germs, Genocides, and America's Indigenous Peoples," 52–76.

23. Jones, "Death, Uncertainty, and Rhetoric," 24.

24. Alchon, *A Pest in the Land*, 2–3.

25. Jones, "Virgin Soils Revisited," 710–15.

26. Kelton, Swedlund, and Cameron, introduction to Cameron, Kelton, and Swedlund, *Beyond Germs*, 13; Jones, "Virgin Soils Revisited," 709, 716–18; David S. Jones, *Rationalizing Epidemics: Meanings and Uses of American Indian Mortality since 1600* (Cambridge, MA: Harvard University Press, 2004), 19–20; Alan C. Swedlund, "Contagion, Conflict, and Captivity in Interior New England: Native American and European Contacts in the Middle Connecticut River Valley of

Massachusetts, 1616–2004," in Cameron, Kelton, and Swedlund, *Beyond Germs*, 162, 165.

27. Kelton, *Epidemics and Enslavement*, 3–10; Kelton, *Cherokee Medicine, Colonial Germs*, 214–15; Paul Kelton, "Remembering Cherokee Mortality during the American Revolution," in Cameron, Kelton, and Swedlund, *Beyond Germs*, 215.

28. Hull, *Pestilence and Persistence*, 222.

29. Jones, "Virgin Soils Revisited," 715.

30. Jones, *Rationalizing Epidemics*, 15, 19–20.

31. Jones, "Virgin Soils Revisited," 714; Scott Lauria Morgensen, "Unsettling Queer Politics: What Can Non-Natives Learn from Two-Spirit Organizing?" in *Queer Indigenous Studies: Critical Interventions in Theory, Politics, and Literature*, ed. Qwo-Li Driskill, Chris Finley, Brian Joseph Gilley, and Scott Lauria Morgensen (Tucson: University of Arizona Press, 2011), 132, 134–35, 138.

32. Jones, "Death, Uncertainty, and Rhetoric," 42; Larsen, "Colonialism and Decline," 88; James H. Merrell, "Second Thoughts on Colonial Historians and American Indians," *William and Mary Quarterly* 69, no. 3 (July 2012): 452, 509, 512.

33. Johnson, "Native American Student at Sac State."

Understanding and Teaching Native American Slavery

From First Slaves to
Early Abolitionists in Four Myths

DENISE I. BOSSY

When I teach Native American slavery or give public and academic talks on the subject, I frequently
come up against a number of brick walls. For a remarkably long time,
we—scholars and the public alike—have collectively denied that millions of Native peoples were the victims of brutal systems of enslavement enacted by European colonizers. That collective denial rests on a
number of myths that serve to explain away Native slavery. As a result,
I often find that the most effective way to teach the topic is by overtly
engaging with these myths. And here I want to emphasize that by no
means are my students the only ones who hold to these problematic
ideas. Rather, many academics—including scholars of slavery—have
propagated these ideas in their published works for over a century.
And some continue to do so today, either overtly or by omission. Many
scholars refuse to consider that some of the enslaved peoples at the
heart of their studies are, in fact, Native people or their descendants.

Myth Number I: All Slaves Were African

This is perhaps the biggest and potentially most politically
sensitive myth. For centuries, most Americans have collectively ignored

a vital truth about slavery: Indigenous peoples were enslaved alongside Africans. In many cases, Natives were the very first enslaved people in the Americas. The trade in their bodies fueled the rise of most European colonies. The Spanish, French, and English all engaged in Indian slave trading and slavery. So, too, did Euro-Americans after them. My students are often shocked to learn that 2.5 to 5 million Native peoples were enslaved from the late fifteenth to nineteenth centuries, and in some cases into the twentieth century. This proves unsettling because it threatens to upend their confidence in what they know about slavery, which opens the door to ask what other lies their teachers told them.

The most empowering way to work through this disorientation is to teach the history of the transatlantic slave trade and slavery in the Americas as a shared story. Millions of Indigenous peoples across both the Americas and Africa were simultaneously enslaved and funneled into expansive, complex networks of trade. Meaningfully including Native Americans in this narrative reveals that the European commercialization of slaving and commodification of enslaved people was even more widespread and even more devastating than previously understood. A total of 14.5 to 17 million Indigenous people from the Americas and Africa were consumed by this ferocious trade, at least 17 to 30 percent of whom were Natives from the Americas. These are truly shocking figures. In some regions of both the Americas and Africa, where slaving was most acute, entire communities were destroyed by slaving and the violence, epidemics, famine, and sociopolitical collapses that came with it. Between 1700 and 1820, the overall population of western Africa fell by 20 percent, a population loss of five million people. Meanwhile in the Caribbean, Gulf Coast, American Southwest, northern Mexico, and Brazil, Indigenous population losses reached a staggering 70 to 90 percent from a combination of the interrelated effects of slaving, warfare, epidemics, and famine. Epidemics often spread along slaving routes through the Americas, prompting further raids for more slaves and the development of large numbers of refugee populations living at risk.[1]

Telling this as a collective story is one way to easily integrate Native American slavery into preexisting course modules on slavery. Not only did Indigenous and African communities experience the same ravaging effects of commercialized slavery, but enslaved Indians and Africans often found themselves thrown together. From the silver mines of northern Mexico to the tobacco fields of Virginia and rice patties of South Carolina, Natives and Africans labored next to one another. In 1712, a British pamphlet promoting colonial settlement in Carolina offered the following advice to prospective planters: purchase both Indigenous and African slaves. The modest farmer was advised to buy one Native woman and one African man, while those with more resources were advised to purchase eighteen Indian women, three African women, and fifteen African men. This pamphlet is a wonderful teaching tool, one that can stimulate really productive conversations with the right questions. For instance, I often ask my students why the author recommended purchasing an equal or greater number of women to men, or an equal number of Natives and Africans when purchasing large numbers of slaves, what kinds of labor the author anticipated Indigenous and African women and African men would do, why he did not recommend purchasing Native men, and what the pamphlet reveals about both the similarities and differences in British constructions of Natives and Africans.[2]

Some Indians and Africans also challenged their enslavement together. In 1721, for example, six enslaved people stole a canoe and fled to St. Augustine, where the Spanish promised freedom to British slaves who converted to Catholicism as a way to destabilize British Carolina. The group included two Native women (one with her two-year-old child), two Native men, and one African man. They lived on three different plantations and had carefully coordinated their escape. It's a remarkable story because they were successful, but not an uncommon one in other ways.[3]

Although it is a good start, it is not enough simply to add Natives to the story. While there are important similarities between Indian and African enslavement, there are also important distinctions that are worth exploring with students. Perhaps the most significant difference is that while African slave trading was broadly a legitimate business venture, Indigenous enslavement was largely illegal. In the late fifteenth century, Queen Isabella of Spain was the first to oppose the enslavement of Indigenous people whom she claimed as her "vassals." In the New Laws of 1542 the Spanish attempted to close previous loopholes exploited by conquistadores and settlers in the Americas by making it illegal to enslave any Native for any reason. In many English colonies Indian slavery was similarly illegal. The Lords Proprietors who owned and governed the colony of Carolina, for instance, issued numerous bans on the enslavement of Native people between 1671 and 1693.[4]

46

Yet, colonial settlers found creative ways to flout these regulations. In South Carolina, colonists and even officials appointed by the Proprietors simply continued to provoke and engage in Native slave wars. Meanwhile, New Englanders used their local courts to create a judicial form of enslavement after King Philip's War (1675–76), when Indian slavery was either outlawed or restricted. Many New England Natives were sentenced to perpetual terms of indentured servitude on trumped-up charges, for debt or alleged criminal behavior. Often their children were born into this perpetual servitude and found themselves trapped in the same corrupt system. New England colonists were not alone in circumventing their own legal systems by calling their enslavement of Natives by another name.[5]

This helps explain to students why, although the numbers were so significant and the devastation so evident, they have not heard much about Native American slavery. Much like human trafficking today—which operated for many decades under our very noses until the late twentieth century—the illegality of Indigenous slavery meant that the people who profited and participated in it left very few (often no) state, company, or private records and did not talk openly about it in their correspondence. Scholars who seek to reconstruct and analyze the enslavement, trade, and sale of enslaved Africans rely on ship manifests, tax records, corporation records, and other official documents produced by accountants, investors, owners, tax collectors, and other government agents. But these records rarely exist for Native people. Scholars have therefore had to piece together extraordinarily fragmentary evidence by searching for evidence of Native slavery. And they are still doing this work.

Myth Number 2: Native Americans Made Poor Slaves

Proponents of this myth suggest that Indigenous peoples made poor slaves because they succumbed to new epidemic diseases, were prone to running away or revolting, and (especially Indigenous men) were lazy. In fact, the enslavement of millions of Natives largely reveals quite the opposite: colonists coveted and valued Indigenous slaves. From the very first Spanish, English, and French colonists to well into the nineteenth century, Native peoples were targeted by slavers. For example, in Charleston, South Carolina—the busiest slave port in the South—more Indian slaves were exported than African slaves imported until the 1720s. And, while Native American enslavement was generally illegal, colonial slave laws from the sixteenth, seventeenth, and even eighteenth centuries overtly list Natives as one of the categories of people subjected to enslavement. Enslaved Indians were the initial targets of the systems of slavery and forced labor enacted by the Spanish and English in the Americas.[6]

The first slaves in the Americas were Indigenous and were victims of none other than Christopher Columbus. Recasting Columbus as the earliest in a long line of Indigenous slavers is often a really effective approach in my courses. Because students are almost universally familiar with Columbus and associate him with the "discovery" of the Americas, taking some time to examine his considerable efforts to found a Native slave trade can have a dramatic effect. Once this point is made through Columbus, students then often are more open to the idea that many European colonizers pursued Indigenous slaves.

Columbus saw great potential in Native slavery. Like many early European explorers after him, he seized Indigenous captives on his first expedition to the Caribbean in 1492 to bring back to Spain. In the early stages of colonial exploration, enslaved Natives served as physical proof of an expedition's success and were often displayed to Spanish, English, and French audiences, much as other exotic animals. Early explorers also hoped to train the Natives whom they kidnapped to serve as translators and guides for future expeditions. But Columbus also schemed to forge a transatlantic trade in enslaved Indians. One that he believed would not only rival but surpass the developing Portuguese trade in Africans.

Inspired by memories of his visit to the first Portuguese slave-trading post on the Guinea coast in sub-Saharan Africa (what would become Elmina), Columbus sent dozens of enslaved Caribs to Spain after his second voyage. He claimed that a Native slave would fetch three times as much as one from Guinea in the Spanish slave markets and proposed that King Ferdinand and Queen Isabella invest. Eager to get started, in 1495 Columbus rounded up some 1,600 Hispaniola Natives, sending 550 to Spain and divvying up the rest among his men. Of the 550 packed into four caravel ships, only 350 survived: a death rate of over 36 percent. This first middle passage of Natives proved remarkably deadly, yet Columbus was not deterred but instead proposed to send another 4,000 Indigenous slaves to Spain. Columbus's transatlantic scheme eventually failed. The Spanish Crown ultimately opposed establishing a state-run slave trade, particularly Queen Isabella, who claimed Natives should be treated as Spanish subjects.

But Columbus and other early Spanish colonizers found even greater demand for slaves in the Americas and enslaved thousands of Indigenous men, women, and children on Hispaniola to pan and dig for gold, dive for pearls, and grow sugarcane in the 1490s and early sixteenth century. As demand quickly outpaced local Indigenous populations, the Spanish launched slave raids from Hispaniola, Puerto Rico, and Jamaica across the Caribbean, to the Bahamas, Florida, the Gulf Coast, and into Central and South America. An enormous amount of energy and organization went into these slaving expeditions, which were often licensed. The Crown allowed the legal enslavement of "cannibals," those who had been taken in "just wars," or those already enslaved by other Natives—leading to false claims in each of those categories. Entire towns and even islands were depopulated by early Spanish slavers. The Spanish Crown responded to the near demographic collapse of the Caribbean by engaging in the first and only imperial debate over the ethics of Indigenous slavery and the bloody conquest of the Americas. But it was too late. Spanish colonizers had created a trans-Americas trade in Native slaves. Alongside Indian slave trading, the Spanish also invented legal systems of forced labor including the *encomienda* and *repartimiento*.[7]

This revised understanding of the centrality of Indigenous slavery to Spanish (and English) colonization also opens room to tackle the related notion that epidemic disease was the major killer of Natives across the Americas. Scholars have made this argument since the 1970s, contending that smallpox (along with measles, yellow fever, malaria, and influenza) resulted in massive depopulation, often up to 90 percent within a generation of contact. This theory has since become so popular that it is often mistaken for fact and applied across the Americas with very little, if any, evidence offered to support it. Although often unintentional, in the process scholars have erased the very real violence of European colonization. In most cases, Indigenous peoples did not quietly die off to make room for European colonists. In fact, American Indians were enslaved, killed, and violently moved off of their homelands in the name of European settlement. It was this intentional settler violence that created the conditions that led to epidemics.[8] This myth erases the violence of colonial slaving, warfare, and settlement and also denies the resiliency of many Native American communities

49

that successfully responded to diseases in innovative ways and whose descendants still survive today, as scholars are increasingly uncovering.

Myth Number 3: Native People Already Enslaved Each Other (So Commercial Slavery Was Nothing New)

This myth is an old one. It was first (and sometimes is still) applied to Africans by apologists for the transatlantic slave trade. The myth goes: Africans enslaved each other long before the Portuguese, English, or other Europeans arrived. Therefore, what Europeans did was not all that different when they created the commercial, transatlantic slave trade. The same myth has been transferred to Native slavery. In my experience, this argument functions as a way to erase European culpability for enslaving millions of Africans and Natives and to also minimize the historical significance of Atlantic world slavery. This is a good reason to spend time unpacking this myth with your students. They likely have heard some form of it.

Yet, there is an element of truth to the argument and one worth exploring because it allows you to engage in a crucially important discussion about what constitutes slavery and how slavery has varied over time and space (and continues to do so). A useful first-day exercise for a course or module on slavery is simply to ask students to tell you what they think when you say the word "slavery" and to write or project their answers on the board. It's crucially important to first offer a disclaimer: no answer is wrong, and no answer is to be judged. Rather, this is about figuring out what the class as a community already knows or thinks about slavery. I find that once a few brave students open up, the rest of the class usually follows suit. (My advice is to be prepared for lots of racially insensitive answers and to see this as a rare opportunity to actually know what your students think. This is, in my mind, the first step to successfully reeducating students.) In addition to the typecasting of slaves as solely African, the vast majority of my students still bring into class the idea that slavery was a static institution. Their definition of slavery is, more often than not, grounded in a cursory knowledge of slavery as practiced in the antebellum South. This form of chattel slavery, to them, is the norm, the standard, what slavery looks like.

For decades, scholars of slavery in Africa have been calling for historians to replace this singular language and construct—the institution of chattel slavery—with a greater sense of how *slaveries* (plural) varied over space and time. Rather than an institution, these scholars contend that we should understand and analyze slaveries as systems, practiced by certain people in distinct places for different reasons. Inspired by this call, the great historian of African American slavery, Ira Berlin, used the framework of generations of slavery not only to assert that there were multiple different systems of slavery practiced by European colonizers and Euro-Americans in the present-day United States, but also to identify structurally what was common among those systems and how they differed.[9]

As archaeologists and historians of the Americas are beginning to uncover, Native societies across the Americas engaged in a variety of forms of captivity before contact with Europeans. In some very rare cases these forms of captivity did resemble the type of slavery that the Spanish, English, Dutch, French, and other Europeans would develop. The Aztecs (or Mexica), for example, practiced different types of slavery including a form of commercial slavery where slaves were exchanged for goods or to cover debts. More generally, Indians violently captured enemies and outsiders, bound them, stripped them of their natal identities, and often forced them to perform demeaning labor. In many Native societies slaves were even deprived of their human identity. From the Pays d'en Haut to the Southeast, the very words and phrases (and even sign language) used to denote an enslaved person communicated this loss of humanity. Captors were understood to transform their captives from people into something akin to a domestic animal (often a dog), through public rituals of humiliation and physical abuse. Slavery was kin based in the majority of Indigenous societies: slaves were denied the family or clan connections that defined the rest of the human beings who made up the community. They existed outside of the human community.[10]

This kinship slavery as practiced by most American Indian communities prior to contact with Europeans—Indigenous slavery—was starkly different from Atlantic-world slavery in a number of significant ways. The biggest distinction, and one worth emphasizing with students, is that Europeans progressively invented and codified race in order to justify their enslavement of Africans and Native Americans. Native polities did vilify enemies, often through gendered language including labeling enemy warriors "women," but they did not create a false notion that some people were naturally inferior by virtue of the color of their skin. Quite to the contrary, Indigenous communities (which were largely exogamous and required their citizens to marry outside of their clan) adopted and married not only Indigenous foreigners but also Africans and Europeans. Only in the second half of the eighteenth century did some communities begin to adopt European racialized constructs. And even so, many communities resisted doing so.

While Natives across the Americas certainly practiced captivity and even slavery, their political and social economies did not rest on them. To draw on Ira Berlin's useful distinction between societies whose economies and social hierarchies were dependent on slavery and those wherein slavery played a minor role in the economy and no role in social hierarchy: there were no Indigenous slave societies in North America, only societies with slaves. Native communities that practiced kinship slavery did not commodify captives and slaves. Slaves belonged to their captors and were exchanged with other communities to solidify peace treaties, but their bodies did not have a cash or other economic value. Rather they had political and social currency. They were slaves because they came from enemy polities.[11]

A second important difference to discuss with students is that Indigenous kin-based slavery was neither inheritable nor necessarily perpetual. The children of Indigenous slaves were free, in stark contrast to Atlantic world slavery where status was both inherited and often matrilineal, with children's legal identities as slaves set by their mothers' status. In addition, many Indigenous slaves were adopted by their captors. This was the main reason for captive-taking among the Haudenosaunees (members of the Great League of Iroquois). Particularly during the 1630s–50s, when they lost over half of their population to epidemic diseases, the Haudenosaunees launched intensive captive wars ("mourning wars") in order to replace their lost loved ones and maintain their family and social structures. Through adoption ceremonies—called Requickening—Haudenosaunee captors transformed their slaves into kin who assumed the identity, name, and place of the lost loved one and who were cherished as family. Slaves might also be repatriated to their original community if, for example, a peace treaty was established.[12]

All the same, some Native communities responded to the disruptive and traumatic effects of European colonization by becoming slavers (as did some Africans). It's important to take some time to explain this decision to students, who are likely to find it confusing for several reasons including their tendency to define "Indians" as a singular political group rather than many distinct polities who did not see themselves as "Indian" until the eighteenth century, at the very earliest. Scholars describe the effects of colonization on Indigenous communities as "shattering." Those communities which survived did so by creatively adapting. For those communities living where slaving was most intense the choice was stark: become slavers or remain targets of slavers. In this context commercial slaving was a tool wielded by Native communities in an effort to survive and also to negotiate the terms of their survival.[13]

Many, but by no means the majority, of the Indigenous slaves sold by Europeans were initially captured by other Natives. In the Southeast, for example, the Westo Indians were major slavers in Virginia, Georgia, South Carolina, and Florida. The Westos were a new society, forged by dislocated Eries who had managed to survive Haudenosaunee captive raids in the 1650s and fled to Virginia, where other refugees joined them. Almost immediately, the Westos began to raid Native communities for war captives, which they exchanged with colonial Virginians and Carolinians for guns, ammunition, and other trade goods. They became a militarized slaving society, using slavery, violence, and guns as tools for survival and geopolitical expansion until Carolina colonists engineered their destruction in order to expand their slave trade enterprises with other Indigenous groups, including the Yamasees and Creeks. In the Southwest, the Comanches were even more successful in using slaving to take over Apache homelands and to foster powerful economic ties to Spanish, French, and English colonies during the eighteenth century. French soldiers and traders, for example, purchased Apache women as sex slaves and also used marriage (and baptism) to forcibly integrate these women and the children they bore into their communities. Like many slaving communities, the Comanches also kept numerous Apache women and children (especially boys who were groomed to become warriors). Some captives were integrated into their kinship networks and others remained slaves in Comancheria. And those captives were not exclusively Indigenous but could also include Americans and Mexicans.[14]

While some Native communities engaged in commercial slaving, European colonists were responsible for creating the conditions that prompted the rise of Native slavery in the Americas. Colonists also transformed Natives from captives into slaves with economic valuations. Indians were enslaved through colonial courts for crimes and debts, through wars waged by colonists, and by colonial raiders who attacked their communities. Even when colonists did not have a hand in the initial enslavement of Indigenous people, they founded the system of slavery that led to the commercial enslavement of millions of Indigenous people.

Myth Number 4: Indigenous Slavery Just Happened in a Few Places and Was a Frontier Phenomenon

Those historians who, prior to the early twenty-first century, admitted that Native slavery did happen tended to argue that it only happened in a few places. South Carolina and Brazil, for example, but surely not Massachusetts or Pennsylvania. Often accompanying this myth was a second argument: that even in these places, Indian slavery rarely lasted beyond the "frontier period." Indigenous slavery, according to this line of thinking, was the aberration and not the norm. Few colonies meaningfully enslaved Indigenous people, and those that did generally did so only until they could economically outgrow it and turn to African slaves for their labor needs. According to this myth, Natives were enslaved in a few (or many) places early on but were quickly replaced by Africans as colonies matured. This myth largely erases colonists' intent to enslave Indians. Native people were there, colonists needed labor, Indians were not their first choice because colonists recognized either their sovereignty or their potential for assimilation, or because they made poor slaves.

Correcting this myth helps students understand that Native slavery was not just a growing pain in early colonial development. Rather, as scholars are increasingly showing, Indigenous enslavement was essential to the broad development of colonial networks across the Americas. Like the Spanish, the English developed a trans-Americas Indigenous slave trade. As they shipped enslaved Natives from places such as Carolina to New York, New England, Jamaica, and Barbados, they knit their empire together. Native people were part of the triangular trade that many of us have taught for some time. Indigenous slavery was also central to settler colonialism. New and forthcoming work on the English Caribbean, for example, reveals just how critical Native slavery was to the rise and expansion of the English empire.[15]

While Indigenous slavery and slave trading varied greatly across the Americas, every major European colonial power was involved in it to some degree. The field is still quite young and developing, but with each new article and book, we find that this was even more the norm than previously thought. One way to approach teaching Native slavery and slave trading, then, is by examining case studies in New France, New England, Virginia, the Carolinas, Louisiana, Texas, New Mexico, the Caribbean, and other regions. Unpacking each reveals a great deal about the particular context of each region and how Native enslavement varied from place to place and over time. In New England, for example, colonists strategically used both war and enslavement to pave the way for the expansion of their colonies into Indigenous homelands. (Contrary to stubborn sectionalist notions, New Englanders were also deeply involved in the slave trade—they owned and sold enslaved Natives and Africans, and slavery was critical to their seventeenth-century economies.)[16]

In many places, Native slavery lasted well into the eighteenth century and in some cases even into the nineteenth and twentieth centuries. Exploring this with students provides an invaluable opportunity to talk openly about how race itself was constructed and reconstructed by European colonizers who sought to codify and justify their enslavement of Natives and Africans. Above all, this is a chance to think about why it is that we still often discuss race as binary, as Black and White, when America is and always has been a far more diverse and pluralistic society. Over the course of the eighteenth century, slavery became increasingly associated with "Africans," even as Natives were still in slavery and actively enslaved. Enslaved Indians were increasingly identified as "negro" in wills, probates, court cases, and statutes. Some owners and merchants intentionally disguised the true identities of Indigenous slaves, while many others were simply recategorized as "negro."[17] By the scratch of a pen, their identities were subsumed under the rubric of slave.

As Native people were rhetorically but not actually erased from the enslaved population, Africans were increasingly conflated with slavery. American Indians were crucial, then, to how Europeans and Euro-Americans grounded eighteenth- and nineteenth-century notions of race in descriptions of alleged physicality. If Natives were poor slaves whose bodies were too frail for the hot sun and hard labor of growing rice, indigo, and sugar, Africans were ideally suited to this work. If Natives were too freedom loving to subject themselves to the indignity of slavery, Africans were—like livestock—able to be broken.

In the second half of the eighteenth century, a small but significant number of enslaved people seized on this racialization of slavery to successfully sue for their freedom. Contesting their enslavement on the grounds that they were the descendants of Indigenous women, they opened the door for others to do the same in Virginia and New England (and likely elsewhere, too). Virginian and New England courts found in favor of these plaintiffs for political reasons. The transatlantic abolitionist movement was gaining ground, and freeing the descendants of Native women proved to be a way for Virginians to demonstrate some morality and for New Englanders to deflect attention away from the gradual nature of abolition in their colonies (and states).[18] Similarly, in the late eighteenth century, the Spanish began to grant freedom to descendants of enslaved Native women in New Orleans.[19]

And yet, the enslavement of Indigenous people persisted in other regions. Most notably, Native slavery was a central component of American expansion into the West. In California, for example, Americans legalized their enslavement under the guise of peonage, apprenticeship, and convict labor leasing programs. And Natives were not included in the 13th Amendment or in subsequent Supreme Court decisions to clarify the amendment's scope. In some parts of the West—New Mexico, for instance—the abolition of African American slavery led to a related increase in Native enslavement. Federal authorities, including President Lincoln and President Johnson, were well aware of this. In 1867, Congress finally passed an act abolishing Native slavery (or "peonage") in New Mexico through Senator Charles Sumner's work, but this led to the liberation of few Natives.[20]

Conclusion: Why Add Slavery to Native American Studies and Native Americans to Slavery Studies?

Telling a more complete story about both American slavery and Native American history requires that we begin to meaningfully include Indigenous people in our classroom discussions of slavery. Enslaved Natives were the first targets of the systems of slavery and forced labor enacted by the Europeans in the Americas. Slaving was also a potent geopolitical tool, enabling European colonizers effectively to remove Native populations from lands they coveted while profiting from the sale of Indigenous peoples. Yet Indigenous people were not silent victims, despite the intentional erasure of their enslavement from our collective memory of slavery.

At times some Natives participated in slaving, seeing in this a chance to survive and even to empower themselves amid the potentially shattering effects of colonization. At other times they contested the enslavement of their kin and friends or even of strangers, including enslaved Africans. The truth is that we are only just beginning to understand Native American slavery: the mechanics of the trade itself, the expansive geographical and temporal scope of Indigenous enslavement, and how Natives understood the new forms of slavery invented by Europeans as they embarked on projects to transform Indigenous places and people into colonies and commodities.

Enslavement lies also at the root of many nineteenth- and twentieth-century systems of exploitation that affected and continue to affect Native people across North America: the reservation movement, racialization in Indian country as many sought to define themselves as not Black in order to avoid enslavement, and the boarding school movement and theft of Indigenous children who were often forced to labor in or by their schools. Present-day issues including the systemic sexual assaults and murders of Native women are also rooted in the historic enslavement and rape of Indigenous women by European colonizers. Future scholars will look back at the first decades of the twenty-first century and mark this as the time when the field of slavery studies was fundamentally and forever changed.

NOTES

1. Andrés Reséndez, *The Other Slavery: The Uncovered Story of Indian Enslavement in America* (Boston: Houghton Mifflin Harcourt, 2016), 5–6, 324.

2. Reséndez, *The Other Slavery*, 110.

3. September 9, 1725, South Carolina Grand Council Journal, no. 3, South Carolina Department of Archives and History, Columbia, South Carolina.

4. Alan Gallay, *The Indian Slave Trade: The Rise of the English Empire in the American South, 1670–1717* (New Haven, CT: Yale University Press, 2002), 62–92.

5. Margaret Ellen Newell, *Brethren by Nature: New England Indians, Colonists, and the Origins of American Slavery* (Ithaca, NY: Cornell University Press, 2015), 131–236. See also Kristofer Ray, "Constructing a Discourse of Indigenous Slavery, Freedom, and Sovereignty in Anglo-Virginia, 1600–1750," *Native South* 10 (2017).

6. Alan Gallay, "Indian Slavery in Historical Context" and "South Carolina's Entrance into the Indian Slave Trade," in *Indian Slavery in Colonial America*, ed. Alan Gallay (Lincoln: University of Nebraska Press, 2009), 1–32 and 109–46.

7. Reséndez, *The Other Slavery*, 1–40; Denise I. Bossy, "16th Century Captivity and Slavery, Indian," in *American Centuries: The Ideas, Issues, and Trends That Made U.S. History*, vol. 1, ed. Karen Kupperman (New York: Facts on File, 2011), 21–29.

8. Paul Kelton, *Epidemics and Enslavement: Biological Catastrophe in the Native Southeast, 1492–1715* (Lincoln: University of Nebraska Press, 2009).

9. Ira Berlin, *Generations of Captivity: A History of African-American Slaves* (Cambridge, MA: Harvard University Press, 2004).

10. Christina Snyder, *Slavery in Indian Country: The Changing Face of Captivity in Early America* (Cambridge, MA: Harvard University Press, 2010), 13–45; Robbie Ethridge, *From Chicaza to Chickasaw: The European Invasion and the Transformation of the Mississippian World, 1540–1715* (Chapel Hill: University of North Carolina Press, 2010), 89–115.

11. Denise I. Bossy, "Indian Slavery in Southeastern Indian and British Societies, 1670–1730," in Gallay, *Indian Slavery in Colonial America*, 207–50.

12. William A. Fox, "Events as Seen from the North: The Iroquois and Colonial Slavery," in *Mapping the Mississippian Shatter Zone: The Colonial Indian Slave Trade and Regional Instability in the American South*, ed. Robbie Ethridge and Sheri M. Shuck-Hall (Lincoln: University of Nebraska Press, 2009), 63–80.

13. Robbie Ethridge, "Introduction: Mapping the Mississippian Shatter Zone," in Ethridge and Shuck-Hall, *Mapping the Mississippian Shatter Zone*, 1–62.

14. Maureen Meyers, "From Refugees to Slave Traders: The Transformation of the Westo Indians," in Ethridge and Shuck-Hall, *Mapping the Mississippian Shatter Zone*, 81–103; Denise I. Bossy, "Negotiating Slavery and Empire: Yamasee Indians in the Early Southeast," in *European Empires and the American South*, ed. Joseph P. Ward (Jackson: University of Mississippi Press, 2017), 57–86; Reséndez, *The Other Slavery*, 172–95.

15. Rebecca Anne Goetz, "Indian Slavery: An Atlantic and Hemispheric Problem," *History Compass* 14, no. 2 (2016): 59–70.

16. Wendy Warren, *New England Bound: Slavery and Colonization in Early America* (New York: W. W. Norton, 2016).

17. Newell, *Brethren by Nature*, 237–54.

18. See Kristofer Ray, "'The Indians of Every Denomination Were Free, and Independent of Us': White Southern Explorations of Indigenous Slavery, Freedom, and Society, 1772–1830," *American Nineteenth Century History* 17, no. 2 (2016): 139–59; and Honor Sachs, "'Freedom by a Judgment': The Legal History of an Afro-Indian Family," *Law and History Review* 30 (February 2012): 173–203.

19. Jennifer Spear, *Race, Sex, and Social Order in Early New Orleans* (Baltimore: Johns Hopkins University Press, 2009), 163–67.

20. Reséndez, *The Other Slavery*, 218–316.

FOR FURTHER READING

Ablavsky, Gregory. "Making Indians 'White': The Judicial Abolition of Native Slavery in Revolutionary Virginia and Its Racial Legacy." *University of Pennsylvania Law Review* 159 (April 2011): 1457–531.

Beck, Robin. *Chiefdoms, Collapse, and Coalescence in the Early American South.* Cambridge: Cambridge University Press, 2013.

Cameron, Catherine. *Captives: How Stolen People Changed the World.* Lincoln: University of Nebraska Press, 2016.

Fisher, Linford. "Why Shall We Have Peace to Be Made Slaves: Indian Surrenderers during and after King Phillip's War." *Ethnohistory* 64, no. 1 (2017): 91–114.

Forbes, Jack D. *Africans and Native Americans: The Language of Race and the Evolution of Red-Black Peoples.* Urbana: University of Illinois Press, 1993.

Kelton, Paul. *Cherokee Medicine, Colonial Germs: An Indigenous Nation's Fight against Smallpox, 1518–1824.* Norman: University of Oklahoma Press, 2015.

Norris, John. "Profitable Advice for Rich and Poor (London, 1712)." In *Selling a New World: Two Colonial South Carolina Promotional Pamphlets,* edited by Jack Greene, 77–147. Columbia: University of South Carolina Press, 1989.

Ray, Kristofer. "Constructing a Discourse of Indigenous Slavery, Freedom, and Sovereignty in Anglo-Virginia, 1600–1750." *Native South* 19 (2017): 19–39.

Ray, Kristofer. "'The Indians of Every Denomination Were Free, and Independent of Us': White Southern Explorations of Indigenous Slavery, Freedom, and Society, 1772–1830." *American Nineteenth Century History* 17, no. 2 (2016): 139–59.

Rushforth, Brett. *Bonds of Alliance: Indigenous and Atlantic Slaveries in New France.* Chapel Hill: University of North Carolina Press, 2014.

Sachs, Honor. "'Freedom by a Judgment': The Legal History of an Afro-Indian Family." *Law and History Review* 30 (February 2012): 173–203.

Van Deusen, Nancy E. *Global Indios: The Indigenous Struggle for Justice in Sixteenth-Century Spain.* Durham, NC: Duke University Press, 2015.

Teaching the Indian Wars

MARK VAN DE LOGT

Warfare and violence shaped American Indian experiences both before and after 1492. Wars redrew territorial boundaries, destroyed some Native civilizations, gave rise to others, determined cultural trajectories, changed economic patterns, and contributed to the greatest demographic disaster in human history. Cultural differences lay at the heart of the causes and character of Euro-Indigenous warfare. Each viewed the other's modes of combat as "savage," although Europeans used "enemy savagery" as justification for conquest and colonization. When Indigenous and European cultures met on the field of battle, the result was an escalation of violence that could lead each side to accuse the other of atrocities. Both sides could adopt strategies of *total warfare*, and occasionally it took on genocidal tendencies.[1]

This chapter explores concepts and timelines for teaching and understanding wars and warfare between Europeans, Euro-Americans, and Native polities (for clarity I shorten it to "the Indian Wars"). Although the chapter cannot cover all aspects of the topic, my hope is that teachers will use it in conjunction with other chapters in this volume to produce more nuanced and effective pedagogies that illuminate Native experiences.

Course Materials

Although textbooks bring structure to a course, primary sources, especially those from Native perspectives, are indispensable. Sources include nonwritten materials such as oral traditions, music recordings, and visual art such as winter counts, ledger drawings, petroglyphs, painted tipi covers, buffalo hides, birch-bark pictographs, bead-work, and wampum belts. There also are a number of written Indigenous-centric sources, although most of these delve into matters of nineteenth-century warfare. Well-known classics include autobiographies by Black Hawk, Geronimo, Black Elk, Lakota chief White Bull, and Cheyenne warrior Wooden Leg, among others. Useful, if biased, non-Native sources include a variety of captivity narratives such as those of Mary Rowlandson, Eunice Williams (as viewed by her father), Mary Jemison, Fanny Kelly, and others. In addition, congressional hearings such as those on the Sand Creek Massacre, treaties, and other government documents are available online and provide teachers with valuable sources.[2]

Rather than presenting ready-made interpretations, the instructor's primary role is to challenge common assumptions and force students to think more deeply and critically. I ask students to debate certain hypotheses or questions. Was Native America more peaceful before the coming of Europeans? Did the European invasion cause the militarization of Indigenous cultures? Was warfare the main reason for the rise and fall of Indigenous nations? Was warfare the main cause of death among Natives? Why did Native people not unite against the invaders? Did Natives who served as scouts or allies of Europeans and the United States betray their people? Was US Indian policy aggressive and militaristic? Should the United States withdraw medals of honor awarded to soldiers of the Indian Wars? And, of course, there are "meta" issues: Did racism cause the Indian Wars, or did the Indian Wars cause racism? Were wars the result of government policy or of "settler colonialism"? Such questions challenge students to look deeper into the subject, and they will soon discover that it is far more complex than they expected.

To facilitate inquiry into the above questions teachers can use "trials" to great effect. The setup is simple: divide the class into three groups. The first group will defend an engagement as a "battle," while the second will criticize the action as a "massacre" (rebuttals are possible). Group three must render a judgment and articulate its reasoning. Instead of "battle" versus "massacre," debates can question whether a certain conflict was genocidal, or whether government/military policy was excessively aggressive. Many variations are possible. Another way to address "big picture" questions is to have students analyze different massacres (defined as the excessive use of violence against both combatants and noncombatants) and then compare notes. It is important here not only to give students examples of massacres perpetrated by Whites (of which there are many, whether Gnadenhütten in 1782, Bear River in 1863, Sand Creek in 1864, Washita in 1868, Marias River in 1870, Camp Grant in 1871, or Wounded Knee in 1890), but also of Natives massacring Whites or of inter-Indigenous attacks. Such assignments are intellectually challenging for students and teachers alike, but the payoffs in terms of learning are considerable.

Concepts and Definitions

The Indian Wars allow teachers to introduce students to military concepts such as limited and total war; strategy, operations, and tactics; annihilation and attrition; asymmetrical warfare; and the principles of war. Admittedly "Western" in origin, these concepts are nevertheless useful discussion points. The *levels of war* (strategy, operations, and tactics) offer a solid starting point because they allow students to consider the objectives, motivations, and ways of thinking of both Natives and Whites. It encourages them to step into the shoes of tribal and army leaders and to think of ways in which these actors made decisions regarding war and peace, neutrality, alliances and diplomacy, and military action or restraint.

In European eyes, Native warfare was mainly a tactical concern. Indigenous leaders, in this line of thinking, lacked strategic vision and operational sophistication—an obviously prejudicial, stereotypical, and incorrect assumption. Perhaps the overarching strategic objective on the part of Native polities was to maintain independence and sovereignty, although there never was a clear-cut means by which to achieve these ends. Whereas some tribes advocated war and armed resistance against invaders, others called for peace, friendship, and accommodation. Such differences sometimes manifested within tribes, as in the nineteenth-century case of the Mesquakies (Sauk and Fox) under Black Hawk and Keokuk. In other examples tribes sought to build alliances (as was Tecumseh's objective in the early nineteenth-century Ohio Valley), but sometimes they sought to exploit rivalries between the European powers. If they chose armed confrontation, they carefully planned operations to weaken the military capabilities of their enemies. On multiple occasions, such as British general Edward Braddock's 1755 defeat along the Monongahela River, Arthur St. Clair's 1791 defeat in Ohio, or the

Fetterman Fight of 1866, Native fighters routed their opponents. Indeed, Native operational abilities were a major source of frustration (and fear) for Europeans and Euro-Americans from 1492 through the end of the nineteenth century.

The concepts of *total and limited war* shed significant light on the character of the Indian Wars. The terms are relative because what is a limited action to one set of combatants may appear as total warfare to their opponents. Also, as often happened, limited wars could escalate into total wars and even massacres, as happened in the Pequot War of 1636–37. Many historians claim that Europeans introduced total warfare into America, and that Native warfare was "limited" (sometimes called "low-intensity"). There is no doubt that it became more deadly after European contact, but pre-1492 warfare was not always limited. Again, the challenge for students is to understand these concepts in relative rather than absolute terms.

There are many methods of warfare, but for the Indian Wars the most useful concept is known to modern scholars as *asymmetrical warfare*. It is also known as "small war," as unconventional, irregular, or guerilla warfare, although those terms can be problematic. "Irregular" and "unconventional," for example, are biased because they imply that Native forms of combat deviated from a European norm. From the Indigenous perspective, of course, European warfare was irregular.[3] Still, the concept has use because it helps explain why Native fighters often avoided pitched battles in favor of pin-prick attacks requiring stealth, surprise, and considerable skill. Put simply, asymmetrical warfare minimized the risk of casualties in their own ranks. Euro-American armies found it frustrating, however, and often attacked friendly camps because they struggled to identify allied from hostile polities.[4]

Nonmilitary historians tend to skim over battles, but if wars are of such defining importance, then these, too, deserve discussion. The *principles of war* (objective, mass, maneuver, unity of command, simplicity, economy of force, offensive, security, surprise, and morale) are useful concepts to help students analyze battles and understand miscalculations made by Custer at Greasy Grass in 1876, Braddock at Monongahela, or St. Clair in Ohio, not to mention numerous crucial but lesser-known battles such as Fallen Timbers (1794), Horseshoe Bend (1814), the Fetterman Fight (1866), and scores of inter-Indigenous battles. Tippecanoe (1811) is a perfect example of a tactical draw but a strategic defeat for the followers of the Prophetstown movement.

Although cultural historians may have to invest a little time familiarizing themselves with these concepts, the payoffs in the classroom are worth the effort.

Also useful are the concepts of annihilation and attrition. *Annihilation* is sought usually by the stronger side that wishes to settle a conflict quickly, preferably in a decisive battle in which it can capitalize on its technological, numerical, and positional strength. *Attrition* is the method often preferred by sides that lack such advantages. In this latter scenario armies hope to frustrate the stronger side over an extended period in order to exhaust its will to fight. Most of the Indian Wars fall into this category. It is important to note that a few tribes sought to escape either annihilation or attrition by seeking refuge across international borders, such as Chief Joseph's Nez Perces and Sitting Bull's Lakotas in Canada, or the Kickapoos in Mexico.

Indian Wars in Euro-American History

Colonial Warfare

When discussing colonial warfare students must understand that context is crucial. Europeans honed their modes of combat through centuries of Old World experience. Seven hundred years of Reconquista on the Iberian Peninsula, for example, directly shaped Spanish willingness to deploy brutal violence for God, Gold, and Glory. Students should view English methods in New England and Virginia against the background of the Irish wars of the late 1500s, while French and Dutch martial codes were shaped by the wars of the Reformation.

Europeans and Native people fought each other not only for land and resources, but also for slaves. Sixteenth-century Spanish conquistadors commonly raided Native polities for labor, but perhaps equally infamous were English efforts to secure Indigenous slaves in New England and Carolina. Adding to this complexity was the fact that as Atlantic World economic imperatives took hold in the late seventeenth and early eighteenth centuries, some American Indian polities became active participants in the Native slave trade. In the South, slaving (along with deerskin trading) catalyzed the collapse of Mississippian chiefdoms and the establishment of newer, "coalescent" societies. Recent research shows that slave trading remained a lucrative and important aspect of Indian-White relations until the late 1800s.[5]

When Europeans and Natives met on the field of battle, different military cultures clashed. Misunderstandings could have dramatic consequences. Seventeenth-century conflicts escalated especially quickly because each side responded violently against perceived abuses of military norms. Misunderstandings also explain why Europeans interpreted traditions such as the Iroquois "running of the gauntlet" as a form of torture rather than as an adoption ritual through which the prisoner emerged from a symbolic "birth canal" as a new person born (though beaten and bloody) into the community.[6] And while Europeans and Natives certainly learned from each other, they interpreted the lessons differently. Euro-Americans, for example, adopted scalping, but they stripped it of its cultural meaning and turned it into a commercial enterprise through scalp bounties. After the Pequot War northeastern tribes combined European scorched-earth tactics with Native asymmetrical warfare that would bring New England to the point of breakdown during King Philip's War (1675–76). The English averted this outcome in part by adopting asymmetrical tactics of their own via ranger units.

A related matter: teachers should challenge students to move beyond the stilted narrative that by the eighteenth century declining political, military, and economic fortunes reduced Native polities to de facto extensions of European projection upon the continent. Ongoing Native military strength reveals a far more complex reality. It allowed the French, for example, to protect their North American interests against a much larger English population—and made French leaders adapt to Native diplomatic protocols rather than vice versa. Teachers can see Native agency particularly well in the era of the Seven Years' War. According to standard descriptions, France's Native partners were utterly dependent upon the French for trade goods, meaning that the destruction of supply lines spelled doom for Franco-Indigenous alliances. But was that actually the case? Historian Michael McDonnell offers an important corrective when he observes that Native polities pursued agendas in support of *their* strategic goals.[7] Sometimes those agendas overlapped with European interests or demands, but many times they did not. Ask your students: Was the Indigenous world really so passive, reactive, and economically hemmed in that it could do little other than "play off" European powers? When looking at a map of eighteenth-century North America, how far does European hegemony actually extend? Would analysis of the rare examples of Native cartography yield similar conclusions? (Having students interpret the so-called

Chickasaw Map or the Catawba Deerskin Map is an excellent exercise to this end.)[8] Could Native polities acquire European goods in ways other than exclusive, one-to-one relationships with Britain, France, or Spain? And how might intra- or inter-Indigenous encounters shape the way *they* understood North America at midcentury?

An example from the Ohio Valley illustrates the point. In August 1764 British lieutenant Thomas Morris left Lake Erie on a twofold mission. First, he was ordered to march to the Ohio River and then to travel to the *pays des Illinois* to proclaim British jurisdiction over the region, as mandated by the 1763 Treaty of Paris. His second mission was to appeal for peace with Indigenous polities then supporting attacks on the newly acquired Fort Detroit. (These attacks were part of what has become known as Pontiac's War.) Long before Morris's expedition could come close to the Ohio, however, Odawas and Miamis diverted it to towns along the Maumee River. Once there, the Odawa sachem Pontiac proclaimed that "the English were liars," that the French were "not crushed (rubbing one hand over ye other) as they said," and that French traders and diplomats continued to encourage westward nations to block the extension of British jurisdiction. A few days later an unnamed sachem donned a British military uniform before informing Morris that the Miamis simply could not "trust the English." Adding insult to that piece of performative symbolism was the fact that an unnamed Mohawk absconded with the expedition's supplies at roughly the same moment, while visiting Shawnees and Lenapes (Delawares) urged neutral Miami sachems to destroy the expedition before it could proceed to the Ohio Valley.[9]

All told, Morris spent roughly three weeks in Ohio before returning to Detroit, during which time (when not fearing the imminence of his death) he described an Indigenous world of remarkable pace and complexity operating according to its own rhythms—not those imposed upon them by European economic restrictions. It is hardly a singular example. Although the British Empire clearly was victorious in the global Seven Years' War, its control of North America existed primarily only on (European-drawn) maps. It is a crucial point: seventeenth- and eighteenth-century Europeans struggled to overcome a dissonance between their claims of continental control and the reality of Native sovereignty and power. To understand (and teach) the coming of the Revolution requires acknowledging this reality and adjusting narratives accordingly.

66

The American Revolution

It is fair to say that for most of the eighteenth-century trans-Appalachian polities would have identified colonial encroachment as merely one—and not the most pressing—of their concerns. It remained the case after 1763, although the situation was changing dramatically. From the Euro-American perspective, however, land was a massive issue. Often overlooked in the cacophony over rights and taxes was the fact that the Proclamation Line of 1763 deeply frustrated many British North Americans (as would the 1774 Quebec Act, which hardened certain boundaries and by implication severely restricted land sales and migration). A deep dive into the matter will help students understand how the Revolutionary moment affected both communities.

The Proclamation established a line along the top of the Appalachian mountains beyond which British North Americans could not cross until the "Royal Pleasure be known." Colonial officials further were required to halt private land sales, cease issuing trans-Appalachian land grants, and ensure that Native people were not "molested or disturbed in the Possession of such Parts of our Dominions and Territories as, having been ceded or purchased by us, are reserved to them, or any of them, as their Hunting Grounds."[10] Not meant to serve as a permanent solution, the Proclamation nevertheless required the colonies to operate within imperial parameters. Any subsequent expansion would have to follow protocols, including that land could only transfer from Native to European control through formal congresses. It is a critical rhetorical point, according to historian Kristofer Ray. "According to the *Oxford English Dictionary*," he notes, "a congress is a 'formal meeting or assembly of delegates or representatives for the discussion or settlement of some question; *spec.* (in politics) of envoys, deputies, or plenipotentiaries representing sovereign states, or of sovereigns themselves, for the settlement of international affairs.' By acknowledging the congressional nature of their diplomacy, the British Empire effectively conceded the fact of Indigenous sovereignty."[11]

Ask students to debate the following questions: What might be the outcome when British North Americans violate protocols agreed between sovereign entities, whether through the Proclamation or at congresses such as at Augusta, Georgia (1764), Fort Stanwix, New York (1768), Hard Labor, South Carolina (1768), or Lochaber, South Carolina (1770)? What might lead Six Nations diplomats to inform British negotiators that although they represented "a Government and Laws[,] you don't prevent" land fraud? Those negotiators found it ironic: "you often tell us we don't restrain our people, and that you do so with yours," they observed, but "your Words differ more from your Actions than ours do."[12] If an empire built on written laws could not make its "People do what they are desired [and] prevent all this, and if they wont let us alone you should shake them by the head."[13] Transcripts of some of these congresses are available online and offer excellent insight into how land catalyzed Revolutionary tensions.

Since the sixteenth century Europeans had accused Native people of "savagery" to justify conquest. Thomas Jefferson revisited this argument in the Declaration of Independence when he charged that George III had "endeavored to bring on the inhabitants of our frontiers, the merciless Indian Savages, whose known rule of warfare, is an undistinguished destruction of all ages, sexes and conditions." Indigenous savagery had become British savagery. And yet the record is clear: a major spark for Revolutionary action was the demand for "liberty" of unfettered access to the west.[14] At the least, land questions should challenge students to see greater nuance in traditional Revolutionary narratives. Like the colonists, Natives fought for liberty. Their struggle, however, did anything but enhance security and independence.[15]

Native responses to the war itself differed from tribe to tribe and could cause significant internal rifts. The Haudenosaunee (Six Nations of Iroquois), for example, temporarily dissolved because of the war, and the followers of Mohawk sachem Joseph Brant ended up living in exile in Canada. The war also provides great lessons about propaganda and double standards, as exemplified by the story of Jane McCrae. McCrae was murdered and scalped by British-allied Natives while traveling to join her fiancée in the British Army. The tragedy made headlines all over the eastern seaboard and in 1804 was immortalized by the artist John Vanderlyn. The actual event is steeped in embellished narratives meant to produce a Eurocentric outcome, but even at its most basic it is not hard to contrast the violence of her death with the actions of American commander George Rogers Clark, who cold-bloodedly executed a number of Native prisoners in full view of British forces at Fort Vincennes in 1779. Thoroughly intimidated, the British surrendered. Americans subsequently honored Clark with an impressive monument, among other accolades.

For all of the patriot movement's condemnation of British and Native savagery, in short, it proved more than willing to commit atrocities in the name of independence. Students need to grapple with issues of bias and mythmaking in this era. Ask them: Why did Europeans see no particular problem with burning Native towns or engaging in mass murder—such as the Paxtonites at Conestoga Manner in 1763, Gnadenhütten in 1782, or John Sevier's 1794 expedition into Chickamauga Country—but fixate on the supposed savagery committed by Delawares, Shawnees, or Cherokees? How have Euro-Americans come to memorialize "atrocities" committed by French-allied forces at Fort Oswego or Fort William Henry in the 1750s (the latter immortalized in *The Last of the Mohicans*) or the death of Jane McCrae? How accurate are the accounts of Native "massacres" upon which Euro-Americans justified military action?

Devastating though it was, the Revolutionary War did not decide the ultimate fate of Native America, whether in trans-Appalachia or in regions further west. The nineteenth-century Indians Wars make that point quite clear.

1790–1846

Although the Northwest Ordinance of 1787, George Washington's factory system, and the Indian Trade and Intercourse Acts established standards of treatment meant to normalize relations with Native polities, pressures from land speculators and settlers moving west made it impossible. The deeply cash-strapped government worsened the situation by pursuing inconsistent military policies that dramatically destabilized the infant Republic. In the Southwest, where land speculators seemed to have laid claim to everything of value, the Washington administration chose not to challenge Native military strength—the result of which to Euro-Americans was a "dark and bloody ground" bordering on Hobbesian. In the Northwest, by contrast, where land seemed abundant for sale to reduce government debt, the administration did send troops. These wars of the Old Northwest are important not only because the United States suffered dramatic defeats under Josiah Harmar in 1790 and Arthur St. Clair in 1791 (when more than eight hundred Americans were killed), but also because they were beaten by supposedly "undisciplined" fighters under Blue Jacket and

Little Turtle. In late 1793 the situation seemed so bleak that President Washington considered banning further American migration into trans-Appalachia. American "fortunes" changed the following year at Fallen Timbers, however, where Blue Jacket's and Little Turtle's outnumbered forces lost control of the battlefield to American troops that were assisted by Choctaws and Chickasaws. Although in the moment victory was unclear, the perception of success became deeply rooted in the American military and public minds. It would not be the last time, as Shawnee sachem Tecumseh's experience makes clear.

Tecumseh, a strategic genius and participant in the Fallen Timbers battle, and his brother Tenskwatawa envisioned a pan-Indigenous movement that would push back against White encroachment in trans-Appalachia. The movement relied not only on Tenskwatawa's vision of spiritual renewal but also on Tecumseh's considerable oratorical and diplomatic skills, and it alarmed the United States, in much the same way as the Ghost Dancers would alarm the American government and military in the lead-up to Wounded Knee in 1890.[16] For now, the question for students to address is why the "Prophetstown" movement ultimately failed. William Henry Harrison's preemptive strike at Tippecanoe (1811) and British reluctance to lend support provide part of the answer, but complex intertribal relations and political considerations are more fundamental.

If the early nineteenth-century vision of pan-Indigenous renewal never came to fruition, Andrew Jackson wanted to make certain that it would not be resurrected. Under his leadership policies of settler colonialism received the stamp of approval from the federal government. His decisions resulted in a number of "Removal Wars," including Black Hawk's War (1833) and the second and third Seminole Wars (1835–42 and 1855–58), both of which present interesting studies of the "guerilla" tactics used by Native fighters and the US Army's so-called counterinsurgency tactics to combat them. In the Seminole Wars, these tactics included destroying food resources and capturing war leader Osceola while under a flag of truce (policies that the army would replicate in the Plains Wars).

Jackson's approach to Indigenous people has become a lightning rod for political conversation in the twenty-first century. Whatever one might think of the man, one point seems inarguable: the vast majority of Jacksonian-era Americans were united by the thought that the United States was a White man's country and that certain ideas (capitalism, individualism, democracy, and Christianity) made them superior. Even humanitarian efforts were tinged with racist paternalism. Such views permeated every level of society, as well as government, the military, and churches. Service in the nineteenth-century Indian Wars became a bonus for presidential candidates, whether Jackson himself (Creek War and First Seminole War), William Henry Harrison (Tippecanoe and War of 1812), Zachary Taylor (Black Hawk War and Second Seminole War), or Abraham Lincoln (Black Hawk War). Confederate president Jefferson Davis served in Black Hawk's War and on the southern plains. George Armstrong Custer told his Arikara scouts during the Little Bighorn campaign that he needed one more battlefield victory against Indians to win election to the presidency.

1846–1890

After the Mexican War, removal of Natives beyond American "Lebensraum" became increasingly difficult. The government instead embarked on a "reservation policy." It was designed to maintain peace by separating Native people from White settlers, and perhaps to keep Indigenous polities from attacking each other. Treaties were at the core of government actions. The 1851 Fort Laramie Treaty, for example, established reservation boundaries and added provisions allowing migrant trails to Oregon and California. The policy proved to be a failure, however. Migrants raised ire by depleting valuable resources (wood, water, grass, and so forth) and disrupting the seasonal bison migrations. Natives demanding payment were accused of begging and stealing, as in 1854 when the Sioux destroyed an American army unit ostensibly because it had come to investigate the theft of a Mormon migrant's cow. On a practical level this explanation is suspect given the depth of anti-Mormon sentiment in 1854, not to mention that the United States would go to war with Mormons in 1857. Certainly Sioux explanations for the event sounded quite different, and these various nuances offer students an excellent avenue for exploring the racist-tinged narratives produced by the US army in this period. At any rate, the following year General William S. Harney destroyed a Sioux camp "in retaliation."

Attempts to relocate and confine Natives onto reservations led to a series of wars in the Pacific West of which the Yakima War (1855–57), the Rogue River War (1855–56), the Modoc War (1874), the Nez Perce War (1877), and the Bannock War (1878) are the best known. The Modoc

71

War is of interest not only because the Modocs killed American general Edward R. S. Canby and put up a powerful resistance using the terrain to their advantage, but also because a subsequent investigation showed that the war cost the United States far more than a peaceful settlement would have. The lesson for students: the war option is expensive and often difficult to reverse without an exit strategy. Meanwhile, a genocide was taking place in California. Because so much of that violence was committed by settlers, militias, and frontier organizations rather than the US Army, it usually is not included under the label of the Indian Wars. Native communities faced devastation not only in wartime, however, but also in supposed times of peace.

The Plains Wars are well known and need little discussion here except to remind teachers that the United States was not the only expanding power there and was on a collision course with the Blackfeet nation on the northern plains, the Lakotas and Cheyennes on the central plains, and the Kiowas and Comanches on the southern plains. Mobility and the ability to live off the land made these powerful equestrian polities major challenges for an overstretched US Army. For this reason, American government and military officials encouraged the annihilation of bison herds (destroying food supplies would starve Plains polities into submission, they believed) and tended to attack settlements in winter, when resistance might be weak. They also came to rely on Indigenous scouts drawn mostly from sedentary tribes such as Pawnees, Arikaras, and Crows. The term "scout" is misleading because these men acted more as special forces and often found themselves in the thick of battle. Military service offered them opportunities to settle old scores, earn war honors, escape the confines of their reservations, earn money, regain self-esteem, and, most importantly, provide safety for people at home by putting enemies on the defensive. Scouts and allies contributed greatly to American success in the Plains Wars. Several were awarded Congressional Medals of Honor for bravery. Arikara scouts even viewed their commander, George Armstrong Custer, with admiration.

As with the Plains Wars, the wars of the American Southwest have been covered in great detail, and teachers will have no problem finding resources. What makes them especially complex are the tangled relations between tribes and Spanish, Mexican, French, and American colonizers. Particularly worth deeper exploration are the Pueblo Rebellion and the "Long Walk" of the Diné (Navajos).

Conclusions

"War," the great military theorist Carl von Clausewitz once suggested, "is politics by different means." In the United States, these violent forms of political confrontation usually began at the local and state levels.[17] Though armies battled and could engage in massacre, "frontiersmen" (surveyors, squatters, settlers, traders, miners, and so forth) inflicted particularly horrific violence against Indigenous polities in the form of militias, volunteer regiments, and paramilitary organizations such as the Texas Rangers. European and Euro-American policies (such as removal) certainly caused war, but war could cause policy shifts as well. Merely a few prominent examples: disastrous campaigns in the 1790s prompted President Washington to adopt the factory system; the Arikara War of 1823 led Congress to create the Office of Indian Affairs and embark on a series of treaties; The Sand Creek Massacre and Red Cloud's War sparked congressional investigations into abuses in the Indian Office and led the government to transfer control over Indian agencies to religious denominations; the Marias River Massacre convinced Congress to outlaw the appointment of military officers as Indian agents.

Indigenous people took on many roles in wars with Europeans and Euro-Americans, sometimes fighting the invaders and sometimes supporting them. Whatever strategic choices they made were based on what was in their best interest. It underscores a crucial point: Indigenous people were never simply passive reactionaries to inexorable American expansion. As with European and Euro-American communities, however, reaching consensus on the best policy to embrace could be a difficult matter.

It is impossible to cover all aspects of Euro-Indigenous war in a single essay, nor is it possible to cover them in a single course. Whatever conflicts upon which teachers choose to focus, I hope that this essay provides some ideas on new ways to approach the subject. One thing is unmistakable: warfare is too important to Native American experiences before and after European arrival not to address.

NOTES

1. Teachers cannot and must not avoid discussing "genocide" in their classrooms, but they should understand that the concept is not without controversy. Perhaps the most conspicuous issue for historians is that of presentism, given

that the term was not defined and codified until 1948. Definitions also have emphasized racial and ethnic groups while leaving out political opponents, homosexuals, the disabled, the old, etc. Finally, some scholars have raised questions regarding the definitional emphasis upon *deliberate* and *physical* destruction. Has US policy toward Native America historically risen to that level? Understanding the nuances of the concept—and drawing respectful and analytically critical conclusions—is crucial to any exploration of Native American history. For more on the complexity of the topic see the chapters in this volume by Tai S. Edwards and Gray H. Whaley.

2. It is crucial to convey that Indigenous understandings of diplomacy and treaty making were not the same as their European and Euro-American counterparts. For more on these topics, see the chapter in this volume by Margaret Huettl.

3. Roxanne Dunbar-Ortiz and Dina Gilio-Whitaker, *"All the Real Indians Died Off" and Twenty Other Myths about Native Americans* (Boston: Beacon Press, 2016), 42.

4. Using asymmetrical strategies should not imply that Native fighters always shied away from pitched battles. When they had a tactical advantage in numbers or in firepower, Indigenous armies could well engage directly.

5. For more on teaching Native slavery, see the chapter in this volume by Denise I. Bossy.

6. Thomas S. Abler, "Scalping, Torture, Cannibalism, and Rape: An Ethnohistorical Analysis of Conflicting Cultural Values in War," *Anthropologica* 34, no. 1 (1992), 3–20.

7. Michael McDonnell, *Masters of Empire: Great Lakes Indians and the Making of America* (New York: Hill and Wang, 2015).

8. Teachers can find a useful introduction to these maps in Kristofer Ray, "Interpreting *Native* Trans-Appalachia, 1670–1770: Or, How I Stopped Worrying and Learned to Read Fanni Mingo's Map," *XVII–XVIII Century Review* 78 (2021).

9. Thomas Morris, "Journal of Trip to the Wabash, August 26–September 17, 1764," cited in Kristofer Ray, "'Our Concerns with Indians Are Now Greatly Extended': Cherokees, Westward Indians, and Interpreting the Quebec Act from the Ohio Valley, 1763–1774," in *The Quebec Act of 1774: Transnational Contexts, Meanings, and Legacies,* ed. François Furstenberg and Ollivier Hubert (Montreal: McGill-Queens University Press, 2020); and Kristofer Ray, "The Indigenous Roots of the American Revolution," in *The Oxford Research Encyclopedia of American History,* ed. Jon Butler and Angela Hudson, 1–2, http://oxfordre.com/americanhistory (2020).

10. The Proclamation attempted to stabilize trade by requiring that licenses would have to come from Royal governors. "The Royal Proclamation—October

7, 1763, by the King," The Avalon Project, Lillian Goldman Law Library, Yale Law School, https://avalon.law.yale.edu/18th_century/proc1763.asp.

11. "Congress, n.," *OED Online*, December 2019, quoted in Ray, "The Indigenous Roots," 6.

12. "Iroquois-Cherokee Congress," Thomas Gage Papers, vol. 75, William Clements Library, University of Michigan.

13. "Iroquois-Cherokee Congress," 19.

14. This is what Jefferson meant when he wrote in the Declaration that the British had tried "to prevent the population of these States [by] raising the conditions of new Appropriations of Lands." Declaration of Independence, July 4, 1776, The Avalon Project, Lillian Goldman Law Library, Yale Law School, https://avalon.law.yale.edu/18th_century/declare.asp.

15. Colin G. Calloway, *The American Revolution in Indian Country: Crisis and Diversity in Native American Communities* (New York: Cambridge University Press, 1995), xiii.

16. See the chapter in this volume by Brady DeSanti for more on Native spirituality.

17. Carl von Clausewitz, *On War*, ed. and trans. Michael Howard and Peter Paret (Princeton, NJ: Princeton University Press, 1989). Section 14, Article 3, of the Northwest Ordinance of 1787, for example, stated, "The utmost good faith shall always be observed towards the Indians; their lands and property shall never be taken from them without their consent; and, in their property, rights, and liberty, they shall never be invaded or disturbed, unless in just and lawful wars authorized by Congress; but laws founded in justice and humanity, shall from time to time be made for preventing wrongs done to them, and for preserving peace and friendship with them." Northwest Ordinance: July 13, 1787, The Avalon Project, Lillian Goldman Law Library, Yale Law School, https://avalon.law.yale.edu/18th_century/nworder.asp.

FOR FURTHER READING

Plains Ledger Art, https://plainsledgerart.org/.
Yale Avalon Project, https://avalon.law.yale.edu/.

Blackhawk, Ned. *Violence over the Land: Indians and Empires in the Early American West*. Cambridge, MA: Harvard University Press, 2006.
Calloway, Colin G. *The American Revolution in Indian Country: Crisis and Diversity in Native American Communities*. Cambridge: Cambridge University Press, 1995.
Calloway, Colin G. *The Indian World of George Washington: The First President, the First Americans, and the Birth of the Nation*. Oxford: Oxford University Press, 2018.

Calloway, Colin G. *The Victory with No Name: The Native American Defeat of the First American Army*. Oxford: Oxford University Press, 2014.

Cozzens, Peter, ed. *Eyewitnesses to the Indian Wars, 1865–1890*. 5 vols. Mechanicsburg, PA: Stackpole Books, 2001–2005.

Dunlay, Thomas W. *Wolves for the Blue Soldiers: Indian Scouts and Auxiliaries with the United States Army, 1860–1890*. Lincoln: University of Nebraska Press, 1982.

DuVal, Kathleen. *Independence Lost: Lives on the Edge of the American Revolution*. New York: Random House, 2015.

Furstenberg, Francois. "The Significance of the Trans-Appalachian Frontier in Atlantic History." *American Historical Review* 113, no. 3 (June 2008): 647–77.

Gallay, Alan. *The Indian Slave Trade: The Rise of the English Empire in the American South, 1670–1717*. New Haven, CT: Yale University Press, 2002.

Greene, Candace S., and Russell Thornton, eds. *The Year the Stars Fell: Lakota Winter Counts at the Smithsonian*. Washington, DC: Smithsonian Institution, 2007.

Greene, Jerome A. *Battles and Skirmishes of the Great Sioux War, 1876–1877: The Military View*. Norman: University of Oklahoma Press, 1993.

Greene, Jerome A. *Lakota and Cheyenne: Indian Views of the Great Sioux War, 1876–1877*. Norman: University of Oklahoma Press, 1994.

Grenier, John. *The First Way of War: American War Making on the Frontier*. New York: Cambridge University Press, 2005.

Hirsch, Adam J. "The Collision of Military Cultures in Seventeenth-Century New England." *Journal of American History* 74, no. 4 (1988): 1187–212.

Jortner, Adam. *The Gods of Prophetstown: The Battle of Tippecanoe and the Holy War for the American Frontier*. Oxford: Oxford University Press, 2011.

Malone, Patrick M. *The Skulking Way of War: Technology and Tactics among the New England Indians*. Baltimore: Johns Hopkins University Press, 1993.

McDonnell, Michael. *Masters of Empire: Great Lakes Indians and the Making of America*. New York: Hill and Wang, 2015.

Mishkin, Bernard. *Rank and Warfare among the Plains Indians*. New York: J. J. Augustin, 1940.

Newell, Margaret Ellen. *Brethren by Nature: New England Indians, Colonists, and the Origins of American Slavery*. Ithaca, NY: Cornell University Press, 2015.

Ray, Kristofer. "Constructing a Discourse of Indigenous Slavery, Freedom, and Sovereignty in Anglo-Virginia, 1600–1750." *Native South* 19 (2017): 19–39.

Ray, Kristofer. "The Indigenous Roots of the American Revolution." In *The Oxford Research Encyclopedia of American History*, edited by Jon Butler and Angela Hudson, 2020. http://oxfordre.com/americanhistory.

Ray, Kristofer. "Interpreting *Native* Trans-Appalachia, 1670–1770: Or, How I Stopped Worrying and Learned to Read Fanni Mingo's Map." *XVII–XVIII Century Review* 78 (2021).

Reséndez, Andrés. *The Other Slavery: The Uncovered Story of Indian Enslavement in America*. Boston: Houghton Mifflin Harcourt, 2016.

Secoy, Raymond F. *Changing Military Patterns on the Great Plains Indians*. Lincoln: University of Nebraska Press, 1992.

Silver, Peter. *Our Savage Neighbors: How Indian War Transformed Early America*. New York: Norton, 2008.

Starkey, Armstrong. *European and Native American Warfare, 1675–1815*. Norman: University of Oklahoma Press, 1998.

Steele, Ian K. *Warpaths: Invasions of North America*. New York: Oxford University Press, 1994.

Tucker, Spencer C., ed. *The Encyclopedia of North American Indian Wars, 1607–1890*. 3 vols. Santa Barbara, CA: ABC-CLIO, 2011.

Utley, Robert M. *The Indian Frontier of the American West, 1846–1890*. Albuquerque: University of New Mexico Press, 1984.

van de Logt, Mark. *War Party in Blue: Pawnee Scouts in the U.S. Army*. Norman: University of Oklahoma Press, 2010.

Teaching the Broad and Relevant History of American Indian Removal

JOHN P. BOWES

If students are going to understand the broader ideas about Indian removal in American history, they need to first know what happened to the Cherokees in the 1820s and 1830s. Students should recognize the names of John Ross, Elias Boudinot, Samuel Worcester, John Ridge, Jeremiah Evarts, Andrew Jackson, and John Marshall, among others. The decisions rendered in the United States Supreme Court cases of *Johnson v. McIntosh, Cherokee Nation v. Georgia,* and *Worcester v. Georgia* should be a part of their knowledge base, and they should be familiar with the debates over and the enactment of the legislation known as the Indian Removal Act.

I have spent the better part of the past twenty years thinking and writing about Indian removal. More specifically, I have focused a great deal of time and energy writing about the ethnic cleansing of Indigenous communities from the Old Northwest Territory. As part of that project I have often asserted that the narrative built around the experience of the southeastern tribes in general and the Cherokee Nation in particular has created a somewhat misguided understanding of how removal occurred on a national scale. Most recently I wrote that the discourse "constructed primarily around the Indian Removal Act and the Cherokee experience, at times hinders a more expansive picture of the wholesale cultural and physical dispossession in the early American republic."[1] Keeping that context in mind, my opening premise for this essay about what students should learn may seem a bit discordant. However, similar to the idea that you should not be allowed to break the rules of writing until you actually learn the rules of writing, I propose that students cannot tackle an expansive analysis of Indian removal until they have a firm grasp of the Cherokee experience and the historical framework within which it exists.

Within any subject or discipline there is a common language that develops based on the creation and distribution of knowledge. For the history of Indian removal, that common language is grounded first and foremost in the Cherokee Nation and the Trail of Tears. But language is not stagnant, and once students become fluent in the common terminology they have the ability to explore new avenues and locate openings for distinct perspectives. The construction of that intellectual opportunity is the real premise of this essay. Expose students to the familiar and most well-known elements of Indian removal history and then demonstrate how that language is still not enough to provide a comprehensive examination of removal in respect to the trauma, the diversity of experiences, and the all-encompassing nature of removal within the American national narrative. The forced relocation of Cherokees and other southeastern tribes in the 1830s comprises one piece of a much larger mosaic. Indian removal encompasses an expansive geography and chronology, and the underlying issues and concepts of removal remain as relevant today as they were two centuries ago.

This essay provides windows into that diverse history of removal and the ways in which students can engage with that material through meaningful analysis. The inherent nature of relocation in the origins and continued existence of the United States is crucial to how we explain not only early American history but also much of the history in the subsequent centuries.[2] Students must understand that this narrative does not and should not have a limited scope. Therefore, even as this essay expounds upon the larger history, it is limited to only a few examples from a wide array of possibilities. The forced removal of American Indian men, women, and children from their homelands was not confined to one region or one historical moment. It stands to reason, therefore, that we should not restrict our examination of that history either. This essay should be just a place to start.

The Cherokees and Removal in the Southeast

Students learning the histories of Indian removal need to understand the Cherokee experience for three reasons. First and foremost, the Cherokee Trail of Tears has long dominated the historical narrative and is thus the most familiar episode. American history text-books rely upon the saga of the Cherokees and their legal battles with Georgia and the United States as one bookend to the American Indian experience in the early American republic. The Indian Removal Act and the presidency of Andrew Jackson are part of the tale that allows text-book authors in particular to tie up the loose ends of early American development before shifting to the period of dramatic western expansion. All of this means that the Cherokee history is omnipresent in the historiography, and students must be familiar with the historiographical canon.[3]

The second rationale for starting with the Cherokee narrative is connected to the accessibility and type of primary sources. Depending on the approach selected or the perspective desired, vast and diverse digitized resources are now accessible. The online repositories of the Library of Congress include the notes for the debates in both the House of Representatives and the Senate over the Indian Removal Act. Students can read through the speeches made on both sides of the debate to see where politicians of the time stood on the issue. The Library of Congress records also contain transcriptions of the petitions sent by citizens throughout the United States who opposed removal legislation. Those petition campaigns were led in part by the American Board of Commissioners for Foreign Missions, and the stance of that religious organization's secretary, Jeremiah Evarts, was known to be opposition to removal. His argument against the policy, outlined in a series of essays written and published under the name of William Penn, can also be found online. Material written by the Baptist missionary Isaac McCoy, a man who supported removal, has also been digitized and is thus available to students with a computer and an internet connection. Even the records for the Supreme Court case of *Cherokee Nation v. Georgia*, as compiled, edited, and published in 1831, can now be found online.[4]

The published account of the *Cherokee Nation v. Georgia* records begins with the document filed with the Supreme Court on behalf of the Cherokee Nation and signed by Principal Chief John Ross to explain the circumstances of the Cherokee complaint and filing. That document speaks to the third and perhaps most important reason for having students start with the Cherokees. Cherokee leaders produced a substantial amount of written material that allows students to examine how the Cherokees responded to the encroachments of Georgia citizens and the ongoing negotiation with the forces that wanted them removed from the state. The *Cherokee Phoenix*, the newspaper established by the Cherokee Nation in 1828 and first edited by Elias Boudinot, has been partially digitized. The first volume of the papers of John Ross, collected and edited by Gary Moulton, is another published collection that can help students gain insight into the struggle from the Cherokee perspective. Students who read through these different sources will thus be able to access more than just one side of the history. Time spent with letters, petitions, and newspapers produced by the Cherokees will give students the opportunity to examine the struggles of the 1820s and 1830s in a more comprehensive fashion.

In brief, the history of Cherokee removal provides a host of entry points into the historical era and enables students to find the larger landscape of ideas and issues involved. Students can use the published Moravian missionary records to gain some insight into the presence of Christian missionaries and their impact on the lives of Cherokee men, women, and children. They can track the political debates on both the American and Cherokee side of the issue in the late 1820s and early 1830s, and they can then look to the records of the removals for accounts of the Trail of Tears.[5] From an introductory standpoint, the document reader edited and compiled by Theda Perdue and Mike Green is one of the best of its kind published to date. It provides an exceptional balance of material that encompasses the state, federal, and Cherokee positions in addition to the products of missionaries and other private citizens. The collection gives students a solid foundation with which to work while providing suggestions for where to turn next for further investigation of the topics.[6]

In all of these sources students will learn the terminology and concepts that shaped the specific history of the Cherokees. The most crucial term at the center of the removal debate was and is "sovereignty." There were certainly other ideas and issues that were part of the larger discussion, but the emphasis on the Cherokee Nation's sovereignty was emphasized most at the time and remains most influential.[7]

Sovereignty within the context of Cherokee removal was political sovereignty, and its importance rested on several foundations. It became a centerpiece of Cherokee resistance because of the words contained within the Cherokee Constitution adopted in 1827. The first sentence of Article I, Section 2, reads, "The Sovereignty and Jurisdiction of this Government shall extend over the country within the boundaries" of the lands that had been specifically described in the first section of the same article. The state of Georgia emphasized the issue of sovereignty because, in the words of Representative Wilson Lumpkin of Georgia, "In all the acts, first by the colonies, and afterwards by the State Governments, the fundamental principle, that the Indians had no right either to the soil or sovereignty of the countries they occupied, has never been abandoned either expressly or by implication."[8] In his first annual address in December 1829, President Andrew Jackson affirmed Georgia's status as a sovereign state in the Union and noted that he had informed the Cherokees "that their attempt to establish an independent government would not be countenanced by the Executive of the United States."[9] And of course there is the famous description of tribal sovereignty that came out of the *Cherokee Nation v. Georgia* case, namely that Indian tribes were "domestic dependent nations." That phrase encapsulated the legal decision that the Cherokees and other Indian tribes did not have standing as a foreign nation in the courts of the United States.

The principle of sovereignty became the cornerstone of the next Supreme Court case, *Worcester v. Georgia*, and the court rendered its decision in March 1832. In this ruling, Chief Justice John Marshall wrote in a different tone than he had one year earlier. "The Indian nations had always been considered as distinct, independent political communities," he asserted, "retaining their original natural rights, as the undisputed possessors of the soil, from time immemorial," and the United States had recognized that sovereignty in the form of treaties.[10] The political sovereignty of the Cherokee Nation meant that they had a special relationship with the federal government that overrode the jurisdiction asserted by the state of Georgia. That principle as written by Marshall continues to serve as a legal cornerstone for tribal sovereignty to the present day.

Sovereignty is the primary thread that connects American political and legal institutions to pivotal events in the Cherokee removal experience. It is the reason why the Cherokee Nation and Andrew Jackson remain at the center of the American public's understanding of Indian removal. The Cherokee Nation asserted its sovereignty in its 1827 Constitution, and that declaration of rights helped frame events of the next decade and more. The court cases that subsequently developed from Cherokee rejection of Georgia's jurisdiction cemented the place of sovereignty in the narrative of Cherokee removal. And thus the Treaty of New Echota and the Trail of Tears highlight not only the human tragedy of this history but also how executive indifference compromised the inherent sovereignty upheld by the judicial branch.

Yet once students have become familiar with this core language of Cherokee removal, it is the very human elements of the history that they must seek. Those elements are not so easily found in the court cases and congressional debates. In the House of Representatives, for example, Edward Everett of Massachusetts was one of the only politicians to stray from the debate over constitutional principles to note that in the removal legislation that stood before them, "The evil, sir, is enormous; the violence is extreme; the breach of public faith deplorable; the inevitable suffering incalculable."[11] Everett's colleagues focused more on constitutional authority, treaty rights, and, yes, sovereignty.

The records that provide windows into the trauma produced by removal in the mid- to late 1830s under the federal government's policies do exist in both hard copy and digitized form. Online, students can access journals and letters relevant to the Cherokee Trail of Tears and other southeastern relocations at the website of the Sequoyah National Research Center.[12] Stories about removal passed down within families can also be accessed through the Indian-Pioneer Papers Collection, where a simple search for the term "Trail of Tears" brings up dozens of interviews that shed light on the personal aspects of that history.[13] Those are just two of the paths available to students looking to expand their understanding of the experience and to teachers seeking source material to use in their classrooms.

A Geographic Shift

Once they have become familiar with the framework of the Cherokee Nation's removal history, the primary question for both teacher and student is where next to apply that knowledge and understanding. Should they stay within the southeast to study the experiences of the Choctaws, Creeks, Chickasaws, and Seminoles, all of whom have also received treatment by scholars? Or should they perhaps shift their chronological or geographic perspectives to gain a more comprehensive understanding of Indian removal?[14]

If one were to shift geographically, it would make sense to examine the history of the Miami Indians. This is not solely because Miami removal took place in Indiana and thus provides a reference point north of the Ohio River, although that is a worthwhile reason. Perhaps most important is the fact that the Miami Indian Tribe of Oklahoma has developed materials to explain their history so that the narrative of Miami removal is not one framed solely by non-Indian scholars. The Miamis are not the only Indian nation using an online presence to accomplish this goal, but they are one of the most effective.

In addition to the benefits that come from the Miamis telling their history is the fact that they consciously present that material within a larger historical context. The Myaamia Center, whose physical location is at Miami University in Oxford, Ohio, maintains a vibrant online presence. As explained on its website, the Center is a tribal initiative "located within an academic setting, [serving] the needs of the Myaamia people, Miami University, and partner communities through research, education, and outreach that promote Myaamia language, culture, knowledge, and values." One of the resources the staff at the Myaamia Center has made available to the public online is a commemoration of the forced removal of their people as they marked its 175th anniversary. Forty separate blog posts examine the context and daily progress of the tragedy that unfolded in October and November of 1846.[15] However, that in-depth examination of removal is only one of many resources that can help teachers and students understand both the history and the contemporary lives of the Miami people. One item that is particularly helpful for teachers is "Telling Our Story: The Living History of the Myaamia," which is a seven-chapter curriculum aimed at grades 3–12.[16] Within that curriculum of seven chapters, removal is at the core of chapter 5, an indication that the history of that experience is only one segment of a longer narrative that explains the Miami world and perspective.

In the case of the Miamis, students and teachers who turn to the tribally produced materials will find a different language for removal and why it matters. The power of the history is present from the beginning. "Emotionally powerful events create big ripples that combine with smaller ripples of less powerful events in unpredictable ways," reads the introduction to a booklet on the removal history produced by the Miami Tribe in 2011. "In our Myaamia pond, the forced removal of 1846 was more like a boulder, which, once dropped into our lives, created a series of waves that changed everything." And instead of a legal fight against state jurisdiction and presidential politics, one finds in the Miami history a hope to remain on individual landholdings that was undermined by the implementation of military force.[17] A relatively brief narrative of the removal written by tribal historian and assistant director of the Myaamia Center George Ironstrack is then followed by transcriptions of primary source documents that frame the history, including a critical treaty signed in 1840, letters written by federal agents describing the removal, and excerpts from contemporary newspapers.

When supplemented by additional scholarly work from outside the Myaamia Center, this examination of the Miami removal history also provides a critical opportunity to expand a student's perspective on the nature of Indian removal in two distinct ways. The Cherokees influenced events in the 1820s and 1830s through their adoption of a constitution and their use of the American legal system to assert political sovereignty. And because of the prominence of the Cherokee narrative, that dialogue has overshadowed other approaches. The Miami's long history of interactions with Europeans and then Americans shaped their response to the calls for their relocation in the 1800s, and that is part of what made their removal experience distinct from that of the Cherokees. In both actions and words, Miami leaders such as Jean Baptiste Richardville expressed a desire to live alongside their non-Indian neighbors even as they maintained their communal and cultural integrity.

The Miamis demonstrated their response to the regional push for removal based on their distinctive historical experience. Meehccikilita, the Miami orator at a treaty council held in northern Indiana in early October 1826, informed the American commissioners that the Miamis wanted "to live like neighbours, and barter and trade with each other."[18] And even as the non-Indian population of Indiana grew in the 1830s, putting increased pressure on the diminishing Miami landholdings, the approach of the Miamis remained the same. Since they had first encountered the French more than a century before, the Miamis had sought to cultivate relationships with outsiders. Over time, like many other Native communities, the Miamis relied on what can be called adaptive resistance to negotiate the changing world around them.[19] In short, the Miamis utilized their alliances and working relationships with traders, missionaries, and other local entities to mitigate the negative impact of state or federal policies. Richardville in particular and the Miamis in general had built strong relationships with traders, and they hoped that these connections to the regional economy might provide one means of avoiding the push for relocation. Up until the moment that soldiers showed up to force them onto canal boats in Peru, Indiana, Miami leaders insisted that they had both the ability and the right to live alongside their non-Indian neighbors.[20]

This history of Miami removal does more than shift the focal point of the larger narrative from the Southeast to the Old Northwest. By following the path of the Miamis from Peru, Indiana, to the banks of the Marais des Cygnes River in what became Kansas Territory, students can soon find their way into the histories of the next phase of removal for eastern Indians. Upon their relocation west of the Mississippi River, the Miamis were placed on lands just south of the reserves established for Potawatomis, Shawnees, Delawares, Kickapoos, and Wyandots, all of whom had endured relocations from the Old Northwest Territory in the previous fifteen years. And for almost all of those tribes that the federal government had relocated to this short-lived Indian Country, a second removal occurred in the aftermath of the Civil War.

The history of the Miamis and their Native neighbors in Kansas from the mid-1850s to the mid-1870s is intertwined with the national narrative of the Civil War, but it is also built on the more specific stories of Indian treaties and allotment policies. Although scholars have written about this historical period, students and teachers can also gain insight into the troubles in Kansas through the digitized offerings of the Kansas Historical Society. Through both the Territorial Kansas Online project and the Kansas Memory digital collections, any researcher can find out about the conditions in the region that shaped the experience of recently removed Indians struggling to maintain both their lands and communal integrity in the midst of territorial battles over slavery and land claims.[21]

As a result of the complicated historical record encompassing the lives of Indians in Kansas, this second removal phase for the Miamis and other tribes is not as thoroughly researched or understood as other periods of their respective histories. Another publication produced by the Miami Tribe described this second removal as "more chaotic" than that of 1846 in part because federal officials "left it up to the Miami to move themselves to their shared reservation in Indian Territory." From the early 1870s to the mid-1880s Miami families moved from Kansas to a reservation in what is now Ottawa County, Oklahoma. This removal was no less traumatic than the first for those involved, and yet more often than not it is left out of the history of Indian removal.[22] Nor is that issue unique to the Miamis, and it serves as a reminder about the expansive nature of forced relocations within the national narrative.

A Chronological Shift

Once students start examining removal within a different-ent geographic context, it automatically follows that they see the need to place the history of removal within a larger chronological frame-work. There is no singular removal era in American history that exists in a decade radius around the enactment of the Indian Removal Act in 1830. Instead, the removal of Indians is an integral characteristic of the creation and growth of the American nation. From the indictment of Native peoples in the Declaration of Independence in 1776 as "merci-less Indian savages" to the construction of dams on the Missouri River in the 1950s that flooded thousands of acres of reservation lands, the life of the United States has depended on the displacement of Native peoples. This final section, then, presents three brief examples that might prove fruitful avenues for teachers and students alike as they explore the ways to understand removal within a more sizeable chrono-logical context.

Expanding the chronology of removal history at times entails only a minor adjustment in perspective. In short, Indian removal was not limited to the forced relocation of eastern Indians to lands west of the Mississippi River. The history of the Ponca removal to Indian Territory in 1877 is one example among many of relocation within the western territories not tied to the Indian Removal Act. Instead, this history is connected to American western expansion and federal policy on the northern and southern plains. Ponca leaders negotiated land cession treaties with the United States in 1858 and 1865, not as a direct conse-quence of military action but because of the increased demand for land in Nebraska in the lead-up to statehood. However, though those two treaties diminished the Ponca landholdings, the most influential accord was one that Ponca leaders did not even sign.[23] In the 1868 treaty that created the Great Sioux Reservation, the United States mistakenly gave the Lakotas the land reserved for the Poncas in their 1865 treaty.[24] And following the military campaigns against the Lakotas in 1876 and 1877, the United States diminished the Lakota landholdings, which meant that the federal government now laid claim to the Ponca lands. Instead of correcting the past error, however, the federal government instead ordered the removal of the Poncas from Nebraska to Indian Territory. That removal was disorganized, and as a result the Poncas suffered tre-mendously during the process and in its aftermath. By the end of their first year in Indian Territory nearly one-third of the tribe had died from disease and the lack of the necessary supplies.[25]

Yet the Ponca removal to Indian Territory is perhaps most well known because of the attempt by the Ponca chief Standing Bear to return to Nebraska with thirty of his followers. Standing Bear's sixteen-year-old son, Bear Shield, was one of those who had died during the first year in Indian Territory, and his father now carried his bones with him so that he could be buried back on their homelands along the Niobrara River. The history of that experience has been incorporated in several different secondary source works, but most recently many of the primary source documents related to both the Ponca removal and Standing Bear's journey have been digitized as part of a larger effort by the Nebraska Commission on Indian Affairs to commemorate the events in question. The website built by the commission has a map and a collection of primary source documents that allows for an in-depth examination of the removal as well as documents related to the court case known as *Standing Bear v. Crook*. The specifics of that case and the assertion by Standing Bear of his individual rights provide the opportunity for an enlightening comparison with the Cherokee assertion of political sovereignty within the context of removal more than forty years earlier.[26]

As illustrated by the expulsion of the Poncas in the 1870s, removal has taken many forms over three centuries of American history. Rather than tied to one specific policy, then, the displacement of Native peoples is inextricably intertwined with the ongoing development of the American nation. That development has also taken many forms, and it appears in both symbolic and physical manifestations.

As both a historian and a devotee of the national park system in the United States, I find myself hounded by *Dispossessing the Wilderness*, a book that describes how Yosemite, Yellowstone, and Glacier national parks are all connected to the removal of American Indians. Mark David Spence is not the only scholar to tackle this particular subject, but his work was the first I encountered that so clearly articulated an ignored aspect of the larger history. "If anything," Spence writes, "national parks serve as a microcosm for the history of conflict and misunderstanding that has long characterized the unequal relations between the United States and native peoples."[27] This is not the same kind of narrative Ken Burns and his team supply in his six-episode documentary titled "The National Parks: America's Best Idea." Yet it is worthwhile for all of us to use such histories to examine the aspects of contemporary life built upon Indian dispossession that are not always emphasized or recognized.

One final example of displacement connected to the growth of the United States originates in the heavy investment in dam construction by the federal government in the mid-twentieth century. The impact of flooding from the Pick-Sloan Plan in the Missouri River Valley devastated reservation communities like that of the Three Affiliated Tribes on the Fort Berthold Reservation. The Garrison Dam created a vast lake upon its completion in 1953, and that lake put whole towns under water along with most of the best agricultural land on the reservation. This history has been captured in books but is also the subject of a documentary titled *Waterbuster*, which was directed by a tribal member, J. Carlos Peinado.[28] Garrison Dam was only one of six built on the Missouri River to control river flooding and provide electricity, and the federal government did not exclusively focus such efforts on the Missouri River. Students can explore similar histories of dispossession, displacement, and dams in the twentieth century on the Allegheny River, the Columbia River, and the Little Tennessee River.[29]

Conclusions

It is necessary for all of us—students and teachers alike—to face the violence and trauma that the removal history encompasses. That process begins when we recognize the extent to which the history of the United States is one predicated on the expulsion of Native peoples from their lands. Indian removal is a core tenet of our nation's founding. It is not a brief time of wrongdoing in the early nineteenth century when Andrew Jackson was president, but is instead a pattern of displacement covering the span of over 240 years that the country has been in existence.

NOTES

1. John P. Bowes, *Land Too Good for Indians: Northern Indian Removal* (Norman: University of Oklahoma Press, 2016), 7.

2. For removal as an imbedded aspect of America's founding and early history, see Samantha Seeley, *Race, Removal, and the Right to Remain: Migration and the Making of the United States* (Chapel Hill: University of North Carolina Press, 2021).

3. For insight into southeastern Native communities that were not removed see the chapter in this volume by Marvin M. Richardson.

4. Richard Peters, ed. and comp., *The Case of the Cherokee Nation against the State of Georgia* (Philadelphia: John Grigg, 1831), at http://archive.org/details/casecherokeenatoogeorgoog.

5. Vicki Rozema, ed., *Voices from the Trail of Tears* (Winston-Salem, NC: John F. Blair, 2003).

6. Theda Perdue and Michael D. Green, *The Cherokee Removal: A Brief History with Documents*, 3rd ed. (New York: Bedford/St. Martin's, 2016).

7. For more on sovereignty, see the chapter in this volume by Margaret Huettl.

8. *Register of Debates*, A Century of Lawmaking for a New Nation: U.S. Congressional Documents and Debates, 1774–1875, Library of Congress, House of Representatives, 21st Cong., 1st. Sess.–page 1024, https://memory.loc.gov/ammem/amlaw/lwrdlink.html.

9. Message from the President of the United States, December 8, 1829, *Journal of the Senate*, 21st Cong., 1st Sess., 5–22.

10. Richard Peters, ed., *Report of Cases Argued and Adjudged in the Supreme Court of the United States: January Term, 1832* (Philadelphia: Thomas, Cowperthwait, 1845).

11. *Register of Debates*, House of Representatives, 21st Cong., 1st. Sess., page 1079, https://memory.loc.gov/ammem/amlaw/lwrdlink.html.

12. "The Trail of Tears through Arkansas," digital exhibit, Sequoyah National Research Center, https://ualrexhibits.org/trailoftears/.

13. Indian-Pioneer Papers Collection, Western History Collections, University of Oklahoma, https://digital.libraries.ou.edu/whc/pioneer/.

14. A recent book that provides a more comprehensive narrative is Claudio Saunt, *Unworthy Republic: The Dispossession of Native Americans and the Road to Indian Territory* (New York: W.W. Norton, 2020).

15. *"Meehkweelintamankwi Aanchsahaaciki: Remembering Our Forced Removal*, https://aacimotaatiiyankwi.org/myaamia-history/removal-commemoration/.

16. "Telling Our Story: A Living History of the Myaamia," http://teach myaamiahistory.org.

17. George Strack et al., *myaamiaki aancihsaaciki: A Cultural Exploration of the Myaamia Removal Route* (Miami, OK: Miami Tribe of Oklahoma, 2011), 1–3.

18. "Proceedings, Potawatomi and Miami Treaty Negotiations, September 30–October 23, 1826," in *John Tipton Papers*, comp. and ed. Nellie Armstrong Robinson and Dorothy Riker (Indianapolis: Indiana Historical Society, 1942), 1584.

19. A more substantive discussion of adaptive resistance can be found in Bowes, *Land Too Good for Indians*, 13, 66–67.

20. Bowes, *Land Too Good for Indians*, 69–77.

21. Links to these Kansas Historical Society collections can be found at https://www.kshs.org/p/online-collections/18942.

22. George Ironstrack and Meghan Dorey, *keehkaapiišamenki: A History of the Allotment of Miami Lands in Indian Territory* (Miami, OK: Miami Tribe of Oklahoma, 2015), 5–14.

23. Treaty of 1858 and Treaty of 1865, in *Indian Affairs: Laws and Treaties*, ed. and comp. Charles A. Kappler (Washington, DC: US Government Printing Office, 1904), 2: 772–75, 875–76.

24. Treaty of 1868, *Indian Affairs*, 998–1007.

25. David J. Wishart, *An Unspeakable Sadness: The Dispossession of the Nebraska Indians* (Lincoln: University of Nebraska Press, 1994), 132–53, 202–11.

26. "Chief Standing Bear: The Trail Ahead," at http://www.chiefstanding bear.org (accessed January 18, 2022); Valerie Sherer Mathes and Richard Lowitt, *The Standing Bear Controversy: Prelude to Indian Reform* (Urbana: University of Illinois Press, 2003), 45–82.

27. Mark David Spence, *Dispossessing the Wilderness: Indian Removal and the Making of the National Parks* (New York: Oxford University Press, 1999), 8; Intermountain Histories has created an online tour of seven different national parks that also illustrate this connection to Native American removal. See "Native American Removal from National Parks," https://www.intermountainhistories .org/tours/show/30 (accessed January 18, 2022).

28. Paul VanDevelder, *Coyote Warrior: One Man, Three Tribes, and the Trial That Forged a Nation* (New York: Little, Brown, 2004). To view the documentary *Waterbuster*, see https://americanarchive.org/catalog/cpb-aacip_508-8k74t6fs54.

29. Colin Calloway, ed., *First Peoples: A Documentary Survey of American Indian History*, 4th ed. (New York: Bedford/St. Martin's, 2012), 502–5; Laurence M. Hauptman, *The Iroquois Struggle for Survival: World War II to Red Power* (Syracuse, NY: Syracuse University Press, 1985).

FOR FURTHER READING

Cherokee Constitution of 1827 as published in the *Cherokee Phoenix*, https:// www.wcu.edu/library/DigitalCollections/CherokeePhoenix/Vol1/no01/ constitution-of-the-cherokee-nation-page-1-column-2a-page-2-column-3a .html.

Cherokee Phoenix, http://onlinebooks.library.upenn.edu/webbin/serial?id=cher okeephoenix; and https://www.wcu.edu/library/digitalcollections/cherokee phoenix/.

Library of Congress, "A Century of Lawmaking for a New Nation: U.S. Congressional Documents and Debates," https://memory.loc.gov/ammem/am law/lawhome.html.

Anson, Bert. *The Miami Indians*. Norman: University of Oklahoma Press, 1971.

Bowes, John P. *Exiles and Pioneers: Eastern Indians in the Trans-Mississippi West*. Cambridge: Cambridge University Press, 2007.

Carson, James Taylor. *Searching for the Bright Path: The Mississippi Choctaws from Prehistory to Removal*. Lincoln: University of Nebraska Press, 1999.

Crews, C. Daniel, and Richard W. Starbuck, eds. *Records of the Moravians among the Cherokees*. Vol. 6, *March to Removal, Part 1, Safe in the Ancestral Homeland, 1821–1824*. Norman: University of Oklahoma Press, 2016.

Dinwoodie, Jane. "Evading Indian Removal in the American South." *The Journal of American History* 108 (June 2021): 17–41.

Green, Michael D. *The Politics of Indian Removal: Creek Government and Society in Crisis*. Lincoln: University of Nebraska Press, 1982.

Haveman, Christopher D. *Rivers of Sand: Creek Indian Emigration, Relocation, and Ethnic Cleansing in the American South*. Lincoln: University of Nebraska Press, 2015.

Herring, Joseph. *The Enduring Indians of Kansas: A Century and a Half of Acculturation*. Lawrence: University Press of Kansas, 1990.

Jacoby, Karl. *Crimes against Nature: Squatters, Poachers, Thieves, and the Hidden History of American Conservation*. Berkeley: University of California Press, 2001.

Kugel, Rebecca. "Planning to Stay: Native Strategies to Remain in the Great Lakes, Post-War of 1812." *Middle West Review* 2 (Spring 2016): 1–26.

Miner, Craig, and William E. Unrau. *The End of Indian Kansas: A Study in Cultural Revolution, 1854–1871*. Lawrence: University Press of Kansas, 1977.

Moulton, Gary E., ed. *The Papers of Chief John Ross*. 2 vols. Norman: University of Oklahoma Press, 1985.

Norgren, Jill. *The Cherokee Cases: Two Landmark Federal Decisions in the Fight for Sovereignty*. Norman: University of Oklahoma Press, 2004.

Paige, Amanda L., Fuller L. Bumpers, and Daniel F. Littlefield Jr. *Chickasaw Removal*. Ada, OK: Chickasaw Press, 2010.

Shuck-Hall, Sheri Marie. *Journey to the West: The Alabama and Coushatta Indians*. Norman: University of Oklahoma Press, 2008.

Snyder, Christina. "Many Removals: Re-evaluating the Arc of Indigenous Dispossession." *Journal of the Early American Republic* 41 (Winter 2021): 623–50.

Teaching the
History of Allotment

ROSE STREMLAU

Allotment receives a few sentences in most high school and college survey textbooks. Students who can define it understand the federal policy entailing the subdivision and privatization of tribal land during the late nineteenth and early twentieth centuries to have been a failed experiment in assimilation and land redistribution. Often described as the end of the reservation era (not true) and the beginning of the forcible integration of American Indian people into mainstream US society (also not true), allotment occurred at the intersection of multiple processes central to settler colonialism that are ongoing. Attention to the policy enables us to consider the forces that led to this sweeping series of laws, the creation of a bureaucracy to implement it, and the dissimulation of its tragic, ongoing impact in history books, museums and historic sites, and popular memory.

When writing my book about allotment, I sought to make clear this complicated process and to humanize the experiences of the allotted. As a teacher, I strive to make past events relevant and empower students to analyze historical topics and correlated or comparable current events with sophistication. With these goals in mind when in my classroom, I teach allotment in four steps to break down the policy into legible components and relate it to critical, controversial questions in our own time: the nature of "proper" family structure and the role of government in promoting it; how bureaucracy shapes individuals' experiences; the ways legal and financial systems limit some people's access to resources while facilitating that of others; and the diverse forms that resistance can take among marginalized people. Understanding allotment is central to

93

understanding American Indian history and contemporary experiences, and this topic also enables us to interrogate main themes and tropes about US history.

Defining Allotment

Between 1882 and 1934, allotment, the subdivision of common land into smaller, individually owned tracts, was a central component of federal-Indian relations. Reformers believed the program would assimilate American Indian people. They reasoned that private property ownership would undermine the communalism characteristic of most Indigenous societies that thus far had enabled resistance to wholesale cultural change and disappearance as distinct peoples. The policy's proponents also sought to open remaining land held in trust for tribes to settlement and development by non-Indians, but they presented this land grab as benevolent. Their unchecked belief in the supremacy of Anglo-American culture justified the destruction of Indigenous ways of life. Individual American Indian people, they reasoned, must be "emancipated" from their tribes.

These critics of decades of negligence and mismanagement of the Indian Service argued for a total overhaul. A coalition of self-appointed "Indian experts" drawn from missionary and educational circles and self-interested commercial and industrial leaders advocated for an end to the reservation system and the initiation of a new era in US-Indian relations. The General Allotment Act of 1887, commonly referred to as the Dawes Act, provided for the allotment of reservations, which were (and are) held in trust for tribes by the federal government. The Dawes Act was one of several laws that applied the policy to federally recognized tribes and their land, and while not the first or final piece of legislation, it had the broadest impact. This process entailed the federal assumption of decisions over tribal citizenship and the creation of tribal rolls, the surveying of tribal property, including the identification of minerals and other resources of commercial value; the issuing of homesteads; and the restriction and ultimate disbanding of tribal governments, which left the administration of allotments and the provision of services to American Indian people to federal Indian Service personnel and, eventually, state and local officials. Not all tribes were subject to the Dawes Act, but the majority of those recognized by the federal government were allotted before the repeal of the policy in 1934. Equally important, even those that were not allotted experienced a shift in the administration of Indian affairs toward deeply intrusive bureaucratic management characteristic of this period.

Allotment resulted in impoverishment, and if desperation was reason to assimilate, then it sometimes caused that, too, although to a much smaller extent than its champions had predicted. American Indian people survived, but their distinct communities frequently did not as non-Indians gained title to land through outright fraud and, more often, the legal but ethically questionable ways in which American Indian estates were managed, taxed, and probated. Advocates for Indians rights and scholars have documented and measured the losses. In the long term, the policy was universally devastating to every community in which it was applied. Across the United States, total tribal land holdings declined from 138 million to 55 million acres before the policy was repealed in 1934.[1] American Indian communities did not experience dispossession evenly, however; those that owned valuable land in desirable areas suffered the most. As a result, some American Indian communities today retain a fraction of their historic homelands and face deeply complicated challenges to economic development and the restoration of sustainability and prosperity.[2]

Teaching Allotment's Lessons

Step One

What was the supposed problem with Native families? What is a family as a legal construct, and what is the role of government and professional experts in defining it? Are some families "right" and others "wrong"?

In our never-ending election cycle, politicians regularly tout family values as the foundation of American civilization and their defense of them as a reason for voters' support. Religious leaders also regularly engage this issue. They generally (and incorrectly) argue that heterosexual, monogamous marriage and nuclear families have been the basic form of social organization throughout the entirety of human history and that demographic trends of the last several decades, particularly a rise in single-parent families and same-sex partnerships, threaten a many millennia-old system sanctioned by God in the Old Testament. If one accepts that ahistorical assertion as factual, then single motherhood and marriage equity seem radical indeed.

Historians and anthropologists who study social organization agree that most human civilizations have not organized themselves into nuclear family units based on monogamous, heterosexual couplings. Extended families and nonmonogamous relationships have been far more common. Native North American societies provide hundreds of alternative examples centered on the concept of kinship. Traditionally, most Native people lived in large, extended families consisting of grandparents, parents, siblings, aunts, uncles, cousins, and children whose presence was valued above that of spouses. Women, especially elders, commonly made decisions regarding the use of resources and parented collectively. A majority (but not all) of American Indian societies recognized descent through the mothers' side, and these matrilineal, extended families remained customary centuries after European contact and even as Native people adopted some elements of Anglo-American culture (including the use of patrilineal surnames) into their own.

Since contact, many Europeans found this lack of male authority to be troubling. Following the Civil War, powerful Anglo-American leaders identified the perpetuation of tribal groupings and women's authority in them to be a national crisis. They believed the federal government needed to act to reform American Indian families because, as philanthropist, educator, and Congregationalist preacher Merrill E. Gates commented in an 1878 report for the Office of Indian Affairs, "The family is God's unit of society. On the integrity of the family depends that of the state."[3] Because most American Indian families were not organized around one heterosexual married couple but around kin groups of those considered to be extended family or even unrelated under American law, Gates and his fellow reformers considered them to be dangerous vectors of social instability. They concluded that American Indian people would only survive in modern society by assuming the gender roles idealized by middle-class, White Americans and that modern American society would only thrive by eradicating alternative social systems.

Allotment was the primary means to this end. These advocates of assimilation theorized that common title to land and resources discouraged American Indian people from living in nuclear families. Reformers intended for the subdivision and privatization of tribal resources among nuclear families headed by adult males to dramatically transform American Indian people and obliterate their distinct cultures within a generation. Although access to tribal resources appealed to some, allotment policy was not just a land grab: it was a tool for state intervention into the private lives of marginalized peoples by imposing the "order" of patriarchal, nuclear families onto the perceived "chaos" of extended, female-headed ones.

I begin my lesson on allotment by assigning Gates's "Land and Law as Agents in Educating Indians: An Address Delivered before the American Social Science Association at Saratoga, N.Y., Sept. 11th, 1885." This primary source is available through several subscription library databases, but I also welcome educators to email me for a PDF if unable to obtain a free copy elsewhere. In his speech, Gates made the case for allotment to skeptical listeners in this organization that evolved into today's prestigious National Institute of Social Sciences. The text effectively serves our purposes by introducing student audiences to reformers' agenda. In successive steps, Gates speculates about how the elimination of communal land bases would ripple through American Indian societies. Organized into about three dozen sections of a few paragraphs each, the report succinctly lists the problems that advocates of uplift identified in America Indian societies; explains how these resulted from family structure; and predicts how private property ownership would correct them and enable assimilation.

Students readily grasp Gates's meaning, and despite some dated language, the document is accessible. Depending on the number of students and their level, I divide sections among individuals or small groups to read in advance. I combine the smaller groups into larger ones based on the portion of the text they read, and we begin our discussion of allotment by creating two cause-and-effect outlines, or fishbone diagrams. Educators unfamiliar with this simple teaching tool can find a range of examples by searching online. In the first step, students break down Gates's explanation for how communal resource ownership created disfunction. We next identify how proponents of the policy believed allotment would rectify this. Students quickly recognize that what he is calling for is a total shift in the ways that American Indian people generated incomes; procured food, clothing, housing, and essential resources; provided education and childcare; accessed health care and tended their sick; and worshipped and expressed their spiritual traditions. Allotment, in other words, was not just about land; it was about the autonomy that access to resources enables when communities can live as they choose.

Students perceive that Gates's ethnocentrism blinded him to the value of Native cultures, that what he called for would be considered unconstitutional today now that American Indians are citizens (most were considered to be wards of the US government during the 1880s), and that some of the evidence to which he referred was factually incorrect. To integrate allotment into the larger history of settler colonialism and correlate this policy to current affairs, I invite students to interrogate his sources. Gates refers to Indian Service reports and missionary publications written by non-Indians who claimed expertise about American Indian people, who had access to institutions of higher learning and media outlets, and whose voices often silenced the dissenting views of marginalized American Indian people. What can this tell us about knowledge production? Who is an authority? Whose perspective is understood to be accurate? Whose is obscured? As a class, we brainstorm responses to Gates's report. If we were to solicit an American Indian rebuttal to Gates, who would we ask to write it? Whose views would we want represented? How do we think it would differ in its conclusions from those of Gates?

I conclude this part of the class by asking students to reflect upon current debates about the accuracy of "facts" and the family. What makes a "good" family today, and what is the relationship between that ideal and the state? How do critics characterize those families that they deem to be deviant? What information or data do they use to prove their point? Are some families today considered to be a threat to the state? Why? How are these families marginalized, and how do local, state, and federal governments use laws, particularly those pertaining to resources such as shared property and benefits such as health care, to force changes in their behavior or punish them for their deviance from social norms?

Step Two

What is the role of bureaucracy in the colonization of American Indian peoples? How did the creation of administrative bodies, particularly those controlling access to resources and monitoring behavior, limit tribal sovereignty and the ability of American Indian people to make autonomous decisions and live self-sufficiently?

I begin this section with a question: what does colonization look like? I use free software that instantly creates a word cloud to generate an instant visualization of their answers. Students generally emphasize military conquest, and their comments reflect the predominance of pop culture representations of armed conflict on the Great Plains and of alien takeovers of earth. From *Dances with Wolves* to *Transformers*, we know what happens when a foreign power invades and decides to stay. Students understand how massacres result in annihilation, but they need help understanding how the establishment of bureaucratic systems often led to destruction, too. Beginning in the colonial period, trading posts shifted patterns of labor and production toward export and non-subsistence consumption and resulted in the loss of traditional ecological knowledge, economic dependence, and environmental collapse. Christian missions and schools continued the work of trading posts in undermining traditional Native ways of thinking and being. British Indian policy was designed to turn Indigenous people into debtors who would surrender land to ensure the continued flow of trade goods into their communities, and our Founding Fathers promoted this practice, which they believed to be the benevolent, cost-effective alternative to frontier warfare. Starting with the Washington administration, federal officials included provisions in treaties that provided for the presence of federal officials as ambassadors of assimilation. This included traders, governments agents, missionaries, and teachers.

Until 1871, when Congress ceased ratifying them, treaties signed with American Indian nations usually included the promise of annuities, cash payments, and provisions in compensation for land cessions and alliances. Federal agents were charged with their distribution, but prior to the allotment era, officials generally did so through tribal leaders, who served as a buffer between American Indian people and the US government. The Dawes Act changed this, however. Congress created a seven-step process through which tribes were allotted, and it empowered non-Indian appointees to make decisions *about* and *for* American Indian people. Although some specific components varied, this generally describes the steps of allotment: (1) the federal government selected tribes to be allotted; (2) federal agents created tribal rolls; (3) federal employees surveyed and divided reservations, generally into 160-acre plots; (4) federal officials assigned allotments to male heads of households and, after 1891, women, too; (5) the federal government held the land in trust for a period of years, during which it managed American Indians' financial affairs, and at the end of this period, it transferred ownership, which entailed full responsibility for the payment of taxes, and extended citizenship rights; (6) the federal government sold natural resources such as timber, mineral and oil rights, and "surplus" land to non-Indians; (7) the federal government removed restrictions on American Indian property owners based on blood quantum.

To begin, federal officials created lists of those eligible for allotted property and, in doing so, usurped the sovereign power of American Indian nations to determine who was (and was not) a member of their families and varying sociopolitical units and who, therefore, had access to shared resources. Federal officials sought to create rolls that would facilitate the economic development of tribal land. They needed to be intelligible to non-Indians seeking to transact real estate deals and probate estates; there was no incentive to reflect Indigenous understandings of relatedness. Officials also saw the regulation of sexuality and reproduction as an appropriate focus of state power, particularly when it facilitated the generation of intergenerational wealth to be transmitted to biological heirs through patrilineal inheritance patterns. Therefore, officials produced rolls using Anglo-American categories and terms for families. In this, allotment agents diverged from precedent. The Census Office, established in 1840, usually defined a family as those who shared a household regardless of whether they were biologically related or conformed to the nuclear ideal. The unrelated residents of a boarding house were listed together, for example.[4] Allotment agents did not organize tribal rolls to provide a comparably accurate reflection of Native societies; rather, they enrolled Native people in the nuclear, patriarchal units preferred in Anglo-American society, whether or not these accurately represented actual living situations.

Although there was variation among specific nations' experiences, enrollment generally consisted of three stages. First, officials arrived in tribal communities; some canvassed individuals in the model of the United States census while others instructed adult men to appear before them to enroll.[5] Second, agents verified the information given to them. This investigative component was arduous. Most often clerks crosschecked individuals with existing tribal rolls and agency records, or they consulted agents and missionaries. The latter sometimes maintained records of marriages, births, and deaths. Because they were determining relatedness to transfer private property at death to biological heirs, agents often asked about sexual fidelity and paternity. Third, clerks organized the information into lists or preprinted cards. They generally listed first the name of the person whom they considered to be the head of household, and they listed others beneath that person and specified their relationship. Again, this head of household often was an adult male—even if that did not correspond with actual family organization. Officials sometimes further identified enrollees by age, sex, and perceived blood quantum. Last, officials commonly assigned individuals a roll number. Federal officials believed that they created a straightforward protocol that would result in accurate rosters. When we consider American Indian perspectives, however, this process was neither simple nor pleasant, and it was inherently inaccurate. American Indians resented and rejected many decisions clerks made, and allotment era rolls remain controversial and contested to this day.

Students are uniquely positioned to appreciate problems with enrollment. Each semester they enroll in classes. Their choices are defined by policies and requirements, and deviation is penalized. Most students believe, however, that no matter their rank, major, or when they enrolled in the class, they should have equal access to me, the professor, and class resources, and they should have equal status in the class. I follow my discussion of enrollment with an exercise in which I create a new roster of the class based on externally imposed hierarchies that students do not recognize as valid. Federal officials allotting American Indian communities favored married adult males. I select history majors to be "heads of households," but teachers could pick members of a team or club, students born in a specific month, or even the first students to arrive to class that day. This example works when a subsection of no more than a fifth of the class is granted this privileged status.

To demonstrate this point, I quickly write the names of history majors in a horizontal line across the dry erase board at the front of the class. I explain that the other students will be included or excluded according to their relationships to the history majors. In my classes, students have done quite a bit of small group work by this point in the semester. I invite majors to quickly note who has worked with them. Usually there are a few students who have never collaborated with any history major, and so some will be left off our new roster while nonetheless remaining in the class. I announce that majors will have priority access to resources such as the course Moodle page and office hours with me and that everyone else's work will be submitted to me through majors, who will receive credit for it. They know I am kidding, but they quickly understand how this reorganization of the class has privileged some, marginalized and excluded others, and imposed a system of inequality upon all of them. We discuss the following: How do human-made systems and the people that enforce them shape our lives? Are there administrative bodies that exert control in our society over marginalized people today?

Step Three

What was/is the role of Indian policy in creating poverty? Did allotment result in the sorts of changes its proponents predicted? Why or why not? If not, what were the results of the policy, and how does allotment continue to impact American Indian communities today?

We next focus on the division and management of tribal resources. While some federal employees created roles, others surveyed and mapped land. In general, the United States Geological Survey (USGS) created plat maps, which divided reservations and communally owned property (like that owned by the Five Tribes in Indian Territory) into uniform townships based on precedents originating in late eighteenth-century federal land ordinances. Notably, surveyors did not always note the location and type of improvements or the owners of these improvements, nor they did appraise the land or the improvements (buildings or other structures, such as fences, barns, mills, and smoke houses; in many late nineteenth-century American Indian societies, family groups or even individuals owned improvements and the products of their labor, while the land beneath improvements remained communal property). Why would surveyors exclude this seemingly relevant information? Plat maps were not designated to document American Indian land use practices but were intended to facilitate the distribution and management of resources, and that step often began while mapmakers completed and corrected their work.

As during the enrollment process, federal officials' approach varied; some invited individuals to select land while others assigned plots to allottees. It is important to recognize the normalization of bureaucratic chaos as a way to frustrate American Indian people and tribal governments defending collective property rights. Agents often attempted to regulate the selection of land, but their efforts did not prevent corruption, which was rampant. People who were not entitled to land occasionally bribed their way onto tribal rolls or onto the claim of improvements that they did not make. Some American Indian people, particularly those who lived on land with valuable mineral or oil deposits, were dispossessed of their improvements when others claimed them. Clerks often assigned to resisters land located at great distances from where they lived or from that of their families. A clerk marked off the allotment on the official map as claimed. Contested claims, which were common, prompted investigation and review by the Office of Indian Affairs and, potentially, the secretary of the interior. Changes to plat maps continued to be made throughout this process and while property distribution proceeded. Allotment typically took years. During this time, some people lost their homes, others who wanted to live on and improve their allotments were prevented from doing so, and familial and community economies were repeatedly disrupted.[6]

A classroom serves as an effective model for property redistribution. Depending on the room layout, the pattern of the flooring, and the placement of furniture, I divide the class in a way that will be logical and obvious to students. For example, if the class has desks, I tell them that each represents one 160-acre section. In classes with square tiles, I often use that as our grid. For the purposes of this essay, let's imagine desks to represent sections of land. Some sections have "improvements" in that they are occupied by students whose laptops, phones, notebooks, and so forth are spread over them. Others are empty. I remind students to be aware of shared resources, such as the door, the computer terminal, the dry erase board, the projector, and the screen that are not on desks but in proximity to them.

I explain that each history major will serve as a head of a household (the groups led by history majors formed in the previous exercise) and will pick one allotment for each group member. Students strategize for a few minutes. I tell students that they can try to work together to obstruct the exercise, and some always try, but inevitably, other students believe they are best served by trying to pick their desks and improvements. I ask students to stand at one side of the room, and I randomly select history majors to pick for their group. Why no obvious order? Because American Indian people experienced the systemic violence of allotment in unpredictable ways. As each group picks, they sit down at their allotted desks. Sometimes they select their own and nearby desks, even if they had been occupied by others. Some pick desks that are in a better location, such as near the door, the computer, and so forth, because they realize that they now can limit others' access to these resources or profit from them. (The question of whether those who control the desks closest to the door will let us leave is always raised!). I invite a student who took the class in a previous offering to represent the squatters and grifters who bribed their way onto tribal rolls to join us; this student simply walks in and claims a desk that had been occupied by another student (students remember this exercise and are glad to come back as the intruders who bribe their way onto the tribal roll).

The exercise moves quickly, and except for the first few to pick, most students end up dispossessed of their original desks and possessions. They also realize that those students left off our roster have been denied access to classroom resources altogether—and yet they remain standing in the room. We consider the following in large group discussion: How do systems of resource distribution create opportunity or inequality among members of a society? What resources are distributed in our society in ways that perpetuate or undermine social hierarchies? Is education one of those resources, or does it subvert inequality?

Once land was distributed, Congress charged federal Indian Service officials with managing American Indian estates during a period of guardianship. Proponents of allotment accepted the paternalistic and pseudo-scientific belief common in the late nineteenth century that human civilizations existed along a hierarchical continuum and that American Indian peoples needed "uplift" and instruction to understand and participate in Anglo-American society. In other words, "giving" Americans Indians private property was not enough; federal officials had to teach them to best utilize it and profit from it. Allotment thus necessitated the creation of exploitative and cumbersome bureaucracies staffed by federal employees who, as political appointees, were not accountable to American Indian people or subject to civil service review. In her account of the administration of American Indian estates, historian Angie Debo described how federal and eventually state and local officials dispossessed Americans Indians through a holistic system of legalized theft based on the removal of restrictions and the transfer of oversight responsibilities.[7]

This occurred in two steps. First, allotment legislation included protections against alienation, which refers to prohibition against the sale of allotted land and its exclusion from taxation for a period of years. White boosters, often representing extractive industries, immediately clamored for their removal. They argued that robust real estate markets uplifted American Indians, and prosperous regional economies benefited all. The removal of restrictions began in 1904 when Congress empowered the secretary of the interior to remove the prohibition against alienation of land allotted to adults on a case-by-case basis.[8] Quickly overwhelmed and unable to effectively manage the estates of hundreds of thousands of allottees, federal officials proposed lifting protections according to the presumed blood quantum, or degree of American Indian versus European or African ancestry, which late nineteenth-century racist thinking correlated with competency. The Restrictions Bill of 1908 was a victory for those who opposed measures protecting against land alienation. Congress authorized American Indian adults and minors registered as having less than one-half Indian blood to sell their remaining land at their discretion; their property became taxable. Those enrolled as having more than one-half but less than three-quarters Indian blood could sell some of their land. Those categorized as having three-fourths or more Indian blood could not sell their allotments, but legal guardians, either Indian Service officials or eventually court-appointment overseers, could negotiate leases for them. In 1919, the commissioner of Indian affairs removed remaining restrictions on all allottees classified as having one-half or less American Indian blood. Only those categorized as full bloods remained fully restricted.[9]

Second, in many regions, Congress incrementally decreased the power of the Office of Indian Affairs and, in response to the vigorous lobby of western congressmen, shifted authority over allottees to state and local authorities. This process escalated in 1907 after Oklahoma statehood. Their congressional delegation complained that restricted land exempt from state and local taxes placed an undue financial burden on the state. Congress transferred the management of estates away from federal officials, who were accountable to at least some minimal oversight through the Department of the Interior, to state and local officials, who were accountable to White voters benefiting from Indian dispossession. Despite concerns raised about the obvious potential conflicts of interest, influential leaders in Congress believed that citizens of each state should be appointed as guardians by county courts and trusted to administer the property of local allottees (referring to those who had received allotments). They argued that local White citizens would tend to their American Indian neighbors' needs with greater concern, efficiency, and economy than the federal government could. (As tribal leaders predicted, this faith in the neighborliness of western Whites was misplaced.) Disillusioned with the long, expensive process of supposedly civilizing and uplifting American Indians, Congress happily shifted the administration of this policy to local authorities, particularly lawyers and judges, who assumed control over the day-to-day management of estates, including probates.[10]

Even when focusing on the management of one tribe's allotments (which most scholars of the topic do), this process is a complicated one, but the outcome was universally the same: land loss over generations through legally but ethically questionable processes, including taxation and probate. To demonstrate this, I instruct students to wear a red, blue, or green shirt to the next class. I bring two kinds of small wrapped candies. I use Hershey kisses and Starbursts because they are available in bulk and easy to count and divide quickly. Educators who can't or prefer not to use food in the classroom can re-create this exercise by using a simple photocopied paper map showing a handful of houses, fields, and so forth overlaid with a grid. Students will simply tear this apart. For the purposes of this essay, I'll describe how I use food to demonstrate dispossession.

What happens next is organized chaos. That's the point. When students arrive at class, I quickly determine which is the least common shirt color. For the purposes of this example, let's say that many students wore red and blue, and fewer students wore green. I ask blue and red students to sit in separate sides of the class, and I tell green students to sit throughout the room among both groups. I explain that the chocolate candy represents land allotments, and every red and blue student, who represent allottees, get ten chocolate kisses representing ten acres. Next, I tell them that the Starbursts represent mineral, oil, or timber resources on the allotment or the cash generated through their sale or that of crops or timber. Some students get a handful of Starbursts. Others get a couple. A few get none. The green students get no candy. I designate the blue students as "full" and red as "part." The green students are nongroup members, which includes government officials and non-Native settlers in allotted regions, particularly those who served as guardians.

I tell blue students that while their chocolate is protected from wholesale loss, guardians will claim fees. Every time I instruct them to do so, they are to give a Starburst to the nearest green student. I do so a few times randomly throughout the next ten minutes. I then explain to red students that they are going to lose protections on their land and pay property taxes. I ask a red student to set their phone timer for sixty seconds, representing a year. Each time the alarm goes off, those students must move a piece of candy—Starburst or chocolate—onto the plate of the nearest green student. I continue to walk around depositing more Starbursts on red and blue students' desks randomly to signify cash income generated or resources available on that land. Inevitably, red students will run out of Starbursts and need to begin giving away their chocolate kisses. While blue students will hold onto their chocolate, they will quickly run out of Starbursts and become indebted to green students. We do this for about ten minutes. At the end, I ask the students to compare their candy stashes. The outcomes are obvious. Green students who had nothing now have a significant percentage and sometimes the majority of the candy. Most red and blue students have lost some but not all candy. A few red students have no candy remaining. I invite them to share candy as they wish and distribute more candy to those who have none. While munching, we discuss. How did the division of the room into groups with different relationships to the candy resources lead to the final distribution outcomes? What would have happened if we kept going? If we were to create another step designed to return candy to red and blue students, what would that look like? (This anticipates our discussions of the Indian New Deal and the Cobell settlement.) Why did no one challenge my rules? Do some systems of resource management in our society and at our school create different rules for different groups? Do we notice them? Do we challenge them?

Step Four

How did American Indian people adapt to and, sometimes, resist allotment and its negative outcomes?

By this point, students understand how allotment was intended to alter American Indian societies. They recognize the differences between the intent of those who created laws reflecting particular ideas about race, gender, civilization, and property and the outcomes shaped by those who implemented the policy. Allotment led to the loss of land and access to the natural resources on it, as well as economic development resulting in environmental decline including soil erosion, the destruction of forests, and the pollution of water by mining tailings. Ironically, the survival of American Indian families on increasingly limited resources was contingent upon kinship and the customs of reciprocity and hospitality and traditional ecological knowledge enabling effective use of the land for subsistence. In contrast to the changes predicted by Merrill Gates and the Friends of the Indian, which refers to the reformers who advocated for allotment policy, those who maintained broad social support systems and utilized a wide range of resources adapted the best by perhaps changing the least.

I have experimented with several methods to help students understand the long-term outcomes of allotment in relationship to individual agency and collective resistance. There are several wonderful books on allotment that explain the diverse ways that American Indian people engaged with, experienced, and resisted the policy. I have found Katherine M. B. Osburn's *Southern Ute Women* to be particularly concise, accessible, and teachable, but one could pick a book from the bibliography I've provided that focuses on a Native nation closest to one's community.[11] Students can read the book or sections of it in preparation for this exercise. I instruct students to pay attention to and note patterns of responses and common variables among their experiences over generations.

For our final exercise, students design a historically accurate and culturally sensitive game that teaches both allotment, in general, and the Southern Ute experience as described by Osburn (or whatever group is the subject of the selected reading). I challenge students to integrate material I have shared, their experiences of the previous exercises, and the reading. I provide markers and flip chart paper, and after a long weekend being able to think and bounce ideas off one another, we take half a class period to work in pairs to prepare; we spend the last part of class sharing their concepts. This opportunity to reflect and consolidate information is essential, and students have produced creative, inciteful projects that have shaped my approach to teaching allotment in subsequent semesters. Some groups design a video game in which individual characters have dramatically different experiences shaped by the players. Others model their game off familiar games of chance and strategy such as Monopoly and Life. We critique and evaluate one another's work. To do so, we ask ourselves, what kind of systems modeled through these games work most effectively to explain the economic outcomes of allotment? Which enable players to understand the complexity of responses and fully humanize American Indian allottees? Which would be the most effective game to play as teaching tools? Students have envisioned a wide variety of creative and engaging games, and this assignment is a pleasure to grade. I have often spun this exercise into an essay question on an exam.

Based on student reflection and my evaluation of these exercises over the years, I've learned that students often expect the time we allocate to

American Indian policy to be boring, but connecting laws to the ideas producing them, the present-day outcomes resulting from them, and the contemporary debates that echo them make history relevant and, therefore, interesting. Some of the reflective questions spark a range of opinions that prompt students to think about their emerging political beliefs, and I also use this as an opportunity to model civil debate. Although I developed this approach to teaching allotment in a two-semester college-level American Indian history course where I have the luxury of time to spend on the topic, I have applied one or two components in US history surveys where I have less time. I encourage those covering allotment in other kinds of courses where they may have one class meeting or a part of it to experiment with one exercise. Many of the techniques described above require just ten or fifteen minutes. Providing these opportunities for interaction and reflection are always valuable, including in small segments.

NOTES

1. Historian Francis Paul Prucha cites these numbers based on tabulations by John Collier, the commissioner of Indian affairs from 1933 until 1945. Prucha, *The Great Father: The United States Government and the Indians*, 2 vols., unabridged (Lincoln: University of Nebraska Press, 1984), 895–96.

2. The Indian Land Tenure Foundation suggests there's been little improvement since the repeal of the policy: https://iltf.org/land-issues/.

3. Merrill E. Gates, "Land and Law as Agents in Educating Indians," Board of Indian Commissioners, Annual Report for 1878, 30–31.

4. The Census Bureau's definition of who and what constituted a family did vary, but significant changes to the described practice did not occur until the 1930 census. Rudy Ray Seward, *The American Family: A Demographic History* (Thousand Oaks, CA: Sage, 1978), 71–74.

5. Kent Carter, *The Dawes Commission* (Orem, UT: Ancestry, 1999), 105–24.

6. Historian Kent Carter described the evolution of this process as it culminated in the system created for the Creeks, who selected allotments according to the terms of the Curtis Act in 1899. Carter, *The Dawes Commission*, 127.

7. Angie Debo, *And Still the Waters Run: The Betrayal of the Five Civilized Tribes* (1940; Princeton, NJ: Princeton University Press, 1973).

8. Debo, *And Still the Waters Run*, 89.

9. Debo wrote the most thorough account of this entire process in *And Still the Waters Run*, and Carter notes these developments throughout his book, *The Dawes Commission*. Prucha provided an abbreviated description in *The Great Father*, 900–903.

10. Carter, *The Dawes Commission*, 207–29; Debo, *And Still the Waters Run*, 159–254; Prucha, *The Great Father*, 759–60, 897–900.

11. Katherine M. B. Osburn, *Southern Ute Women: Autonomy and Assimilation on the Reservation, 1887–1934* (Lincoln: University of Nebraska Press, 2009).

FOR FURTHER READING

Indian Land Tenure Foundation, "Indian Lands in Indian Hands," https://iltf .org/.

Berthrong, Donald J. *The Cheyenne and Arapaho Ordeal: Reservation and Agency Life in the Indian Territory, 1875–1907*. Norman: University of Oklahoma Press, 1977.

Carter, Kent. *The Dawes Commission and the Allotment of the Five Civilized Tribes*. Orem, UT: Ancestry.com, 1999.

Chang, David A. *The Color of the Land: Race, Nation, and the Politics of Land Ownership in Oklahoma, 1832–1929*. Chapel Hill: University of North Carolina Press, 2010.

Chang, David A. "Enclosures of Land and Sovereignty: The Allotment of American Indian Lands." *Radical History Review* 109 (Winter 2011): 108–19.

Debo, Angie. *And Still the Waters Run: The Betrayal of the Five Civilized Tribes*. Princeton, NJ: Princeton University Press, 1973.

Genetin-Pilawa, C. Joseph. *Crooked Paths to Allotment: The Fight over Federal Indian Policy after the Civil War*. Chapel Hill: University of North Carolina Press, 2014.

Justice, Daniel Heath, and Jean M. O'Brien, eds. *Allotment Stories: Indigenous Land Relations under Settler Siege*. Minneapolis: University of Minnesota Press, 2022.

Knack, Martha C. "The Sage of Tim Hooper's Homestead: Non-Reservation Shoshone Indian Land Title in Nevada." *Western Historical Quarterly* 39, no. 3 (Summer 2008): 125–51.

Mark, Joan T. *A Stranger in Her Native Land: Alice Fletcher and the American Indians*. Lincoln: University of Nebraska Press, 1989.

Meyer, Melissa L. *The White Earth Tragedy: Ethnicity and Dispossession at a Minnesota Anishinaabe Reservation, 1889–1920*. Lincoln: University of Nebraska Press, 1999.

Osburn, Katherine M. B. *Southern Ute Women: Autonomy and Assimilation on the Reservation, 1887–1934*. Albuquerque: University of New Mexico Press, 1998.

Osburn, Katherine M. B. "'To Build Up the Morals of the Tribe': Southern Ute Women's Sexual Behavior and the Office of Indian Affairs, 1895–1932." *Journal of Women's History* 9, no. 3 (Autumn 1997): 10–27.

Palmer, Mark H. "Sold! The Loss of Kiowa Allotments in the Post-Indian Re-organization Era." *American Indian Culture and Research Journal* 35, no. 3 (2011): 37–57.

Stremlau, Rose. "Allotment, Jim Crow, and the State: Reconceptualizing the Privatization of Land, the Segregation of Bodies, and the Politicization of Sexuality in the Native South." *Native South* 10 (2017): 60–75.

Stremlau, Rose. *Sustaining the Cherokee Family: Kinship and the Allotment of the Cherokee Nation.* Chapel Hill: University of North Carolina Press, 2011.

Storied Lands;
Storied Peoples

*Teaching the History of Federal Indian
Law through Native American Literature*

N. Bruce Duthu

Native American history is indispensable to a proper
understanding of federal Indian law, both in terms
of appreciating the complexity of the field's foundational principles
and in developing students' capacity to assess whether contemporary
legal and policy developments advance or impede the Republic's commitment to tribal self-determination. Without historical perspective
the vast body of treaties, statutes, regulations, and cases that make up
the field of federal Indian law would be devoid of substantive context, rendering the legal principles unintelligible for most readers. For
the instructor desiring to present a more inclusive account of American history, one that treats Native peoples as fundamental, not incidental, players in the national origin story, the challenges can indeed
be daunting.

One pedagogic response to this dilemma is to employ Native American literature—fiction, poetry, memoir—to serve as an entry point into
this legal and historical universe. A prominent, if not defining, feature of Native American literature is its engagement with *Indigenous
political narratives*,[1] or stories of contestation in which Indigenous and
non-Indigenous individuals or communities strive to assign enduring
meaning to notions of identity, place, and relationships and, in the process, offer important understandings about sovereignty, justice, and

pluralism. These stories of contestation are similarly embedded within historical and legal texts involving Native and non-Native peoples, albeit in forms that may be difficult to discern upon casual reading. The Acoma Pueblo poet Simon Ortiz once noted that "because of the insistence to keep telling and creating stories, Indian life continues, and it is this resistance against loss that has made life possible."[2] The regenerative and reaffirming force of tribal stories has been most severely tested when confronted by the overwhelming, and often destructive, power of federal law in Indian affairs. Reconceptualizing the legal texts of federal Indian law as forms of political narratives helps avoid ascribing to those texts undue weight and authority and opens them up for closer and more critical interrogation than may otherwise be the case. This approach helps achieve a certain *narrative symmetry* (at least analytically) when legal texts are brought into critical dialogue with Indigenous political narratives. The resulting analysis, as I've argued elsewhere, "serves to awaken the mind to reconceptualize the place of Native people within American society and to ignite the imaginative possibilities of more inclusive, respectful, and peacefully co-existing communities" in our constitutional democracy.[3]

A critical feature of this narrative symmetry is its focus on textual language and the related inquiry of how language functions as domination or as resistance. To illustrate, consider the text of the so-called Commerce Clause of the United States Constitution: "The Congress shall have Power . . . To regulate Commerce with foreign Nations, and among the several States, and with the Indian Tribes."[4] Contrast that with the US Supreme Court's language in *United States v. Wheeler* (1978) describing the nature of tribal sovereignty: "The sovereignty that the Indian tribes retain is of a unique and limited character. It exists only at the sufferance of Congress and is subject to complete defeasance."[5] The former text situates Indian tribes within the constellation of discrete and enduring political bodies, while the latter text envisions tribal sovereignty as a vulnerable, ephemeral concept. Even the casual reader will appreciate the dissonance between constitutional life, on the one hand, and the specter of juridical death, on the other.

Consider now an excerpt from *Anchorage*, a poem by Mvskoke/Creek writer and artist Joy Harjo:

Everyone laughed at the impossibility of it,
but also the truth. Because who would believe

the fantastic and terrible story of all of our survival

those who were never meant

to survive?[6]

The literary scholar Eric Cheyfitz has argued that Western imperial-ism "founds its program on the disappearance of the 'other.'"[7] The text above from the US Supreme Court would certainly seem to confirm that view. On the other hand, the text from the Constitution and from Harjo suggest a different trajectory for the development and evolution of relations between Indigenous and non-Indigenous societies. They point to new and different outcomes, ones made possible by the addi-tion and critical examination of Indigenous voices and narratives.

This essay presents a series of political narratives from Indigenous and non-Indigenous authors to illustrate the pedagogic value of teaching the history of federal Indian law through the lens of Native American literature. The first set of narratives feature contestations over ancestral tribal homelands during the formative years of the United States. The second set of narratives concerns the operation of the criminal justice system in the modern era, especially in the context of justice for Amer-ican Indian women. In both instances, the critical element for interro-gation is the systems of power that enable resolution of these disputes and the relative capacity of those systems to produce justice in the cir-cumstances for all concerned.

Contestations over Tribal Homelands

Disputes over land have a long lineage in Native Ameri-can history, dating back to the earliest years of contact between Native peoples and Europeans. Some of these contestations were resolved more or less consensually while others involved warfare or outright theft of Indigenous lands. Until 1823, however, US law offered no defini-tive guidance on the nature of Indigenous rights to their ancestral home-lands. In *Johnson v. McIntosh* (1823), the US Supreme Court ruled that while tribal nations held rights of possession to their ancestral home-lands—a so-called Indian title—they did not hold rights of ownership over those lands. The rights of ownership belonged to the United States as the successor sovereign to earlier Christian colonizing nation(s). We explore the court's opinion in a bit more detail below and bring it into textual dialogue with the writings of two Native authors, one historical—William Apess (Pequot)—and one contemporary—Louise Erdrich (Ojibwe). These literary texts provide an important critique of the broader colonial project, particularly as that project coupled Christian ideology with Euro-American political and military might to overwhelm or marginalize Indigenous rights.

Johnson v. McIntosh *(1823)*

The practical challenge for the court was to find a way to accommodate the fact of Indigenous prior occupancy of their lands within the structure of a national land tenure system that had already authorized title to millions of acres of land held by Euro-American settlers. The court's response was to import the "discovery doctrine," a centuries-old rule of European international law, into US domestic law of property. Under the doctrine, the European nation making initial discovery of "countries then unknown to all Christian people" held absolute title to those lands, subject only to an Indian right of occupancy. The discovering nation further held the exclusive right to extinguish the Indian right of occupancy (also known as "Indian title") by purchase or conquest. According to the court, the United States, as the successor sovereign to the British Crown, "have unequivocally acceded to that great and broad rule by which its civilized inhabitants now hold this country. They hold, and assert in themselves, the title by which it was acquired. They maintain, as all others have maintained, that discovery gave an exclusive right to extinguish the Indian title of occupancy, either by purchase or by conquest."

In arriving at this conclusion, the court drew sharp sociocultural distinctions between Indigenous and non-Indigenous societies, some quite dubious from the standpoint of history and others inescapably racist. Indigenous societies are described as "fierce savages," "heathens," "hunters," and "conquered," while Europeans/Americans are described as "Christian people," "civilized," "agriculturists," and "conquerors." Casting all Indigenous peoples broadly as hunter/gatherer societies ignores the historical record, but this mischaracterization may have been intentional. Otherwise, the court would have had to explain how or why Indigenous agriculturists did not acquire the same property interests in their ancestral homelands as their White neighbors. Related to this, Indigenous societies are depicted as a dying race. According to the court, "Frequent and bloody wars, in which the whites were not always the aggressors, unavoidably ensued. European policy, numbers, and skill, prevailed. As the white population advanced, that of the Indians necessarily receded. The country in the immediate neighbourhood of agriculturists became unfit for them. The game fled into thicker and more unbroken forests and the Indians followed." In embracing the "dying race" thesis regarding Indigenous peoples, the court reflected widely held sentiments of the day, perhaps as a signal to itself and others that any accommodation of Indian title necessitated by its ruling would inevitably be short-lived.

From the standpoint of judicial rhetoric, the *Johnson* case is noteworthy for the numerous instances where the court expresses ambivalence about the moral integrity of its opinion. After concluding that the United States had, in practice and policy, endorsed the doctrine of discovery, the court states the following:

> We will not enter into the controversy, whether agriculturists, merchants, and manufacturers, have a right, on abstract principles, to expel hunters from the territory they possess, or to contract their limits. Conquest gives a title which the Courts of the conqueror cannot deny, whatever the private and speculative opinions of individuals may be, respecting the original justice of the claim which has been successfully asserted.... Although we do not mean to engage in the defence of those principles which Europeans have applied to Indian title, they may, we think, find some excuse, if not justification, in the character and habits of the people whose rights have been wrested from them.

The court describes the "character and habits" of Indigenous peoples in the following language:

> The tribes of Indians inhabiting this country were fierce savages, whose occupation was war, and whose subsistence was drawn chiefly from the forest. To leave them in possession of their country, was to leave the country a wilderness; to govern them as a distinct people, was impossible, because they were as brave and as high spirited as they were fierce, and were ready to repel by arms every attempt on their independence.

In a remarkable concluding passage, the court acknowledges the moral shortcomings of its ruling but portrays the judiciary as institutionally incapable of doing anything about it. "However this restriction may be opposed to natural right," wrote the majority, "and to the usages of civilized nations, yet, if it be indispensable to that system under which the country has been settled, and be adapted to the actual condition of the two people, it may, perhaps, be supported by reason, and certainly cannot be rejected by Courts of justice."

For the student of Native American history, *Johnson v. McIntosh* offers an excellent opportunity to examine critically the legal and moral justifications asserted by the emerging United States for dispossessing Native peoples of their ancestral homelands. The case has generated its own cottage industry of critical commentary, including studies that confirm that the underlying "controversy" between the two competing non-Indian landowners in the case was, in fact, the product of collusion by the proprietors of early land syndicates who concocted the case as a means of achieving legal recognition of their titles to lands west of the Appalachian Mountains.[8]

Notwithstanding the critical attention the case has attracted, there are still glaring omissions in the broader narrative of tribal dispossession during the early American period. The Indigenous voice is severely muted in the nation's formative legal narrative. As scholarship from recent decades demonstrates, this is not because Native peoples were not speaking or writing or otherwise contesting the developments that were quickly enveloping them. They most emphatically were. William Apess, for example, a Pequot Indian and Christian minister, published a series of books from 1829 to 1836 whose focus was less about converting Indians to Christianity than controverting the historical exclusion of Native peoples from the nation's emerging origin story.[9] Apess's writings are particularly relevant given their temporal proximity to landmark legal cases such as *Johnson v. McIntosh* and the famous *Cherokee* cases from the early 1830s that confirmed the legal status of Indian tribes as political bodies with rights of self-governance.[10] I turn now to place some of Apess's writings, along with more contemporary literary texts from Native writers such as Louise Erdrich (Ojibwe), into textual dialogue with legal narratives like *Johnson* to demonstrate one pedagogical strategy for restoring a critical Indigenous voice into the nation's formative legal narrative.

Indigenous Literary Narratives by William Apess and Louise Erdrich

Apess regularly appropriated the rhetoric and values of American nationalism and Christian doctrine in order to offer stinging criticism of early nineteenth-century US society's treatment of marginalized peoples, including Indigenous peoples. In his 1833 text, *An Indian's Looking Glass for the White Man*, Apess turned Christian doctrine and ideology onto White society itself to expose the hypocrisy and damage done to Indigenous peoples in the name of God, as in the following excerpt:

> Now let me ask you, white man, if it is a disgrace for you to eat, drink, and sleep with the image of God, or sit, or walk and talk with them. Or have you the folly to think that the white man, being one in fifteen or sixteen, are the only beloved images of God? Assemble all nations together in your imagination, and then let the whites be seated among them, and then let us look for the whites, and I doubt not it would be hard finding them; for to the rest of the nations, they are still but a handful. Now suppose these skins were put together, and each skin had its national crimes written upon it—which skin do you think would have the greatest? I will ask one question more. Can you charge the Indians with robbing a nation almost of their whole continent, and murdering their women and children, and then depriving the remainder of their lawful rights, that nature and God require them to have? And to cap the climax, rob another nation to till their grounds and welter out their days under the lash with hunger and fatigue under the scorching rays of a burning sun? I should look at all the skins, and I know that when I cast my eye upon that white skin, and if I saw those crimes written upon it, I should enter my protest against it immediately and cleave to that which is more honorable. And I can tell you that I am satisfied with the manner of my creation, fully—whether others are or not.[11]

Apess took care to acknowledge those individuals who worked actively in support of Indian rights and causes, framing their actions as consistent with, not departures from, Christian doctrine and ideology. Among those whom Apess singles out for praise are William Wirt, a former attorney general of the United States and legal advocate for the Cherokee Nation in their cases before the US Supreme Court, and Daniel Webster, one of the advocates in *Johnson v. McIntosh* who argued that Native tribes ought to be recognized as the first and true owners of their ancestral homelands. Highlighting the beneficial work of these individuals, Apess again turned his interrogative eye to the dominant society:

How are you to love your neighbors as yourself? Is it to cheat them? Is it to wrong them in anything? Now, to cheat them out of any of their rights is robbery. And I ask: Can you deny that you are not robbing the Indians daily, and many others? But at last you may think I am what is called a hard and uncharitable man. But not so. I believe there are many who would not hesitate to advocate our cause; and those too who are men of fame and respectability—as well as ladies of honor and virtue. There is a Webster, an Everett, and a Wirt, and many others who are distinguished characters—besides a host of my fellow citizens, who advocate our cause daily. And how I congratulate such noble spirits—how they are to be prized and valued; for they are well calculated to promote the happiness of mankind. They well know that man was made for society, and not for hissing-stocks and outcasts. And when such a principle as this lies within the hearts of men, how much it is like its God—and how it honors its Maker—and how it imitates the feelings of the Good Samaritan, that had his wounds bound up, who had been among thieves and robbers. Do not get tired, ye noble-hearted—only think how many poor Indians want their wounds done up daily; the Lord will reward you, and pray you stop not till this tree of distinction shall be leveled to the earth, and the mantle of prejudice torn from every American heart—then shall peace pervade the Union.[12]

According to Barry O'Connell, literary scholar and Apess biographer, Apess sought nothing less than to redirect the trajectory of Indian-White relations and, in the process, tilt the nation toward a more just, egalitarian, and inclusive society. For O'Connell, "[Apess advanced] an idea of American history which, had it been accepted, would have denied to Euro-Americans the conviction of superiority and of divine mission they needed to conduct their conquests. Indians and black people had, in different ways, to be rendered culturally and morally negligible if the White settlement of the West and the full operation of the slave system were to proceed."[13]

Pursuing similar goals, but working in the modern era, the celebrated Ojibwe writer Louise Erdrich also challenges Euro-Americans' "conviction of superiority" in their relations with Indigenous peoples. For Erdrich, as with Apess, Christian institutions and ideology regularly come under critical scrutiny, and no wonder, given the massive influence this ideology has had in shaping Indigenous/Euro-American relations in the political and legal spheres (as evidenced in the *Johnson* case). A chapter entitled "Saint Marie" from Erdrich's first novel, *Love Medicine* (1984), offers a powerful and poignant meditation on moral authority and political power in the setting of a Christian convent located on an Indian reservation.

Marie is a thirteen-year-old mixed-blood Chippewa girl whose quest to attain sainthood within the Catholic Church leads her to enter the convent on her home reservation. There, she confronts Sister Leopolda, a complex and frightening figure whose distaste for Indians is apparent but who nonetheless finds Marie a worthwhile "project" in terms of helping advance her own religious aspirations. A battle of wills ensues with both characters using everything at their disposal, including physical violence, to establish their moral and spiritual superiority over the other. In the midst of this conflict, Marie envisions herself resplendent and dominant over Leopolda:

> I was rippling gold. My breasts were bare and my nipples flashed and winked. Diamonds tipped them. I could walk through panes of glass. I could walk through windows. She was at my feet, swallowing the glass after each step I took. I broke through another and another. The glass she swallowed ground and cut until her starved insides were only a subtle dust. She coughed. She coughed a cloud of dust. And then she was only a black rag that flapped off, snagged in bob wire, hung there for an age, and finally rotted in the breeze.[14]

Emboldened by her vision (or perhaps deluded by it), Marie attempts to thrust Leopolda headlong into the convent's large oven. She fails. Leopolda responds by raising a steel poker and striking Marie, first through her hands and then across her head, knocking her out. When she revives, Marie finds herself surrounded by the nuns of the convent, all kneeling in apparent adoration of her. From the soft murmurings among the nuns, Marie quickly surmises the reason: on her hands, she bore the miraculous stigmata, the nail marks of Jesus crucified on the cross. Leopolda had manufactured a lie to cover up her act of physical violence. Marie, however, played along: "I lifted up my hand as in my dream. It was completely limp with sacredness. 'Peace be with you.'" She calls Leopolda forward to kneel before her, her ultimate conquest about to be confirmed, when the following transpires:

"Christ has marked me," I agreed. I smiled the saint's smirk into her face. And then I looked at her. That was my mistake. For I saw her kneeling there. Leopolda with her soul like a rubber overboot. With her face of a starved rat. With the desperate eyes drowning in the deep wells of her wrongness. There would be no one else after me. And I would leave. I saw Leopolda kneeling within the shambles of her love. My heart had been about to surge from my chest with the blackness of my joyous heat. Now it dropped. I pitied her. I pitied her. Pity twisted in my stomach like that hook-pole was driven through me. I was caught. It was a feeling more terrible than any amount of boiling water and worse than being forked. Still, still, I could not help what I did. I had already smiled in a saint's mealy forgiveness. I heard myself speaking gently. "Receive the dispensation of my sacred blood," I whispered. But there was no heart in it. No joy when she bent to touch the floor. No dark leaping. I fell back into the white pillows. Blank dust was whirling through the light shafts. My skin was dust. Dust my lips. Dust the dirty spoons on the ends of my feet. Rise up! I thought. Rise up and walk! There is no limit to this dust![15]

In earlier writing, I provided this analysis of Marie's visionary triumph over Leopolda and her unsettling response to "sainthood":

In her "visionary triumph" over Leopolda, Marie shatters false, corrupt ideologies, the pieces of which are swallowed by the propagators leading to their eventual demise. That vision is juxtaposed against her real knowledge of Indians who swallowed pieces of holy cloth believing it would cure fever, only to contract smallpox from the contaminated material, killed with belief. In the end, however, Marie's "real triumph" over Leopolda and her temporal ascension to power is joyless because she knows that this power, like Leopolda's earlier exercise of power over her, is anchored in deceit, violence, perversion, and self-denial. Far from shattering false, corrupt ideologies, Marie finds herself complicit in them and now relying on them to maintain her position. The dust that envelopes her, like the dust in her vision, reveals the empty, lifeless and spent force of ideology run amok. This represents a return to transpositional discourse, but only in the sense that each character ultimately realizes, or at least must confront, the morally bankrupt nature of her pretensions to power.[16]

Returning to the legal narrative in *Johnson v. McIntosh*, I noted earlier how the court revealed its ambivalence about the moral integrity of its opinion. Reading *Johnson* in dialogue with the literary texts by Apess and Erdrich allows us to view the opinion as a meditation on political and legal power. As in *Saint Marie*, the *Johnson* court's rhetoric reflects an understanding, but also disquietude, that the dispossession of Indigenous peoples from their ancestral homelands is rooted in deceit, violence, and perversion of justice. One imagines how the opinion might have evolved differently if the audience were to shift from the "courts of the conqueror" to the imaginative "assembly of nations" conjured in Apess's essay. At the least, such a reading suggests the complexity of historical intersocietal relations and the serious challenges that arise in crafting arrangements for peaceful coexistence when the Indigenous voice is included and given due attention. Those challenges are as urgent in the modern era as they were in the formative years of the nation, as the next series of narratives demonstrates.

Justice and the Criminal Law

Government power often operates at its most coercive in the administration of criminal law since in this arena, a person's liberty or life can be taken in the name of the people and in pursuit of justice. No wonder then that the Constitution's Bill of Rights are framed largely as a set of protections for individuals unfortunate enough to face this massive power. The Constitution, however, only constrains the exercise of federal and state governmental power; it does not serve as a constraint on the exercise of tribal power. Not surprisingly, US law and policy has interpreted the scope of tribal criminal authority to be exceedingly narrow, extending only to Native peoples who are citizens of federally recognized tribes. Until recently, non-Indians were deemed completely out of the reach of tribal criminal law. This posed tremendous problems for tribal nations trying to redress reservation-based crimes, including the pernicious issue of sexual violence against Native women where the overwhelming majority of alleged perpetrators are non-Indian men.

In this portion of the essay, I briefly examine the Supreme Court opinion in *Oliphant v. Suquamish Indian Tribe* (1978), the landmark case that addressed the issue of inherent tribal criminal jurisdiction.[17] I approach this opinion in parallel with another literary work by Louise Erdrich, her prize-winning novel *The Round House* (2012), which offers a gripping fictional account of a Native family torn apart by the crime of sexual violence. Finally, I assess the relative merits and shortcomings of Congress' legislative remedy to help tribal governments confront this serious problem.

In the *Oliphant* opinion, the Supreme Court held that Indian tribes lacked the inherent sovereign authority to prosecute non-Indians. The court could point to no federal statute, treaty provision, or presidential order that compelled this result. Instead, the court relied on federal common law (or judge-made law) principles to hold that inherent tribal powers could be divested either *explicitly*, by statute or treaty, or *implicitly*, if determined by courts to be "inconsistent with their status" as domestic dependent nations. While *Oliphant*'s "implicit divestiture" rule originated in a criminal case, the court has since extended it to cases involving civil or regulatory tribal powers as well.[18] As a result, tribal nations have experienced the diminishment of huge swaths of jurisdictional power, only a small portion of which has been remedied through federal legislation.[19]

The court's principle concern in *Oliphant* was to guard against "unwarranted intrusions" on personal liberty, an unquestioned cornerstone value of our democratic system. The opinion thus reminds tribes of their subordinate position within the nation's constitutional framework: "Upon incorporation into the territory of the United States, the Indian tribes thereby come under the territorial sovereignty of the United States and their exercise of separate power is constrained so as not to conflict with the interests of this overriding sovereignty. [T]heir rights to complete sovereignty, as independent nations, [are] necessarily diminished."[20] The trope of "incorporation" is nowhere defined or explained, but its effects parallel the results in *Johnson* in terms of the lethal consequences for tribal nations. In short, the rhetorical "conquest by incorporation" of *Oliphant* and the "conquest by discovery" of *Johnson* both impoverish tribes and reveal law's awesome capacity to accomplish by the stroke of a pen what once required force of arms.

The court acknowledges that while tribal courts "have become increasingly sophisticated and resemble in many respects their state counterparts," and are obligated to enforce the protections under the federal Indian Civil Rights Act (1968), there remain "dangers" for non-Indians if subjected to criminal prosecution in tribal courts. Again, the court offers no explanation for what "dangers" means in this context. In relying heavily on nineteenth-century precedents and historical events, the court unwittingly frames tribal courts as judicial analogues to early American captivity narratives, where White pioneers wrote of their travails living within and escaping from tribal communities.

In Erdrich's *The Round House* we learn about the devastating effects of sexual violence against Native women through the eyes of thirteen-year-old Joe, whose mother was sexually assaulted by a White man. Through Joe, we also learn about the limits of tribal court authority as he comes to understand the legal constraints confronting his father, a tribal court judge. Rummaging through his father's case files, Joe narrates his reaction as follows:

> I'd thought I was being excluded from weightier matters, upsetting or violent or too complex, because of my age. I had imagined that my father decided great questions of the law, that he worked on treaty rights, land restoration, that he looked murderers in the eye, that he frowned while witnesses stuttered and silenced clever lawyers with a slice of irony. I said nothing, but as I read on I was flooded by a slow leak of dismay. For what had Felix S. Cohen written his Handbook [of Federal Indian Law]? Where was the greatness? the drama? the respect? All of the cases that my father judged were nearly as small, as ridiculous, as petty. Though a few were heart-breaking, or a combination of sad and idiotic, like that of Marilyn Shigaag, who stole five gas station hot dogs and ate them all in the gas station bathroom, none rose to the grandeur I had pictured. My father was punishing hot dog thieves and examining washers—not even washing machines—just washers worth 15 cents apiece.[21]

Later, Joe's father uses a rotten casserole from the refrigerator to illustrate the layers of "rotten decisions" from the US Supreme Court that stripped tribal nations of much of their sovereignty, leaving them shadows of their former states and entrusted with matters of little concern to the dominant society. "But this one—my father teased a particularly disgusting bit of sludge from the pile with the edge of his fork—this one is the one I'd abolish right this minute if I had the power of a movie shaman. *Oliphant v. Suquamish*. He shook the fork and the stink wafted at me. Took from us the right to prosecute non-Indians who commit crimes on our land." When Joe asks why his father persists, he gets this response:

> These are the decisions that I and many other tribal judges try to make. Solid decisions with no scattershot opinions attached. Everything we

do, no matter how trivial, must be crafted keenly. We are trying to build a solid base here for our sovereignty. We try to press against the boundaries of what we are allowed, walk a step past the edge. Our records will be scrutinized by Congress one day and decisions on whether to enlarge our jurisdiction will be made. Some day. *We want the right to prosecute criminals of all races on all lands within our original boundaries. Which is why I try to run a tight courtroom, Joe. What I am doing now is for the future, though it may seem small, or trivial, or boring, to you.*[22]

The day Joe's father envisioned arrived in 2013. In reauthorizing the federal Violence Against Women Act (VAWA), Congress enacted a partial repeal of the *Oliphant* case and affirmed inherent tribal criminal jurisdiction over all individuals, *including non-Indians*, who commit a limited class of sexual crimes. The price tag, however, was steep. Tribal nations wishing to exercise this authority are required to conform to all legal protections guaranteed under the US Constitution and adapt their trial procedures and court personnel so that they resemble their state counterparts. For some tribes, the judicial makeover is well worth the opportunity to prosecute sex offenders. For others, there is resistance—for reasons both pragmatic (the costs are not insignificant) and ideological (the net result constitutes a form of judicial assimilation and a rejection of greater, more respectful forms of legal pluralism).

Conclusions

Teaching the history of federal Indian law through intertextual analysis of legal and literary texts is certainly an unconventional approach or methodology. As the materials above suggest, however, they provide an opening for the critical addition of long-ignored Indigenous voices and perspectives. The approach challenges many of the assumptions that are so deeply entrenched in Western legal discourse as to seem normative, including the moral "rightness" of legal systems operating on lands usurped from their original owners. It also stimulates within our students the capacity to ask—even demand—greater attention to and inclusion of Indigenous voices in the presentation of our national story. Such efforts lend weight to the aspirations of many tribal nations and their leaders—finally to have their sovereign status understood, accepted, and made a critical part of the everyday functioning of our evolving constitutional democracy.

NOTES

1. This borrows from David Luban's notion of "political narrative," which, in the form of legal argument, represents "a struggle for the privilege of recounting the past. To the victor goes the right to infuse a constitutional clause, or a statute, or a series of prior decisions with the meaning that it will henceforth bear by recounting its circumstances of origin and assigning its place in history." See David Luban, "Difference Made Legal: The Court and Dr. King," 87 *Michigan Law Review* 2152 (1989).

2. Simon J. Ortiz, "Towards a National Indian Literature: Cultural Authenticity in Nationalism," *MELUS* 8, no. 2 (Summer 1981): 11.

3. N. Bruce Duthu, "Incorporative Discourse in Federal Indian Law: Negotiating Tribal Sovereignty through the Lens of Native American Literature," 13 *Harvard Human Rights Journal* 141, 143 (2000).

4. US Constitution, Article 1, Section 8, Clause 3, https://www.archives.gov/founding-docs/constitution-transcript.

5. *United States v. Wheeler*, 435 U.S. 313, 323 (1978).

6. Joy Harjo, "Anchorage," from *She Had Some Horses* (New York: W. W. Norton, 2008). Also found at https://poets.org/poem/anchorage.

7. Eric Cheyfitz, "Savage Law: The Plot against American Indians in *Johnson and Graham's Lessee v. M'Intosh* and *The Pioneers*," in *Cultures of United States Imperialism*, ed. Amy Kaplan and Donald E. Pease (Durham, NC: Duke University Press, 1994), 109.

8. See for example Lindsay G. Robertson, *Conquest by Law: How the Discovery of America Dispossessed Indigenous People of Their Lands* (Oxford: Oxford University Press 2007); Stuart Banner, *How the Indians Lost Their Land: Law and Power on the Frontier* (Cambridge, MA: Harvard University Press, 2007); Blake A. Watson, *Buying America from the Indians: Johnson v. McIntosh and the History of Native Land Rights* (Norman: University of Oklahoma Press, 2012); Steven T. Newcomb, *Pagans in the Promised Land: Decoding the Doctrine of Christian Discovery* (London: Fulcrum Press, 2008); Robert J. Miller, *Native America, Discovered and Conquered: Thomas Jefferson, Lewis & Clark, and Manifest Destiny* (Lincoln, NE: Bison Books, 2008).

9. See, generally, Barry O'Connell, *On Our Own Ground: The Complete Writings of William Apess, a Pequot* (Amherst: University of Massachusetts Press, 1992).

10. *Cherokee Nation v. Georgia*, 30 U.S. 1 (1831); *Worcester v. Georgia*, 31 U.S. 515 (1832).

11. Barry O'Connell, *On Our Own Ground*, 157.

12. O'Connell, *On Our Own Ground*, 160–61.

13. O'Connell, *On Our Own Ground*, lxxvi.

14. Erdrich, *Love Medicine* (New York: Henry Holt, 1984), 64.

15. Erdrich, *Love Medicine*, 71–72.

16. Duthu, "Incorporative Discourse in Federal Indian Law," 141–89.

17. 435 U.S. 191 (1978).

18. See for example *Montana v. United States*, 450 U.S. 544 (1981); *Strate v. A-1 Contractors*, 520 U.S. 438 (1997); *Atkinson Trading Company v. Shirley*, 532 U.S. 645 (2001).

19. In *Duro v. Reina*, 495 U.S. 676 (1990), the court held that Indian tribes also lacked inherent criminal jurisdiction to prosecute nonmember Indian defendants. In 1991, Congress acted with uncharacteristic speed to overturn that result and reaffirmed tribal criminal jurisdiction over nonmember Indians. See 25 U.S.C. 1301(2), amended by Act of October 28, 1991, 105 Stat. 646. The *Oliphant* ruling, however, was left intact.

20. *Oliphant v. Suquamish Indian Tribe*, 435 U.S. 191, 209 (1978).

21. Erdrich, *The Round House* (New York: Harper, 2012), 48.

22. Erdrich, *The Round House*, 229–30.

FOR FURTHER READING

For instructors wishing to apply the methodology described above to other topical areas, here are some suggested pairings of literary and legal texts.

Contestations over Individual and Tribal Identity

Alexie, Sherman. *Flight*. Sydney, Australia: Turtleback Books, 2007.

Mississippi Band of Choctaw Indians v. Holyfield, 490 U.S. 30 (1989), dealing with the Indian Child Welfare Act of 1978.

Santa Clara Pueblo v. Martinez, 436 U.S. 49 (1978), involving a challenge to tribal membership criteria under the Indian Civil Rights Act of 1968.

Contestations over Treaty Promises, Particularly Reserved Lands

Erdrich, Louise. *Tracks*. New York: Henry Holt, 1988.

Momaday, N. Scott. *The Way to Rainy Mountain*. 50th anniversary ed. Albuquerque: University of New Mexico Press, 2019.

Lone Wolf v. Hitchcock, 187 U.S. 553 (1903), holding that Congress has power unilaterally to abrogate or break treaty promises.

Lyng v. Northwest Cemetery Protective Association, 485 U.S. 439 (1988), rejecting tribal claims to off-reservation sacred lands under the Free Exercise Clause of the US Constitution, which protects free exercise of religion.

United States v. Sioux Nation of Indians, 448 U.S. 371 (1980), ordering compensation from the US government for its unconstitutional "taking" of the Black Hills.

Contestations over Natural Resources and Sustainable Living Practices

Hensley, William Iggiagruk. *Fifty Miles from Tomorrow: A Memoir of Alaska and the Real People*. New York: Sarah Crichton Books, 2008.

Hogan, Linda. *Power*. New York: W. W. Norton, 1998.

Alaska v. Native Village of Venetie Tribal Government, 522 U.S. 520 (1998), holding that lands assigned to Native Alaskans under the Alaska Native Claims Settlement Act of 1971 are not "Indian Country."

US v. Billie, 667 Federal Supplement 1485 (SD Florida 1987), a criminal case against a Seminole political leader charged with killing an endangered panther.

Nation to Nation

Understanding Treaties and Sovereignty

MARGARET HUETTL

"Save a walleye, spear an Indian." The words were there in red letters on the back of my uncle's truck, a narrow, six-inch rectangle that opened a wedge of division in my family. For my father's family, the descendants of German and French immigrants to North America, recreational hunting and fishing were treasured seasonal pastimes. They owned a cabin on one of the many pine-edged lakes in Wisconsin's Northwoods. When Ojibwe spearfishers legally crossed reservation boundaries to harvest walleye, my uncle reacted with outrage that "those Indians," defeated by his ancestors long ago, had special privileges to hunt and fish in ways that he could not, all because of some old treaties. He joined the upsurge of White Wisconsinites who lobbied politicians to abrogate or dissolve treaties, fundraised, held public rallies, and, at their worst, violently threatened spearfishers with rocks and guns from docks and boats.

That bumper sticker meant something very different to my mother, one of "those Indians." My father's family cabin stood in the middle of her ancestral homeland. She and my grandfather are enrolled members of the Lac Courte Oreilles Band of Lake Superior Ojibwe. Two brothers from Lac Courte Oreilles had started the round of litigation and non-Indian backlash that became known as the Walleye Wars, and my mother understood that they exercised a right that her ancestors had protected when they negotiated the treaties that made it possible for migrants like my father's family to settle in Wisconsin. When we pulled up in my grandparents' driveway behind my uncle's truck, she made my father turn the car around. We missed Christmas that year.

Events throughout the country replicated the tension in my family on a larger scale. In 1969, dozens of Native men and women seized Alcatraz Island for more than a year, citing treaties that promised the return of abandoned federal land. During the summer of 1971, a group of Natives led by the American Indian Movement occupied Mount Rushmore's summit to demand that the United States honor the Treaty of Fort Laramie, which acknowledged Lakota rights to the Black Hills. There were fish-ins in Puget Sound and confrontations between spearfishers and state game wardens on lakes throughout northern Wisconsin. In Washington and Wisconsin, courts upheld the treaty-protected right to hunt and fish beyond the limits of state laws and reservation boundaries. With attention came backlash from non-Indians who saw treaties as outdated relics and modern Indians as opportunistic anachronisms.

I was barely out of preschool when I came face-to-face with that bumper sticker from the back seat, but my uncle's anger at "those Indians"—which I thought might include me—stuck with me. Later, as I became a historian and professor, I encountered that anger again in some of my classrooms, not only in small-town Wisconsin but also in Las Vegas and Lincoln, Nebraska. My uncle and my students thought they knew the history of Native American treaties, and they felt certain that this history was in the past. They saw treaties as yellowing documents in distant museums, their relevance disintegrating along with the paper on which they were written. However, the more than five hundred treaties negotiated between the United States and Native Nations remain in effect. Treaties represent relationships—peace and friendship, trade, access to land and resources. They connect the people of different nations through the rule of law, and neither the United States nor Native polities have ever dissolved these relationships, although one side has ignored, violated, and even forgotten their promises. Understanding treaties and contemporary Indigenous People's treaty rights requires us to simultaneously recognize two seemingly contradictory truths: treaties functioned as tools of dispossession in the effort to transfer Native lands and resources to Euro-Americans, but they also serve as powerful and enduring statements of Indigenous sovereignty.

More than written documents forced on helpless Indigenous peoples, treaties are agreements negotiated between sovereign entities that protected Native nations that reserved rights to self-governance and resource access. This chapter begins by defining the sovereignty that underwrites treaty relationships and then explores both Native and United States perspectives on treaty making. The best way to learn about treaty rights is to focus on specific treaties and their local contexts; therefore, this chapter uses Ojibwe treaties as an example. In the decades that followed treaties' creation, federal and state governments violated their agreements, breaking up reserved lands and denying hunting, fishing, and gathering rights. Native nations such as the Ojibwe returned to the rights and relationships symbolized by the written documents to fight back. Today, treaties remain testaments to the sovereignty of Native peoples.

Understanding Sovereignty

Treaties represent nation-to-nation agreements. Native tribes—the Ojibwe, the Cherokee, the Narragansett, and more than five hundred others—are and were sovereign nations. At its most basic, sovereignty refers to the right to self-rule. Diné scholar Jennifer Nez Denetdale provides a straightforward definition that makes sense to students and holistically encapsulates Indigenous sovereignty's scope: sovereignty means "concrete rights to self-government, territorial integrity, and cultural autonomy under international law."[1] Sovereignty, then, consists of more than centralized laws and mapped borders; it includes cultural aspects such as everyday relationships with land, language, sacred history, ceremonies, and kin.

Indigenous sovereignty predates Europeans' arrival on the shores of Turtle Island. Sovereignty is not a status given to Natives by the United States or previous European powers. It is inherent. This distinction matters when talking about treaty rights. In the classroom, students frequently default to the verb "to give": the United States "gave" Indians land for reservations, or treaties "gave" them the right to spearfish. However, the United States cannot give Native peoples something they already possessed. Understanding sovereignty helps us see how Native Americans' rights to land and resources originated from Native power, not United States beneficence.

The American legal system recognizes tribal sovereignty. The United States acknowledged this sovereignty not only by entering into treaties with individual Native nations but also in the Constitution, which, in addition to federal and state governments, refers to Indian tribes as distinct entities. The Supreme Court further entrenched the legal reality of Native sovereignty in a series of court cases known as the Marshall Trilogy, after Chief Justice John Marshall. The court's ruling in *Worcester v. Georgia* (1832) most clearly confirms tribal rights by describing Native peoples as

> distinct political communities, retaining their original rights as the undisputed possessors of the soil from time immemorial. . . . The very term nation, so generally applied to them, means a people distinct from others, having territorial boundaries, within which their authority is exclusive, and having a right to all the lands within those boundaries, which is not only acknowledged but guaranteed by the United States.[2]

Native peoples possessed the inherent right, rooted in "time immemorial," to govern themselves and their territory. Of course, we are talking about the legal system of the colonizer, which sought to cut tribal sovereignty down to a more manageable size. Even while making strong statements for sovereignty, the Marshall Trilogy reaffirmed the doctrine of discovery, which held that title to the land in North America belonged to the European nation that "discovered" the territory and relegated Indigenous People's land rights to temporary occupancy. From the perspective of the United States, the federal government may unilaterally—without Native input—limit tribal sovereignty. For instance, *Johnson v. McIntosh* (1823), the first case in Marshall Trilogy, rules that Native nations may not sell land to any party other than the federal government. Areas where the United States, via Congress and the Supreme Court, has acted to curtail sovereignty include limiting tribal governments' powers of taxation, restricting tribes' jurisdiction over non-Natives, and regulating commercial ventures such as casinos. Nevertheless, the Constitution and the Marshall Trilogy not only confirm but also guarantee Indigenous sovereignty, and treaties emerge from this nation-to-nation relationship.

Different Views

When Indigenous leaders and United States officials met around campfires or across tables, each brought their own expectations and worldviews. Contrary to popular belief, Native people did not universally negotiate from a position of weakness and dependency. Native communities and their leaders made difficult and sometimes limited choices while facing newcomers who took their lands, resources, and sometimes their lives, but they entered into negotiations with the understanding that they stood on equal footing as sovereign entities.

Native nations brought a long history of negotiating with outsiders to eighteenth- and nineteenth-century treaty councils. The Ojibwe, for instance, belonged to the Three Fires Confederacy with the Odawa and Potawatomi peoples since at least 796 AD, united along a network of kinship ties reinforced by military, economic, social, and spiritual relationships. Eastern Ojibweg entered into an agreement with their Haudenosaunee (Iroquois) neighbors, themselves a powerful alliance of five, later six, nations who had come together to end generations of violent conflict. Rather than defining exclusive land title, their treaty, known as the "Dish with One Spoon," acknowledged the reality of shared territory and resources and established the rights and responsibilities of both nations to each other and the natural environment. Neither the Ojibwe nor the Haudenosaunee used writing, but they exchanged a belt of purple and white shells known as wampum to signify the agreement. Today, this belt resides at the Royal Ontario Museum, a reminder of both nations' mutual responsibilities, including period renewal of the relationship through ceremony and gift giving.[3]

The first treaties between Native nations and Europeans followed Native protocols and took Native forms. The Two Row Wampum Belt represents one of these earliest agreements between the Dutch and the Haudenosaunee, who in 1613 agreed to open their territory for the Dutch to access furs while recognizing each nation's independent, sovereign status. The two parallel rows of purple wampum on a white background embody that equal relationship.[4] From the earliest encounters, Native perspectives shaped treaty making in North America.

From an Indigenous perspective, treaties were living relationships. As the Dish with One Spoon and Two Row Wampum treaties demonstrate, Native peoples understood alliances and their formal agreements as opening shared access to land and resources, which depended on continuous actions from both parties. Rather than one-time, exclusive transfers of territory, treaties manifested ongoing relationships between nations. For Euro-Americans, however, treaties served as a tool of dispossession—or, perhaps, from their perspective, possession. Understood primarily as written documents, treaties ceded land—gave up title—in exchange for payments in cash or goods. These were one-time transactions, although compensation might be spread out in annual payments known as annuities. Treaties were, as George Washington's secretary of war Henry Knox put it, "expansion with honor," conquest via diplomacy rather than war, which could more easily be reconciled with America's vision of itself as a bastion of justice and liberty.[5] Treaties by which money and goods extinguished Indigenous claims facilitated the inevitable (from a US perspective) transfer of the continent.

The final documents shelved in the Library of Congress represent merely one aspect of alliance formation that included ceremonies and the spoken word. Gift giving both opened and closed treaty negotiation across the continent, a diplomatic procedure that established mutual obligations between the negotiating parties. US treaty commissioners carefully calculated how much food they needed to supply to sustain negotiations that often lasted weeks, and Native people greeted US officials with dances, feasts, and other ceremonies, welcoming outsiders into their community. One of the mythologized ceremonies involved smoking tobacco, referred to in popular culture as the "peace pipe." The ceremonial role of tobacco was so important to negotiations that in the Ojibwe language the word for "council" is *zagaswe'idiwin*. Its root, *zagaswe*, means tobacco smoke.[6] Feasting, exchanging gifts, and smoking tobacco were more than window dressing—they initiated diplomatic relationships that treaties signified. Similarly, spoken words meant as much as those that found their way onto paper.[7] From our perspective as scholars and teachers of Native American history, recognizing that treaties were more than written documents and that Native perspectives actively shaped these agreements means that we must take into account multiple sources when interpreting this history, from journals and transcripts of negotiations to statements by Native leaders objecting to misinterpreted agreements and the treaty documents themselves.

Examples from nineteenth-century Ojibwe treaties help illustrate how bringing various documents together results in a more complete understanding of treaties and treaty rights. Indigenous peoples including the Ojibwe entered into treaties with the United States to address territorial, economic, and military concerns. The Ojibwe had a long history of close relationships with French, English, and American fur traders, often integrating traders into economic and kinship networks via marriage. Throughout the nineteenth century, Ojibweg in Wisconsin,

Michigan, and Minnesota agreed to allow their American allies and trading partners access to their homeland's resources, but they did not sell the land.

In 1837, *ogimaag* (leaders) signed the White Pine or Pine Tree Treaty, which granted the United States timber rights in central Wisconsin and Minnesota. In 1842, the Copper Treaty, concerning lands north of the 1837 boundaries, opened the rich mineral deposits within Ojibwe territory to American mining companies.[8] In an 1864 bilingual petition, ogimaag explained that they had agreed to let American interests harvest timber, but "I reserve the root of the tree" for the Ojibwe people.[9] In other words, the Ojibwe understood that they had granted Americans access to resources, but only under specific conditions and without altering Ojibwe rights to their homeland. These treaties granted access to certain resources—white pine trees and copper—while protecting Ojibwe homelands and sovereignty.

In both the 1837 and 1842 treaties, Ojibwe ogimaag protected future generations' rights to the land. Both treaties contain articles explicitly reserving hunting, fishing, and gathering in ceded territory. During negotiations in 1837, ogimaa Magegawbaw of Leech Lake placed an oak leaf on the table before US representatives and explained his people's position, "We wish to hold on to a tree where we get our living, and to reserve the streams, where we drink the waters that give us life."[10] In the written document, Magegawbaw's assertion of the Ojibwe People's ongoing rights became the "privilege of hunting, fishing, and gathering the wild rice," with an added provision that this would persist "during the pleasure of the President of the United States."[11] The language of the written document suggests that Ojibwe rights were conditional, subordinated to US interests. The larger context, however, makes it clear that the Ojibwe had secured a more permanent safeguard.

At every step of the negotiations, the Ojibwe articulated their intent to remain on their lands. Immediately following the 1842 treaty, which reiterated the rights reserved in 1837, local and federal officials started pressuring the Ojibwe to remove west of the Mississippi as part of a larger federal policy of removal. Ojibwe leaders referred back to their treaties as they refused to leave their homes. Gichi-Waabizheshi, an ogimaa from Lac Courte Oreilles, explained how he and his fellow ogimaag had understood the 1842 treaty: "We were told by the commissioner that our grand father [*sic*] wanted our lands for the sake of the mines, but that we might remain on them as long as our grand father see[s] fit. But I and my brother chiefs refused to touch the pen unless . . . we should be permitted to live on the land as long as we behaved well and are peaceable with our grand father [*sic*] and his white children."[12] Gichi-Waabizheshi only signed the written document when US representatives assured him that the United States agreed that the Ojibwe could stay in their homeland forever, or as long as the relationships that formed the treaty remained. The US documentary record supports Ojibwe assertions. Treaty Commissioner Robert Stuart, who led the US side of negotiations, confirmed that removal "would not be in conformity with the spirit of the treaty."[13] Nevertheless, President Zachary Taylor signed a removal order in 1850, and the US resorted to trickery and force to coerce the Ojibwe to remove, transferring treaty payments from the more central Madeline Island to Sandy Lake in Minnesota. Payments and other supplies such as flour and meat never arrived, and winter set in. Several hundred Ojibwe men, women, and children died as a direct result of the federal government's attempt to unilaterally rewrite the treaties of 1837 and 1842.[14]

The Ojibwe, confident that their treaties protected them, defied the removal order and traversed frozen rivers and snowy woods to return to their homes. In 1854, after a delegation of ogimaag traveled to Washington to demand that the US honor its treaty obligations, US and Ojibwe officials returned to negotiations in La Pointe, Wisconsin. This time, the Ojibwe demanded explicitly reserved lands in supposedly ceded territories. The 1854 Treaty of La Pointe carved nine reservations or *ishkoniganan* ("lands that we saved for ourselves") from the Ojibwe homelands.[15] Likewise, the Treaty of La Pointe reaffirmed the 1837 and 1842 treaties' commitment to reserved rights beyond the new reservation boundaries. The Ojibwe used treaties to defend their homelands and their interests as a sovereign nation.

Treaty Rights in the Twentieth Century

The story of US-Ojibwe treaties did not end in the nineteenth century. Ojibwe people continued to rely on treaties to protect their sovereignty, even as the United States reinterpreted or overlooked these agreements to carry on their goals of securing Indigenous lands and resources.

The reservation system, implemented via treaties, provided space to isolate and ultimately erase Indigenous peoples. The federal government launched attacks on land and culture under the umbrella of assimilation policies. Boarding schools separated Indian children from their families and communities to, in the words of Carlisle Indian Industrial School founder Richard Pratt, "kill the Indian in him, and save the man."[16] Allotment policies broke up reservations. Across the United States, Native nations lost two-thirds of their reserved territory—nearly ninety million acres—by the 1930s as a direct result of allotment. Together, these assimilation programs compelled Native people away from the seasonal labor that had sustained them for generations, pushing them toward low-skilled wage work or, more often, farming. As the Northwoods tourist industry grew in the twentieth century, state governments restricted Ojibwe people's access to resources coveted by vacationing sportsmen.[17] Despite the legal history going back to the Marshall Trilogy affirming Native peoples' unique relationship with the federal government, Wisconsin and other states asserted their jurisdiction over all inhabitants within their borders. They arrested Native Americans for hunting, fishing, and gathering in violation of state laws.

From an Ojibwe perspective, activities such as hunting or spearfishing provided more than physical sustenance. Hunting, fishing, and harvesting wild rice connected Ojibwe people to the land even as the United States chipped away at their territory. These activities provided opportunities to engage in ceremony, offering tobacco to a deer that gave its life to feed one's family or drumming at a rice camp. Meat and wild rice could be distributed to elders, honoring essential kinship obligations. These activities were part of being Ojibwe. As Lac du Flambeau spearfishing activist and cultural educator Nick Hockings explained, "It's a strong feeling knowing your ancestors traveled this way, so being able to do as our ancestors have done, this is who were are as a people."[18] These were the rights their ancestors had the foresight to protect.

Generations of Ojibwe kept the knowledge of their treaties alive. They continued to hunt, fish, and gather in so-called ceded territory, despite harassment from state and federal officials. Curt Kalk of Mille Lacs remembered his family's efforts to exercise their treaty-protected rights during the mid-twentieth century. He told anthropologist Larry Nesper,

> I would say that we were raised netting fish. And we'd harvest fish and deer out of season, which was against state law back then. . . . My

137

grandparents always told me, "You have a right to do that." You can't imagine a parent telling, or a grandparent, telling their kids to do something that's considered illegal. But here on the reservation my grandparents said "It's not illegal." The state guys think so, but it's not illegal. There's nothing wrong with you doing this, you have your rights that we've never given up.[19]

The risks from state law enforcement were real. In 1894, for example, two Wisconsin Department of Natural Resources (WDNR) wardens murdered Lac Courte Oreilles ogimaa Giishkitawag, or Joe White, for hunting deer out of season. An all-White jury cleared the state employees of wrongdoing.[20] More often, hunters and fishers faced arrests and fines. In 1901, after John Blackbird fought his conviction for fishing in Lake Superior off the shore of the Bad River Reservation, a federal court acknowledged that the state of Wisconsin lacked the jurisdiction to interfere with reservation hunting and fishing. Wisconsin, however, ignored the ruling. Through the 1950s, its courts upheld the state's ability to curtail Ojibwe resource access both on and off the reservation.[21] Nevertheless, more than a century of setbacks proved insufficient to quash either Ojibwe resilience or their legal knowledge of their treaties.

The Ojibwe won important treaty rights recognition in *Wisconsin v. Gurnoe*. In 1969, the same year that dozens of Indian men and women occupied Alcatraz Island while invoking broken treaties, a group of Ojibwe fishermen from Bad River tested their treaty rights in the waters of Lake Superior. Known to Ojibweg as Gichigami, Lake Superior had provided fish to sustain Ojibwe families for hundreds of years. In the nineteenth century, when ogimaag, or leaders, negotiated treaties to protect their rights to their homeland, that included Gichigami. The Bad River ishkonigan, or reservation, protected seventeen miles of shoreline. While the states of Wisconsin, Michigan, and Minnesota tried to extend their authority over the lake, Ojibweg continued to make a living on its waters. Many worked in non-Indian commercial fisheries until the trout population collapsed in the 1950s, after which they transitioned to working in the cargo freight industry. Additionally, individuals fished for their families, using the netting methods they had learned from their parents and grandparents.

In the late 1960s, a confrontation with WDNR wardens brought a century of tensions to a head. Richard "Dick" Gurnoe, Vietnam veteran and tribal vice chairman, noted that by 1969, he and the rest of the Bad

River Ojibwe had grown increasingly frustrated by the WDNR's constant arrests and confiscations targeting those who simply exercised their legal rights. After a heated disagreement with a WDNR warden at a local bar, Gurnoe, tribal chairman Philip Gordon, and four others decided that enough was enough. "We knew we had treaty rights to fish," Gurnoe recalled, and so they decided to initiate a test case to fight the WDNR in court.[22]

On September 17, 1969, hours before dawn, Gurnoe, Gordon, and several others pushed their boats into the water. The boats leaked so badly that the men had to bail them out with buckets just to stay afloat. They had chosen the "worst gear" they could find, knowing that the WDNR, whom they had tipped off, would confiscate the boats and equipment. The Ojibwe fishers dropped their nets in the water and pulled them in. Gordon freed a single sucker from the net and held it up to cheers from the crowd that had gathered on the shore. And then the waiting WDNR boat arrived and arrested all six Ojibweg, towing the now-submerged boats to Bayfield.[23] The confrontation moved from the waters to the courtroom. *Wisconsin v. Gurnoe* resulted in an Ojibwe victory over the WDNR. The case affirmed the Ojibwe peoples' right to fish on Gichigami according to nineteenth-century treaties.[24]

The *Gurnoe* case represented part of a larger national pattern of treaty-rights activism. Between the 1960s and 1980s, Native People from the Great Lakes to the Pacific Northwest forced US courts, both state and federal, to honor their treaties. The Indigenous peoples living along the Puget Sound, who like the Ojibwe had used treaties to protect their hunting, fishing, and gathering rights, held widely publicized fish-ins during the 1960s and initiated a court case that impacted Indigenous communities throughout the United States. *United States v. Washington* (1974), better known as the Boldt Decision after US district court judge George Hugo Boldt, affirmed that treaties remained the supreme law of the land and dismissed the argument that state laws could override federal treaties. "The mere passage of time has not eroded, and cannot erode, the rights guaranteed by treaties," Boldt wrote in his opinion.[25] The Supreme Court upheld the Boldt Decision in 1979.

At first, *Gurnoe* did little to change the state of Wisconsin's policy toward the Native nations within its boundaries. In 1974, game wardens arrested Lac Courte Oreilles brothers Fred and Mike Tribble for spearfishing through the ice across the reservation border. The Tribble brothers, who expected the arrest, showed the wardens a copy of the

1837 treaty. The wardens arrested the brothers anyway, and Lac Courte Oreilles brought the case to the Wisconsin Supreme Court. In 1983, the outcome, known as the Voigt decision, affirmed off-reservation treaty rights throughout the state of Wisconsin and established an important precedent for interpreting the reserved rights in 1837, 1842, and 1854 treaties. In *US v. Michigan* (1979), a federal court held that Ojibwe living in Michigan had retained their resource rights in nineteenth-century treaties, and those rights superseded the state's interest in regulating hunting and fishing. For Ojibwe in Minnesota, the legal battles culminated in *Mille Lacs v. Minnesota*. In 1999, the Supreme Court once again confirmed the sovereign right, protected by treaties, to access resources beyond reservation boundaries without interference from the state—what Ojibwe people had been saying for one hundred years.[26]

In exercising their newly acknowledged rights, the Ojibwe faced backlash. The state of Wisconsin repeatedly appealed the Voigt decision, drawing litigation out over nearly two decades. Non-Indian sportsmen and other locals who did not like the idea of Indians spearfishing when they could not fought to suppress treaty rights. Anti-treaty protesters accused Ojibwe spearfishers of decimating walleye and muskie populations, despite the fact that Ojibwe harvests remained between 1 percent and 2 percent of sports fishing harvests even during peak spearfishing years.[27] They spoke of reverse racism and "unequal rights." Their anger manifested in more than merely bumper stickers and racist slogans. Tina Kuckkahn (Lac du Flambeau Ojibwe) remembered that "there were pipe bombs, there were rocks being thrown, there were bottles being thrown. People would go out in their powerful boats to try to make waves to swamp our boats."[28]

Regardless of anti-treaty anger, however, the treaty rights debate was not dependent on public opinion. It remained fundamentally a question of legal rights, and one that the United States courts have repeatedly answered in favor of Native interpretations of their treaties. The Ojibwe and other Native people retain rights not because of race or blood but because of their political status as members of sovereign nations. The Voigt decision, for instance, explicitly excludes the Ojibwe bands such as St. Croix and Mole Lake that did not sign the 1854 treaty.

While the tensions that sparked the Walleye War have yet to dissipate, the Ojibwe people and their allies achieved several positive outcomes. The six bands of Wisconsin Ojibwe included in the Voigt decision finally reached a settlement with Wisconsin in February 1991 after seventeen years of contentious litigation. The agreement included joint regulation by the Ojibwe and the state. The Ojibwe people came together to create the Great Lakes Indian Fish and Wildlife Commission (GLIFWC), a Native-run conservation and law enforcement agency that also engages in education and public awareness activities. Data collected by the Bureau of Indian Affairs, US Fish and Wildlife Service, GLIFWC, member bands, and the WDNR indicates that spearfishing has not damaged fish populations. In fact, seven of eleven GLIFWC member bands operate fish hatcheries to stock both on-reservation and off-reservation lakes. They played an instrumental role in restoring lake trout to Lake Superior.[29] GLIFWC's environmental and regulatory efforts have helped to ensure that future generations of Ojibwe, as well as their non-Indian neighbors, retain access to fish, wildlife, and wild rice.

A Long and Ongoing History

Understanding the long history of treaties and sovereignty allows us as teachers and learners to see treaty rights as manifestations of inherent Indigenous sovereignty. Treaties were more than written documents imposed upon desperate Native peoples. The perception of treaties as one-sided, foreign documents derives largely from the events that followed their signing. Seeing Indigenous peoples as powerless victims of greed and manipulation overlooks the active, central role of Native Americans in the treaty-making process. Undeniably, these treaty documents put in place the legal mechanisms that the United States used to override Indigenous sovereignty and control their lands and resources. Just as importantly, however, treaties represent mutually beneficial agreements that established protocols for living and governing in shared territory.

More than 150 years after touching the pen, the Ojibwe continue to use their treaties to protect their existence as a sovereign people. As treaty ogichidaa, or warrior, Mike Tribble recently reflected, "There's a lot more spearers out there. There's a lot more wild ricers out there. Even the schools take the classes out harvesting maple sugar, all things that their ancestors have been doing for generations. It's maintaining a way of life."[30] The history of treaties remains ongoing.

NOTES

1. Jennifer Nez Denetdale, "Naal Tsoos S001: The Navajo Treaty of 1868, Nation Building, and Self-Determination," in *Nation to Nation: Treaties between the United States and American Indian Nations*, ed. Suzan Shown Harjo (Washington, DC: National Museum of the American Indian, 2014), 118.

2. *Worcester v. Georgia*, 31 U.S. 515 (1832).

3. Leanne Simpson, "Looking after Gdoo-naaganinaa: Precolonial Nishnaabeg Diplomatic and Treaty Relationships," *Wicazo Sa Review* 23, no. 2 (Fall 2008): 29–42.

4. Jon Parmenter, "The Meaning of *Shwetha* and the Two Row Wampum Belt in Haudenosaunee (Iroquois) History: Can Indigenous Oral Tradition Be Reconciled with the Documentary Record?" *Journal of Early American History* 3 (2013): 82–109. The Onondaga Nation has created an excellent digital resource, described as "an educational and advocacy project," for exploring the Two Row Treaty: Two Row Wampum Renewal Campaign, honorthetworow.org.

5. Frederick Hoxie, "Why Treaties?" in *Buried Roots and Indestructible Seeds: The Survival of American Indian Life in Story, History, and Spirit*, ed. Mark A. Lindquist and Martin Zenger (Madison: University of Wisconsin Press, 1994), 90–92; Paul Rosier, *Serving Their Country: American Indian Politics and Patriotism in the Twentieth Century* (Cambridge, MA: Harvard University Press, 2009), 4.

6. Cary Miller, *Ogimaag: Anishinaabe Leadership, 1760–1845* (Lincoln: University of Nebraska Press, 2010), 108–9, 276.

7. Colin G. Calloway, *Pen and Ink Witchcraft: Treaties and Treaty Making in American Indian History* (New York: Oxford University Press, 2013), 12–48.

8. Ronald N. Satz, *Chippewa Treaty Rights: The Reserved Rights of Wisconsin's Chippewa Indians in Historical Perspective* (Madison: Wisconsin Academy of Sciences, Arts, and Letters, 1991).

9. "Ojibwe treaty statement and related papers, 1864, 1881–1882," original manuscript in the Wisconsin Historical Society Archives (SC-O 40), online facsimile at: http://www.wisconsinhistory.org/turningpoints/search.asp?id=40.

10. W. H. C. Folsom, *Fifty-Years in the Northwest* (St. Paul: Pioneer, 1888), 233–36.

11. "Treaty with the Chippewa, 1837," in *Indian Treaties, 1778–1883*, ed. Charles J. Kappler (New York: Interland, 1972), 491–92.

12. Folsom, *Fifty-Years in the Northwest*, 233–36.

13. Quoted in Satz, *Chippewa Treaty Rights*, 39.

14. Child, *Holding Our World Together*, 64–70.

15. The Ojibwe saw reservations as a strategy to protect their homelands. For some Native nations, the United States forced reservations on them, either with military force or through threats of withholding food and other supplies. For more on military issues, see the chapter in this volume by Mark van de Logt.

16. Official Report of the Nineteenth Annual Conference of Charities and Correction (1892), 46–59. Reprinted in Richard H. Pratt, "The Advantages of Mingling Indians with Whites," in *Americanizing the American Indians: Writings by the "Friends of the Indian," 1880–1900* (Cambridge, MA: Harvard University Press, 1973), 260–71.

17. Child, *Holding Our World Together*, 85–120.

18. Nick Hockings, *Lighting the 7th Fire*, directed by Sandra Osawa (1994; Upstream Productions), film.

19. Larry Nesper, "Twenty-Five Years of Treaty Rights and the Tribal Communities," *Minwaajimo Symposium* (Odanah, WI: Great Lakes Indian Fish and Wildlife Commission, 2009).

20. Eric Redix, *The Murder of Joe White: Ojibwe Leadership and Colonialism in Wisconsin* (Lansing: Michigan State University Press, 2014). Additionally, the Wisconsin Historical Society has an online archive of documents related to the case at https://www.wisconsinhistory.org/turningpoints/search.asp?id=1626.

21. Chantal Norrgard, *Seasons of Change: Labor, Treaty Rights, and Ojibwe Nationhood* (Chapel Hill: University of North Carolina Press, 2014), 59–78.

22. Sue Erickson, "True Grit Red Cliff Style: Looking Back with Red Cliff's Dick Gurnoe," *Mazina'igan: A Chronicle of the Lake Superior Ojibwe*, Fall 2003, 11.

23. Patty Loew and James Thannum, "After the Storm: Ojibwe Treaty Rights Twenty-Five Years after the Voigt Decision," *American Indian Quarterly* 35, no. 2 (Spring 2011): 161–91.

24. Erickson, "True Grit Red Cliff Style," 11.

25. *United States v. Washington*, 520 F.2d 676, 692 (9th Cir. 1975).

26. "Ojibwe Treaty Rights: Understanding & Impact" (Odanah, WI: GLIFWC, 2016). Online facsimile available at https://glifwc.org/publications/pdf/OTRUI2006.pdf.

27. Loew and Thannum, "After the Storm," 169.

28. Suzan Shown Harjo, "Rights We Always Had: An Interview with Tina Kuckkahn," in *Nation to Nation: Treaties between the United States and American Indian Nations*, ed. Suzan Shown Harjo (Washington, DC: National Museum of the American Indian, 2014), 195.

29. Loew and Thannum, "After the Storm," 179.

30. "Crossing the Line: Tribble Brothers," GLIFWC video, 4:52, https://www.youtube.com/watch?v=KSpEGhWR44Q&feature=youtube.

FOR FURTHER READING

Great Lakes Indian Fish & Wildlife Commission, https://glifwc.org/.
Two Row Wampum Renewal Campaign, http://honorthetworow.org.
Wisconsin Historical Society, "Turning Points in Wisconsin History," http://www.wisconsinhistory.org/turningpoints/.

Adams, Hank. "The Game and Fish Were Made for Us: Hunting and Fishing Rights in Native Nations' Treaties." In *Nation to Nation: Treaties between the United States and American Indian Nations*, edited by Suzan Shown Harjo, 181–85. Washington, DC: National Museum of the American Indian, 2014.

Calloway, Colin. *Pen and Ink Witchcraft: Treaties and Treaty Making in American Indian History*. New York: Oxford University Press, 2013.

Child, Brenda. *Holding Our World Together: Ojibwe Women and the Survival of Community*. New York: Penguin Books, 2012.

Harmon, Alexandra, ed. *The Power of Promises: Rethinking Indian Treaties in the Pacific Northwest*. Seattle: University of Washington Press, 2008.

Lomawaima, K. Tsianina. "Federalism: Native, Federal, and State Sovereignty." In *Why You Can't Teach United States History without American Indians*, edited by Susan Sleeper-Smith et al., 273–86. Chapel Hill: University of North Carolina Press, 2015.

Wilkinson, Charles. *Blood Struggle: The Rise of Modern Indian Nations*. New York: W. W. Norton, 2005.

Teaching Indigenous Environmental Histories

PAUL KELTON AND JAMES D. RICE

We have taught Native American/Indigenous history for over twenty years, at public and private universities in New York, Kansas, Washington State, and Connecticut, and Massachusetts. The majority of our students have been non-Natives. These students have brought a diverse set of experiences and assumptions about Indigenous peoples to our courses, but most do have one thing in common: they generally believe that Indigenous peoples have a spiritual connection to the natural world that non-Natives lack. Such statements as "Indians were at one with nature" or "Indians understood humans belong to Mother Earth rather than the earth belonging to humans" are frequently offered in essays and discussions.

Students make such utterances with ease and without much reflection, which we find troubling. Such statements reveal a superficial understanding of who Native people are and present a constant challenge in the classroom. They reflect Euro-Americans' need to persuade themselves to treat the environment better, which is admirable, but they do so by embracing the same racial essentialism that has so often been wielded as a weapon against Native Americans—in this case, by implying that Native peoples' connection to the natural world is encoded in their DNA. This essentialism erodes an awareness of cultural and environmental differences among Native people, of the complexity of both Native societies and of nature, and of history itself—that is, of change (and continuity) over time. It glosses over the destructive power of colonialism, and by reflexively employing the past tense to invoke the trope of the Vanishing Indian it renders invisible the continual struggle of modern Native people to protect their identity and the natural environments that sustain them.

We focus on three themes selected with an eye to getting our students beyond these clichés and into a closer engagement with Native peoples and their pasts: first, the *diversity* of Native ways of living within nature; second, the *complexity* of each of those ways; and third, the *historical specificity* of Native peoples' relationships with nature. Because each of these three themes could itself become a cliché, we guide students through deeper, more detailed explorations of a few carefully selected and highly specific peoples, places, and times. We seek to put Native voices at the center of the discussion, but we also seize opportunities for students to become more conscious of disciplinarity; that is, of the existence of academic disciplines and of some of the central concerns and concepts of those that come into play when studying Native American environmental history.

Diverse Cultures, Diverse Environments

We start our classes—and our discussions of the diversity of Native environmental history—with origin stories. Although each is culturally specific, origin stories have in common that they explain how particular environments came to be and the relationships people ought to have with other beings that inhabited their shared world. Whether assigning the widely available Diné (Navajo), Cherokee, Haudenosaunee (Iroquois), or other stories, we challenge our students to discern the multiple actors—often animals—involved in creation, in contrast with the solitary God of the Judeo-Christian Genesis. We ask them to think about the implications of believing that birds, animals, rocks, rivers, mountains, and other entities are spiritual beings and having spiritual guardians. Here, students often will seize the opportunity to retreat to the mantra that "Indians lived in harmony with nature," but we close off that path by asking them to identify the most fundamental differences between the several origin stories they've studied and challenging them to take those differences seriously. (Our students are eager to show respect toward Native people and cultures and thus respond well to such exhortations.)

We emphasize, moreover, that Native communities have rarely, if ever, taken harmony and balance within nature for granted. Indigenous people in general have conceived of the world as a place of competing spiritual powers, and one that can potentially descend into chaos and disorder. In the Pacific Northwest, for example, the trickster-creator Raven (or Crow) brought the sun, stars, moon, salmon, humans, and other elements of the natural world together through a series of accidents, most of which were a product of his selfishness, lust, and gluttony rather than of a coherent, benevolent grand design. Raven tales describe a world of instability and even arbitrariness rather than of permanence, which fits rather well with the Pacific storms, extreme tides, earthquakes, volcanic eruptions, and occasional tsunamis of the coastal Northwest. In the Puebloan towns of the Southwest the world is more the product of intelligent design yet is equally unstable; in most tellings this is but the most recent world to have been created for humans, having been preceded by several previous cycles of world creation and destruction.

Origin tales also make it clear that the people must take active measures against the world's inherent instability. People must cultivate reciprocal relationships with all spirits around them through the observation of taboos, ritual performances, and regular ceremonies. Both the bodies and the spirits of game animals or fish, for example, must be treated with respect through taboos and rituals performed before and after they've been killed. Similarly, Hopi and other Puebloan Kachina dances maintain proper relationships with numerous spirits representing elements of nature, from thunderstorms to the germination of seeds to the winter solstice. Colonizers of course attempted to stamp out such practices.

Indigenous ways of living within nature are as diverse as their creation stories, in part because of North America's remarkable ecological diversity. It's no coincidence that people in today's interior Alaska and Canadian North have always spent a great deal of time hunting caribou and other cold-hardy animals rather than planting crops that would have been unsuited to that climate; that salmon, berries, and camas roots figured so prominently in the lives of Pacific Northwest groups; that acorns, fish, and deer occupied a central place in much of today's California; or that the "Three Sisters"—maize, beans, and squash—structured the lives of people in the well-watered, temperate Eastern Woodlands. North America's ecological diversity, in short, ensured that its human inhabitants would adapt to their environments in equally diverse ways.

Local environmental conditions, however, did not determine a people's culture. Each group also made choices about what resources to access, when, and how. The importance of contingency and choice is clearest where immediate neighbors adapted to their natural surroundings in radically different ways. The Wendats (Hurons), for example, gravitated toward viable farmlands near Georgian Bay in today's northern Ontario, while their Algonquian neighbors directly to the east and north adopted a far more mobile hunting lifestyle; not surprisingly, they traded a great deal with one another. Similarly, the sedentary Mandans and Hidatsas farmed maize, beans, and squash on the rich bottomlands of the Missouri River basin in today's Dakotas, while all around them other nations such as the Lakota, Cheyenne, and Crow chose to build their lives around the buffalo hunt.

Neighboring peoples could also make very different choices about who should do the work, how the fruits of that labor would be distributed, and who should be in charge of such decisions. By about 1300, for example, the thirty-plus nations of the Chesapeake Bay region were all agricultural societies—that is, societies that organized their ceremonial calendars, gender relations, child-rearing, and other central aspects of their existence around the demands of cultivating domesticated plants (particularly the Three Sisters). By the sixteenth century, most of these Algonquian-speaking peoples had abandoned the relatively egalitarian organization that had previously sustained them in favor of more hierarchical societies composed of commoners, elites, and powerful hereditary chiefs (including Wahunsenacawh, or Powhatan). The Iroquoian-speaking Susquehannock nation, located immediately to the north of this cluster of chiefdoms and paramount chiefdoms, adopted the same crops at the same time and lived in roughly the same climate. Their villages, fields, and surrounding landscapes looked very similar. Yet the Susquehannocks governed themselves without creating a highly stratified society or hierarchical political system like that of their neighbors. Their leaders achieved power and authority rather than having it ascribed to them by birth or office, as was the case among their Algonquian neighbors. Clearly, the fact that everyone was forced to adapt to their natural environment did not force everyone to adapt in the same way.

Complexity

The day-to-day, season-to-season, and year-to-year lives of Native people required a tremendously wide array of skills and knowledge. Every day, season, and year required extensive planning

148

and preparation, as well as a high degree of flexibility in order to adapt to unforeseen circumstances such as weather events, failed crops, or fluctuating fish or animal populations. Elders were critical to community survival, for they retained knowledge of the seasonal cycles, of natural products that could be used, and of techniques to acquire what people needed to survive. Elders handed down this knowledge to younger generations through hands-on apprenticeships, stories, songs, and prayers. Our students tend to bring to class a deep-seated, though rarely spoken or examined, belief that their world is somehow more complex than that of Indigenous peoples who had long inhabited the Americas. However, a close examination of any people—of how, for example, a band of Mushkegowuk (Swampy Cree) hunter-fisher-gatherers to the west of Hudson Bay made it through any given year—makes it difficult to sustain this illusion of modern complexity (and superiority).

That is why we also punctuate our courses with deeper dives into the histories of a few carefully selected peoples and places. Take, for example, Celilo Falls in the Columbia River Gorge, where, during the spring and summer salmon runs, a few year-round residents once hosted annual gatherings of thousands of Native people from all over the coastal Pacific Northwest and as far inland as today's Montana. Some came mainly to trade, find marriage partners, and feast. Others fished, taking large quantities of salmon with nets held by men perched on rocks or precarious platforms over the thundering rapids of the powerful Columbia River. Suitable fishing perches were hard to come by. Contrary to prevailing stereotypes about the absence of "property" in Native societies, the possession and use of each fishing perch, as historian Richard White writes, "made visible and reproduced the social structure" of the people who fished the rapids. "Space was not empty or free"; rather, access to each fishing station was secured by kin connections. With rights to a fishing perch determined by the clan and lineage of the particular man wielding the net, possession and ownership were not individually based. Equally intricate rules governed the presence of women, the processing and preservation of salmon, the treatment of their bones and innards, and the observance of ceremonies to maintain a proper reciprocal relationship between humans and salmon.[1]

The example of Celilo Falls illustrates a particular community—a collection of people who recognized themselves as a people who have mutual obligations to one another—that utilized certain territories as theirs to hunt, fish, gather, or farm on and defended these territories from outsiders. The Pacific Northwest as well as the entire North American continent was indeed home to multiple communities that often competed with each other for territories. A consequence of this competition was the creation of buffer zones wherein people feared to travel because of war parties traversing them during the summer months. Game animals proliferated due to the relative absence of humans, which paradoxically made them attractive to late-autumn and winter hunting parties after the prime season for war had passed. That was the case along the upper St. Lawrence and lower Ottawa Rivers in the sixteenth and seventeenth centuries, as well as across an enormous swath of central Pennsylvania and western Virginia and Maryland during the seventeenth and eighteenth centuries. An in-depth focus on the interplay between environment, society, and external relations of any one of the First Nations ringing one of these buffer zones, if sufficiently detailed, will disabuse students of the idea that such relationships lacked complexity. For the seventeenth and eighteenth centuries, the Haudenosaunee, Wendats, Chesapeake Algonquians, Catawbas, and Cherokees are especially well documented.

Historical Specificity

A third major point that we impress upon students is that Native relationships with the environment were not static. The environment itself was in profound flux when people first emerged onto the continent: the Pleistocene epoch (from about 2.6 million to 11,700 years ago) was just beginning to give way to the relatively warm stable Holocene era of the last 11,700 years. The massive ice sheets of the last glacial maximum still covered much of the north, sea levels were rapidly rising, and regional climates were very different from today's climate. Indigenous peoples adapted to these ongoing transformations and in fact changed the land through their own activities; moreover, the ways in which Indigenous people chose to engage with the environment changed over time. The first major transition occurred with the decline of large game animals. Mammoths, mastodons, ancient species of camels, horses, and elephants once roamed North America, but these animals one by one became extinct during the late Pleistocene and early Holocene. Thereafter, Indigenous peoples depended more heavily on smaller game animals such as deer, turkey, and bison. The reasons for the extinction of some species and the survival of others are hotly debated, with scholars increasingly citing climate change as the major factor, but with others suggesting that overhunting played a role.

Less debatable is that Native people significantly altered their surroundings by using fire. They purposefully set fire to forests and grasslands to herd animals into smaller areas so that they could be more easily killed. They also used fire to clear underbrush, a process that promoted regeneration of grasses and shrubs upon which animals fed. This common practice created a park-like environment in much of North America, one that only developed with purposeful human management via fire. Consequently, the Great Plains extended further east than they otherwise would have done, and wooded areas lacked the heavy underbrush that is common to today's forests. Europeans often found Native fire practices a nuisance, particularly to the livestock they imported.

Native agricultural practices also changed the land. Most of your students will have at least a vague understanding that Indigenous peoples practiced agriculture and may be able to recite "corn, beans, and squash" when asked what crops Natives grew before Europeans arrived. We strive to go beyond this static understanding. Cultivation developed only slowly, after multiple generations of trial and error. Native communities were also understandably reluctant to depend too heavily on a farm crop that might fail or be destroyed by a storm or enemy attack; thus, for centuries they added a few cultivated plants to their diverse array of food sources, using them to expand their options rather than to limit them. Still, Indigenous peoples continued to select seeds from wild cultigens, plant them, and repeat the process year after year, which eventually resulted in the evolution of carbohydrate-rich species that could sustain increasingly sedentary human populations. Maize cultivation spread from Mesoamerica to the American Southwest, where Indigenous communities constructed elaborate irrigation systems and canals to bring water to their fields. After 800 AD maize production proliferated in the fertile and well-watered areas of the Eastern Woodlands as far north as southern Ontario and Quebec, leading Indigenous communities to clear the river valleys of trees and cultivate large fields.

Agriculture centering on calorie-rich crops such as maize sustained larger populations but also came with its own problems. Years of use depleted the soil of nutrients and led to smaller crop yields; concentrated populations increased infections from bacteria, fungi, and worms; surrounding forests receded as humans harvested more and more wood for buildings and fuel; nearby game became depleted amid increasing human demand for meat and hides for clothing; and competition with other communities escalated in the centuries preceding European colonization, resulting in increased warfare across North America.

There was quite an eventful environmental history before Europeans arrived, in other words, with agricultural communities growing and developing and then dispersing, with constituent groups relocating and reforming. The most dramatic example of this cycling occurred in southern Illinois. Around 650 AD, Natives of the area began to grow maize intensively. Within a few hundred years, the population boomed. Permanent towns surrounded by palisades and containing large earthen mounds developed, and outlying areas became agricultural colonies of the more urban core. The largest town—Cahokia—contained somewhere between ten and thirty thousand inhabitants at its height in the twelfth century, making it one of the world's largest urban centers. It covered much of today's St. Louis region and southern Illinois and had dozens of human-made earthen mounds. The largest of these, Monk's Mound, was larger by volume than the famed pyramid of Giza. Following the common pattern that was also emerging in the agricultural Southeast, though, Cahokia collapsed as a large polity in the thirteenth century. Its people reorganized into smaller, less archaeologically visible groups. Oral history indicates that many Cahokians gravitated to the south and west and became the Osages, Omahas, and Quapaws.

European invasion, of course, presented a far larger challenge to Indigenous peoples. Many students may come into your course with a ready and simple explanation for what happened: Europeans brought germs that wiped out Indigenous peoples. Tai S. Edwards in this volume explains the fallacy of this notion, but we would like to emphasize here that biological determinism has pervaded the way many high schools teach the European invasion, with some teachers requiring their students to read all or part of Jared Diamond's problematic *Guns, Germs, and Steel* (1997). Diamond's work, of course, is derivative of Alfred Crosby's works *The Columbian Exchange* (1972) and *Ecological Imperialism* (1986). Crosby explained that Europeans brought not only germs but also weeds, new crops, and domestic livestock that transformed the Americans into "Neo-Europes," wherein settler populations thrived and Indigenous populations dwindled.

This simplistic explanation obscures how Europeans deliberately changed the land to facilitate conquest. Early colonizers allowed their livestock to roam freely and at times purposely herded them into Native fields. Native people understandably tried to protect their crops by killing the animals, thus engendering European retaliation that sometimes escalated into warfare. Deliberate environmental change that undermined the ecological basis for Indigenous communities became a constant in the conquest of Native America. Settlers understood that remaking the landscape according to a European vision would force Native Americans into submission. Among many things that undercut the livelihoods of Indigenous peoples, settlers and their governments purposely erected mill dams at Indian fishing places beginning in the seventeenth century, commercialized hunting in the eighteenth-century Eastern Woodlands, employed the US Army and commercial hunters to slaughter the bison herds in the nineteenth century, and drained the vast wetlands of California's Central Valley in the late nineteenth and early twentieth centuries.

The policies of the US government also explicitly sought to destroy Indigenous cosmologies and cultural practices that had served them well for hundreds of generations. Euro-Americans saw the diversified economies of Indigenous peoples—gathering, fishing, farming, and hunting—as uncivilized, especially because females controlled their own labor and often committed that labor to agricultural work. From the very beginning, the US government aimed to coerce Natives into ceding hunting grounds, force Native men to abandon hunting and take up herding and planting, and make Native women move their labor from the fields into the home exclusively.

Missionary organizations, largely funded privately but after 1819 supplemented by federal funds, played a key role in this civilization process. Missionaries attacked Native environmental beliefs and in their place promoted the Judeo-Christian system in which a singular deity commanded his followers to subdue Nature and to convert diverse landscapes into an homogenous array of family farms. Andrew Jackson based his removal policy of the 1830s on the premise that this was not occurring fast enough and that Indigenous nations ought to be forced from the lands to western territories farther from Euro-Americans. This removal of nearly a hundred thousand Indigenous people severed the connection with homelands in which they were rooted by centuries of intimate familiarity, their creation stories, and their ceremonies. After removal they had to produce new knowledge about even the most basic matters: where and when to plant, where to fish, and where to find medicinal plants as well as fresh springs. Western reservations on which Natives were forced to live on small patches of land, surrender access to sacred sites, and commit to farming in climates too dry to sustain agriculture thus became the testing grounds for the US civilization program. US policy makers, moreover, crafted a system of compulsory education that aimed to deprive Indigenous children of their ancestors' cumulative environmental knowledge and indoctrinate them with Euro-American agricultural and mechanical knowledge.[2]

By the 1880s, US policy makers sought a more permanent solution to sever the communal relationship Indigenous peoples had with their environment. Various allotment policies—the Dawes Act (1887) and laws that led to the dissolution of nations of Indian Territory to create the state of Oklahoma—divided Native lands among individual indigenous families who would then ultimately have private ownership of the land. Allotted reservations, federal officials believed, often had too much land, and surplus land had to be sold on the market. The process of allotment ended up with Native American communities losing even more land. In 1887, Natives held 138 million acres of land; by 1934, when the allotment process ended, Natives held just 48 million acres. Much of the remaining land consisted of small allotments that were too small to farm or ranch successfully. Poverty, not prosperity, was the end result.

The Dawes Act and the dissolution of Indian Territory coincided with the height of America's Industrial Revolution, in which nature was celebrated as something to be subdued and its resources tapped and converted into commodities to be bought and sold on an international market. Natural resource extraction and industrialization were very much connected: hides from the massive buffalo hunts of the late nineteenth century, for example, were used as high-quality conveyor belts in eastern factories. The bisons' bones were used in making fertilizer. Their flesh fed crews building the railroads that were so instrumental in reducing Native communities to reservations. This was "progress" via colonialism. Progress meant, on one hand, deforestation, deep wells, species extinction, and so forth, while on the other hand, it meant material comfort, technological breakthroughs, and enrichment of stockholders. The high levels of consumerism of the modern capitalist economy, moreover, seemed to leave vast numbers of Natives behind. It was during this period that Indians became a pervasive symbol of a lost world and lost values. Ironically the stereotype became revered in some circles. These included the Boy Scouts of America, an organization formed in 1910 because of the fear that the new, increasingly white-collar post-frontier economy threatened Euro-American masculinity.

The assault on Indigenous peoples' environments that had begun with seventeenth-century colonists' free-range livestock rampaging through Natives' fields actually intensified in the early twentieth century. Nearly 20 percent of natural gas and oil deposits in the United States and a third of the western United States' low-sulfur coal deposits lay under Indian reservations.[3] The Bureau of Indian Affairs, invoking its trustee relationship to the tribes, exercised almost total control over the natural resources on reservations. It seldom engaged in meaningful consultation with tribal governments over the extent to which they wished to exploit those resources, and routinely sold mining, timber, and other rights at rates far below market value. Thus members of even energy-rich tribes such as the Diné (Navajo) and timber-rich tribes in the Pacific Northwest benefited far less than did shareholders in the outside corporations that harvested the bulk of the profits. At the same time, the federal government actively interfered in Native peoples' use of reservation lands, most notably on the Navajo reservation where a decades-long federal program forced the Diné to destroy over half of their livestock, ostensibly to reduce soil erosion. The federal government also did little to protect individual Native owners of allotted lands, so that, for example, Native owners of land on top of Oklahoma's oil fields were easily separated from their extremely valuable property.

Then came the dams and irrigation projects that remade the American landscape in the twentieth century. Beginning in the 1910s, large dams provided cheap hydroelectric power that made possible energy-dependent industries throughout North America, sprawling air conditioning–dependent cities such as Phoenix, and a vast expansion of American agribusiness into the arid West. The dams drowned Indian peoples' fisheries and fields and even—as in the case of the Senecas and Kinzua Dam in New York, or the Mandan, Hidatsa, and Arikara/ Sahnish and Garrison Dam in North Dakota—their towns. Local environments thus became damaged without enriching tribal members, many of whom in fact had less water than before the dams as development drew down the massive underground aquifers necessary to sustain the economy of tribes in the Great Plains and Southwest.

In the wake of World War II, the Cold War inspired renewed attacks on Native control over their land and environments. Part of the program was driven by ideology, as anticommunist zealots in Congress interpreted communal Native land-use practices as "socialist" and became determined to liberate Indians from this communist yoke through "termination" — that is, by eliminating Indigenous governments, turning their citizens into undifferentiated Americans, and privatizing tribal lands. About 3 percent of all enrolled tribal members, and 2.5 million acres of their land, were subjected to termination. Another part of the program was driven by the arms race. The uranium necessary to build thousands of atomic bombs, and the sites chosen to build and test these weapons, were disproportionately located on or near Indian reservations and communities. Numerous Diné and other Native workers in the Southwest, for example, found employment in the region's uranium mines. They suffered from spectacularly high levels of cancer and respiratory illnesses. So too did the largely Indigenous neighbors of those mines who washed in, bathed in, and drank from streams downriver from uranium mines and tailings. The livestock upon which many relied also suffered; ten thousand sheep, for example, perished in one incident after millions of gallons of radioactive water contaminated the Rio Puerco River.

Termination and other midcentury assaults on Indigenous lands and people, however, inspired a strong reaction from Native people. The residential schools and other attempts at forced assimilation, for all their horrors, created a substantial class of Indigenous leaders who possessed both a dense web of intertribal connections and an intimate understanding of the system that oppressed them. Despite their exploitation by outsiders, moreover, some tribes were able to use their natural resources to rise somewhat from the impoverishment that more than century of colonialism had created. These developments, combined with selective borrowings from the legal and political strategies being employed in the African American civil rights movement, made it possible for Native people mostly to turn back attempts at termination and, increasingly, to control their own land and resources.

From the Osage, whose underground resources produced substantial profits in oil drilling in the 1920s, to today's Three Affiliated Tribes of North Dakota (Mandan, Hidatsa, and Arikara), who have generated sizeable revenue through fracking, tribal governments managed to gain an increasing degree of sovereignty in the last half of the twentieth century. In 1975 Native leaders came together to form the Council of Energy Resource Tribes (CERT) to pressure both corporations and the government to offer tribes better terms. Recently, Native cooperation led to a class action lawsuit against the US Bureau of Indian Affairs for squandering tribal funds held in trust. The lawsuit ended in a settlement in which $1.4 billion went to Indigenous plaintiffs and an additional $2 billion to a fund for land purchases and scholarships.

Not all tribes who have mineral resources, however, have jumped at the opportunity to exploit them, while even those that do tend to impose stricter environmental regulations on their reservations than the federal and state agencies do on non-Native lands. In the 1970s, for example, the Northern Cheyennes of Montana stopped leasing tribal lands for the strip mining of coal due to their concerns for scarring the land and polluting the air. The Diné had a more difficult time severing their relationship with mining, as some tribal officials saw coal and uranium mining as a way out of their nation's poverty. The Diné have created their own Environmental Protection Agency to minimize pollution and scarification, and in 2005 they voted to ban uranium mining, but the nation still depends heavily on revenues from coal mining.

Native assertions of rights to fishing and whaling were critical in the rise of modern tribal sovereignty and control over their environments. Numerous Indigenous communities have looked to the sea as the source of their food and culture, and from the very beginning of colonization non-Native commercial fishing and whaling, with its ever-increasing pressure on marine species, has threatened this connection. In the 1950s Native peoples in Washington State, Oregon, and the Great Lakes began fishing off their reservations in ways that violated state fishing regulations. Citing treaties signed in the 1850s in which they retained their rights to fish in their "usual and accustomed places," Native tribes argued that they could fish off their reservations and obey tribal, rather than state, fishing regulations. Ultimately the courts agreed. Fishing has thus become increasingly important to Washington tribes, who regulate their activities through restocking programs and sustainable yield measures.

Tribes throughout North America continue their fight for access to fish and game that they had traditionally relied upon for food. The

Makah of the Olympia Peninsula in Washington State present a case that your students will find particularly interesting. By treaty rights they retained access to whales but did not exercise those rights for most of the twentieth century. In 1999, though, shortly after the gray whale was removed from the endangered species list, the Makahs harvested a gray whale despite opposition from environmental groups such as Green Peace. Since then, the federal government has halted Makah whaling pending an environmental review, and as of this writing related litigation is likely bound for the Supreme Court—the outcome of which is the subject of considerable suspense. Still, Native communities in general lack the access to the marine life that once sustained them. Dams throughout North America block salmon, steelhead, and other anadromous species from swimming upstream to spawn; this, combined with commercial fishing at sea, has caused these fish runs to collapse. Elsewhere, industrial and agricultural pollution has killed off fish populations or made fish too toxic to eat.

Conclusions

So where are we today? Each of the more than five hundred federally recognized Indian tribes has its own unique environmental history. Colonialism in general has undermined the environmental relationships that Native communities have had, but environmental knowledge persists. The stereotype of the ecological Indian endures, but there are also hopeful signs that Euro-Americans are listening to real Native voices and engaging real Indigenous communities. The career of Winona LaDuke (Anishinaabe) exemplifies this. Her active role in the environmental movement, the popularity of her books and essays, and her nomination as the vice-presidential candidate for the US Green Party in 1996 and 2000 are important for your students to consider, especially because she has criticized tribal governments' relationships with the fossil fuel industry. Scientists also show signs of a willingness to learn from Indigenous peoples, especially about climate change. And most recently, Lakota of the Standing Rock Reservation have brought international attention to the destructive potential that oil pipelines buried underneath their land and under the Missouri River have not only for their water supply but also for a broad swath of communities in the Great Plains and Midwest. Protests against the Dakota Access Pipeline (DAPL)—so vividly captured in the free-to-stream documentary *Black*

Snake Killaz—provide a fruitful opportunity for your students to think about the interconnectedness of the fossil fuel industry, increasingly militarized police forces (including private security forces), and global environmental changes that impact us all.[4]

Given the current political climate in the United States and abroad, Native environmental history has a direct application outside the classroom. Many indigenous communities are on the front lines of efforts to reverse our dependence on fossil fuel and deal with climate change, and the stakes for their communities are extraordinarily high. In one sense, then, Native environmental history might inspire your students to take actions to protect their own environments and ally with Indigenous groups struggling to protect their lands from further degradation. Such an alliance must begin, however, with a realization that it was Euro-Americans' own actions—given validity in the policies of the US government—that created Indigenous poverty, and that stereotypes of Indigenous peoples as children of nature have hidden the destructive forces of colonialism.

Notes

1. Richard White, *The Organic Machine: The Remaking of the Columbia River* (New York: Hill and Wang, 1996), 15–24.

2. For more on systems of compulsory education, see the chapters in this volume by Margaret Huettl, Devon A. Mihesuah, and Donald L. Fixico.

3. Colin Calloway, ed., *First Peoples: A Documentary Survey of American Indian History*, 6th ed. (New York: Bedford Press, 2018), 517.

4. *Black Snake Killaz: A #NoDAPL Story*, Unicorn Riot, April 17, 2017, https://www.unicornriot.ninja/2017/black-snake-killaz-documentary-production-support-fund/.

Teaching and Understanding Genocide in Native America

G RAY H. W HALEY

G enocide is a politically charged topic when applied outside of the universally accepted context of Nazi war crimes during World War II. By contrast, the applicability of the term "genocide" in the context of the history of American Indians has been widely contested in the public, political, and academic realms. As a recent example from 2017, the dean of my college requested that a colleague from anthropology coauthor a press release about the approaching solar eclipse. My rural college town just happened to be at the geographic center of the longest duration of the eclipse in North America, everyone expected throngs of visitors, and NASA rented out athletic facilities for their measuring equipment and carnival-like public education efforts. To showcase liberal arts, our dean selected an image of a sixteenth-century woodcut depicting the famous episode in which Columbus exploited the Tainos of Jamaica with his foreknowledge of the eclipse in 1504. She recruited anthropologist John McCall to provide context for early modern European knowledge of eclipses and specific historical context for the woodcut's scene. McCall was livid when the piece appeared in the local newspaper having been cleansed of any mention of the genocide associated with Columbus's "trick," which the conquistadors used to begin the conquest, enslavement, and rapid extermination of the Jamaican Tainos. Spanish "rape and pillage" became "unwelcome behavior," and his explanation of the brutal colonization of Jamaica as genocide was scrubbed.[1] The dean wanted fluff, not controversy, and unfortunately, I think most Americans do prefer whitewashed history, particularly when confronted with perceived national or cultural culpability. Related scenarios have played out numerous times as Americans seek to reconcile past horrors with the desire to commemorate everything from the so-called battlefields of Sand Creek and Wounded Knee Creek to the Spanish missions in the Southwest to Sutter's Mill in northern California to the origin stories of New England and Virginia.

Indeed, genocidal acts occurred episodically throughout the history of the European and Euro-American colonization of the Americas, but the term "genocide" hardly accounts for the diversity of Native experiences since 1492. Where does genocide fit into a course on American Indian history? How and when should a class return to it? In my own research in colonial Oregon, Americans targeted specific bands and tribes for extermination, especially in the southern Oregon goldfields during the 1850s. Not all Americans agreed, and not all Native peoples were necessarily targeted, but these caveats do not make the extermination efforts any less genocidal. Genocide is a crime against a group of people, an attempt to eliminate the corporate body; thus, targeting a band, village, or tribe is genocidal, and American Indians, as a whole, need not be the target for the action to be genocidal. California followed suit and sustained its genocidal efforts well into the 1870s with the US Congress reimbursing the state for scalp bounties.[2] Despite the accuracy of the term in given situations, genocide's utility as a central organizing theme for teaching general American Indian history courses is debatable, and not one I recommend.

Over the past twenty years of teaching American Indian history, I have instead opted for more broadly applicable (and empowering) course themes such as sovereignty, colonialism, and cultural adaptation. I include genocide as a recurring topic that I approach cautiously and often in open-ended dialogue with students. For example, when we cover Columbus and the Tainos, we analyze the so-called Black Legend both as contemporary accounts by witnesses, participants, and chroniclers and as politically charged literature of the Reformation, and we discuss whether the Spanish conquest of the Greater Antilles offers cases of genocide or merely recurring tragedies on a grand scale. Given the undeniable factor of new epidemic diseases carrying off Tainos en masse, can the Spanish conquistadors who attacked, exploited, and brutalized the febrile Tainos still be guilty of genocide? That is, does the role of so-called Virgin Soil epidemics remove culpability from colonizers who took advantage of and worsened conditions for the Native peoples?

As suggested above, this story did not stop in the sixteenth-century Caribbean. We revisit the dynamics again and again in the colonial wars of southern New England, Virginia, the Ohio Country of the imperial and early republic American periods, the California gold rush, the Plains Wars, and elsewhere in the history of early colonization by Europeans and Euro-Americans. Western newcomers did not have a grasp of pathogens and microbiology, and with the exception of Lord Jeffrey Amherst in 1763 did not engage in germ warfare, as we know the term today, but they certainly took advantage of the opportunities and worsened conditions for Native peoples, including displacing them and sometimes attacking remnant survivors.[3] Textbook publishers seem to struggle with the issue as much as my college dean. Although the treatment of genocide is not the reason I select a textbook for my introductory course, the one I most often assign does indeed follow my basic strategy of confronting the difficult topic in concrete terms with appropriate examples but otherwise keeping it lurking in the background. By comparison, two of the leading competitors in the American Indian history college textbook market avoid the topic without a single indexed reference of genocide.[4]

Genocide currently exists as both a legally defined crime against humanity under the auspices of the United Nations Genocide Convention (UNGC) and as a broader category of scholarly investigation in the global field of genocide studies. The scholarly field tends toward more liberal definitions of genocide, as intended by Rafael Lemkin, the principal architect of genocide both as a concept and as a crime. At the outset in the 1970s, genocide studies confronted the "Holocaust problem": not all genocides resemble the Nazi archetype as reflected in the UNGC, including my example from colonial Oregon. At different times and places, Native peoples faced extermination attempts by colonial powers in the Americas. However, there was no consistent, coherent, and coordinated effort to make all indigenous Americans extinct as a race, let alone a systematic attempt at group murder by a modern, industrialized nation-state such as Nazi Germany. The comparison creates problems for teachers and scholars. Does inclusion of Native genocide undercut the study of the Shoah, the Jewish Holocaust of World War II? Must there be overwhelming similarities to merit use of the term? The UNGC was indeed adopted in the wake of the Shoah, and the specific language owes much to the events of the 1930s and 1940s, the crimes perpetrated by German Nazis and their allies in France, eastern Europe, and the Balkans. Lemkin, leading author of the UNGC, sought to include a wider, historical understanding of this ancient crime with a new name, as he put it. Indeed, Lemkin began his crusade years before the rise of Hitler, seeking to avoid anything comparable to the Armenian genocide in the wake of World War I. For Lemkin, genocide was the murder or attempted murder of a *group* of people as opposed to the mass murder of individual people. The target is the group, a people, a culture, an identity.[5] Lemkin continued his broader work on a multivolume history of genocide going back to antiquity, but his own death left much undone in his ambitious project. For Lemkin, American Indian experiences were among the many that needed to be documented and understood if humanity was to eliminate genocide in the future. Colonial empires with significant indigenous populations, including Canada and the United States, had resisted a broader definition in the 1948 declaration. Similarly, when the United Nations finally adopted the Declaration of Rights for Indigenous Peoples (UNDRIP) and unequivocally included the language of genocide, the same resisting nations held out, with the United States becoming the last to endorse the document when President Obama did so in late 2010. Not surprisingly, the declaration does not include language for past crimes, although the preamble does acknowledge the importance of considering historical relations when addressing contemporary problems and solutions.[6]

Among scholars of American Indians, many of whom identify as Indian or First Nations themselves, genocide presents a thicket of thorny issues. Does a colonial ideology of Native erasure count as genocide? That is, the widespread belief that Native peoples must make way for the progress of an advancing Anglo-Saxon civilization and vanish as distinct cultures and people. Settler states, including the United States, certainly enacted assimilation efforts and sporadic military efforts to bring such an erasure about, and the general faith in the vanishing Indian of North America maintained a nearly hegemonic status well into the twentieth century. Or do there have to be genocidal actions specifically accompanying those general ideologies in specific places and times that add up to an overall genocide? Can disconnected massacres of distinct Native *groups* add up to this specific crime against humanity by the United States as well as Canada, Australia, and New Zealand? To answer these questions, I explain a few relevant things about the scholarship of genocide studies, particularly regarding language.

For this chapter, I draw mostly on the published proceedings from a conference on North American genocide in which I participated in

Winnipeg, Canada, in 2012. The academic conference complemented the then ongoing Canadian Truth and Reconciliation Commission and included the participation of commission chair Justice Murray Sinclair. Editors Andrew Woolford, Jeff Benevenuto, and Alexander Laban Hinton assembled a dense but relatively brief text that covers a wide breadth of genocide scholarship particularly regarding Native North Americans and the various arguments within the literature.[7] Importantly, a point of contention among the scholars emerged between taking a broad view of genocide as applying to both an ideology of erasing ethnic minority cultures in addition to attempts at their physical destruction, and the narrower view of labeling only specific instances of group murder as genocide. Joseph P. Gone, a Gros Ventre Indian, scholar, and clinician, made the latter point most effectively.[8] The crux of the argument is the power of language. Gone asserts that stretching the term "genocide" to include forced removals, assimilation efforts, and sundry cruel acts and policies by colonial powers blunts the most important accomplishment of the UNGC: humanity now has an unambiguous, internationally accepted word for group murder. Any other use of the term waters it down and weakens its effect. He cites my own work among others in which the lines were often blurred in history, and can render blanket statements regarding US guilt in genocide weak if not misleading. In my work, I found that while some American citizens did attempt genocide during the gold rush of 1850s Oregon, the US Army acted to mitigate the slaughter and even threatened to attack their countrymen to protect Native people under their watch at the Table Rock Reservation in southern Oregon.[9]

Were US citizens guilty of attempted genocide in southern Oregon in the 1850s? Yes. Was the United States as a nation guilty of attempted genocide? No, not according to the stricter usage of the term by Gone. Still, if one extends the term to include the broader, dominant culture, then a case can be made. The United States did establish the conditions for its citizens to assert dominion over the land and resources, and neither the territory of Oregon nor the federal government spent much effort to prevent violence that was a long-established part of frontier conditions. Citizen miners and their supporters readily cited historical precedent to justify extreme violence from previous colonization in other parts of the United States, especially the relatively recent armed occupation of Florida in which the US government formally supported private warfare to rid that territory of Indians. "Exterminators," as one miner militia fancied themselves, expected support from the territorial and federal governments, including reimbursement from the national treasury. Indeed, the United States had done so in the past and even had a formal path via the category of Indian Depredations in the US Court of Claims. However, the dispute that arose over the attempted genocide of Oregon Indians between the militias and their supporters and their adversaries, particularly General John Wool of the US Army, dragged out for decades and demonstrates that genocide in American history is not always a simple matter of US national culpability.[10]

As a counterpoint, sociologist David MacDonald asserts that the US and Canadian residential schools represent clear examples of article 2(e) of the genocide convention, "forcibly transferring children of one group to another group," and argues that a case can be made for other clauses as well.[11] While the United States ceased mandatory attendance at off-reservation schools by the early 1930s, and began to phase the institutions out even earlier, Canada continued the practice into the 1950s. Without doubt, policy makers beginning in the 1870s intended to "kill the Indian to save the man" and designed these total institutions to bring about the end of Native cultures partly by separating children from their families and communities. The Americanization project, as it was known in the United States, had unintended consequences, not the least of which was contributing to an increased pan-Indian identity rather than an eradication of Native cultures, but the intent was undeniably cultural eradication. That the United States had to pass the Indian Child Welfare Act in 1978 to keep Native children in their communities instead of being adopted out, as was the common practice, and given the continuing violations of the federal law by states to the present day, is testament to the ongoing need to come to terms with article 2(e) of the UNGC and its possible applicability in the United States.[12] Indeed, the residential schools were the main focus of the Canadian Truth and Reconciliation Commission. In my classes, one of the ways in which I have made this connection between early and late twentieth-century child welfare in class is via a documentary called *The Canary Effect*.[13] The movie is polemical and not without its problems, but I represent it to the students as advocacy, not fact, and as a discussion piece. The filmmakers make historical connections explicit between the massacres and cultural genocide of the nineteenth and early twentieth centuries and more contemporary problems such as forced sterilization of Native women in the 1970s, current poverty, and poor health and sanitation conditions on many reservations today. I ask students to use other course materials, many of them primary documents from the Calloway textbook, to consider the filmmakers' claims critically. Now that the UN has completed a study of American Indian reservations, teachers can also draw on that critical report for recent data.[14]

Regarding Indian child welfare and other contemporary matters, the discussion often turns to cultural genocide or, as some scholars prefer, ethnocide. I provide the students with copies of the UNGC to remind them that Lemkin did not make that same distinction. Genocide was the crime whether killing the group physically or culturally. As stated, I generally come down on the side of Dr. Gone and others who prefer to make distinctions between physical and cultural extermination, but I do not press my students to agree. Lemkin provided an excellent framework, but the UNGC did not represent his full thinking on the matter, nor frankly does his 1940s understanding of the slippery concept of culture hold much utility. Lemkin worked with a fixed, reified, and singular definition of culture whereas scholars of his day were already developing more fluid, dynamic understandings of culture that treated it as more of an approximate term. My students are, of course, steeped in the modern conception. For the sake of accuracy regarding culture and in support of Gone's argument for preserving the potency of the term "genocide," I argue for a distinction between biological genocide and cultural genocide (ethnocide). Cultural eradication was indeed a concerted national effort by the United States and Canada (and elsewhere), whereas physical extermination attempts were much more localized and complex. I feel that when addressing such sensitive matters, specificity helps us understand the many ways in which US colonization was a multidimensional and often dark enterprise, especially as experienced by American Indians.

NOTES

1. Meera Komarraju, "Eclipse Legend: Here's How Christopher Columbus Used an Eclipse to Trick Native Jamaicans in the New World," *The Southern Illinoisan*, July 31, 2017. John McCall, who largely wrote the original version, entitled it "The Dark Shadow of Columbus."

2. Gray H. Whaley, *Oregon and the Collapse of Illahee: U.S. Empire and the Transformation of an Indigenous World* (Chapel Hill: University of North Carolina Press, 2010).

3. Colin Calloway, ed., *First Peoples: A Documentary Survey of American Indian History*, 5th ed. (New York: Bedford/St. Martins Press, 2016), 203.

4. Calloway treats genocide well but only intermittently and distinguishes "cultural genocide" as the term for forced assimilation attempts and policies. For comparison, see R. David Edmunds, Frederick Hoxie, and Neal Salisbury, *The People: A History of Native America* (Belmont, CA: Wadsworth, 2006); and Michael Leroy Oberg, *Native America: A History* (Hoboken, NJ: Wiley Blackwell, 2010).

5. Convention on the Prevention and Punishment of the Crime of Genocide. Adopted by the General Assembly of the United Nations on December 9, 1948. Article II states: "In the present Convention, genocide means any of the following acts committed with intent to destroy, in whole or in part, a national, ethnical, racial or religious group, as such: (a) killing members of the group; (b) causing serious bodily or mental harm to members of the group; (c) deliberately inflicting on the group conditions of life calculated to bring about its physical destruction in whole or in part; (d) imposing measures intended to prevent births within the group; (e) forcibly transferring children of the group to another group."

6. United Nations Resolution adopted by the General Assembly, 61/295. September 13, 2007. The preamble to "United Nations Declaration on the Rights of Indigenous Peoples" states: "Concerned that indigenous peoples have suffered from historic injustices as a result of, inter alia, their colonization and dispossession of their lands, territories and resources, thus preventing them from exercising, in particular, their right to development in accordance with their own needs and interests."

Article 7 specifically addresses genocide with section one pertaining to individuals and section two is closer to Lemkin's 1948 formulation of a corporate body: "1. Indigenous individuals have the rights to life, physical and mental integrity, liberty and security of person. 2. Indigenous peoples have the collective right to live in freedom, peace and security as distinct peoples and shall not be subjected to any act of genocide or any other act of violence, including forcibly removing children of the group to another group."

7. Andrew Woolford, Jeff Benevuto, and Alexander Laban Hinton, eds., *Colonial Genocide in Indigenous North America* (Durham: Duke University Press, 2014) [hereafter cited as *Colonial Genocide*].

8. Joseph P. Gone, "Colonial Genocide and Historical Trauma in Native North America: Complicating Contemporary Attributions," in *Colonial Genocide*, 273–91.

9. Gray H. Whaley, "American Folk Imperialism and Native Genocide in Southwest Oregon, 1851–1859," in *Colonial Genocide*, 131–48.

10. Whaley, "American Folk Imperialism." See also Whaley, *Oregon and the Collapse of Illahee*.

11. David B. MacDonald, "Genocide in the Indian Residential Schools: Canadian History through the Lens of the UN Genocide Convention," in *Colonial Genocide*, 306–24.

12. *Oglala Sioux Tribe v. Luann Van Hunnik*, 993 F.Supp.2d 1017 (2014). This ruling was upheld January 2016.

13. Robin Davey and Yellow Thunder Woman (The Bastard Fairies), dirs., *The Canary Effect*, 2006.

14. "United Nations; United States: First U.N. Investigation of Native American Rights," Library of Congress, 2012, http://www.loc.gov/law/foreign-news/article/united-nations-united-states-first-u-n-investigation-of-native-american-rights/.

For Further Reading

United Nations, Office on Genocide Prevention and the Responsibility to Protect, "Genocide," https://www.un.org/en/genocideprevention/genocide.shtml.

Edwards, Tai S., and Paul Kelton. "Germs, Genocide, and America's Indigenous Peoples." *Journal of American History* 107, no. 1 (June 2020): 52–76.

Madley, Benjamin. *An American Genocide: The United States and the California Indian Tragedy, 1846—1873*. New Haven, CT: Yale University Press, 2017.

Ostler, Jeffery. *Surviving Genocide: Native Nations and the United States from the American Revolution to Bleeding Kansas*. New Haven, CT: Yale University Press, 2019.

Woolford, Andrew, Jeff Benevuto, and Alexander Laban Hinton, eds. *Colonial Genocide in Indigenous North America*. Durham, NC: Duke University Press, 2014.

PART TWO

Reflections on Identity and Cultural Appropriation

An Appropriate Past

Seminole Indians, Osceola, and Florida State University

A N D R E W   K .   F R A N K

lorida State University's use of the Seminole's name
and a mascot named for their famed leader Osceola
stands out as an anomaly in the contemporary history of Indian mascots. FSU, despite its visibility, has largely avoided the sustained opposition that has been directed against the Cleveland Indians, Washington
Redskins, and University of Illinois. In fact, as the voices of protest have
swelled nationally and have made impressive gains in the world of athletics and in shaping public opinion, the protests have largely fallen
silent at Florida State University. Exploring this contrast with students
allows me to examine issues of tribal self-determination and culture appropriation. I make this exploration through a combination of lectures
and source discussions.

FSU's contrast from the typical Indian mascot story does not, by
and large, reflect a distinctive approach to using the Seminole image
and name. Much of its contemporary and historic iconography mimics
that which the NFL's (National Football League) Washington team and
MLB's (Major League Baseball) Cleveland team have employed. This
can be seen in FSU's Seminole logo that depicts an Indian head, the
performance of a White student in red face and regalia pretending to
be Osceola at football games, a fight song that includes the phrase
"scalp 'em," and a "tomahawk chop" and "war chant" that are routinely performed at sporting events, graduation, and community events

in general. Currently and in recent years, the university's buses and buildings have been decorated with tomahawks and arrows; an on-campus convenience store was called the "Trading Post," the MBA program declared that it provides "warpaint for today's business world," and an on-campus recreation area was until very recently called the "Reservation." There are "chiefs" everywhere—with a "Marching Chiefs" band, donors to its booster club earning "Golden Chief" status, and a homecoming Chief and Princess. FSU has even borrowed the self-proclaimed "Unconquered" status of the Florida Seminole Tribe. In short, the incorporation of the Seminole name extends throughout the university, and protesters have routinely characterized these acts with the same language that they chastise Indian mascots elsewhere.

Because I teach at Florida State I routinely have my students examine the iconography and behavior deployed around campus and online. I focus our conversation on a few of the "traditions" listed above to start the discussion. Every semester I learn about more places and ways that the Seminole name and ideas of Native people permeate the campus and wider Tallahassee community. Yet there is remarkable futility in the discussions that ensue. Our discussions quickly descend to the chaos of dozens of students deciding for themselves what they deem to be offensive or racist. The more we talk, the less historical the conversation becomes and the less I hear about the Seminoles themselves. Students who find Indian mascots offensive struggle with FSU's use of the Seminole; those who do not find Indian mascots offensive do not.

I interrupt the conversation with a short historical lecture that inserts the Seminole Indians and the issue of self-determination. It is not the story that my students are often familiar with, and it not the story that most scholars and activists explore. It is also not the story typically told in public, but rather one gleaned from the behind-the-scenes discussions of the participants. It is not that my students never bring historical background to the conversation. When pressed, my students (and the university community more generally) occasionally point to the Seminole Tribe of Florida's very public statements of support for the university in the 2005 fight against the NCAA's ruling regarding "hostile and abusive" mascots. In this manner, these students approach the topic in ways that are remarkably similar to those used by academics and American Indian activists. They, broadly speaking, come to opposing conclusions about the appropriateness of using the Seminole name and iconography. Yet, both groups focus on the public events of 2005, and they both refrain from taking the Seminoles and tribal sovereignty seriously.[1] My students say it is ok because the Seminoles said it was ok. Other voices do not matter. Scholars and many others have hypothesized that the Seminole Tribe receives lucrative cash payouts (not true), while many others have ridiculed the tribe for being sell-outs.[2] Chairman James E. Billie received the nickname "Uncle Tom-Tom" for his four decades of support for the university, and the Seminoles as a whole are repeatedly derided for not knowing what outsiders declare is in their best interest.[3] Scholars, for their part, acknowledge that the history begins with FSU's decision to become the Seminoles in 1947, but they only look for a Seminole voice after the protests in the late 1990s that culminated in the NCAA's ruling in 2005. C. Richard King and Charles Springwood typified this approach to the dispute by writing "Tellingly, concern for Seminole involvement and Native responses to Chief Osceola apparently were never of interest to FSU supporters until the mascot became contested."[4] King and Springwood offer a compelling critique of the use of the name and various iconographies, but they falsely imagine that the relationship between the Tribe and FSU began as a sudden reaction to the NCAA ruling and the national debate that ensued. The Seminoles, in this interpretation, can respond to but not initiate the conversation.[5]

Instead of beginning with the 2005 NCAA ban, I begin my classroom discussion in the early 1990s. In January 1994, shortly after he was appointed president of Florida State University, Talbot "Sandy" D'Alemberte faced a public controversy over the university's use of the Seminole name and its nineteenth-century war leader Osceola. Members of the American Indian Movement and various other protestors took aim at Indian mascots nationwide and at FSU more particularly. Michael Haney, an Oklahoma Seminole and chairman of the United Indian Nations Repatriation Committee, had recently left Tallahassee after he had led protests at various sporting events, attracted local and national media attention, met with university officials, and threatened to sue the university for civil rights violations. His activism paralleled protests against Indian mascots across the country. Local newspapers published debates over the proper course forward, the state legislature considered action, and a university task force explored issues related to the university's representation of the Seminoles.[6]

D'Alemberte, the former president of the American Bar Association and Democratic representative in the Florida legislature, considered all of this when another protestor, Bryan St. Laurent, demanded to present his concerns directly to him. Before a scheduled meeting with St. Laurent, D'Alemberte received some advice from Beverley Spencer, the vice president of university relations. Chairman of the Seminole Tribe of Florida James E. Billie, she explained, "felt that the meetings of Mr. Haney with University officials and an appointment of a symbolism committee was patronizing. He felt the recognition of Haney questioned the legitimacy of the Seminole Tribe to make judgments about the use of its name and created the perception that the University knew more about the use of the name than the tribe." The Seminole Tribe of Florida had for several years already voiced its support for the name, the university and tribe had discussed the issue many times in the past, and Billie insisted that their support should settle the issue. Spencer urged the president to follow the guidance of the Seminole Tribe rather than the well-intentioned protests of outsiders. D'Alemberte did as he was advised and refused to meet with St. Laurent. Instead, he chose to "develop a relationship with Chief Billie" and the Seminole Tribe in general. This was an issue for Seminoles to decide and not a decision for all Native Americans.[7]

My students struggle and debate whether D'Alemberte did the right thing. Should he have listened to the concerns of a Native person representing a large and influential pan-Indian group? Do only elected officials get to speak for Native people? Do only Florida Seminoles get to speak on behalf of all Seminoles? Is it appropriation if the Florida Seminole's Tribal Council gives consent but individual Seminoles and other Natives voice their opposition? As they discuss these questions, they realize that D'Alembert's decision complicates the widely presumed dualism between those who maintain Indian mascots and thereby ignore Indigenous concerns and those who listen to Native American concerns and abandon mascots. President D'Alemberte's deliberation and decision opens the discussion of tribal sovereignty, political representation, and cultural appropriation.

After this discussion, I remind my students that the conversation about the FSU Seminoles neither began nor ended in 1994. The university decided to take the Seminole name in 1947, shortly after the university admitted men and changed its name from the Florida State College for Women. The decision and the subsequent creation of Native iconography and performances in the following decades took place without any input from the Seminole Tribe in Florida or Native peoples in general.

There is no evidence that university officials reached out to tribal members or vice versa in the first decade of use, and therefore it provides a clear case of cultural appropriation. The lack of permission or participation by Seminole Indians led FSU to make choices that my students describe as peculiar and offensive.

As a class we explore how the university embraced the idea of the Indian more than the distinctive culture or history of the Florida Seminoles. As much as FSU cheerleaders occasionally wore traditional Seminole patchwork skirts, most of the iconography on campus was far more generically "Indian" than distinctively Seminole.[8] The university formally called its homecoming celebration "Powwow," invited "All Squaws and Braves" to attend, and anointed the year's queen with an all-white feathered war bonnet.[9] A humor magazine on campus took the name *Smoke Signals*, and in countless promotional materials for the university illustrators placed a single feather on top of the heads of students.[10] Several homecoming Powwows in the 1950s included an "Indian Ceremonial Dance" performed by cheerleaders and other students, and skits routinely evoked Indian stereotypes including an "Indian Love Call." Gymnasts dressed up with feathers and donned red face as they somersaulted on the sidelines, whooped and hollered, and otherwise donned clothing that mirrors attire in 1950s westerns. In 1958, a gymnast portraying a caricature of an Indian named Sammy Seminole patrolled the sidelines. Later, the university briefly had a basketball counterpart in Chief Fullabull.[11]

Exploring the first decade of FSU's use of the Seminole name allows my class to establish a baseline for three important concepts. First, the absence of permission by Seminoles makes for clear definition of cultural appropriation. FSU used the name "Seminole" and images of Seminoles without the consent of the Seminoles (the owners). Second, the lack of Seminole participation allows my students to see a lack of tribal self-determination. Seminoles had no power or voice in the conversation, and as a result they could not pursue their self-interests or assert their tribal sovereignty. Third, the Seminole traditions that FSU created illuminate the concept of "playing Indian." These traditions lacked anything from the culture and traditions of Seminole Indians but instead allowed outsiders to perform stereotypically "Indian" behavior.[12]

Armed with this shared vocabulary, the class discussion turns to the history of the FSU-tribal relationship. Before I begin to lay out a narrative of the relationship, I present students with a series of questions to get them thinking about the terms in historic rather than absolute ways. Is FSU's use of the Seminole always an act of cultural appropriation? What kind of control (if any) do the Seminoles have in this conversation? Is FSU performing Native stereotypes, or are they embracing something Seminole? Students are free to disagree over how to answer these questions over time, but they need to keep track. I also urge them to pay attention to the tensions within these questions. Does tribal participation erase concerns for cultural appropriation? To help them, we create a simplified timeline to keep track of changes in how these terms apply.

I begin this part of the discussion in 1957, the same year that the Seminole Tribe of Florida obtained federal recognition and wrote a constitution that created a democratically elected tribal council. That year, the Seminole Tribe reached out to FSU and offered to attend homecoming and other public events. The Seminoles' participation with FSU was an extension of their cultural performances elsewhere. For several decades, Seminoles had participated in a series of pay-per-view demonstrations of so-called Indian culture in newly formed "villages" in south Florida. During tourist season Seminole men and women wore traditional patchwork clothing, built thatched-roof chickee homes, cooked sofkee and other distinctively Indigenous foods, and carved canoes. They also created a host of items designed to meet tourist demands rather than Seminole customs. They made tomahawks, drums, and various dolls specifically designed for the trade; they wrestled alligators for paying audiences; and they built totem poles and tepees for tourists who expected to see iconic "Indian" items even if they were not authentically Seminole.

The Seminoles' performances at FSU in 1957 followed similar lines. While they "played Indian" publicly at homecoming and other events, tribal members and leaders met with deans and other university officials behind the scenes.[13] These meetings, which took place outside of the spectacle of Miss Seminole Tribe crowning the homecoming court, provided Seminoles with opportunities to have their voices heard. These sporadic meetings were initially confined to homecoming and other public events, but they provided opportunities for Seminoles to assert their interests. In one instance, Chairman Howard Tommie announced his disappointment with some of the iconography being used at FSU. In particular, he pointed to the homecoming court's use of stereotypical Indian clothing and headdress rather than the traditional patchwork and turban, and he echoed the complaints of many others that Chief Fullabull was offensive. After a series of informal conversations in 1970 and not much public comment, the university implemented a series of changes. Seminole women thereafter made the traditional turban and clothing, and the university retired Chief Fullabull. In 1971, members of the Seminole Tribe from Florida and Seminole Nation from Oklahoma performed dances at homecoming. The following year, FSU said goodbye to the highly racist and stereotyped Sammy Seminole. Most FSU "traditions" remained intact, but the two most visible spectacles were gone.[14]

As the university abandoned some of its most egregious "Indian" traditions, it created new "Seminole" ones. In 1977, a local booster and horse trainer worked with then football coach Bobby Bowden to create a new sideline mascot. They arranged for a White student to dress in redface and "Indian clothes" and to ride an Appaloosa horse named Renegade before and during the game. At first, the student wore pantyhose and a "really colorful bathrobe" and went by the name "Savage Sam." In 1978, in part out of discussions with the Seminole Tribe, who pride themselves on their long history in the cattle industry, he was renamed Chief Osceola. Shortly after, the rider added a flaming spear to the highly choreographed performance. His appearance also changed, and on the advice of Seminole elders the rider's clothing began to change. A similar metamorphosis occurred at homecoming, as Seminole elders and others insisted that the homecoming court wear Seminole turbans made by Seminole women rather than generic Siouan headdresses.[15] Discussing these changes forces students to think carefully about the nature of the FSU-tribe relationship, and it allows us to debate the significance of our three terms. How sovereign is the tribe in this era? How significant were these changes? How significant is the transition from "playing Indian" to "playing Seminole"?

The next part of the class explores how FSU explicitly dealt with the issues of sovereignty, cultural appropriation, and playing Indian. In the early 1990s, the university faced internal and external pressures to rethink its use of the Seminole name. Responding to a national discourse on racist Indian mascots, some administrators, professors, staff, and students pushed for some changes to campus culture. With protests around the country and in Tallahassee, FSU president Dale W. Lick convened a President's Study Group on the Use of Seminole Symbolism and Tradition in order to see if "there may be some things that we are doing that may need refinement." The committee met in 1993 and called for the elimination of stick art that was "silly" and "offensive," reviewed licensing procedures, and reduced the use of the otherwise ubiquitous "scalp 'em,'" terminology.[16] They also met with Joe Quetone (executive director of the state's Governor's Commission on Indian Affairs) to explore issues as wide-ranging as the lack of Seminole graduates, the use of the tomahawk chop, and concerns of some tribal members that Osceola's appearance and "attire is not authentic and that, in fact what he wears appears to be Apache." In the end, though, Quetone reinforced the idea that "Chairman Billy [sic] does have the authority to say what is appropriate for Seminole Indians and the tribe."[17]

For various reasons, the committee met "without fanfare, as low key as possible, and quickly" and did so intentionally. The university was likely concerned about arousing the ire of its alumni and fan base, but the committee was more concerned with trampling over the sovereignty rights of the Seminole Tribe and therefore angering its leadership. "Whatever we do should be done. We do not want to allow ourselves to be drawn into political issues that Indian people are quite capable of handling themselves." Concern for the Seminole Tribe led Anthony Paredes, an anthropologist and leader of the committee, to ignore the concerns of nontribal members. Listening to non-Seminoles would "disrespect . . . the Seminole people, their right to self-government, and the larger principal of tribal sovereignty. That's not to say, however, that there is no room for improvement in the way FSU uses so-called 'Indian symbolism.'" Paredes was even hesitant for the group to self-police as it too would counter tribal sovereignty. "The very existence of the group could be construed as an insult to legitimate tribal governments and Indian people in general." In a memo to other committee members, he explained, "Through their elected head of government, the Seminole Tribe of Florida, in particular, has advised the university in no uncertain terms that it should give no credibility in self-appointed spokesmen (Indian or otherwise) for American Indians who take it upon themselves to criticize what legitimate tribal governments have approved." Rather than meet as a group, Paredes urged them to "quietly disband" and leave the issue to a "case-by-case consultation with the Seminoles of Florida."[18]

Paredes got his wish, but not before the university began to implement some changes quietly. By the following year, university officials were privately and then publicly urging coaches and the community to start referring to Seminole Indians, Osceola, and Renegade as university spirits, legends, and names rather than as "mascots."[19] They continued to have students ride in redface, but they began to wear Seminole-made clothing that mimicked the appearance of Osceola in George Catlin's famous portrait. Other changes were more central to the university mission. On campus, several administrators and faculty members began to promote Native American studies and to alter behavior they deemed inappropriate. These acts of outreach largely remained confined to the Southeast, but they extended outside of the Seminole Tribe of Florida. In 1993, the chairman of the Seminole Nation attended homecoming events after being invited.[20] A few months later, in February 1994, former chairwoman of the Seminole Tribe Betty Mae Tiger Jumper received an honorary PhD from the university. The planning for this event began a year and a half earlier, but she served as a keynote speaker for the Women's History Celebration.[21] A few months later, Cherokee chairwoman Wilma Mankiller participated in the Distinguished Lecture Series on campus. Her speech focused primarily on gender equality, but while she was on campus she reiterated the growing sense that the Seminole Tribe of Florida should be free to decide how its name is used.[22]

Paredes's concern for tribal sovereignty was not overblown. As the committee met to discuss the issue, representatives of the Seminole Tribe of Florida left little room for FSU to respond. Many tribal members viewed the protests as an attack on tribal sovereignty—the right of the Seminoles to make decisions for themselves even if they were unpopular or considered by outsiders not to be in the Seminoles' best interest. In 1992, for example, the tribe countered an American Indian Movement (AIM) demonstration in Tallahassee by asserting their own tribal desires. "We enjoy the football team. It doesn't insult us," Chairman Billie stated.[23] The attack on the mascot by nontribal members and the university's concern for the feelings of nontribal members, however, did. "I am surprised and disappointed that sophisticated Florida State University is allowing itself to be sucked into the tornado of this issue," Billie declared in a widely reported and published letter. "Nothing has been broken. Nothing needs fixing. We Seminoles have no objection to Florida State University using the Seminole mascot. In fact, as long as the Seminoles keep winning, we're happy. We do not want to participate in this ridiculous debate just to fan the flames of news hype."[24] In the late 1990s, as the opposition to Indian mascots gained new traction, tribal leadership insisted that this was a local rather than national issue. Billie, who served more than twenty-seven years in his two stints as chairman and oversaw the tribe's emergence at the forefront of the national legal fight for tribal sovereignty, declared in 1999, "We have never gone to North Carolina or Navajo Country and protested."[25] A year later, he proclaimed, "Some people eat bear; some don't," and that it is not his place to comment. "I stay away from your culture."[26]

I then return to our conversation about D'Alemberte's decision by reminding my class that university administrators routinely make decisions that upset students, alumni, faculty, staff, and other members of their community. They raise tuition, cut classes, fire employees, and alter mascots. Dozens of schools changed their mascots in the name of progress, and nearly all of them faced a backlash from their student and alumni base. D'Alemberte could have pushed the university to change the mascot and then deal with the fallout. He chose not to. Did FSU use the sovereignty of the tribe in order to shield itself from criticism, or was the support of sovereignty the main ambition? What was the importance of allowing Seminoles to speak for themselves? Do the motives of the university matter?

We pick up our discussion of FSU in the early 2000s, when the NCAA explored and then finally announced its ruling to eliminate the use of Indian and other "hostile and abusive" mascots. When the NCAA made its ruling in 2005, FSU and the Seminole Tribe already had a relatively unified script on how to respond. Rather than emphasize issues of iconography or the psychological impact in Indigenous communities, both made the issue about tribal self-determination. The approach disarmed most of the opposition as it put activists in the awkward position of opposing the sovereignty of a federally recognized tribe. University and state leaders offered vigorous defenses of the Seminole name, but their voices proved significantly less influential than tribal ones.[27] Leaders from the tribe immediately addressed the NCAA's concerns about iconography with the language of sovereignty. Acting Chairman Max B. Osceola Jr. for example, stated: "Members of the Seminole Tribe do not consider it derogatory, demeaning or insulting. . . . We do not look at it as a mascot, we look at it as a representation of the Seminole Tribe." Osceola explained, "They [FSU administrators] work with us in representing our heritage. This is our tribe, and the tribe that is represented needs to have final say, and they need to respect that."[28] Like Billie before him, Osceola insisted on the Seminoles' right to speak for themselves. "It's like history—they left the natives out. They have non-natives telling natives what's good for them or how they should use their name. You have a committee of non-natives telling people that they cannot use a native name when you have a native tribe—a tribal government, duly elected and constituted—that said they agree with Florida State."[29] Tribal leaders even disarmed protestors who targeted the use of a White student dressing up in redface to be "Osceola." Jim Shore, the lawyer and Tribal citizen who fought for the Seminole's right to self-determination for decades, made an impassioned defense of the mascot. "Look, those little differences don't bother us. An actual Seminole warrior of the 1800s couldn't be depicted in modern times. But this character has a great resemblance to what he should be. It's modernized, not theatrical. The school has checked with us, over and over again. And we have no objections to how he's portrayed. It's always respectful."[30]

The tribe's insistence on the right to self-determination did not disarm Indigenous opposition immediately or completely. Clyde Bettincort, a founder of AIM and perhaps the loudest critic of the Seminole decision, derided the Seminoles for being sellouts. Chairman Billie, he stated, "is a puppet of the US federal government. He doesn't represent the people. We've always had Indian scouts willing to ride with the calvary." Billie would not take this lightly. "I was elected by the tribe to take care of its interests," he noted. "If the Seminole people think it's insulting or undignified, I'm sure I'll be the first to know."[31] Other protests came from Seminoles in Oklahoma, where a larger Seminole Nation had issued a statement that disapproved of the use of Indian mascots. When the Seminole Tribe voiced its support, the Seminole Nation changed its tune. They continued to oppose the use of Indian mascots but reaffirmed the right of the Florida Seminoles to decide for themselves. In short, as the voice of the Seminole Tribal Council became more clear, Indigenous opposition dissipated. Native peoples were unwilling to trample on the self-determination of other Natives.

At this point in the lesson, my students can understand why the NCAA ultimately exempted FSU from the prohibition on Indian mascots. The NCAA, my students conclude, ultimately came to the same conclusion as President D'Alemberte in 1994. Their personal opinions about whether Indian mascots were appropriate did not particularly matter. Instead, they both determined that the Seminole Tribe of Florida had the right to decide the issue for itself. Once sanctioned by the tribe, the university's use of the Seminole name and image of Osceola ceased to be "hostile," "abusive," or "appropriated." The discussion that ensues allows us to discuss and clarify the meaning of Indian sovereignty and cultural appropriation. I remind students that the issue is not settled and that the debate over mascots is only one issue where Native Americans have insisted on their right to speak for themselves.

NOTES

1. David Eugene Wilkins, *American Indian Politics and the American Political System* (New York: Roman and Littlefield, 2007), 235.

2. Steve Ellis, "Tribe Not Paid for Nickname," *Tallahassee Democrat*, August 11, 2005.

3. "The Real Inspiration of the Seminole Tribe," *Overtime Times*, December 30, 1995. For background on Billie see Patricia Riles Wickman, *Warriors without War: Seminole Leadership in the Twentieth Century* (Tuscaloosa: University of Alabama Press, 2012); Andrew K. Frank, "An Unconquered Statesman: James E. Billie and the Florida Seminoles," in *"Our Cause Will Ultimately Triumph": The Men and Women Who Preserved and Revitalized American Indian Sovereignty*, ed. Tim Garrison (Durham, NC: Carolina Academic Press, 2014), 157–72.

4. C. Richard King and Charles Fruehling Springwood, "The Best Offense," in King and Springwood, eds., *Team Spirits: The Native American Mascots Controversy* (Lincoln: University of Nebraska Press, 2001), 146.

5. Harry A. Kersey Jr. *Assumption of Sovereignty: Social and Political Transformation among the Florida Seminoles, 1953–1979* (Lincoln: University of Nebraska Press, 1996).

6. Beverley Spencer to Talbot D'Alemberte, January 14, 1994, Seminole Mascot 1993–1994, Box 1817, Folder 2, Mss 2008–023, Florida State University, Special Collections [hereafter cited as FSU SC].

7. James E. Billie to Emile Whitehead, April 2, 1993, Seminole Mascot Materials, Box 1817, Folder 2, Mss 2008–023, FSU SC; "Real Issue Is Not Mascot but Instigators and Egotists," *Seminole Tribune*, April 9, 1993; Bryan St. Laurent to D'Alemberte, January 5, 1994, Seminole Mascots, Box 1817, Folder 3, Mss 2008–023, FSU SC; Spencer to D'Alemberte, January 14, 1994.

8. "Yell Louder, Florida State," *Florida Flambeau*, November 14, 1952. See the photographs, Special Collections, Manuscripts Box 1817, Folder 1, Football Players, Cheerleaders, Homecoming Princess, Seminole Mascot Materials, FSU SC.

9. For example, see Sign for the First Florida State University Pow Wow—Tallahassee, Florida, 1948 or 1949, Photograph in Florida Memory Collection, State of Florida Archives, RC01370, https://www.floridamemory.com/items/show/25300.

10. *Smoke Signals: Florida State University's Humor Magazine*, 1956, in Heritage Protocol, Miscellaneous Documents, Box 2, FSU SC. See also *Time for Homecoming*, 1951, FSU Homecoming Files, Box 1343, Mss 90:18, FSU SC. Coincidentally, the Seminole Tribe used the same name when it published its first newspaper in 1963.

11. Florida State University, Press Kit for Homecoming 1955, FSU Homecoming Files, FSU SC; Powwow 1956, FSU Homecoming Files 18, FSU SC.

12. Phillip J. Deloria, *Playing Indian* (New Haven, CT: Yale University Press, 1998).

13. "Seminole Princess Contest Winners: August 1957–1986," *Seminole Tribune*, August 10, 1987; Photo of Dean Ottis McBride with Seminole Chief, *Tally Ho*, 1960, Donna McHugh Collection, Heritage Protocol, 2014–18, FSU, Unprocessed Box 30, FSU SC.

14. Donna McHugh Collection, Heritage Protocol, 2014–18, FSU, Unprocessed Box 30, FSU SC. The internal discussions also included Jean Chaudhuri (a Muscogee Creek) and her husband Joyotpaul Chaudhuri (an FSU political scientist).

15. Evalyn Beck, "With a 4.0 and an Ability to Ride, He Gets the Job," *Florida Flambeau*, November 17, 1978; "Seminole Spirit Personified," *Florida Flambeau*, October 10, 1980.

16. "FSU Task Force on Seminole Symbols Formed," Seminole Mascot Materials, Box 1817, Folder 2, Mss 2008–023. FSU SC; Anthony Paredes to the Editor of the *FSView*, January 25, 1993, Seminole Mascot, Box 1817, Folder 3, Mss 2008–023, FSU SC.

17. Freddie Grooms to President Lick, Memo, January 20, 1993, Seminole Mascot Materials, Box 1817, Folder 2, Mss 2008–023, FSU SC.

18. Paredes to President's Study Group on the Use of Seminole Symbolism and Tradition, April 15, 1993, Seminole Mascot Materials, Box 1817, Folder 2, Mss 2008–023, FSU SC; Paredes to Rep. Al Lawson, March 17, 1994, Seminole Mascot, Box 1817, Folder 3, Mss 2008–023, FSU SC.

19. Spencer to Annette Lee, March 31, 1994, Seminole Mascot, Box 1817, Folder 3, Mss 2008–023, FSU SC; Douglass L. Mannheimer to Charles Erhardt, March 9, 1994, Seminole Mascot, Box 1817, Folder 3, Mss 2008–023, FSU SC; Bob Goin to All Athletic Staff, March 9, 1994, Seminole Mascot, Box 1817, Folder 3, Mss 2008–023, FSU SC.

20. James H. Melton to Freddie Grooms and Joe Dalton, September 27, 1993, Seminole Mascot Materials, Box 1817, Folder 2, Mss 2008–023, FSU SC.

21. Press Release, February 1993, "Seminole Leader to Speak, Receive Honorary Degree," Seminole Mascot, Box 1817, Folder 3, Mss 2008–023, FSU SC.

22. Tom Fields, "Cherokee Chief Determined to Set the Historical Record Straight," 1994, Seminole Mascot, Box 1817, Folder 3, Mss 2008–023, FSU SC.

23. Donna Leinwand, "Seminoles Refuse to Join Protest of FSU Mascot," *Miami Herald*, December 22, 1992.

24. Billie to Emile Whitehead, April 2, 1993, Seminole Mascot Materials, Box 1817, Folder 2, Mss 2008–023, FSU SC; "Real Issue Is Not Mascot but Instigators and Egotists," *Seminole Tribune*, April 9, 1993.

25. Billie to James H. Melton, March 24, 1999, Seminole Mascot, Box 1817, Folder 4, Mss 2008–023, FSU SC.

26. Niala Boodhoo, "FSU Nickname Not Offensive, Seminole Chief Says," *Tallahassee Democrat*, June 16, 2000.

27. Governor Jeb Bush, for example, echoed Billie by stating that "I think it is offensive to Native Americans . . . the Seminole Indian Tribe who support the traditions of FSU." "Wow Jeb! NCAA Needs to Hear This," *Tallahassee Democrat*, August 11, 2005.

28. Nancy L. Othón, "Seminoles Give Blessing to FSU Tradition," *Orlando Sentinel*, April 3, 2003.

29. Steve Ellis, "FSU Vows to Keep Name," *Tallahassee Democrat*, August 6, 2005.

30. Jim Shore, quoted in *Tampa Tribune*, August 16, 2005,

31. Donna Leinwand, "Seminoles Refuse to Join Protest of FSU Mascot," *Miami Herald*, December 22, 1992.

Looking Past the Racial Classification System

Teaching Southeastern Native Survival Using the Peoplehood Model

M A R V I N   M .   R I C H A R D S O N

Perhaps the least studied and least understood histories of Native America in the nineteenth and twentieth centuries are those of the southeastern United States. Historians and teachers tend to cover the struggles, decimation, and survival of southeastern Native peoples during the colonial and Revolutionary eras up through the era of removal, but even there the focus chiefly is on the so-called Five Civilized Tribes: the Seminoles, Creeks, Chickasaws, Choctaws, and Cherokees. These tribes held vast swaths of land and retained a significant political, military, and economic presence in the Southeast. They signed treaties and secured government-to-government relationships with the United States.[1] Though this history is much more nuanced than teachers often have conveyed in classrooms, we at least have the tools and resources to follow the history of these tribes from contact to the twenty-first century.

Unremoved tribal groups in the Southeast have largely been left out of this conversation due to their small populations, loss of communal lands, cultural change and adaptation, and the lack of historical government-to-government relationships with the United States. Most importantly, they have been made invisible due to the South's imposition of a Black/White binary and the racial classification of many Native southerners as non-Native. But if we look past the racial classification system imposed on southeastern Native peoples and listen to their voices, what emerges is a powerful story of survival, adaptation, and resilience.

As a Haliwa-Saponi Indian of northeastern North Carolina, I bring my life and academic experiences to the classroom so that unremoved southeastern tribes remain an integral part of Native and American history. I explore how and why the Haliwa-Saponi Indians endured a social and legal system that denied their separate racial and ethnic identity as Indians by imposing a Black/White binary and White supremacy. I explain how Haliwa-Saponis maintained a separate Native identity despite these hardships and impositions. They have done so by continuing what scholars such as Tom Holm, J. Diane Pearson, Ben Chavis, and others call "peoplehood."[2] My work relies heavily on oral histories so that the voices of the Haliwa-Saponi people and other unremoved southeastern Natives are heard and respected. I use primary sources to gauge and understand the worldview and motivations for historical action of Natives and non-Natives alike. Genealogical tools and resources are important for describing the racial classification system at play in the lives of many southeastern Indians, but also for explaining how they maintained autonomous communities. Finally, presenting the story of the Haliwa-Saponi Indians contributes to knowledge about both the diversity and commonality of the Native experience in the Southeast and propels so-called marginalized peoples into the conversation about Native identity, politics, and culture in the nineteenth and twentieth centuries. Using episodes in Haliwa-Saponi history, this chapter demonstrates how and why to use these tools and methods to understand and teach the history of little known southeastern Native peoples.[3]

Genealogy is one of the most useful methods to describe and teach the complications of race and to demonstrate resiliency and the maintenance of community autonomy. In North Carolina and many other southeastern states Native peoples lost or abandoned their communal lands and became individual landowners, renters, laborers, or squatters. In the process their identity as Natives was challenged. Nonreservation Native peoples were classified as "free persons of color," as early as the 1790 census, for example. Without knowing or describing the history of Native land loss, one would assume that these "free people of color" were free Blacks and emancipated slaves. Resources such as court records, land deeds, marriage bonds, and military papers, however, allow us to reconstruct these communities and show how Natives maintained their peoplehood despite losing their communal lands and legal identity.

Both communal and individual landowning Natives protected their lands and used similar strategies to maintain them. For example, the Cherokees (as well as other southeastern tribes) adopted American-style governments to demonstrate their "civilization" and to protect their lands from encroachment, and they even proved willing to use US courts to affirm their sovereignty. They mostly were removed nonetheless.[4] Prominent and educated leaders, such as Cherokee Chief John Ross, led these engagements on behalf of their people.[5]

Though Haliwa-Saponis owned their property legally and individually, it did not stop Whites from swindling them for their lands. They, too, used the court system to seek relief. John Richardson, a Haliwa-Saponi ancestor, should be viewed in much the same light as John Ross in his actions to protect his land. In 1795 the Halifax County sheriff arrested Richardson for allegedly harboring an escaped slave belonging to a local White man named William Brinkley. Richardson offered bail to secure his release, but the sheriff refused and Richardson was left a prisoner overnight and into the next day in the care of Brinkley. To Brinkley the only thing that would satisfy the misdeed was land. Under "circumstances of confinement and terror" Richardson deeded one hundred acres to Brinkley, and the sheriff let him go. After Brinkley died a few years later, Richardson successfully sued Brinkley's heirs in Halifax County Superior Court and recovered his land.[6] That he owned the land individually should not take away from the importance of him protecting the land not only for his family but also for the community at large. The Richardsons and other large Native landowners provided the land for their peoples' livelihood and protected their territories to maintain their way of life and autonomy.

In the classroom teachers can describe how and why Native peoples lost communal lands and draw useful comparisons between removed southeastern peoples and those who remained. Most removed southeastern Native peoples maintained communal lands until the Dawes Allotment Act of 1887 and the Curtis Act of 1898, which targeted the "Five Civilized Tribes" of Indian Territory.[7] Unremoved southeastern Native peoples, such as Haliwa-Saponi ancestors, lost or abandoned their communal lands as early as the 1720s and as late as 1800 but maintained or formed new tribal communities. Early on, Haliwa-Saponi ancestors accepted and used the Anglo land tenure system. After the American Revolution they participated in civil affairs under the jurisdiction of the state and county court system. Both unremoved and removed southeastern Natives changed and adapted to the circumstances of colonialism.

Other important events in North Carolina and southern history could seem insignificant to southeastern Native history if we rely solely on racial categorization and labeling. At the North Carolina Constitutional Convention of 1835 delegates debated the voting rights of nonwhites. For years free people of color, including Indians, voted in elections and participated in other civil affairs. Slaveholders feared slave uprisings, however, and collaboration between those free and those in bondage. To limit the political and economic power of free people of color, the delegates narrowly passed an amendment taking away their right to vote.[8] The amendment as passed ignored the ethnic diversity of free nonwhites, as well as their contributions and participation in civic affairs. Nonreservation, unremoved southeastern Natives lived with the added pressure of protecting their identities as Indigenous peoples, as well as having their rights stripped away. Race-based restrictions carried a significant burden on unremoved southeastern Natives and helped shape their strategies to maintain autonomous communities or to seek better opportunities elsewhere.

Oral traditions of these important and tragic events continued in the memory of both those who stayed and those who left. George W. Hillyard, a Native of Halifax County whose family removed to Indiana, remembered that a large group of people left the state because "they passed a law down there that all free born people and the mixed bloods would have to get out inside of 90 days or they would be put back into slavery."[9] Though in actuality these laws did not apply to Indians unless they had been enslaved, his statement nevertheless represents the spirit of terror and confusion over race-based restrictions in the South. During an era when Haliwa-Saponi ancestors tried to regain recognition as Indians through the US Court of Claims, Alfred Richardson Jr. remembered that it was difficult because "from the year 1835 to 1865 we had no one to vouch for us and by being cut Short from all our privileges." Part of the privileges had to do with participating in civil affairs as they had done before. As late as 1944 community leader P. A. Richardson remembered how "after the restrictions of 1835 in North Carolina, many [Indians] emigrated on ox carts and wagons . . . to the State of Ohio, and a large settlement was made near Chillocotha [*sic*], Ohio."[10] It is important for instructors to use and teach about the oral traditions and use primary sources of southeastern Native peoples, because they provide voice and perspective. These Native peoples may not have been forcefully removed but left for principles and reasons felt across their communities: encroachment of lands by Whites, restrictive laws and policies based on racism and ethnocentrism, and lack of autonomy and access to justice through government.

Events from the late eighteenth and early nineteenth centuries highlight the importance of race and genealogies in understanding, narrating, and teaching the story of surviving unremoved southeastern Indians. Few contemporary records describe community members as Indian, but through genealogy, historical research, and oral tradition we know that the Meadows community was and still is a community made up mostly of Native descendants. Marriage and land records clearly show that Haliwa-Saponi ancestors married (almost exclusively) other community Indians and maintained close-knit community boundaries. A look at census records from Halifax and Warren Counties, North Carolina, show clusters of families named Richardson, Lynch, Evans, Silver, Copeland, Hedgepeth, Hawkins, Mills, and others living closely together. Recovery of hidden Native histories would be almost impossible if not for the memories of tribal elders and the narratives pieced together using genealogical records.

The focus on Native voice and perspective also shows how unremoved southeastern Natives negotiated the Black/White binary and maintained peoplehood in the post-Reconstruction South through Indian-built and -controlled churches and schools. Haliwa-Saponi ancestors established Jeremiah Methodist Church and Pine Chapel Baptist Church. Even so, Meadows Indians still dealt with the intrusion of a Black/White binary, which only intensified with the introduction of former slaves into their midst. Haliwa-Saponi ancestors debated how much to cooperate with former slaves within the context of the racial binary. During and immediately after Reconstruction nonwhites finally had the legal means to pursue an education, and Haliwa-Saponis took advantage of that opportunity. Tribal ancestor Alfred Richardson Jr., for example, served as a Warren County school committeeman. In 1882, he persuaded the Warren County Board of Education to support a school in his section, and his brother Reese Richardson and family donated one acre of land to erect a school in the heart of the Native community.

Even though the school was under the "colored" school system, the Indians tried their best to control the school for use of the Indian people. When the county sent a former slave to the school to teach, parents withdrew their students until an acceptable teacher was appointed.[11] Eventually, however, Indians lost control of the school. Not only were African American teachers employed, but Haliwa-Saponis were ostracized for being Indian.

Haliwa-Saponi history and the decisions made by many unremoved southeastern Natives were affected both by the White supremacy campaigns of the Progressive Era and the "vanishing policy" (a term created by historian Tom Holm) enacted toward American Indians. During the late nineteenth and early twentieth centuries southeastern Natives dealt with White insistence on industrialization and change while limiting nonwhite economic progress and civic participation. Reformers during the Progressive Era had "an assumption of the superiority of their new, modern culture over rural culture—or over the culture of southern blacks" and other racial minorities. Reformers acted in a contradictory manner since "they were fervent advocates of democracy, yet also endorsed measures of coercion and control."[12] The federal government enforced the vanishing policy "to integrate an Indigenous group into the colonial socioeconomic structure," according to Holm.[13] To Haliwa-Saponis and other unremoved Natives of the South, "integration" held several connotations. It could mean that racial segregation was expected, that ethnic differences among nonwhites were nonexistent, and that Native labor and resources could be exploited.

In the Meadows, Indigenous integration and the vanishing policy merged with the arrival of Fosburgh Lumber Company, which brought hundreds of non-Native workers and created a town to support the infrastructure of the lumber industry. Fosburgh executives had established a railroad by 1906 and by November 1908 had bought rights-of-way and timber rights from Meadows residents. They moved their main camp to the Meadows community to exploit the huge timber resources of the area. By 1916 Fosburgh had established the town of Hollister near the lumber mill. Outsiders described the Meadows community as "uncivilized." African Americans also placed a tremendous strain on the established school systems, thereby threatening to erase the distinctiveness of the community.[14]

Oral traditions and obscure documents allow us to demonstrate how Meadows Indians, when faced with an influx of outsiders, took actions to maintain control over their establishments and to draw a distinction between themselves and African Americans. In 1912 longtime community leader Norman L. Keen asked the Halifax County Board of Education to consolidate the schools of the Pine Chapel district, which the Meadows Indians controlled.[15] The request was an effort to maintain autonomy in light of the hundreds of outsiders in the community. Because of drastic changes to their social and economic lives, Native leaders instructed families how to maintain their identity as Native peoples. Inez Lynch recalled that her grandfather T. P. Lynch told her and her siblings, "you know you are nothing but just an Indian people." Lynch told the children, "when you go to school we want you to be nothing but an Indian child."[16] Native children practiced social avoidance and used social restrictions to portray a distinct identity as Indigenous within a social system that legally ignored ethnic differences among nonwhites. Regulating relationships with outsiders was a powerful method for Haliwa-Saponis (and other unremoved Indians) to maintain their autonomy as Native peoples. Instructors and teachers can use examples like these to draw contrasts and similarities between the experiences of unremoved southeastern Natives and other Indigenous peoples.

Between World War II and the 1960s Haliwa-Saponis became politically active to gain recognition as Indians. World War II was a significant time when racial minorities began forcefully to demand inclusion in the political system, equal education, and humane treatment from Whites. Haliwa-Saponis demanded the same rights but focused primarily upon challenging their racial classification as non-Natives. White draft registrars, probably judging based upon physical appearances, classified some Haliwa-Saponi people as Indian and others as "Negro" or "African." Even after they insisted upon their Indigeneity, the registrars went back and checked another race. Meadows Indians responded by writing letters to the federal Office of Indian Affairs and having meetings to strategize how to deal with the problem. Racial classification as non-Native and placement in the racial hierarchy with African Americans became an ever-growing point of contention to Haliwa-Saponi Indians.[17]

By the late 1940s Haliwa-Saponi men began holding meetings in the yards of public schoolhouses they had helped start but that were part of the "colored" school system. Local non-Natives did not support or understand the Indians' political goals, so the group moved the meetings to individual homes. John Conrad (J.C. or Johnsy) Hedgepeth and others visited homes throughout the community encouraging Native descendants to assert their identity and join the Native political movement.[18] Around 1952 Hedgepeth and others traveled to Robeson County to meet with Lumbee leaders, who served as mentors to help establish the Haliwa Indian Club by 1953. The Haliwa Indian Club found a semi-permanent home at the pack house (farm storage house) of B. B. Richardson. In the civil rights era violence was a constant threat, so the club kept armed guards to patrol the yard in case anyone wanted to disrupt their meetings. W. R. Richardson moved back home from Philadelphia and served as leader and chief of the tribe for forty-four years. He explained that the club had organized because "they were Indian blood and sometimes that they would have to accept a title that they did not agree with, but that was put up on them by non-Indians." The leaders "called the people together and told them that we were being misrepresented."[19] Membership in the club steadily grew, and the members gave donations to help correct vital records and to build a clubhouse.[20]

News of the Indian club drew the ire of local and statewide non-Natives who questioned its authenticity and whose responses promoted in policy and expression an outside expectation of Nativeness. Non-natives believed Indigenous people should have stereotypical physical features, possess arbitrarily defined Indigenous "blood," live in an Indian community, practice Native culture, and descend from a widely known "tribe." To reach their goals Haliwa leaders believed they needed to engage with outsiders' expectations and portray themselves as authentic Indians. They adopted policies such as forbidding associations with non-Natives, especially African Americans. These policies were controversial and caused a rift between families and other community members. In addition, the club researched their origins and history to provide a better explanation of the historic polities from which the group descended.[21]

Haliwa strategies to maintain a distinct identity, and the internal and external forces that shaped those strategies, demonstrate how instructors can discuss the issue of Native authenticity, expectations, and stereotypes, as well as the experiences and voices of Native peoples themselves.[22] Discuss with students how and why outsiders have those expectations about Native peoples. Then discuss what is important to Native peoples and how they have maintained their peoplehood and distinct identities. What are the points of overlap between these two perspectives? How have Native peoples responded to outsiders' views about Indian authenticity? For unremoved southeastern Natives, issues of race, the imposition of a Black/White binary, and the Natives' interactions with it through institutions such as churches, schools, and governmental structures shaped outsiders' perspectives about Native authenticity.

The Haliwa Indian Club continued its civil rights era advocacy by founding an exclusive Indian School (the Haliwa Indian School) in 1957 and an Indian church in 1958. With the help of the Lumbees and Ray Holy Elk, a Lakota man married into the Lumbee community, the Haliwas lobbied the Halifax and Warren County school boards to fund a segregated school for Native people, distinct from "colored" and "Negro" schools they long had attended. Officials questioned their authenticity and delayed supporting it, so the Haliwas funded the school operations out of their own short pockets. Their segregated school was controversial as well because it flew in the face of the *Brown v. Board of Education*. In an unexpected twist, the Haliwas proposed to fund their school using North Carolina's Pearsall Plan, which provided state funds to operate private schools. The Pearsall Plan was seen as a tactic for Whites to keep schools segregated, but Haliwa Indians turned the strategy to suit their purpose. In so doing, they gained the favor of White segregationists. Eventually, the Haliwas satisfied governmental questions of their Native authenticity and convinced Halifax and Warren Counties to fund the operation of their school, which stayed open until 1969. And when locals questioned how and why the Haliwas would continue attending "colored" churches such as Pine Chapel, the Haliwas founded the Saponi Indian Baptist Church, renamed the Mount Bethel Indian Baptist Church, in 1958.[23]

Haliwa-Saponi (and unremoved southeastern Native) activism followed patterns used by other Indigenous communities, but their motivations were different. One useful example draws from these tribes' participation in the national American Indian Chicago Conference (AICC) of 1961. University of Chicago anthropology professor Sol Tax envisioned a national movement to update the federal government's Meriam Report of 1928, which assessed the economic, health, and education conditions of Native peoples. The AICC was designed to encourage Natives to compile their own problems and propose solutions, through the *Declaration of Indian Purpose*. In a bit of controversy, Native organizations such as the National Congress of American Indians pushed to include only federally recognized tribes in the conference, but Tax insisted on the participation of all Native people, including nonfederally recognized polities and urban Natives. Before the national meeting in June 1961, the conference held regional meetings. Judge Lacy Maynor, a Lumbee, led the southeastern regional meeting held at Pembroke State College (now University of North Carolina at Pembroke). Other participating tribes included the Haliwas, Mississippi Band of Choctaws, the Waccamaw-Siouans, and several Virginia tribes. Southeastern tribes cited education, housing, and basic skills such as reading and writing as issues, but overwhelmingly they believed that racism and a lack of official recognition and classification as Indians were most important. Tribes from other regions had similar concerns but spoke in terms of sovereignty and self-determination as it relates to the federal government. By contrast, many unremoved southeastern Natives viewed sovereignty as their right to be recognized as Natives first. The AICC prompted unremoved eastern Natives to push for state and federal recognition and to better organize themselves.[24]

Because of its diverse participation and attendance, the AICC and the *Declaration of Indian Purpose* provide an excellent opportunity for students to discuss Native diversity, viewpoints, and political activism during the Red Power era. Teachers and professors should spend time sharing the political, cultural, and social history of unremoved southeastern Natives and comparing their history and contemporary status with other Natives. Why did some Native peoples reject the idea of allowing all Natives to participate? Ask students: Who or what is an Indian, and how many ways can someone be Native? Have them explore issues of genealogy, culture, kinship tribal enrollment, reservation or no reservation, physical traits, intermarriage, and governmental relationships with the United States. Next, have them read the *Declaration of Indian Purpose* and discuss what portions of the document may have represented the perspective of all Natives, and what portions may show diversity and why.[25]

Events such as the AICC encouraged unremoved southeastern Natives to assert greater autonomy to escape the social, political, and cultural shackles of the Black/White binary and gain recognition as Indians. After a lengthy period of lobbying by Chief W. R. Richardson and others, North Carolina finally recognized the Haliwas as a tribe on April 15, 1965. The tribe celebrated by organizing a small gathering that grew into an annual powwow. The powwow spurred a cultural revitalization for the tribe, including arts, regalia, dancing, history, and language.[26] Like the AICC, the powwow facilitated exchanges with tribes from all over the United States and Canada. Today the powwow is like a tribal holiday and the tribe's biggest homecoming. It is the oldest and largest powwow in North Carolina and one of the largest on the East Coast. Instructors should understand (and explain) that while the powwow is important to internal tribal identity and pride, it is also an important display of Native distinctiveness to outsiders. Each year approximately eight thousand visitors attend the powwow and have an opportunity to learn and share with Haliwa-Saponis and other Native peoples.

The political, cultural, and social activities of the Haliwa-Saponi and other unremoved southeastern Natives should be viewed as actions of Native sovereignty and autonomy. These peoples overcame the challenge of asserting their race distinctiveness before tackling recognition by the state and attempting recognition by the federal government. Unremoved southeastern Native history should be viewed as integral to the southern and southeastern Native story. In order to do so, however, we must broaden our analytic and interpretive lens to account for race, loss of communal lands, and change over time by capturing Native voices. Various resources are available to instructors to assist in their incorporation of unremoved southeastern Native history and contemporary issues.

NOTES

1. For more on treaty relationships, see the chapter in this volume by Margaret Huettl.

2. Tom Holm, J. Diane Pearson, and Ben Chavis, "Peoplehood: A Model for the Extension of Sovereignty in American Indian Studies," *Wicazo Sa Review* 18, no. 1 (Spring, 2003): 7–24. The Peoplehood Matrix provides an excellent model to examine, understand, and teach Indigenous survival. According to its creators, the peoplehood model consists of four interrelated and intertwined elements: language, sacred history, place/territory, and ceremonial cycle. These four interwoven factors are universal for all tribes and are equally important in the matrix; they "make up a complete system that accounts for particular social, cultural, political, economic, and ecological behaviors exhibited by groups of people indigenous to particular territories" (12).

3. This essay relies heavily on Marvin M. Richardson, "Racial Choices: The Emergence of the Haliwa-Saponi Indian Tribe, 1835–1971" (PhD diss., University of North Carolina at Chapel Hill, 2016).

4. For more on removal issues, see the chapter in this volume by John P. Bowes.

5. Duane H. King provides a good summary of Cherokee removal and the issues surrounding it. See King, "Cherokee in the West: History since 1776," in *Handbook of North American Indians*, vol. 14, *Southeast*, ed. William Sturtevant and Raymond D. Fogelson (Washington, DC: Smithsonian Institute Press, 2004), 354–72.

6. John Richardson vs. Estate of William Brinkley, 1798 Halifax County District Superior Court Minutes, Court of Equity, 1797–1805. 1798: 25–31: Friday, May 4, 1798.

7. Donald L. Fixico, "History of the Western Southeast since Removal," in *Handbook of North American Indians*, vol. 14, *Southeast*, 166–68.

8. The amendment read: "No free negro, free mulatto, or free person of mixed blood, descended from negro ancestors to the fourth generation inclusive (though one ancestor of each generation may have been a white person,) shall vote for members of the Senate or House of Commons." *Journal of the Convention Called by the Freemen of North Carolina to Amend the Constitution of the State: which assembled in the City of Raleigh, on the 4th of June, 1835, and Continued in Session Until the 11th Day of July Thereafter*, 98.

9. George W. Hillyard, "To Whom This May Concern," Eastern Cherokee Applications of the U.S. Court of Claims, 1906–1909, Eastern Cherokee Application, RG 123, Roll 0272, Application #34532.

10. P. A. Richardson, "To Whom This May Concern," 1940, Haliwa-Saponi Indian Tribe, Hollister, North Carolina.

11. Haliwa-Saponi Petition for Federal Acknowledgment, 112. For more information see the Haliwa-Saponi website, https://www.haliwa-saponi.org/.

12. William A. Link, *The Paradox of Southern Progressivism, 1880–1930* (Chapel Hill: University of North Carolina Press, 1992), xii.

13. Tom Holm, *The Great Confusion in Indian Affairs: Native Americans and Whites in the Progressive Era* (Austin: University of Texas Press, 2005), 2.

14. Richardson, "Racial Choices," 107–12.

15. Halifax County Minutes, Board of Education, October 7, 1912, 26.

16. Inez Lynch, interviewed by Marvin M. Richardson, December 4, 2000, Haliwa-Saponi Indian Tribe, Hollister, North Carolina.

17. Richardson, "Racial Choices," 129–44.

18. Jesse McGee, interviewed by Marvin M. Richardson, October 19, 2017, Haliwa-Saponi Historic Legacy Project, Haliwa-Saponi Indian Tribe, Hollister, North Carolina.

19. W. R. Richardson, interviewed by Helen Maynor Scheirbeck, September 20, 1977, Helen Maynor Scheirbeck Papers, UNC Chapel Hill, Southern Historical Collection Number 05526.

20. Richardson, "Racial Choices," 146.

21. Richardson, "Racial Choices," 149–67.

22. Related issues—along with the appropriateness of Native mascots—are explored in the chapter in this volume by Andrew K. Frank.

23. Richardson, "Racial Choices," 158–75.

24. Richardson, "Racial Choices," 178–86.

25. *Declaration of Indian Purpose: The Voice of the American Indian*. Proceedings of the American Indian Chicago Conference, University of Chicago, June 13–20, 1961, https://eric.ed.gov/?id=ED030518.

26. Richardson, "Racial Choices," 194–96.

FOR FURTHER READING

Adams, Mikaëla M. *Who Belongs? Race, Resources, and Tribal Citizenship in the Native South*. Oxford: Oxford University Press, 2016.

Bates, Denise E., ed. *We Will Always Be Here: Native Peoples on Living and Thriving in the South*. Gainesville: University Press of Florida, 2016.

Klopotek, Brian. *Recognition Odysseys: Indigeneity, Race, and Federal Tribal Recognition Policy in Three Louisiana Indian Communities*. Durham, NC: Duke University Press, 2011.

Lowery, Malinda Maynor. *Lumbee Indians in the Jim Crow South: Race, Identity, and the Making of a Nation*. Chapel Hill: University of North Carolina Press, 2010.

Lowery, Malinda Maynor. "On the Antebellum Fringe: Lumbee Indians, Slavery, and Removal." *Native South* 10 (2017): 40–59.

Oakley, Christopher Arris. *Keeping the Circle: American Indian Identity in Eastern North Carolina, 1885–2004*. Lincoln: University of Nebraska Press, 2005.

Osburn, Katherine M. B. *Choctaw Resurgence in Mississippi: Race, Class, and Nation Building in the Jim Crow South, 1830–1977*. Lincoln: University of Nebraska Press, 2014.

Teaching Native American Religions and Philosophies in the Classroom

BRADY DeSANTI

Teaching Native American religious beliefs and practices affords a unique opportunity to inform students about subject matter that initially will strike many as both intriguing and incomprehensible. Students are often oblivious to the diversity and sophistication of the hundreds of tribal nations and cultures in Native North America. Their initial assumptions regarding Native religions tend to reflect two stereotypes: (1) Indigenous religions represent exotic and "primitive" superstitious holdovers from earlier eras in human history; and 2) they offer well-intentioned but unrefined "hippie"-type platitudes about nature and "Mother Earth."[1] Neither accurately represents Indigenous realities. With care and reasonable intellectual lifting, your students can develop a better understanding of Native traditions and epistemologies ("ways of knowing") regarding the natural world, its inhabitants, and the cosmos. In so doing they will gain greater respect both for historical nuance and for contemporary Native peoples and issues.

Due to the large number of Indigenous nations in North America, I intentionally limit this chapter to those traditions and communities with which I have extensive experience. I focus on general spiritual and philosophical ideas and upon connections between diverse traditions that I have found most useful to emphasize in class.[2] Specifically, I examine the biases historically displayed by Western academia toward Indigenous spiritualities, some significant features of creation stories, and the concept of interrelatedness. I conclude by offering suggestions for teaching about sacred lands and sites.[3]

Given the complexity and sensitivity of this material, I feel it prudent to say a few words regarding my own background. I am an enrolled citizen of the Lac Courte Oreilles Ojibwe Nation and maintain an abiding interest in my heritage. I was also adopted and made connections with Ojibwe relatives in my late teens. While I continue to learn about Ojibwe and other Native traditions, I do not claim to be a master of Ojibwe practices. I make a conscious effort to conduct myself responsibly when discussing them, which means being honest with my peers and students about who I am.

My background provides an important reminder that teachers should approach Native students about this subject with sensitivity and honesty. Native students often bring different life experiences and levels of cultural knowledge to class. I do not single them out to provide "expertise" to their colleagues but readily welcome their contributions, particularly if we are covering their traditions. In my experience, respecting one's position within this field and allowing Native students to share and reflect in accordance with their own comfort level results in a satisfying learning experience for everyone. One should never assume that because someone is Native that they automatically know everything about their culture or wish to share it publicly. This holds true for teachers like me. We are capable of articulating general philosophical beliefs about Native religions but make no claim of authority as to how they should operate within the "lived experiences" of Native medicine people and Indigenous communities.

Early Scholarly Misappraisals of Native Religions

The renowned twentieth-century Lakota scholar Vine Deloria Jr. once noted, "Anthropology has taken the values and institutions of Western civilization, acted as if they represented normality, rationality, and sanity, and leveled severe criticism of tribal societies, finding them lacking in the rudiments of civilized behavior."[4] His words capture perfectly the manner in which scholars once viewed Indigenous religious traditions, particularly British and American anthropologists in the late nineteenth and early twentieth centuries. Essentially, cultural evolutionary theory provided an organizing scheme through which contemporary Indigenous peoples became living fossils from an earlier stage in humanity's slow march toward "civilization." Western social scientists believed that by observing contemporary Indigenous cultures they could reveal how societies move from a state of "savagery" to one of enlightenment. Indigenous peoples would one day catch up, the theory held, but they would first need to rouse from their slumber and complete the great racetrack already trailblazed by their more advanced Western counterparts.

Western scholars applied this framework to the study of religion as well. One popular theory held that people in a savage state maintained a "primitive" form of spirituality referred to as animism: the belief that all things in nature possessed a soul. As humanity progressed from savagery to barbarism, animism gave way to polytheism (multiple gods). And as barbarians morphed into "civilized" nations, monotheism replaced polytheism. Finally, in the post-Enlightenment age many scholars have believed that science will replace religion altogether. Academia today by and large rejects this scheme, of course, but old habits die hard. A cursory look at many introductory world religions textbooks begin with Indigenous religions and end with the monotheistic traditions, suggesting a teleology moving from simplistic beliefs to the advanced monotheisms of Judaism, Christianity, and Islam. I recommend turning this arrangement on its head: beginning with the Abrahamic traditions, ending with Native spiritualities, and explaining to students the reasons for doing so.

A personal experience demonstrates how portions of these anachronistic theories often remain—even in the minds of people who should know better. A colleague from another institution at dinner a few years ago asked me what I taught. After I described my classes, this colleague questioned whether there was enough "stuff" available to teach an entire semester's worth of content. I am confident that this person meant no disrespect, but it is a testament to how thoroughly entrenched are Western stereotypes and frameworks, even in the minds of people who should know better.

A good way to begin to address these outdated ideas is to use the first day of class asking students to share whatever comes to their mind about Native religions. Emphasize to them that they do not have to worry about saying anything inappropriate, that these may be stereotypes, images, and assumptions to which they may have been exposed. I write these ideas on the board, stopping after around thirty selections. If my experience is any indication, you will find ample opportunity to categorize and discuss myriad popular misunderstandings of Native peoples and religious traditions. I also have each of my students turn in a one-page paper the second day of class sharing their own familiarity with and assumptions about Native religions. This exercise provides insight into what all students think, not just those brave enough to share their ideas on the first day. It is a great way to break the ice with your class and to help educate them on the matters outlined above.

Creation Stories

Native creation stories comprise a major element of my classes. While they share some characteristics with origins narratives of major world religions, they differ in fundamental ways. Because so many modern American students are at least somewhat familiar with the biblical story of Adam and Eve, I begin by contrasting the order in which God (Yahweh) created humans with their emergence in Native creation accounts. Without asserting the superiority of one account over the other, I highlight the unique aspects of Native stories by placing the main characteristics of each in two columns on the board. As distinctive as the Abrahamic traditions (Judaism, Christianity, and Islam) can be from one another, all three believe that humanity is God's most important, intelligent, and worthy creation, standing shoulders above other lifeforms on the planet. All three also adhere to the idea that creation happened ex nihilo, or out of nothing. Only God existed, who then proceeded to fashion the cosmos out of the darkness that sat "upon the face of the deep."[5] And while Middle Eastern creation stories (including Genesis) once were limited to local communities or nations, today most members of the Abrahamic faiths view the biblical creation narratives as universal in scope, accounting for everything in existence.

Most Indigenous origins stories also understand humanity to have been created very late in the process. Rather than interpreting this sequence as an indication of human superiority, however, Indigenous traditions make people the younger siblings of everything that came before them. I tell my students the key to understanding these traditions is to define personhood much more expansively than is commonly accepted in Western (and Eastern) societies. In most Indigenous traditions, plants, animals, stars, clouds, bodies of water, and the other manifold aspects of the natural world are understood as different types of "people," with their own inherent worth and ways of being.[6] It goes well beyond the adoration students may have for their pets, or the aesthetic appreciation they may have for nature and wildlife in general. Rather, it is an acknowledgment of the fundamental worth of "people" who came into the world long before humans. They are our elder siblings, and it is incumbent on humans to abide by a set of intricate kinship obligations toward them. When an animal was hunted, for example, its spirit was thanked for giving its life, ensuring that it and its species would continue to return and participate in a reciprocal relationship. Beyond mere sentimentality, Native people understand the order of creation as inaugurating a complex system of reciprocal kinship bonds and corresponding obligations between human communities and the rest of the natural world.

Unlike biblical creation accounts, Indigenous narratives are not intended to explain the creation of the cosmos. They do not speak for the creation of communities or nations beyond their own cultural purview. They are also traditionally told orally, which means they are understood to be "alive" with power and the ability to inform contemporary Native communities. Those tribal members designated to tell the stories know the protocols that come with being a custodian of sacred narratives. They know the appropriate times to tell the stories, and how to tell the stories.

Being "alive" with power also means that these stories are malleable. They can incorporate new experiences and developments within the life of the community, thereby keeping pace with the lived experiences of the tribe itself. What I call "mythological fluidity" allows these stories to retain their original and core meanings while simultaneously addressing the radical changes and hardships experienced during colonization.[7] An example comes from a Mandan story told by John Brave to an anthropologist during the early twentieth century. This period was a particularly difficult time for Native people, who had dealt with the loss of their lands and much of their lifeways. For example, Native religions were banned from the late 1880s through 1934 as part of the federal government's assimilationist policies. Particularly devastating to tribal peoples was the near extinction of the bison, with which they had maintained kinship ties for millennia. The introduction of cattle and other livestock brought over from Europe was not always welcomed by Native people. According to Brave, the creator made "white man's cattle." The horns were so crooked and bent out of shape they had to walk "funny." "Save those strange animals for later, for now I'll make buffalo for the Indians," God commented. European livestock devastated the crops of Native people, and this story condemns the animals brought through waves of European immigration. In another tale Brave recounted how God and "Lone Man" were out walking and came across a wolf's carcass covered in red-headed maggots. Lone Man threw the carcass and maggots across the lake, stating: "In the days to come, they'll have intelligence." Brave added additional commentary: "When you see white men, some of whom have red heads, they are descendants of those maggots. And today these white men are very intelligent, as it was promised. Today they are doing everything which seems impossible." While it is impossible to know exactly what this story references, it may be regarding the completion of the Garrison Dam project along the Missouri River, which forever altered the lives of the Three Affiliated tribes in North Dakota.[8]

As an example of a unique feature of Native creation stories, a likely intention by John Brave was to take the known consequences of White colonization on his people and project some of those consequences backward into the form of an origin narrative. He provided commentary on the creation of White people as undesirable and the introduction of cattle, which eventually offset bison populations. This demonstrates the creative ability of storytellers to incorporate recent events that impacted their communities. The stories remain "alive" so long as they can keep pace with the lived experiences of the tribe, while providing a sense of emotional agency during great hardships.

The last aspect of Native creation stories I cover with my students explores the issue of interrelatedness—how the process of creation was a cooperative endeavor by the animals and other "people" in existence before humans. Unlike creation ex nihilo, many of these origin stories begin with something already in existence. Some sort of calamity ensues, followed by the establishment of the present world. There are many possible examples to use, but an excellent one comes from the Haudenosaunee. According to their creation narrative, before the earth existed a powerful husband and wife lived in the Sky World, where a great tree resided. The tree's roots spread to all four sacred directions: North, South, East, and West. At some point, the tree fell through a hole in the Sky World, and the spirit woman fell with it. As she fell, she grabbed some of the life-giving seeds from the tree. Below her was a vast body of water inhabited by water "people," such as Turtle, Duck, Beaver, Muskrat, and Loon. The turtle offered his back for the Sky

Woman to land upon, but the other animals insisted that something more was needed. Each of the animals took turns diving to the bottom of the water to retrieve a little bit of mud to place on Turtle's back, but they all failed until Muskrat dove deep enough and succeeded in gathering a tiny ball of mud. He placed it on Turtle's back, who proceeded to create and sustain the present world. The Sky Woman's fall was stopped by two swans that flew up and carried her safely to the earth, where she proceeded to distribute the seeds, creating the first plant life.[9]

This creation story's "earth diver" motif is shared by many other Great Lakes and Eastern Woodlands communities, albeit with some distinctions due to cultural emphases. I stress to my students that the story makes no attempt to explain the existence of the earlier world. The emphasis instead is placed on the kinship bonds and cooperative efforts that took place between these different groups of people that resulted in creation. The Sky Woman, despite her great power, was dependent on the water animals' kindness and cooperation to land safely, which resulted in the creation of the earth. Furthermore, plant life depended on the water animals and the quick actions of the Sky Woman, who brought the seeds with her as she plummeted from the heavens. The lives of all "people" in the natural world, in short, are interrelated. None is superior to another.

Creation stories such as the Haudenosaunees' serve as a roadmap, charting out the proper behavior that humans would later seek to emulate. They continue to orient contemporary Indigenous peoples' behaviors toward each other and their "other-than-human" kinfolk. They remain a living, dynamic aspect of Native lifeways and offer a great entryway for thinking about the issue of interrelatedness more broadly. Indeed, just as learning how relationships originated is important, the guidelines on how to maintain them are equally crucial.

Interrelatedness

Native people understand their communities to be engaged in profound relationships of reciprocity with the lands they inhabit, the plant and animal relatives that reside on those lands, and the larger natural and cosmological forces that surround them. This is not mere sentimentality or abstraction. Phrases in Lakota such as *Mitakuye Oyasin* or the Ojibwe expression *Nindinawemaaganidog* translate into English as "all of my relations" or "all of my relatives," highlighting the holistic inclusiveness of the bonds between the human and nonhuman world. Most tribal nations have phrases in their own languages that convey similar sentiments. One of the more engaging examples of this complex set of ideas comes from the Ojibwe, which also gives teachers an opportunity to approach the topic from multiple angles and source materials.

The Ojibwe concept of *mino-bimaddiziwin* means "to live a good life." A central component is one's ability to abide by kinship obligations toward land as well as nonhuman and human relatives. A person must approach spirit beings with respect. One must also maintain balance among one's tripartite self (two souls and physical body). The first— often referred to as the ego soul—resides near a person's chest and is responsible for a person's sense of self (rational thought, reasoning, and intellect). The second is a free-floating or dream soul residing in a person's head. It is responsible for dreaming, intuition, and following one's "gut instinct."[10] Living a life exemplifying mino-bimaddiziwin means utilizing these two souls at the appropriate moments. At times, using a rational approach to a dilemma is most appropriate. At other times, listening to the wisdom of dreams or following one's intuition is necessary. Maintaining equilibrium between them is crucial, because a person's internal balance (or imbalance) extends to their external relationships.

Traditional stories starring the Ojibwe trickster figure Nanaboozho offer excellent insight into this concept. Often placed in situations where he must correctly utilize the two souls, Nanaboozho sometimes uses the wrong soul at the wrong time and place.[11] For centuries his experiences have taught Anishnaabe the importance of keeping their two souls balanced, ensuring that their other relationships are harmonious.[12] They in turn can give your students insight into the importance of inner equilibrium between the souls and the concept of interrelatedness more broadly.

Properly contextualized, another entryway into these philosophical/ spiritual ideas is for students to examine the dreaded windigo. In Ojibwe cosmology the windigo can exist as an entity that stalks the woods in the winter, preying on hunters or lost persons. It can also impart cannibalistic tendencies to human beings, especially if they (intentionally or unintentionally) eat human flesh. Essentially, an imbalance in a person's ego or free-floating souls can serve as a gauge for the likelihood that the person is (or could become) a windigo. If they have transformed, it would mean that the person is internally imbalanced and estranged from their human and animal relatives.[13]

One last example I discuss with my students regarding interrelatedness is the Navajo (Diné) concept of Hozho, which is intimately connected to the Holy Woman named Changing Woman, who played a foundational role in the creation of the Diné people. Hozho stresses the interconnectedness of all things in the universe and the need to maintain balance and harmony among all aspects of creation. When there is balance among the various facets of creation, the Diné refer to it as "Walking in Beauty."[14] I have enjoyed success in discussing this topic using Navajo physician Lori Arviso Alvord's book *The Scalpel and the Silver Bear: The First Navajo Woman Surgeon Combines Western Medicine and Traditional Healing*. One example suffices: her description of a curious disease outbreak while working for Gallup Indian Medical Center in New Mexico on the Navajo Reservation in 1993. Dr. Alvord was treating a few young and healthy Navajo patients for colds and other minor ailments when, shockingly and seemingly overnight, their conditions took a drastic turn for the worse. They died within a day or two of their appointments when their lungs shut down. The mysterious illness then spread to their relatives before moving into the wider Navajo community. Eventually, it affected non-Navajo residents in New Mexico and Arizona.

Dr. Alvord and other physicians were at a total loss as to the cause of this mysterious illness. The mainstream press began referring to it as the "Navajo Plague," which had the effect of encouraging racist stereotypes of supposedly unhygienic Indians. Looking for deeper insight into the problem, one of Alvord's Navajo friends, Dr. Ben Muneta, consulted an *hataalii* named Andy Natonabah. An hatalii is a traditional Diné healer who uses songs as medicine to heal various ailments over the course of four night ceremonies.[15] Without hesitation, Natonabah blamed the disease on too much rainfall. It was a surprising diagnosis for Western-trained physicians, given that New Mexico and Arizona are part of the arid Southwest. Natonabah explained further: excessive rainfall that year had resulted in an increased harvest of pinon nuts. Since mice and rats consume pinon nuts, the outsized harvest in turn increased the rodent population. As a result, humans came into closer proximity to rodents and their droppings. Natonabah also showed Dr. Muneta a sand painting depicting a mouse and said that the Navajo had contended with this same illness decades before this most recent outbreak. The CDC (Centers for Disease Control and Prevention) came to agree with Natonabah, determining that the illness was the hantavirus, which is spread by inhaling rodent droppings. It is an important lesson in Hozho, which stresses that all of reality is intertwined and interrelated. Impacting one aspect of creation influences the whole, and relationships between water, pinon nuts, and rodents were out of balance.

Through Alvord's anecdote students gain insight into multiple avenues for acquiring knowledge. On the one hand, Western science worked from the microlevel and discovered that the illness was the hantavirus. On the other hand, Natonabah used Hozho to understand relationships between different types of "people" in a broader sense. In the case of the hantavirus, an imbalance in rainfall adversely affected the relationships between pinon nuts, rodents, and human beings. Such observations come from developing a profoundly intimate relationship with one's homeland and sacred places.

Land and Sacred Sites

Land as "Mother Earth" remains one of the more entrenched stereotypes non-Natives ascribe to Indigenous people and beliefs. It is at best a shallow generalization. I stress to my students that Native communities relate to their lands and specific sacred sites in a deeply personal manner—expressing similar kinship connections and obligations to their homelands that they do toward their plant and animal relatives. Native communities understand their identity based upon the land and the ceremonies they conduct and participate in at certain places and times of year. Because Native ceremonies are so intricately tied to the "power of place" and the nonhuman "people" who reside on these lands, great effort is placed on performing rituals and ceremonies in areas that have been understood as sacred since time immemorial. I tell my students that this approach to land distinguishes Native religions from those within the Abrahamic family. While Judaism, Christianity, and Islam all have sacred places in their respective traditions, it is not necessary to practice these faiths in the lands in which they originated. This is not necessarily the case with Indigenous religions, where tribal communities place great emphasis on attempting to perform major ceremonies at long-held sacred geographical locations.

I also point out to students that Native traditions do not stress temporal or chronological considerations, as do Western traditions. Rather, they stress spatial considerations. For Indigenous people, *when* something occurred is much less important than *where* and *what happened*. Sites become a way of recalling local history and the ceremonial obligations placed on the community as a result. One of the best sources to learn more about this phenomenon is Keith H. Basso's *Wisdom Sits in Places: Landscape and Language among the Western Apache*. Understanding how this particular Apache community understands its homelands as a living and dynamic history book, with each place associated with a story and sacred event that is evoked through storytelling and ceremony, is enlightening and gives students an opportunity to appreciate how land is not understood by Native people in a general, romantic fashion, but through deeply intimate and specific connections.[16]

I also recommend having your students read Lakota scholar Vine Deloria Jr.'s chapter "Sacred Lands and Religious Freedom" from his book *For This Land: Writings on Religion in America*. Deloria felt that the wider non-Native public needed a way to appreciate why certain places are so sacred to Native people and how to understand the various levels of sacredness they assign to these places. He establishes four categories of sacredness (although he stresses that they are not immutable). The first regards places in which nothing supernatural occurred but are important due to historical actions. Unfortunately, these sites are often memorialized because of acts of violence—the site of the 1890 Wounded Knee Massacre, for example. Wounded Knee is sacred both to the Lakota people and to many other Native people because of that senseless slaughter as well as the occupation of the same site in 1973 during the Red Power movement. Your students can probably identify non-Indian places with similar vibes—the Alfred Murrah Building in Oklahoma City or Ground Zero in New York City, for example.[17]

Deloria's second category includes places where the sacred or holy manifested during ordinary circumstances. These sites have become the focal points of ceremonies in which a given community renewed and rejuvenated its relationship with the powers that now reside there permanently. An example may be Mato Tipila (Lodge of the Bear) in the Black Hills of Wyoming. Some Lakota traditions place Mato Tipila as the place where the Holy Woman, White Buffalo Calf Woman, revealed herself to a few hunters and gave them the sacred pipe for the Lakota people.[18] There are many other examples that could be used, too.

Deloria's third category of sacredness includes places Native people have always understood as sacred in themselves. They may not have a definitive explanation for how they became so crucial to a tribe's ceremonial life. In my classes I stress that it is not a matter of Native people declaring a place sacred because of expediency. They emphasize that certain places take the initiative and reveal their sacredness, through visions and healings that take place there. With Western traditions, it is acceptable to build a place of worship anywhere that is deemed convenient. This is not the case with Native traditions. It also is crucial to understand that these places are not deemed sacred because of their aesthetic qualities. What appears to be a barren piece of land or unattractive mountain peak may be deeply holy because of the power imbued within it.

Deloria's final category reinforces that Native people can remain open to revelation of new places and the initiation of new kinship and ritual obligations. This openness is particularly important in light of centuries of forced removals. Many sacred sites are today located off reservation lands, creating a host of access obstacles. A good example draws from the process forced upon Native southerners in the 1820s, 1830s, and 1840s. These Trail of Tears episodes severed Indigenous communities from their sacred lands and places in the Southeast. Many of their descendants recount eventually developing close relationships with their new lands in Oklahoma in large part due to their openness to the ongoing revelations so characteristic of Native religious traditions.

Native communities often find it difficult to access traditional sacred places to perform ceremonies without interference by non-Indians and federal and state authorities. Many rituals necessitate solitude and up to four days of unfettered access to the site. To highlight these issues and to give your students firsthand Native perspectives, I recommend showing them the extraordinary documentary *In the Light of Reverence*.[19] The Lakota struggle to stop recreational rock climbing on Mato Tipila is profiled, as are Hopi efforts to protect sacred mountain shrines from being used as gravel to pave interstate highways and Winnemem Wintu struggles to prevent a ski resort from destroying their sacred spring at Mount Shasta, California. These examples should lead to larger conversations about how activities such as rock climbing, oil drilling, mining, and pipelines often compete with Native ceremonies on their sacred lands.

To engage students in active learning I recommend having groups debate whether Native people should have unrestricted access to some of their sacred sites, or whether they should compromise and allow multiple use of the lands in question. I have two groups, each with four or five students, take opposing sides of the argument. Each student presents for four to five minutes on a specific sacred place, explaining why it is important to particular tribes and why the location is controversial. After these mini-presentations the groups debate their respective positions. Along with the readings and documentary, this exercise gives students an opportunity to learn about and appreciate the unique aspects of how Native people relate to land in ways that go beyond the "all land is sacred" generalities many non-Native people hold.

Land is a central component to Native traditions, but it is important to stress that the ceremonies and pilgrimages made to sacred sites cannot be separated from the larger themes of Native spiritual traditions of relationships, kinship bonds, and acts of reciprocity between humans and nonhumans. Land is not worshipped any more than are plant and animal relatives. Rather, Native people understand the land as embodying their identity and providing the frame of reference in which they engage in extended kinship bonds and play their part in upholding the principles of cosmological harmony and balance.

Conclusions

My goal in this chapter is to provide an introductory roadmap for teaching elements and expressions commonly found within Native American religious traditions. I focus heavily on the ways in which Native peoples traditionally relate to their homelands and the nonhuman relatives that inhabit those lands and with whom they enjoy kinship bonds of reciprocity. The ideas of interconnectedness and interrelatedness found within Native philosophical traditions are living teachings that remind Native peoples of their close relations with their nonhuman relatives and the land itself. Maintaining balance and harmony are not just abstract concepts; they are ever-present teachings that demand action and accountability for Native people.

By no means do I address every facet of Native religions, which would be an impossible and irresponsible task. Other scholars may emphasize different things and use different examples. I focus on what I feel has worked best for my classes and the students with whom I have worked. And due to cultural sensitivities, I deliberately omit references to healing and specific ceremonies. I would approach such matters cautiously, but they are important dimensions to Native religious traditions. Nevertheless, I hope that this chapter imparts complex ideas to fellow teachers on how to speak to students about some of the major themes found in Native American religions, particularly when the teacher may only have a few days to a week at most to cover the subject matter.

NOTES

1. I focus on Native American religious beliefs and practices in this chapter, but I also teach another course titled "Shamanism" that examines spiritualities and philosophies from global Indigenous perspectives.

2. Spatial limitations as well as the complexities and cultural sensitivities inherent in the subjects make it impossible to devote much space to another crucial element of Native lifeways: approaches to healing or to specific ceremonies.

3. Numerous definitions of religion—both good and bad—exist. This chapter explicitly avoids delving into that issue, except to say that Native traditions do not distinguish between the "sacred" (spiritual or religious) and the "profane" (ordinary, nonreligious) dimensions of life. Moreover, many Native people would disagree that their beliefs and practices constitute "religion." It is possible to mollify objections that religion only refers to formalized and organized institutions and traditions, however, which is often what troubles many Native people about the word. A good way to think about the distinction is through the Lakota expression wićoh'aŋ, which can be translated to mean "ceremony"; however, it can also refer to ways of life, activity, or tradition. This one phrase captures the holistic nature of Native religions. See Joseph Carol, ed., *Everyday Lakota: An English-Sioux Dictionary for Beginners* (St. Francis, SD: Rosebud Educational Society, 1971), 13. This meaning of wićoh'aŋ was confirmed by fluent Sicangu Lakota speakers Dr. Susana Geliga and Gary Saul.

4. Vine Deloria Jr., "Conclusion: Anthros, Indians, and Planetary Reality," in *Indians & Anthropologists: Vine Deloria, Jr., and the Critique of Anthropology*, ed. Thomas Biolsi and Larry J. Zimmerman (Tucson: University of Arizona Press, 1997), 220.

5. Genesis 1:1–2, *The Oxford Annotated Bible*, revised standard edition. The Qur'an has multiple passages referring to the fact that God "created the heavens and the earth and ordained darkness and light." *The Koran, with Parallel Arabic Text*, trans. N. J. Dawood (London: Penguin Classics, 1994), 127. It is worth noting that most biblical scholars accept that the Book of Genesis contains two different creation accounts. In chapter 1 God creates woman and man simultaneously, while in chapter 2 he creates Adam, followed by animals, followed by woman (Eve). Scholars generally agree that the two accounts were written at vastly different times in Hebraic history. See Richard Elliot Friedman, *Who Wrote the Bible* (New York: Simon & Schuster, 2019).

6. A. Irving Hallowell describes Indigenous understanding as a belief in "other-than-human persons." See Hallowell, "Ojibwa Ontology, Behavior, and

211

World View," in *Teachings from the American Earth: Indian Religion and Philosophy*, ed. Dennis and Barbara Tedlock (New York: Liveright, 1975), 145.

7. For an examination of this phenomenon involving Southeastern Native traditions, see Brady DeSanti, "'I Can Come into Your World but You Can't Come into Mine': John Swanton and Southeastern Oral Narratives," *Chronicles of Oklahoma* 94, no. 1 (spring 2016): 32–57.

8. Peter Nabokov, *A Forest of Time: American Indian Ways of History* (Cambridge: Cambridge University Press, 2002), 94–95.

9. Jerry H. Gill, *Native American Worldviews: An Introduction* (Amherst, NY: Humanity Books, 2002), 50–51.

10. Theresa Smith, *The Island of the Anishnaabeg: Thunders and Water Monsters in the Ojibwe Life-World* (Moscow: University of Idaho Press, 1995), 132–33; Christopher Vecsey, *Traditional Ojibwa Religion and Its Historical Changes* (Philadelphia: American Philosophical Society, 1983), 60.

11. A great way for students to learn about this is to have them read one of the Ojibwe creation stories where a flood ensues after Nanaboozho successfully kills the water monster. Tricksters can be found within most Native traditions. Like Nanaboozho, they are understood to be crafty spirit beings, sometimes even elder siblings to human beings. They exhibit both proper and improper behavior, and the stories told about them teach Native communities how to conduct themselves and treat the other relatives in the natural world.

12. While there are many versions of this story, I recommend having your students read the version in Theresa Smith's *The Island of the Anishnaabeg* (157–89). Smith does a masterful job of describing Nanaboozho's exploits throughout the creation narrative utilizing his two souls correctly, along with respecting the limits of his physical body.

13. Although teachers must be cautious, film and popular media can serve as good tools for teaching about the intersection of the windigo and the Ojibwe concept of interrelatedness. For more on this possibility, see Brady DeSanti, "Classroom Cannibal: A Guide on How to Teach Ojibwe Spirituality Using the Windigo and Film," *Journal of Religion & Film* 22, no. 1 (2018), https://digitalcommons.unomaha.edu/jrf/vol22/iss1/36; and DeSanti, "The Cannibal Talking Head: The Portrayal of the Windigo 'Monster' in Popular Culture and Ojibwe Traditions," *Journal of Religion and Popular Culture* 27, no. 3 (Fall 2015): 186–201.

14. Lori Arviso Alvord and Elizabeth Cohen Van Pelt, *The Scalpel and the Silver Bear: The First Navajo Woman Surgeon Combines Western Medicine and Traditional Healing* (New York: Bantam Books, 1999), 14–15.

15. Alvord and Van Pelt, *The Scalpel and the Silver Bear*, 6–7.

16. Keith H. Basso, *Wisdom Sits in Places: Landscape and Language among the Western Apache* (Albuquerque: University of New Mexico Press, 2010). It is important to note that while Basso's work has been mostly praised, Apache

scholar Martin Ball leveled some serious criticisms of Basso's findings and methodologies. I recommend having students also read Martin Ball's essay "People Speaking Silently to Themselves: An Examination of Keith Basso's Philosophical Speculation on 'Sense and Place' in Apache Cultures," *American Indian Quarterly* 26, no. 3 (Summer 2002): 460–78. This allows your students to discuss both works and obtain different opinions on this important subject matter.

17. For this entire chapter and a discussion of Deloria's four categories of sacred sites, see Vine Deloria Jr., *For This Land: Writings on Religion in America* (New York: Routledge, 1999), 203–14.

18. There are many variations on the appearance of White Buffalo Calf Woman and the introduction of the sacred pipe to the Lakota people. See Mark St. Pierre and Tilda Long Soldier, *Walking in a Sacred Manner: Healers, Dreamers, and the Pipe Carriers—Medicine Women of the Plains Indians* (New York: Simon & Schuster, 1995), 38–45.

19. *In the Light of Reverence: Protecting America's Sacred Lands*, produced and directed by Christopher Mcleod (Oley, PA: Bullfrog Films, 2002).

Sustenance as Culture and Tradition

Teaching about Indigenous
Foodways of North America

DEVON A. MIHESUAH

One might think that teaching and writing about Indigenous foods is innocuous and simple. Some of my students think exactly that when they sign up for what they believe will be an easy class. Granted, Indigenous foodways really *is* easy to teach if one provides only laundry lists of what tribes ate historically. In most "American Indian" or "Native American" history courses, what tribes ate and how they procured sustenance are usually incidental to the main topics—such as the English colonists arguing that northeastern tribes were "uncivilized" because they did not farm even though they produced millions of bushels of corn per year. Or that the decimation of bison herds by non-Indians was a purposeful act designed to deny the Plains tribes' their main food source. Then there is the romanticized First Thanksgiving. Even those instructors who stereotype that event as one big happy multicultural feast at least get one thing right, and that is to recount some of the Western Hemisphere's bounty: turkey, venison, squashes, and potatoes. There was, however, much more, including cacao, cranberries, elk, bison, tomatoes, salmon, peanuts, vanilla and manioc.

Providing students with only catalogs of flora and fauna misses opportunities for more thorough discussions about social, political, religious, and economic aspects of tribal life and Indian-White relations. The issues swirling around hunting, gathering, and growing food are complex. The production and sharing of food provided social cohesion and identity. Everyone had to eat, and in order to procure food they had to understand and respect the Natural World. Therefore, their emotional, spiritual, cultural and physical well-being depended—and still does depend—on the condition of the environment.

I am a historian, and in my writings and teachings I connect the past to the present. In any course dealing with Indigenous issues, it is crucial to remind students that Natives are not memories from the misty past. Natives are still alive, and many are suffering from food-related maladies such as diabetes, obesity, and heart disease. How did this happen, and what can be done about it? That question is the foundation of the classes I teach on Native North America and Latin America foodways. Environmental degradation, poverty, and the adoption of processed foods, in addition to the loss of knowledge of how to save seeds, plant, cultivate, and harvest according to the seasons and ceremonial prescriptions are ongoing results of colonization and have caused tribespeople to develop unprecedented health problems. Today, many Natives are attempting to revitalize foodways traditions. In order to accomplish that, they have to contend with environmental pollution, climate change, treaty rights, racism, and impoverishment. Teaching about foods and health, therefore, requires a complex meshing of social, economic, political, religious, environmental, and ethical topics.

Colonialism has shaped the attitudes of tribal groups in the United States toward food and eating, and the relationship between ethnicity, religion, culture, and food choices offers many opportunities for classroom discussion. There is a difference, however, between an introductory course and upper-division and graduate classes in which students are expected to have prior knowledge of Native North American tribes, ethnobotany, and nutrition. What follows is for an upper-division course for students without background knowledge of Indigenous peoples. Still, discussions and research assignments require critical thinking. Some aspects are controversial, and not everyone in the classroom will agree. For a course on Indigenous foodways, there is a plethora of topics to address:

- how the influences of social, economic, cultural, religious, environmental, and psychological factors have affected the attitudes of

tribal groups in the United States toward food, eating, and the
environment;

- the relationship between ethnicity, religion, culture, and food choices
and respect for the natural world;
- historic diets of tribes, including cultivation of crops, hunting and
fishing methods, food preparation, and seed preservation;
- policies and ideologies that caused the cultures to alter their ways of
eating, resulting in health problems and environmental degradation;
- challenges to food sovereignty and food security;
- strategies for health recovery, including traditional ways of governance, a return to egalitarianism (so women have more of a say about
food and meal preparation), language recovery, and the use of oral
traditions to maintain cultural knowledge and pride.

The *course description* might look something like this:

This class will spur discussions about how the significant differences in
tribal foodways and interactions with the natural world relate to tribal
cultures, beliefs, religions, gender roles, economies, worldview, and
environmental changes. Because tribes historically did not suffer from
the obesity, high blood pressure, diabetes, and related maladies that
they do today, this course necessarily explores the connection between
good health and traditional ways of eating, and the effects of colonization on how modern Indigenous peoples procure and prepare foods.
This class will examine changing cultural influences and environmental
degradation on health and nutrition among the various tribal peoples of
the US. In so doing, the methods used to examine tribal foodways will
enable students to explore their own ancestries and the impact of socio-
economics, religion, politics and identity have on their attitudes toward
foods, eating, and the environment. This course is multidisciplinary in
approach. Lectures will mesh archival data, oral testimonies from tribal
individuals, and scientific data in order to present more complete versions of the past.

The first day of my classes begins with discussion about terminology.
Students need to understand commonly used terms such as colonialism,
multi-heritage, mixed-blood, full-blood, progressive, minority, majority, ethnobotany, food justice, sovereignty, food sovereignty, food sustainability. A key term used throughout the course is "traditional"

food. Does that refer to precontact times or last week? Restaurants such as the Smithsonian's *Mitsitam* Native Foods Café, cookbooks, and online recipe sites feature Indigenous dishes, but the majority of ingredients are not from this hemisphere. This is important when considering tribal foodways, because many refer to popular non-Indigenous foods, such as unhealthy frybread, as "traditional." Warning: discussions about frybread can become heated and personal.[1]

Often tribes are designated agricultural, hunter, or gatherer. That is a misnomer. Many tribes were mainly agriculturalists but also hunted and gathered. Hunters mainly utilized game, but they also foraged and sometimes planted gardens. Comanches were hunters, for example, but they also gathered wild foods and traded (and raided) for agricultural crops such as corn, squash, beans and melons.

What They Ate

Prior to colonization peoples of the Western Hemisphere had access to a vast array of edible flora and fauna in mountains, deserts, rivers, lakes, oceans, and forests. A way to make an impression on students about the importance of these nutritious foods is to discuss how they changed the rest of the world. In 1492 the European population was approximately 70 to 88 million. By 1900 it had exploded to 435 million.[2] Better health care and awareness of sanitation accounted for some of this rise, but corn, potatoes, manioc, sweet potatoes, and peanuts provided calories and nutrition.

Several class sessions provide overviews of where tribes lived and what they ate based on the resources available to them. The geographical areas I use are the Southwest, Northeast, Old Northwest (or Great Lakes), Alaska, Canada, California and Northwest, Plateau, Northern and Southern Great Plains, Arctic, Southeast, Indian Territory, and Hawaii.[3] Within these areas, however, tribes are culturally different, and there are multiple ecosystems that determined how the people lived. For example, California supplied Natives with a plethora of flora and fauna and supported hundreds of thousands of people. The environment ranges from mountains, deserts, coasts, rivers, lakes, valleys, and extreme heat and cold. Those who gathered acorns spent days preparing the nuts to eat, and it was in many cases a necessary social activity. Around the San Francisco Bay area, Costanoans speared fish and gathered shellfish, insects, fruits, acorns, and honey. They also killed seals and whales.

Tribespeople historically ate foods that many students have not tried. For example, peoples of the Southwest often consumed insects, and today insect consumption is common in Mexico. They ate offal—that is, brains, entrails, kidneys, tongue, and marrow—animal parts that many people in the United States consider undesirable because they have access to other cuts of meat. There are exceptions, of course, and mentioning those exceptions help students understand the importance of those foods. For example, ingredients in hot dogs span the spectrum of animal parts. More restaurants offer expensive organ meats as haute cuisine entrees. Many families use turkey giblets in their Thanksgiving gravy, and liver and onions remains a popular dish. Menudo (tripe stew) remains a staple in many Latino homes.

A subheading in this section is how tribes acquired foods. Corn, for example, is considered a major food plant of tribes in the Northeast, Southwest, and Southeast. It was developed from a grass called teosinte about seven thousand years ago and then spread north from Mexico.[4] Today, tribes grow several kinds of corn: dent, flint, flour, pop, and sweet. Chile peppers, many kinds of squashes, and sunflowers also originated in Mexico. Tribes organized trade networks throughout the continent to acquire resources from various environments.

This section also includes what tribes adopted from the colonizers.[5] Choctaws in the Southeast, for example, utilized pigs brought by the Spanish in the 1500s. After the tribe's removal to Indian Territory, they continued to raise pigs, and pork became a daily ingredient for many families. Navajos adopted European sheep, and even their religious stories changed to incorporate the animals that came to symbolize sustenance and wealth. Many Cherokees, Choctaws, and Chickasaws used homemade gardening tools and rabbit sticks, ate traditional corn-based dishes such as *tamfulla* and *sofkey*, and eschewed European foods such as wheat, barley, and rye. Others integrated non-Native materials (manufactured tools and clothes), methods (gristmills, muley cultivators) and medicinal concoctions learned from Black slaves into their cultural repertoire. Still others, especially some Cherokees, had already abandoned traditions while living in the east; they were acquisitive, owned slaves, wore Victorian fashions, and made significant profits from cattle ranching. Assimilated Cherokees and Choctaws, at least, have referred to traditional tribal dishes as "peculiar" and folk cures using medicinal plants and ceremonies as "mythical doctoring." However, some of these acculturated individuals occasionally consumed traditional food and consulted with spiritual leaders when they became ill or injured.[6]

Importance of Place

Homeland is where tribes believe they emerged, the site of ceremonies, resources, animal and plant foods, and medicinal plants. Where one's ancestors lived determine one's identity. The loss of those homelands, because the tribes were forcibly driven out or removed, was and still is disastrous for tribes and is a major factor in mental and physical health problems today. Being removed from one's homeland means one has been taken away from the site of worship, burial sites, and medicinal plants and foods. *Indigenous knowledge* is the basis for local decision-making about fundamental aspects of day-to-day life, such as hunting, farming, gathering, seed saving, fishing, water, health, and adaptation to environmental change. Indigenous knowledge includes codes of conduct for how to behave as a member of the group. A tribe's traditional Indigenous knowledge defines that community's uniqueness and explains its relation to the world. This knowledge is maintained and developed by peoples with long histories of close interaction with the natural environment of their homeland. Tribes needed to understand the seasons and weather patterns in order to hunt and farm success-fully. Tribes followed their own calendars—often thirteen months—that included ceremonies corresponding with the seasons.[7] Seed saving was crucial to tribes' survival. If they had nothing to plant, then there was nothing to cultivate. Saving seeds meant that those plants that had adapted to a particular environment would continue to procreate. Today there are 150 crop plant species, whereas there used to be at least 7,000. Without great diversity, food plants are much more susceptible to dis-ease, insects, and climate changes.

Women and Tribal Foodways

Tribes spanning the Western Hemisphere had complex creation stor-ies that in large measure included female deities that brought food to the people and ceremonies to celebrate the seasons, planting, harvest-ing, seed saving, and meal preparation. Since interacting with Euro-Americans much of the Indigenous knowledge related to foodways has been lost because of cultural disconnect or has been purposefully ignored because Natives perceive that the "old ways" are archaic and inferior to mainstream society's mores. For example, in the Northeast, women of the Iroquois tribes held substantial power within the tribal structure. Women cultivated the corn fields. Elder women, also known as Clan Mothers, controlled and divided the agricultural goods. They owned what they harvested and then determined the value of the corn in trade. After contact, however, European men refused to negotiate with females, and women's roles faded. Indeed, across Indigenous America, the status of women diminished as male power increased. Missionaries dedicated themselves to making sure tribes understood God was male and females were subservient to men. Cherokee women also were the farmers, but they were moved inside from the fields and were taught to weave, and men took their places outside.[8]

Tracing the Decline of Health

Colonization has affected tribal cultures in myriad ways. Some were positive. Colonizers brought new plants (oat, rye, barley, asparagus, garlic, and so forth) and animals (cattle, sheep, goats, chickens, pigs) that altered the social construction of Indigenous culinary practices, beliefs, and traditions. However, colonization has been devastating to tribes from loss of tribal land and sacred sites; a disconnection from their cultures, their ties to land, and the natural world; and cessation of a diet of unprocessed natural foods acquired by hunting, gathering, or cultivating. Food-related diseases developed after contact, and diabetes exploded around the 1950s.[9] Indigenous peoples are also suffering from cancers not only because of their choice to smoke commercial tobacco products but also because of environmental influences.

Boarding Schools

Loss of Indigenous knowledge is devastating to tribal societies. When one teaches about oppressive boarding schools, that is also an opportunity to discuss how the curricula caused a disconnect with their cultures that taught them ceremonies about food and how to hunt, fish, and gather. Government-run boarding schools in the nineteenth and early twentieth centuries punished Native children who spoke their tribal languages and prohibited their participation in ceremonies and their communicating with tribal elders who could teach them cultural mores (i.e., customs and traditions), including foodway traditions. Consequently, they lost the ability, or even the desire, to save seeds, cultivate plants, and hunt game. This "Boarding School Syndrome" also affects subsequent generations who learned from boarding school survivors that the "white way" is the best way, including eating nontraditional, processed foods. And boarding schools, such as the Cherokee Male and Female Seminaries, fed students nontraditional fare such as white flour, sugar, candy, and fats, resulting in serious food-related health problems.[10]

Environmental Issues

One of the most dangerous effects of our industrialized society is climate change and the detriment to the environment. This environmental damage is inexorably linked to humans' physical and mental well-being. Plants and animals have disappeared or are endangered, and many ecosystems have been destroyed or imperiled by pollution, damming, overgrazing, erosion, deforestation, invasive flora and fauna, and development. Genetically modified plants and animals are now commonplace, and tribal crops are endangered from pollen and pesticide drifts. Fracking in Oklahoma and pipelines such as the Dakota Access Pipeline and Diamond Pipeline potentially threaten multiple waterways, ground water, and soils.[11] The loss of pollinators such as bees, moths, butterflies, wasps, hummingbirds, and flies threatens the survival of fruits and vegetables.

Indigenous Food Sovereignty and Food Sustainability

Modern Indigenous peoples are suffering from diabetes, obesity, high blood pressure, and related maladies. It is not only because they lost traditional knowledge necessary to plant, cultivate, and save seeds. What tribes want is to recover food sovereignty, including sustainable agriculture and cultural educational programs, but there are significant challenges in creating a self-sufficient food system and reconnecting tribal members with their traditional foodways. Many Indigenous people cannot access fresh foods, much less culturally connected ones, because of federal policies, treaty abrogation, climate change, environmental degradation pollution, racism, and poverty.[12]

Indigenous food sovereignty is a common phrase we see today, but there is no agreed-upon meaning. This lesson requires analysis of the term "sovereignty" and discussion of the challenges to tribes producing and distributing their own food.[13] Treaties are legally binding contracts between tribes and the federal government. They are declarations that promise self-determination, health care and educational services, religious freedom, and rights to hunt and fish. The federal government is required to protect tribal treaty rights, tribal lands, and resources. Treaties agreed upon and signed by the federal government and the tribes guaranteed—depending on the arrangement—food, shelter, clothing, lands, or education and farming monies. Any discussion about the challenges of food sovereignty and food justice for tribes necessarily includes an understanding of the relationship between tribal, federal, and state jurisdiction and Indian self-determination. Discussions about food sovereignty will include tribal food initiatives, such as stores that stock culturally relevant foods, community and backyard gardens, large farms to feed the entire tribe, bison ranching, heirloom seed distribution, and economic development.

Health Care

Historically, tribal doctors (that is, medicine men and women) treated physical and emotional ailments. Ceremony was a part of the rituals, as were flora and fauna with medicinal properties. Many Indians still prefer the treatment of medicine men and women, although they also seek treatment from non-Indian physicians. Many Native students have experiences with Indian Health Service (IHS) hospitals and clinics, but what they do not know are overall health statistics within tribal nations. Food related issues such as diabetes, obesity, and tooth decay require medical treatment, but so do other maladies tribes face—alcoholism, drug abuse, and emotional problems. The section on Indigenous health care meshes with the question of whether tribes can achieve food sovereignty. The topic offers an opportunity to debate the question "Are foods medicine or are they preventatives?" Can eating right, being physically active, and caring for the environment reduce your risk of diabetes, obesity, and cancers? Because of the costs of health care, this is an important question. Also, there is a need for more Native health care professionals, and discussions can spur students to explore careers in the fields of health and nutrition.

222

Activities

Food Tastings

I bring food samples for students most class periods, including cacao nibs, dark (90 percent) and milk chocolate, boiled flint, flour and sweet corn, blue corn tortillas, venison (white-tailed deer and elk), chili pepper slices, grilled nopales (prickly pear cactus paddles), wild and domestic turkey, crickets and mealworms (farm-raised from Educational Innovations), and a variety of Indigenous and introduced Latin fruits (grilled plantain, mango, papaya, breadfruit). Students have shared nettle tea, dandelion honey, and cattails. In my Latin American foodways course, I have many more foods from which to choose. Warning: Check with your university about distributing food products.

Diet Documentation

Have students keep a diary of what they eat for one week and determine how many calories and which nutrients each meal contained. In combination with a lack of exercise, diets of sugary, salty, and fatty foods has created tribal nations of overweight and unhealthy Natives. Many of my students have been surprised to discover the unhealthiness of their daily routines.

Term/semester projects give students an opportunity to focus on a topic of importance to them. Examples include

- History of a tribe's health and food
- History of your culture's food (traditional foods and how they are used today)
- How Indigenous women are strengthening food economies
- Environmental health issues as related to food
- Slow Food movement
- Challenges to achieving food sovereignty
- Indigenous protests of pipelines
- Controversies over genetically modified plants
- Successful tribal health initiatives
- Challenging the food industry
- School food and health curriculums
- Problems with the Indian Health Service

- How diets of specific tribespeoples were altered because of colonization
- Strategies for health recovery of a certain tribe (recovery of agricultural techniques, tribal health efforts, etc.)
- Food in fiction, film, and art
- Traditional foods cookbooks with photographs.

University Connections

Many students who enroll in my Indigenous foodways courses are interested in agriculture, nutrition, and cooking. Any related initiatives, organizations, clubs, and projects on university campuses related to foodways, environmental and plant protection, and food sustainability reinforces what they learn in class and inspires them to complete their degree. At the University of Kansas, for example, there are opportunities for students to connect with the Center for Sustainability, the Native Medicinal Plant Research Garden, the School of Pharmacy Medicinal Plant Garden, Monarch Watch, Kansas Biological Survey, the student-led environmental advocacy group Environs, KU Farm Hands, and the American Indian Health and Diet Project.

Traditional and modern tribal foodways are complex topics. In order to impart information to students, anyone who teaches such a course needs to explore the vast amount of information in the fields of history, anthropology, literature, religion, law, political science, and nutrition. This is a crucial topic and should be taught more. Food is a necessary part of Indigenous concepts of decolonization, empowerment, and nation building.

There are myriad books, articles, blogs, and websites pertaining to the course topics. I have only listed a few.

NOTES

An earlier version of this chapter appeared in *Recovering Our Ancestors' Gardens: Indigenous Recipes and Guide to Diet and Fitness* by Devon Abbott Mihesuah and is reproduced here by permission of the University of Nebraska Press. Copyright 2005 by Devon Abbott Mihesuah.

1. See Devon Mihesuah, "Indigenous Health Initiatives, Frybread, and the Marketing of Non-Traditional 'Traditional' American Indian Foods," *Native American and Indigenous Studies* 3, no. 2 (Fall 2016): 45–69.

2. Russell Thornton, *American Indian Holocaust and Survival: A Population History since 1492* (Norman: University of Oklahoma Press, 1990).

3. Teachers can find an extensive compilation of plants used by tribes for food, medicine, dyes, and so forth in Daniel E. Moerman, *Native American Ethnobotany* (Portland, OR: Timber Press, 1998). There also is an online database at Native American Ethnobotany, http://naeb.brit.org/.

4. Betty Fussell, *The Story of Corn* (Albuquerque: University of New Mexico Press, 2004).

5. While his interpretation of disease epidemics is dated, for the broad contours of the "Columbian Exchange" see Alfred Crosby, *The Columbian Exchange: Biological and Cultural Consequences of 1492*, 30th anniversary edition (Westport, CT: Praeger, 2003). For more on disease epidemics, see the chapter in this volume by Tai S. Edwards.

6. Where does one obtain this information? I utilize eighteenth- and nineteenth-century diaries, journals, sketchbooks, and reports of travelers, Indian agents, ethnographers, and military personnel who made observations of flora, fauna, and terrain. The Oklahoma Natural Heritage Inventory links plants and animals to specific historical habitats. Tribal census records itemize tribal citizens' lands and resources, and surveys at the Oklahoma State Archives detail the Tribal Nations' topography, vegetation, bodies of water, and soil types. See Devon A. Mihesuah, "Sustenance and Health among the Five Tribes in Indian Territory, Post-Removal to Statehood," *Ethnohistory* 62, no. 2 (April 2015): 263–84.

7. See, for example, Choctaw seasons at "Choctaws and a Cornucopia of Food," American Indian Health and Diet Project, http://www.aihd.ku.edu/foods/choctaw.html.

8. Devon Mihesuah, *Indigenous American Women: Decolonization, Empowerment, Activism* (Lincoln: University of Nebraska Press, 2003), 41–61.

9. Centers for Disease Control and Prevention, "Native Americans with Diabetes," *Vitalsigns*, January 2017, https://www.cdc.gov/vitalsigns/aian-diabetes/.

10. Devon Mihesuah, "Historical Research and Diabetes in Indian Territory: Revisiting Kelly M. West's Theory of 1940," *American Indian Culture and Research Journal* 40, no. 4 (2016): 1–21.

11. For more on environmental issues, see the chapter in this volume by Paul Kelton and James Rice.

12. Devon Mihesuah, "Searching for Haknip Achukma (Good Health): Challenges to Food Sovereignty Initiatives in Oklahoma," *American Indian Culture and Research Journal* 41, no. 3 (2017): 9–30.

13. Kyle Whyte's multiple writings about sustainability and food sovereignty at Michigan State University, https://kylewhyte.seas.umich.edu/articles/; Alfred Taiaiake, "Sovereignty," in *A Companion to American Indian History*, ed. Philip J. Deloria and Neal Salisbury (Malden, MA: Blackwell, 2004), 460–74.

For Further Reading

American Indian Health and Diet Project, "Choctaws and a Cornucopia of Food," http://www.aihd.ku.edu/foods/choctaw.html.

American Indian Health and Diet Project, "Foods Indigenous to the Western Hemisphere," http://www.aihd.ku.edu/foods/western_hemisphere.html.

American Indian Health and Diet Project, "Medicinal Plants Used by the Five Tribes in Indian Territory," http://www.aihd.ku.edu/health/MedicinalPlants oftheFiveTribes.html.

Centers for Disease Control and Prevention, "Native Americans with Diabetes," https://www.cdc.gov/vitalsigns/aian-diabetes/.

Environmental resources, https://kylewhyte.seas.umich.edu/articles/.

"From Garden Warriors to Good Seeds: Indigenizing the Local Food Movement," https://gardenwarriorsgoodseeds.com/.

Intertribal Agriculture Council, Technical Assistance Program, https://www .indianag.org/technicalassistance.

Native Food Systems Resource Center, *Gather: The Fight to Revitalize Our Native Foodways*, http://www.nativefoodsystems.org.

Nutritional Value of Insects, "Are Edible Insects More or Less 'Healthy' Than Commonly Consumed Meats?," https://www.ncbi.nlm.nih.gov/pmc/arti cles/PMC4781901/.

Seed Savers Exchange, "Our Mission," http://www.seedsavers.org/mission.

Shakopee Mdewakanton Sioux Community, "Seeds of Native Health: A Campaign for Indigenous Nutrition," http://seedsofnativehealth.org/partners.

University of Arkansas School of Law, Indigenous Food and Agriculture Initiative, "About Us: Meet Our Team," http://Indigenousfoodandag.com/about -us/.

Anderson, M. Kat. *Tending the Wild: Native American Knowledge and the Management of California's Natural Resources*. Berkeley: University of California Press, 2013.

Guarino, Julia. "Tribal Food Sovereignty in the American Southwest." *Journal of Food Law and Policy* 11 (Spring 2015): 83–105.

Hoover, Elizabeth. *The River Is in Us: Fighting Toxics in a Mohawk Community*. Minneapolis: University of Minnesota Press, 2017.

Jordan, Julia A. *Plains Apache Ethnobotany*. Norman: University of Oklahoma Press, 2008.

Kimmerer, Robin Wall. *Braiding Sweetgrass: Indigenous Wisdom, Scientific Knowledge and the Teachings of Plants*. Minneapolis: Milkweed Editions, 2015.

Kindscher, Kelly. *Medicinal Wild Plants of the Prairie: An Ethnobotanical Guide*. Lawrence: University Press of Kansas, 1992.

LaDuke, Winona. *Recovering the Sacred: The Power of Naming and Claiming*. Chicago: Haymarket Books, 2016.

Mihesuah, Devon. *Recovering Our Ancestors' Garden: Indigenous Recipes and Guide to Diet and Fitness*. Lincoln: University of Nebraska Press, 2020

Mihesuah, Devon, and Elizabeth Hoover, eds. *Indigenous Food Sovereignty in the United States: Restoring Cultural Knowledge, Protecting Environments, and Regaining Health*. Norman: University of Oklahoma Press, 2019.

Milburn, Michael P. "Indigenous Nutrition: Using Traditional Food Knowledge to Solve Contemporary Health Problems." *American Indian Quarterly* 28, nos. 3–4 (2004): 411–34.

Minnis, Paul E. *People and Plants in Ancient Eastern North America*. Tucson: University of Arizona Press, 2010.

Minnis, Paul E. *People and Plants in Ancient Western North America*. Tucson: University of Arizona Press, 2010.

Salmon, Enrique. *Eating the Landscape: American Indian Stories of Food, Identity, Resilience*. Tucson: University of Arizona Press, 2012.

Wall, Dennis, and Virgil Masayesva. "People of the Corn: Teachings in Hopi Traditional Agriculture, Spirituality, and Sustainability." *American Indian Quarterly* 28, nos. 3–4 (2004): 435–53.

Native American Art 101

NANCY MARIE MITHLO

There is considerable disagreement in Native arts circles about what constitutes an Indigenous arts practice and theory. Some of this confusion originates in the academic disciplines that have historically laid claim to or rejected Native arts, namely anthropology and art history. It is not uncommon today to see displays of American Indian arts within a natural history context. One of our field's leading artists, Allan Houser (a member of my tribe), was at the height of his career in 1992 when he was famously exhibited at the Natural History Museum of Los Angeles County along with the stuffed bison, not in the Los Angeles County Museum of Art as he anticipated.[1] This categorization of American Indian art tells us much about the reception of American Indian intellectual knowledge systems in non-Native settings.

This confusion about the place of Indigenous arts is echoed throughout the history of museums, especially in the United States, where anthropologists collected American Indian materials under the assumption that the race was "vanishing."[2] For American Indian graduate students wishing to work in American Indian arts, advisers typically recommended careers in the fields of museum studies and anthropology in order to have access to collections of Native materials housed in anthropology and history museums. The problem with this approach is that the discourses and methodologies of anthropology were starkly different than the connoisseurship of fine arts, even given the great "museum turn" of inclusion in the 1990s.[3] This disciplinary rift remains contested, resulting in uneven scholarship and widely divergent research and exhibition practices.[4]

While it is easy to assert that a multidisciplinary approach might serve the scholarship needs of American Indian art studies, it is not so simple in practice. Consider for a moment the vast difference between the Western concept of curation, as in "to care," and the Zuni equivalent of curation, which connotes disintegration. In the Zuni philosophy, to take care of an object means to let it erode naturally in the open elements of wind and sun.[5] Of course, Zuni scholars and museum professionals understand mainstream curatorial mandates to protect objects using environmental controls. The community, however, also retains the authority to treat their own ceremonial objects in the manner in which they choose, which may be by exposure to the elements. These diametrically opposed values of conservation expose a divergence of deep philosophical values.[6] For Zuni ethnologist Ed Ladd, the time frame of conservation is considered over thousands of years, not simply a few generations. In this ontology of thought, it is foolish to try to keep an object the same over a thousand years, as objects by their nature decay over time. Why, then, pretend that one could stop that natural process? Why not embrace it? These opposing philosophies are indicative of what Vine Deloria Jr. termed "absolute conflict" between Western and Indigenous value systems.[7]

This chapter does not attempt to dissuade the reader from adopting a multidisciplinary or even a disciplinary-specific lens. Rather, what I am suggesting is that educators prioritize a coeval and contemporaneous interpretation that incorporates Native voices while advancing the thesis that Native arts are essential tools for learning Native culture. The recognition of living cultures should be complemented by a frame that considers a holistic thematic, such as family and tribe, land and dislocation, commercialization and internal consumption or conceptions of gender. These interrelated and tangled topics lend themselves to student participation and encourage an investigative attitude that rejects the standard frames of geography, medium or era-driven research, and writing. heather ahtone, senior curator at First Americans Museum (FAM) in Oklahoma City, describes an Indigenous aesthetic as one in which a complex sociocultural community is recognized by using art as a mnemonic reference to understanding traditional values. In other words, the arts are an instrument for transmitting cultural knowledge.[8]

This chapter employs a research methodology known as American Indian Curatorial Practice, defined as work that is long-term, mutually meaningful, reciprocal, and with mentorship. First articulated at a Ford Foundation seminar at the University of Wisconsin in 2008, this methodology has been adopted for educational publications and exhibit practices both nationally and globally.[9] A long-term academic project necessarily means that educators do not strive to address in a survey manner the arts of a dozen tribes, each articulated by geographic region. This type of descriptive analysis tends to alienate student interest. A far more effective approach is to craft a syllabus around "defining moments of conflict," meaning addressing central tensions, events, and themes such as artist biographies, portraiture, relationships to land, or the spirituality of dance.[10]

Framework

American Indian Curatorial Practice, defined as mutually meaningful and reciprocal, signals the importance of community-based learning pedagogies. Tribal resources available in print publications or on the web are more readily available today than even twenty years ago. Tribal nations commonly provide their own data on dedicated websites authored by their nations, and tribal museums dedicated to interpreting the arts are numerous. Many museums with large holdings of American Indian materials host online research tools in addition to extended resources such as interviews and videos via their educational resource offices. The Smithsonian National Museum of the American Indian, for example, has free online lessons and resources that tie objects to makers and cultures.[11]

For an example of how educators might take advantage of these types of resources, consider Cherokee ceramicist Anna Belle Sixkiller Mitchell (1926–2012), known for revising the art of Cherokee pottery. Mitchell experienced the loss of Cherokee language and culture as a boarding school student. When asked by her husband to construct a pipe similar to the one that Cherokee leader Sequoya used, she embarked upon a decades-long process of discovering how to make Cherokee ceramics. An online video of Mitchell produced by the Cherokee Nation contains interviews with the artist and demonstrations of not only how the clay is processed, but also how it is viewed as a living entity.[12] This contemporaneous material can be linked to the ancient history of mound cultures by using the online catalog *Cherokee Pottery, People of One Fire* (produced by the Cherokee National Historical Society), which features a timeline stretching back 4,500 years.[13] This bridging of contemporaneous nationhood with continuous traditions demonstrates the longevity of American Indian culture, knowledge, and artistic practice.

The frames traditional and modern create a false dichotomy and should ideally be avoided. While chronological comparisons may seem innocent enough, these mutually exclusive categories have expanded to describe inaccurately and unevenly the content of artwork, the rendering of the work in terms of medium and method, and even the intent of the work. While appearing simply to describe the time an object was manufactured, overuse of the term "traditional" has resulted in an ill-defined concept that has wrought much harm by justifying a number of flawed conclusions including notions of authenticity and aesthetic worth. Artist and curator Jaune Quick-To-See Smith explains: "Authentication is an imperial rationalization for increasing or decreasing value. Terms such as contemporary, traditional or modernist have mixed meanings and are tossed around with abandon depending on each writer's personal notions."[14] Often the terms "traditional" and 'modern" are used as easy tools for novice writers and educators to try and grasp the complexity of American Indian arts in a shorthand fashion. Scholar and artist John Paul Rangel states, "The dichotomous taxonomy of 'traditional' and 'contemporary' utilized in interpreting Native art results in a reductive privileging of the non-Native voice and authority on what constitutes the field."[15]

With the advent of the internet and online resources, there are more opportunities for Native-led publishing including magazines, brochures and catalogs, and blogs. Cherokee Nation artist and publisher America Meredith established style guidelines for *First American Art Magazine* that mandate the avoidance of these terms altogether. "Do *not* pair the terms *traditional* and *contemporary*; they are trite and create a false dichotomy. Find more precise pairings, e.g., *historical* and *contemporary,* or use new terms that aren't clichés. Minimize the use of *tradition* and *traditional* due their vagueness and overuse."[16]

Educators should employ the same high-level standards (cross-referencing, referencing of primary and secondary sources, transparency of their own subjectivity, and clarity of scholarly purpose) in American Indian art studies as any other field. Be aware of the quality of resources referenced, the time frame in which the work was produced, and the audience for which it was intended. Do not be fooled into citing whatever resources are most readily available; be resourceful. Jaune Quick-To-See Smith advises: "Learning or knowing about this art is the same process as discovering a New York Euro-American artist. One must read the reviews, the critical writing and the monographs. This is the issue that isolates contemporary Native art and keeps it in the dark. There is a scarcity of monographs, critical writing and certainly no encyclopedic cataloging of who these artists are. Their work is a hidden treasure within the mainstream art world."[17]

Interpretation

Having established certain guidelines and values, let us consider the interpretation of Native arts for an unversed audience. I begin with one of the founders of the American Indian art movement from the last century, Chiricahua Apache artist Allan Houser (1914–1994), who was mentioned in the introduction to this chapter. Houser was the first child born free from the tribe's twenty-eight years as prisoners of war, or more appropriately described as political prisoners indefinitely detained (1886–1914). Of his career Houser stated: "I was twenty years old when I finally decided that I really wanted to paint. I had learned a great deal about my tribal customs from my father and my mother, and the more I learned the more I wanted to put it down on canvas. That's pretty much how it started."[18] Houser lived in an era when American Indians lacked basic rights as citizens, such as the right to vote, receive integrated public school instruction, or own individual property. His choice to depict his own culture as beautiful, intact, and thriving was a revolutionary act. Although he experienced racism in overt and covert ways, Houser devoted his career to filling the American imagination with new images of Indian people who loved their children, who bravely fought for their rights, and who enjoyed the simple pleasures of dance and song. This creation of an alternative universe for the unversed viewer simultaneously served the needs of American Indian peoples to see themselves in a positive light—thriving, well, and happy.

Houser's *Apache Crown Dance* (1953) is a masterpiece in demonstrating tribal cohesiveness, cultural specificity, and the expression of human joy. Small details of family and community are present everywhere—the two dogs to the upper left side of the frame, sniffing each other hesitantly, one with a paw tentatively raised; the small child to the right of the frame who stretches at his father's grip, eager to run while his father remains engaged in a serious conversation; the old man limping at the top, leaning against his cane; two boys in the foreground chasing each other with hardly a stitch on while most of the adults have

232

Apache Crown Dance by Allan Houser, 1953. Photo courtesy of Allan Houser, Inc., copyright Chiinde LLC.

shawls and blankets wrapped around themselves for warmth. These endearing details of community life are clearly read across cultures. While the term "universal" has so often been used as a tool to erase cultural distinctions and flatten inequities, we can say with confidence that almost any viewer could find warmth and compassion for those depicted.

The challenge for the unversed viewer is to withhold or delay other readings of the work—particularly the dancers, the clothing, and the dwellings depicted, all of which contain specific cultural and religious values rooted in deep ancestral knowledge. In a study titled "Seeing American Indians," funded by the National Endowment for the Arts, I, along with my co-researcher cognitive scientist Aleksandra Sherman, authored an approach to interpreting Native culture that recommends the viewer pause and embrace uncertainty prior to formulating any conclusions.[19] This approach to interpreting art directly conflicts with standard interpretive models such as the Visual Thinking Strategies (VTS) approach to learning about art that is widely incorporated in many (if not most) museum educational departments.[20] VTS does not interpret the unique cultural registers of religiosity, social standards, and non-Western aesthetic appreciation that are demonstrated so clearly in

Houser's drawing. A program cofounded by cognitive psychologist Abigail Housen to foster aesthetic development, VTS asks only three questions when viewing a work of art: *What's going on in this picture? What do you see that makes you say that? What more can we find?*

The teacher remains nonintrusive and keeps the discussion moving only by repeating the questions, paraphrasing the answers, and linking remarks. The assumption in this approach is that any art may confidently be interpreted without supporting contextual data. VTS's aim to "support aesthetic growth" is far from the goal of most Indigenous artists, who wish to retain cultural knowledge and to enhance the strength and resilience of Indigenous communities.[21] Curator heather ahtone states, "Every time an Indigenous artist creates an object that reflects concepts rooted within her culture this same artist is perpetuating that culture one more day as an act of self-determination." She observes: "Their survival can be partially attributed to the continued production of the visual and performance arts. As long as Indigenous people continue to use the arts to reflect unique experiences within a contemporary society, they are fundamentally breathing life into these cultures."[22]

Houser "breathes life" into community by seamlessly sharing a visual narrative of Apaches as intact, happy, and safe. These simple human experiences were unavailable to the generations of his family that had experienced genocidal efforts to eradicate our tribe.[23] Houser's *Apache Crown Dance* is a remarkable testimony to our way of life, with men and women participating in the beauty and power of dancers and singers while their babies nurse and children sleep. It is a magical moment, revolutionary in its simple insistence on humanity and joy. As aesthetically pleasing as this canvas is, the joy of survival and the layers of meaning behind the dancers are unavailable to the unversed public. This magic will not come about from a universalistic Visual Thinking Strategy. Redeeming this image in all of its complexity requires that the viewer admit they do not know the purpose of the dance, why the people dress that way, or how their homes are constructed. In short, they have to delay interpretation and accept that not all knowledge is available to them, not only because of their lack of background but also because not everything is shared.

To refuse to share is a right of any person, but this right takes on particular significance when considering the imperialist histories of the United States against the Indigenous inhabitants of North America. Artists are well-versed diplomats. They can tell something visually that can be read in multiple ways by audiences with very different knowledge systems at play. For a tourist in Santa Fe or a visitor to the Autry Museum of the American West, *Apache Crown Dance* could easily engender reactions such as, "The Apaches were warlike people, you know Geronimo." It is a typical response from an uneducated audience rooted in the all-pervasive Western value of freedom of knowledge. If Houser had said, "I will not tell you about the beauty of White Painted Woman and the Gaan dancers because I do not want you to know," a negative reaction would likely follow. Anthropologist Audra Simpson states, "To speak of limits in such a way makes some liberal thinkers uncomfortable, and may, to them, seem dangerous. When access to information, to knowledge, to the intellectual commons is controlled by the people who generate that information, it can be seen as a violation of shared standards of justice and truth."[24]

The refusal to share particular knowledge is not a rejection of intellectualism as much as it is a refusal to share knowledge that one is fairly certain the recipient cannot process. An analogy might be what a parent decides to share with a child, saying "someone got hurt" rather than stating an individual was murdered. *Apache Crown Dance* is a depiction of a blessing ceremony with the Mountain Spirit dancers, a sacred event. Houser does not say too much, however, which leaves the viewer with a number of choices. They can research what our dances look like, they can attend a dance, or they can start a long conversation with a tribal historian. As Simpson states, "Rather than stops, or impediments to knowing, those limits may be expansive in what they do not tell us."[25]

To redeem the VLS method of artistic interpretation, then, one would have to add another question to the standard "What is going on here?" and "What do you see that makes you say that?" The question "How would I find out more?" offers an expansive vision to complement the acceptance of a lack of knowledge. It is difficult for a person of the modern world to state they do not know something. For many researching American Indians, this may be a shameful or guilt-ridden space: "I should know something about Native Americans and I do not. I live as a settler in a land that is not mine. I thought that by simply looking at Native art or even buying Native art, I could assuage this guilt." Guilt does not wash out easily. Critical race and cultural studies scholars Eve Tuck and K. Wayne Yang remind us to slow the impulse of those who wish to alleviate the impacts of colonization: "Yet, this joining cannot be too easy, too open, too settled. Solidarity is an uneasy, reserved, and unsettled matter that neither reconciles present grievances nor forecloses future conflict. There are parts of the decolonization project that are not easily absorbed by human rights or civil rights–based approaches to educational equity."[26] The American Indian Curatorial Practice norms (long-term, mutually meaningful, reciprocal and with mentorship) encourage slow-learning, deep curiosity, mutual respect and a comfort with not knowing.

Photography provides another excellent medium for deploying this form of interpretation. Ho Chunk photographer Tom Jones is known for his sensitive and evocative portraiture. Jones's series Strong Unrelenting Spirits is part of a continuing body of work that documents his own community. Jones states:

> Through the use of portraiture I am giving both the tribe and the outside world a perspective from someone who comes from within the community. I have incorporated the beading of traditional floral designs directly onto the photograph, in order to give a symbolic representation of our culture. I am interested in broadening the conversation of portraiture in mainstream art and to present a nation that is generally unseen in popular culture.[27]

Portraiture is a rich genre to explore Indigenous arts in a classroom setting. The medium of photography is one that all students relate to given the rise of the smart phone, social media, and "selfies." In terms of scholarly literature, the portrait raises questions about authority and control. Who is in charge, the sitter or the photographer? There is a vast amount of interest in photographs of Native people yet often less interest in how American Indians photograph themselves (students should not confuse images of American Indians with American Indian art). Native self-portraiture is growing, and Jones's work finds a solid presence in the larger field of Native photographers, many of whom respond to the legacy of prior non-Native photographers.[28]

Like Houser, Jones works to mitigate the damage done by popular culture icons of Nativeness, what I term "conventional narratives" (rather than stereotypes, which are problematic, densely packed, and solely negative interpretations).[29] Jones does more than simply substitute positive images for those that disparage. His work actively engages with Indigenous aesthetics. What is an Indigenous aesthetic? Is it something one can see visually, or is it solely present only in the process and intent of Native arts?

The photo of Pendalton Price shows a young man gazing upward in a highly meditative and almost reverent gaze. His physical attributes, the tattoos, black T-shirt, denim work apron, skull cap, and piercings, identify him as a contemporaneous person. The food thermometer in his pocket gives evidence of his status as a manual laborer, in this case working for his father, who runs a barbecue restaurant. The addition of the floral beadwork used by Ho Chunk people to embellish their regalia challenges and complicates the everyday quality of the photo. Many unversed viewers might ask, "Is this American Indian art?" Within an American Indian studies lens, one might pay attention to the cultural icons that accompany the sitter. These indicators of belonging could take several visual forms, such as the type of clothing, body adornment, or background. Are these accruements consistent with the lives of the subject, or do they appear as props? Alternately, one might try to assess the relationship between the sitter and the photographer by the prevalence or absence of eye contact or posture.

Jones's work exceeds these more obvious physical attributes by incorporating three opaque variables. First, one must consider the manner in which he selects and communicates with his subjects. He restricts his portraiture to his own community in and around Black River Falls, Wisconsin. This deliberate choice positions his oeuvre in a social world to which he is responsible and liable in rich and compelling ways. Referencing American Indian Curatorial Practice, his work is long-term, mutually meaningful, reciprocal, and with mentorship. Second, once photographing, his manner is informed by noninterference. His photographic practice is noncontrolling. He does not instruct the sitter how to dress or pose, aside from the unavoidable need to adjust for correct lighting. This noninterference betrays a social attribute commonly associated with Indigenous peoples that is viewed as a means of ensuring group unity and cohesion.[30]

A critique of non-Native photographers is often based on the fact that they photograph Native peoples using interference tactics, for example, telling someone what to wear or how to look.[31] In the context of American Indian peoples being photographed by non-Native photographers, the potential for an exertion of power and abuse is always present. Jones's methodology of taking portraits of only his community and not posing his subjects are Indigenous registers of practice. Finally,

Portrait of Pendalton Price by Tom Jones, 2017, from the series Strong Unrelenting Spirits. Photo courtesy of Tom Jones.

Jones's addition of beadwork to the surface of the print encodes specific Ho Chunk signifiers for religious and metaphysical power. These overt marks are rich with interior meaning and place the whole composition in an inescapably Ho Chunk frame of analysis.

Scholar Richard Brilliant concludes that portraits whose references are intentionally socially enabled are no longer really portraits but so-called ethnographic portraits. He explains, "The subjects are so often

238

ignored as subjects of portraiture or they are strongly subordinated to other agendas of representation."[32] Such duality of the individual and society runs counter to an Indigenous interpretative model in which individual autonomy is highly valued alongside a higher communal good. While generalizing what constitutes an "Indigenous value" is always suspect, these diametrically opposed viewpoints—the portrait as an individualistic subject or as an expression of larger social values—are instructive. The self/collective divide inherent in the portrait provides a rich framework from which to debate representations of race in photography.

But what of three-dimensional objects? In the late nineteenth century Cahuilla basket weaver Juana Apapos of the Soboba Reservation in Southern California created a piece known as the *Milky Way*. The basket was featured in the Autry Museum of the American West's exhibit *California Continued* that opened in 2016. Los Angeles public television station KCET's video *Tending the Wild* accompanied the exhibit. The online image and description of the basket in concert with the full KCET video available online gives students access to rich cultural interpretations of the Autry Museum collections, including explanations of Traditional Ecological Knowledge (TEK). What is TEK? In *Tending the Wild*, biologist Liz Roth Johnson summarizes:

> We can see the natural world as something to exploit or we can see the natural world as something to keep precious and protect. In both of those cases, humans are separate from nature. Traditional Ecological Knowledge is a different perspective of knowing a place or knowing the natural world. TK is not just information; it is how people do things. It's how people practice their culture. How you do and collect material for a basket. It's how you actually go fishing or set up your society in a particular place.[33]

A discussion of Traditional Ecological Knowledge can enhance an appreciation of Native arts made from natural materials by addressing environmental concerns.

We know that the diamond pattern on the basket is a reference to the galaxy Milky Way, but what exactly is the Milky Way?[34] Educators can productively draw from scientific resources provided by NASA in addition to American Indian resources that convey the complexity of Indigenous science (such as AISES, American Indian Science and Engineering

Society). Native knowledge of astronomy is historically rich, as the stars and planets provided navigation tools, indicated the timing of planting and hunting seasons, and served as a mnemonic device for origin stories.

Consider the date of the manufacture of the basket—over a hundred years ago. How might people have collected deer grass and sumac at that time? Do students think that the environment in Southern California has changed over this period of a hundred years? What was the Soboba Reservation like at that time? Cultural resource management records, including studies conducted for development projects in Southern California, are rich repositories of historic data. A report completed in 2014 and presented to the city of San Jacinto (the city nearest the Soboba Tribe) for consideration of a levee project, for example, identifies a "cottonwood grove of traditional cultural value" as a potential "historic property" as defined by the National Historic Preservation Act and a potential "historical resource" as defined by the National Register of Historic Places and the California Register of Historical Resources. The cottonwood grove was demonstrated to have cultural importance by researchers, who observed that "it is reportedly the physical embodiment of the Luiseño practice of collecting tree mushrooms that grows on dead or dying cottonwood trees, known as shakapish in the Luiseño language, as well as other materials gathered from live cottonwood trees for medicines, rattle handles, stick game pieces, and ramada frames." The report concludes that this particular cottonwood grove is especially important because of the way land was cleared for agriculture, residential development, and levee construction along the river. According to the authors, "it is that remnant of what was once a dominant part of the landscape that has dwindled greatly over the last 100 years."[35]

Drought, wildfires, overpopulation, and environmental warming are all critical topics that impinge on the access to materials used to make baskets and the ability of weavers to sustain their practice. Advocacy groups such as the California Indian Basketweavers Association (CIBA) make the general public aware of the fragility of the California ecosystem, particularly in terms of access to materials needed for this art form and of the dangers of pesticides that may damage the health of basketmakers. CIBA's mission is to "preserve, promote and perpetuate California Indian basketweaving traditions while providing a healthy physical, social, spiritual and economic environment for basketweavers."[36] Land sovereignty should be a central component of any educational discussion of Native basketry, making this cluster of resources particularly helpful in approaching the topic in a socially and politically aware manner.

When the *Milky Way* basket was chosen for the *California Continued* exhibition at the Autry Museum, an interview was conducted with cultural consultant Lorene Sisquoc, a member of the Fort Sill Apache Tribe of Oklahoma and a descendant of the Mountain Cahuilla. Sisquoc's comments reference a historic interview with Soboba basketmaker Juana Apapos by writer and collector George Wharton James (1858–1923). Students can use online Autry Museum collection resources to further research the work of James, Apapos, and the Soboba community. In the process, they will gain insight into cultural resource management, archival studies, oral histories, and library sciences, fields that are increasingly central to the study of American Indian arts.[37] A high-resolution scan of a hand-written Soboba Day School newsletter from 1893 is available in the Autry Museum Collections (object ID MS.1268) documenting the daily life of the community.[38]

Sisquoc states of the *Milky Way* basket:

> The basket here was made by a Cahuilla basket weaver Juana Apapos. She was a well known weaver, created many, many beautiful baskets. The one here today is the Milky Way. Milky Way is very significant for our people, for many tribal people, as that's where we go when we pass away, to telmikish. When you see the designs that look like a net or the diamond patterns, a lot of time that represents the Milky Way. We were fortunate enough that Mrs. Apapos was interviewed, and she was able to tell a little bit about those baskets and what they meant.
>
> In her interview, she talked about how she would lay there at night and look up to the sky and look at the Milky Way knowing her ancestors are up there she wished she could join them because things were so bad down here for her people. One thing she said was that she would look down upon the people here that are doing harm to her people and she would wish bad on them. I was surprised at that because we were always told we had to weave good thoughts; but it was so hard back then, the times, the changes, and everything that was happening. You can just feel her feelings in that.[39]

This compelling narrative presents an evocative question. If a cultural mandate is to do no harm or not think bad thoughts while creating a basket (similar to the discussion of noninterference above with the work of Tom Jones), how could a revered artist "wish bad on" the people doing harm to her people? Teachers and students should ask what Sisquoc means by "doing harm to her people." What exactly is the history of Indigenous peoples in California?

The legacy of colonization in California is now accepted as a cultural genocide. UCLA historian Ben Madley documents how California's Indian population plunged from approximately 150,000 to 30,000 from 1846 and 1873 due to state and federal policies of violence, relocation, and starvation.[40] A "war of extermination" was declared at the time of statehood, with state money used to arm local militias to slaughter Native Americans.[41] Despite this horrific history, today California is home to the largest population of Native Americans in the United States with 109 federally recognized tribes.[42]

Conclusions

The general American consciousness continues to distort and submerge the history and present conditions of Native Americans. In the arts, as in the other subdisciplines of American Indian studies, there are endless avenues of research where educators can learn more and do better. The resources are more easily available than ever, but what is often missing is the willingness to "speak the hard truths of colonization," as historian Amy Lonetree reminds us.[43] Artist Erica Lord suggests that we question our preconceived knowledge. "Whether change comes from Natives who hold leadership roles or from our friends and family," she argues, "it will take an intelligent and conscious analysis of our own colonized minds, understanding and critiquing our own preconceived notions, characters, and stereotypes."[44] The arts are an accessible way to learn more in an expansive and inclusive manner. Especially in an era where hybridity, movement, and incessant change blur previous intellectual approaches, the arts can serve as a means of holding conflicting knowledge, of delaying conclusions. As Lord states, "To sustain a genuine self, art becomes my means, creating a world in which I can shift and become one or all of my multiple visions of self."[45]

This chapter advocates a contemporaneous interpretation that incorporates Native voices, with an acceptance that Native American arts are essential tools for understanding Native American cultures. A holistic approach, fueled by curiosity and self-guided open research, involves methodologies that can empower students and teachers to create their own templates for learning. The American Indian Curatorial Practice mandate of doing work that is long-term, mutually meaningful, reciprocal, and with mentorship can help guide these explorations.

NOTES

1. "Allan Houser: A Life in Art," touring exhibition, Museum of Fine Arts, Museum of New Mexico, Santa Fe, 1991–1994," listed in "Allan Houser Chronology," New Mexico History, State Records Center & Archives, http://newmexicohistory.org/people/allan-houser-chronology. Also confirmed in personal communication with Allan Houser Incorporated agent David Rettig via email communication on September 29, 2017: "His 1991 retrospective organized by the Museum of New Mexico traveled to the Los Angeles County Museum. As it was related to me, Allan assumed that it would be at the Los Angeles County Museum of Art. As the exhibition dates approached, he was informed that it would be in the Los Angeles County Museum of Natural History [Natural History Museum of Los Angeles County], about which he was very disappointed. I believe this was 1993. It started in Santa Fe, jointly hosted by the Fine Arts Museum and MIAC. It also went to the Eitlejorg and the University of Oklahoma and was at the Palm Springs Desert Museum when Allan passed away in 1994."

2. George W. Stocking Jr., *Objects and Others: Essays on Museums and Material Culture* (Madison: University of Wisconsin Press, 1988).

3. See Steven D. Lavine, *Exhibiting Cultures: The Poetics and Politics of Museum Display* (Washington, DC: Smithsonian Institution Press, 1991).

4. See "Facts and Resources: Jimmie Durham," *First American Art Magazine*, June 8, 2017, http://firstamericanartmagazine.com/facts-resources-jimmie-durham/.

5. Nancy Marie Mithlo, "'Red Man's Burden': The Politics of Inclusion in Museum Settings," *American Indian Quarterly* 28, nos. 3–4 (2004): 743–63.

6. For a more thorough discussion see Marisa Elena Duarte and Miranda Belarde-Lewis, "Imagining: Creating Spaces for Indigenous Ontologies," *Cataloging & Classification Quarterly* 53, nos. 5–6 (2015): 677–702.

7. "A Conversation with Vine Deloria, Jr.," ca. 1978, in *Words and Place: Native Literature from the American Southwest*, University of Arizona and KUAT-TV. For the transcript see http://wordsandplace.arizona.edu/deloria.html.

8. heather ahtone, "Designed to Last: Striving toward an Indigenous American Aesthetic," *International Journal of the Arts in Society* 4, no. 2 (2009): 373–85.

9. A free online educational resource is available at my website: http://www.nancymariemithlo.com/. See the subheading under "Teaching" and click

on the link for the downloadable "Visiting: Conversations on Curatorial Practice and Native North American Art," from which excerpts are taken for use in this present essay.

10. Nancy Marie Mithlo, ed., *Making History: IAIA Museum of Contemporary Native Arts* (Albuquerque: University of New Mexico Press, 2020.)

11. "Transforming Teaching and Learning about Native Americans," Native Knowledge 360° Education Initiative, National Museum of the American Indian, Smithsonian Institution, https://americanindian.si.edu/nk360.

12. "Anna Mitchell: Grandmother of Cherokee Pottery," Cherokee Media Production for the Cherokee National Living Treasure Program, 2008, the Cherokee Nation, https://www.youtube.com/watch?v=bRiXFsgGyO4.

13. Barbara Duncan, Brett H. Riggs, Christopher B. Rodning, and I. Mickel Yantz, *Cherokee Pottery, People of One Fire* (Tahlequah, OK: Cherokee Heritage Press, 2007), www.cherokeeheritage.org/wp-content/uploads/2013/08/Cherokee PotteryCat.pdf.

14. Jaune Quick-To-See Smith, "Scattergories, the Categories Game in Native American Art History: A Commentary," in *Visiting Conversations on Curatorial Practice and Native North American Art: The American Indian Curatorial Practice (AICP) Symposium*, University of Wisconsin–Madison, Department of Art History, September 25–27, 2008, Ford Foundation sponsorship; Nancy Marie Mithlo, AICP Project Director and "Visiting" Senior Editor, "American Indian Curatorial Practice," http://nancymariemithlo.com/American_Indian_ Curatorial/index.html.

15. John Paul Rangel, "Moving beyond the Expected: Representation and Presence in a Contemporary Native Arts Museum," *Wicazo Sa Review* 27, no. 1 (Spring 2012): 31–46.

16. "FAAM Style Guide," *First American Art Magazine*, http://firstamerican artmagazine.com/submissions/faam-style-guide/.

17. Jaune Quick-To-See Smith, "Scattergories."

18. "Biography," Houser, https://allanhouser.com/the-man.

19. Nancy Marie Mithlo and Alexandra Sherman, "How Perspective-Taking Can Lead to Increased Bias: A Call for 'Less Certain' Positions in American Indian Contexts," *Curator: The Museum Journal* 63, no. 3 (July 2020): 353–69, https://doi.org/10.1111/cura.12373.

20. Mike Murawski, "Openthink: Visual Thinking Strategies (VTS) & Museums," Art Museum Teaching: A Forum for Reflecting on Practice, April 29, 2014, https://artmuseumteaching.com/2014/04/29/openthink-visual-thinking-stra tegies-vts-museums/.

21. Abigail Housen, "Eye of the Beholder: Research, Theory and Practice," presented at the "Aesthetic and Art Education: A Transdisciplinary Approach" conference, sponsored by the Calouste Gulbenkian Foundation, Service of Education, September 27–29, 1999, Lisbon, Portugal.

22. ahtone, "Designed to Last."

23. I am a member of the Fort Sill Chiricahua Warm Springs Apache Tribe of Oklahoma and New Mexico. See the tribal website, https://fortsillapache-nsn .gov/.

24. Audra Simpson, "On Ethnographic Refusal: Indigeneity, 'Voice' and Colonial Citizenship," *Junctures* 9 (December 2007): 67–80.

25. Simpson, "On Ethnographic Refusal."

26. Eve Tuck and K. Wayne Yang, "Decolonization Is Not a Metaphor," *Decolonization: Indigeneity, Education & Society* 1, no. 1 (2012): 1–40.

27. Tom Jones website, http://tomjoneshochunk.com/.

28. Nancy Marie Mithlo, "The Encyclopedic Gaze," in *Knowing Native Arts* (Lincoln: University of Nebraska Press, 2020).

29. See Mithlo, "'The Manner in Which Knowledge Grows,'" in *Knowing Native Arts*.

30. Joe Wark, Raymons Neckoway, and Keith Brownlee, "Interpreting a Cultural Value: An Examination of the Indigenous Concept of Non-interference in North America," *International Social Work*, September 15, 2017.

31. Christopher M. Lyman, *The Vanishing Race and Other Illusions: Photographs of Indians by Edward S. Curtis* (New York: Pantheon Books, 1982).

32. Richard Brilliant, *Portraiture* (London: Reaktion Books, 1991), 106.

33. Liz Roth Johnson, in *Tending the Wild*, KCET, https://www.kcet.org/shows/tending-the-wild/episodes/tending-the-wild. *Tending the Wild* was a presentation of KCETLINK and the Autry Museum of the American West for the exhibit *California Continued*, produced by Juan Devis and Stacey Lieberman, 2016.

34. See http://collections.theautry.org/mwebcgi/mweb.exe?request=record ;id=M132527;type=101.

35. Bai "Tom" Tang, Daniel Ballester, and Nina Gallardo, "Identification and Evaluation of Historic Properties: San Jacinto River Levee Project (Stage 4), in and near the City of San Jacinto, Riverside County, California," 2014. See http://content.rcflood.org/Documents/CEQA/San%20Jacinto%20Levee%20 Stage%204%20and%20River%20Expansion%20Project%20Draft%20Environ mental%20Impact%20Report.pdf.

36. California Indian Basketweavers' Association, "Our Vision," https:// ciba.org/our-vision/.

37. Association of Tribal Archives, Libraries, and Museums, "About ATALM," http://www.atalm.org/node/1.

38. The Autry's Collections Online, "Milky Way Basket," http://collections. theautry.org/mwebcgi/mweb.exe?request=keyword;keyword=milky%20way %20basket.

39. Lorene Sisquoc, 2016 interview with Autry Museum of the American West curatorial team.

40. Ben Madley, *An American Genocide: The United States and the California Indian Catastrophe, 1846–1873* (New Haven, CT: Yale University Press, 2016).

41. Erin Blakemore, "California's Little-Known Genocide," History A&E Television Network, November 16, 2017, https://www.history.com/news/californias-little-known-genocide.

42. "California Tribal Communities," California Courts, Judicial Branch of California, http://www.courts.ca.gov/3066.htm.

43. Amy Lonetree, *Decolonizing Museums: Representing Native America in National and Tribal Museums* (Chapel Hill: University of North Carolina Press, 2012).

44. Erica Lord, *Wretched*, in *Visiting Conversations on Curatorial Practice and Native North American Art: The American Indian Curatorial Practice* (AICP) symposium, 2008.

45. Lord, *Wretched*.

Land Acknowledgments in Higher Education

Moving beyond the Empty Gesture

JOSHUA THUNDER LITTLE AND
MIYE NADYA TOM

Some Native groups have pushed for the recognition of local tribes as original stewards of the land through land acknowledgments. These statements are utilized to honor local Indigenous communities and begin a conversation about the relationships between Indigenous people, the land, and settler society. Recent years have seen a rise in the number of land acknowledgments at various institutions, conferences, political functions, and public events—all of them meant to improve relationships between Natives and non-Natives. By addressing harmful actions committed toward local Indigenous populations, acknowledgments theoretically provide a space for remediation. Many Native people, however, have come to regard them as problematic because they do little to enact meaningful change. Land acknowledgments are merely empty gestures.

This chapter first highlights shortcomings of land acknowledgments as part of a genealogy of institutional approaches for diversity. It then provides examples of how land recognition can promote change in our educational institutions while also serving as a tool for understanding the history of American settler colonialism, land rights, and the contemporary realities of Native peoples. Schools and universities have much to learn from local Indigenous peoples and need far greater commitment to teaching Indigenous ways of knowing.[1] We believe such reflections will lead us toward the next steps to be taken collectively.

Territory acknowledgments have traditionally existed in many Indigenous communities as a way for guests to show respect to those whom they visited. In Canada, they became widespread with non-Indigenous populations following the Truth and Reconciliation Commission report of 2015. They became a way of addressing the legacies of violence that have shaped contemporary First Nations communities, starting with residential school survivors and their families. First Nations populations are proportionally larger than their counterparts south of the border, and they wield considerable influence in their public sphere. Their actions also influence aspects of Indigenous struggles in the United States.

To date there are no publications that comprehensively detail the recent history of land acknowledgments in the United States, but it is safe to say that they increased at schools and universities at the height of the 2016–17 NoDAPL movement in Standing Rock, North Dakota. Resistance to the Dakota Access Pipeline drew attention to the rights of Indigenous people in universities and private and public spaces, places where such attention was once largely absent.[2] Major television networks and social media coverage of NoDAPL brought more national (and global) attention to the Indigenous presence in the United States, with protests organized from major urban epicenters to even the smallest universities.

Today, land acknowledgments present an awkward contradiction. On the one hand, they recognize tribal lands after centuries of genocide, theft, displacement, and contemporary invisibility. On the other hand, they do not actually give any real power back to Native peoples in their traditional homelands. Prior to colonization, Indigenous people stewarded their lands and understood the geography through their intricate relationship with human and nonhuman entities.[3] When Native people lose their autonomy on their traditional homelands, it disrupts entire communities on a profound level. As such, the ultimate goal for Native people is to regain this autonomy. In effect, land acknowledgments point out territory once occupied by Native people but fail to restore relationships with the land. Often, land acknowledgments are gestures that read as: "We recognize that this was once the traditional territories of x, y, and z peoples, the lands on which our institution stands today. Let us congratulate ourselves for saying so, but today it is ours." Even in the rare cases in which the names of local tribes and nations are pronounced correctly, the verbiage of recognition does little to restore power to Indigenous people.

Comprehending the flaws in land recognitions rests upon understanding settler colonialism itself. As Patrick Wolfe famously observed, settler colonialism is a structure that seeks to remove Natives and replace them with the settlers in their own lands.[4] It is both a historic and ongoing project. Historically, diverse populations of Indigenous peoples were racialized as primitive and ill-equipped for the onward march of Western progress. They were relics of some unfortunate past, incapable of making proper use of land (as Europeans understood the phrase). Once the Natives were displaced, the territories in which they once lived became available for acquisition and exploitation. In the present era, individual landowners, government agencies, and corporations maintain ownership of most Indigenous lands. The power dynamics are not equal and have diminished the authority of Native people in their traditional territories. Unfortunately, the return of stolen territories is unfeasible for the foreseeable future because of existing power structures. Schools and universities must consider this history and reality, especially when it comes to acknowledgments and diversity.

Institutional Approaches to Diversity: Empty Gestures?

In many ways, land acknowledgments are no different than previous efforts at "inclusivity" or to "decolonize" education. While well intentioned, neither have done much to change institutions beyond providing the illusion of embracing diversity. Empty gestures do nothing for historically underrepresented groups. Following the civil rights and Red Power movements of the post–World War II decades, multicultural (or intercultural) education emerged during the 1970s. Multiculturalism emphasizes the role of curriculum to create societal change by raising awareness of cultural differences. In fact, "a central claim has been that multicultural education can foster greater cultural interaction, interchange, and harmony, both in schools and beyond. It has also regularly been touted as the best educational means of addressing and redressing longstanding paradigms of differential achievement for minority students."[5]

In common with land acknowledgments, however, celebrations of diversity can reinforce the racial/ethnic "othering" inherent in modern schooling and associated academic discourses.[6] These approaches were enunciated from within the Western epistemology, wherein difference is created, taught, and interpreted as an active process of self-assimilation.[7] "Minoritized" populations were expected to aspire to values of dominant American society and culture (White, middle class, English-speaking, Protestant) as a model of success. This approach neither challenges structures of settler colonialism nor embraces the linguistic, cultural, and intellectual contributions of diverse populations.

In response to these shortcomings, decolonizing and anti-colonial education emerged in the early 2000s. George Sefa Dei argues that "anti-colonial thought is about a 'decolonizing of the mind' working with resistant knowledge and claiming the power of local subjects' intellectual agency. Resistance in this context is about fighting for survival and beyond. It is about resistance to domination of the past, contamination of the present and the stealing of a people's future."[8] Decolonizing education looks toward undoing the impacts of colonialism on schooling. It has done little, however, to move beyond rhetoric and to create meaningful change. In their widely cited article "Decolonization Is Not a Metaphor" Eve Tuck and K. Wayne Yang observe that decolonization has become little more than an overused metaphor. It is not, the authors insist, "a swappable term for other things we want to do to improve our societies and schools."[9]

Despite the growing influence of decolonial rhetoric, the tone for multiculturism in the public sphere is still mostly set from above rather than below, reinforcing the old colonial dynamic. Over the last decade, universities, schools, and companies have emphasized diversity, equity, and inclusion. As Benjamin Reese notes, diversity, equity, and inclusion often translate into a statement such as the following: "Our organization respects all differences, and we work to create an environment where everyone feels included and can do their best work."[10] The problem is that this approach attempts to work around the spaces ascribed for difference but does little to challenge categories of difference in themselves nor does it address systemic racism, much less encourage conversations about land repatriation.[11] Nor does it deal with how genocide, displacement, and race are endemic to the United States' settler-Native-slave structure.[12]

Marta Araújo argues that most occidental countries are colonial societies, each one having its own depoliticizing myths of anti-racism embedded in colonial discourses.[13] She illustrates how some of these discourses celebrate how multiculturalism was created through colonial encounters, such as the notion that the United States is a nation of immigrants (settlers, occupiers, and racialized arrivals). Readers should take that in tandem with the understanding that colonization is inherently about controlling land and maintaining a structure that has proliferated racial hierarchies. Both remain endemic in American settler society. As such, the act of decolonizing needs to include struggles for recognition of sovereignty and the repatriation of land to Native peoples.[14] The question then becomes, How might educational institutions move past empty gestures and contribute to such meaningful change?

Beyond the Recognition of Land

We might presently "acknowledge" that our schools, universities, and major cities and small towns sit on Indigenous lands. But what further steps might we take to build upon the dialogues opened by territorial recognition? Universities should hold themselves accountable to support Native students, from developing accessible pathways to higher education to improving student retention. They should offer culturally relevant courses, increase Native staff and faculty to support Indigenous students, and expand financial aid to the extent possible. Additionally, Indigenous histories and knowledges must be more widely incorporated into disciplines that might otherwise overlook potential contributions of Native American and Indigenous studies. We believe moving beyond empty gestures to implement such changes can equally benefit Native and non-Native students.

Financial Aid and Tuition

As stated by Megan Red Shirt Shaw, one of the meaningful ways to give back to Native people is by providing free tuition and university attendance.[15] Notably, some states are beginning to implement such reforms, especially for Native students from local tribes and nations. In 2021, for instance, Colorado governor Jared Polis signed into law Senate Bill 29, which provides support to Native American students who are federally recognized and maintain a historic connection to the current borders of Colorado starting in the 2021–22 academic year. Out-of-state tuition prices out many Native students seeking to attend public universities in Colorado; therefore, in-state tuition offers them a more affordable path to higher education. Also in 2021, Nevada governor Steve Sisolak signed a law waiving registration and other fees for students enrolled in Nevada tribes. Each of these states show how local institutions may take meaningful steps to help American Indian students afford college, even if they stop short of offering higher education tuition free.

Programming, Curricula, and Indigenous Studies

Additionally, universities can implement a number of changes that can benefit programs within and beyond Native American and Indigenous studies. Including Native ways of knowing in curricula will initiate Native approaches to established disciplines. As it currently stands, schools preserve inequality by affirming the cultural legitimacy of Western-based knowledge over others. What is considered "official" or "legitimate knowledge" at the level of curriculum, pedagogy, and forms of classroom evaluation may disqualify or marginalize other communities' knowledge, histories, languages, and cultures, including those of Native students.[16] Incorporating Native ways of knowing would address this error and would benefit all students as future professionals, (global) citizens, and allies long after their graduation. Access and acknowledgments alone do not create change—it also must come from what students learn in schools.

America's history of education is rich with ethnocide, segregation, and cultural alienation. It is also rich in histories of resistance, however. In the United States and globally, colonized peoples and marginalized populations have survived these legacies and made critical reflections on the role of education in defining resistive strategies. During the late 1960s and early 1970s, for instance, Native American student activists perceived education as a tool to dismantle the economic, cultural, and political apparatuses of oppression. In 1968, Indigenous, Chicano (today Latinx), Asian American, and African American students marched together in the famed Third World Liberation Front strike. What brought them together? The demand for ethnic studies and Native American studies at the University of California, Berkeley. Within the broader

Red Power movement, part of the struggle involved revitalizing Native American education and tribal governments, forcing the federal government and public schools to provide quality education and to incorporate Indigenous perspectives. In so doing Native people would have an active voice in educating their children in institutions on and off reservations. As Vine Deloria Jr. and Daniel R. Wildcat contend, Indigenous peoples and communities could once again determine their fates and the futures of their communities through indigenized education.[17] Ethnic studies and Native American studies, however, are not quite what these students (or "epistemic insurgents") envisioned. According to Ramón Grosfoguel, liberal multiculturalism merely allots each racialized group a space to celebrate identity and culture, which is unproblematic so long as ethnic/racial hierarchies are not questioned. He further contends that "Ethnic studies in the United States is at present torn between two problems of the coloniality of global power: 1) the "identity politics" of liberal multiculturalism in the United States and 2) the disciplinary colonization of the Western colonial human sciences (social sciences and the humanities) over these spaces."[18]

Within the colonial logic of multiculturalism, difference is pigeonholed and reduced. Native American and Indigenous studies encapsulate a vast interdisciplinary field, however, including history, art, science, literature, math, community/land-based educational models, and traditional ecological knowledge. Too often this vast wealth of knowledge is marginalized into an increasingly underfunded space. Western-centric knowledge and disciplines reign supreme. Few students who do not major or minor in Native American studies find purpose in the coursework beyond fulfilling diversity requirements. In our experiences teaching Native American Studies, some students have sought out courses due to the lack of information provided in their major and future profession of choice, such as social work or education. How might Native American studies be incorporated into other disciplines to broaden understandings of Native peoples and intellectual contributions and to work with our communities?

Working with Communities

Even as institutions might purport diversity, equity, and inclusion, there is general unfamiliarity with Native peoples, including local tribes frequently rattled off in superficial land acknowledgments. Learning about past injustices toward Native people and the relationships tribes still hold to land is imperative to understand the past, present, and future of Native America. It is also crucial for building relationships with local communities. The University of California, Riverside (UCR) provides a positive example of an institution incorporating Indigenous voices. UCR worked with the local tribes in the Inland Empire of Southern California to produce a statement aiding in the awareness of local Indigenous communities. UCR staff, faculty, and students made an effort to work with Tongva, Cahuilla, Luiseño, and Serrano peoples to create a land acknowledgment that honors the local Native nations. These tribes all maintain a shared, although complex, history of the land UCR occupies.

The input of Native faculty was crucial. Some UCR faculty are of the local tribes. Other Native faculty also contributed to the dialogue of creating the statement. Faculty further reached out to local tribal people not affiliated with the university in educational or professional capacities but who remained connected to the land that the university occupies. Speakers from the Serrano, Tongva, Cahuilla, and Luiseño also came forth. They brought their perspective and demonstrated their willingness to work toward a future where Native lands are recognized in the Inland Empire (a region in California east of Los Angeles and centered around Riverside and San Bernardino). After the finalization of the land recognition statement relationships with local tribes did not stop. UCR continues to work with the local tribal communities, the faculty and staff from the local tribes, and the larger Indigenous population to continue working toward a better future.

Staff and Faculty

The question of faculty hires amid budget cuts and overall institutional apathy also hangs over this conversation. Efforts to include local Indigenous populations vary from institution to institution. At roughly one percent of the US population (and even less in many universities), the realities of Indigenous peoples and the needs of Native students often remain trivial to larger racial and ethnic groups. Current budget cuts, the elevation of STEM (science, technology, education, and mathematics) over the social sciences and humanities, and other structural problems negatively affect institutional willingness to serve Native students. The gradual disappearance of tenure-track positions heavily impacts the retention of quality Native faculty. As with many other departments, Native American studies programs rely on low-wage, unstable, and exploitative adjunct positions.

Despite these challenges, long-term Native staff and tenured faculty can strengthen existing Native American studies programs. They can contribute to the edification both of students and of unknowledgeable administrative personnel, some of whom might oversee student support services. We do not intend this observation to put the work on the shoulders of Native professionals. Instead, we believe that an active presence on campus will contribute to changing university culture. In addition to Native staff and faculty campus leadership, trained professionals should be hired to educate staff and faculty on the needs of Native people within the academy. In short, Native students need to see themselves represented.[19] At the same time, non-Native students will benefit from a truly diverse faculty that can provide unique contributions to various fields, enhancing each student's ability—as future professionals—to work with and serve Native, other American, and even global populations.

Land Recognition as an Educational Tool for Change

Incorporating Indigenous knowledge will introduce new ways of understanding responsible environmental stewardship. It benefits Native students but can also help guide non-Indigenous people toward developing appropriate relationships with the land. As previously mentioned, the American education system draws exclusively from a Western knowledge system. Utilizing a land acknowledgment can start a conversation on Native perspectives on the proper relationship to the Earth. It is therefore imperative that educators find meaningful ways to incorporate local histories and Indigenous knowledge into classrooms.

By centering on the Lakota worldview, for example, we can see how land recognition can promote justice and the intellectual traditions that Lakota knowledge systems can provide. *Unci Maka* (the Lakota word that translates to "Grandmother Earth") as a concept explains the relationship of the *Oyate* (the word for "the people" in the Lakota language) and the land. The relationship between the Lakota and the land mirrors human relationships with grandmothers and their relatives. In Lakota culture, grandmothers are highly respected and valued. Grandmothers instill knowledge, continue cultural traditions, and provide support for families raising future generations. The Earth's relationship is paralleled in this same way with humans: if humans take care of the land, then people will continue to have lives that the Earth sustains.

Teaching non-Native people about embedded relationships between *Unci Maka* and the *Oyate* will reinforce the powerful relationship between the two entities. The Lakota always remind themselves that taking care of *Unci Maka* will ensure that they are taken care of. Reciprocity is essential in this relationship. Teachers can explore this theory and praxis of Lakota relational knowledge via land acknowledgment statements.

All non-Native people in the United States occupy Indigenous territories. They also have a relationship to the land, albeit different from Indigenous peoples, and need to learn how to interact with it responsibly. Non-Native people can learn a Lakota worldview on how to interact with the land in a good way. Instructive here is the issue of the Dakota Access Pipeline. The Standing Rock Sioux Tribe and their relatives who fought against the installation of the pipeline did so for more than just themselves. They believed the pipeline was dangerous and decided to stand up for environmental rights for all American citizens living along its path. Environmental rights are not just an Indian issue, in other words, but a human issue. Regardless of race, age, gender, nationality, and sexual orientation, all people need clean water to survive. If made tangible in such a manner, implementing land acknowledgments with a curriculum can be an effective teaching tool in the classroom.

A worldview that includes Native environmental stewardship will consider other options for taking care of the land—many of which have existed for millennia. Teaching core concepts such as the Lakota worldview of *Unci Maka* or other Native ways of knowing will promote improved ways of thinking about the lands we inhabit and our relationship to the Earth. In other words, Indigenous knowledge offers a humanistic approach to treating the land as a relative rather than a mere commodity.

Conclusions

As land acknowledgments began in Canada and eventually gained traction in the United States, educational administrators have come to see them as a positive step toward justice and inclusivity. Creating these statements with the input of local Indigenous communities can broaden conversations about Native American experiences, thought, issues, and future well-being. Properly conceived and written, they can stir productive conversations for changing how settler society can respect local Native communities and how all populations can relate to the land.

In practice, however, territorial recognition has mostly only served the non-Native population. The American educational system seems to position diversity and multiculturalism as tools of change, but to date it has done little to engage local tribal communities in meaningful ways. One need look no further than the lack of funding for Native studies programs to observe how indifferent the academy is to Native histories and knowledges. Building upon recent efforts such as those in Colorado and Nevada would go a long way toward improving the situation. Providing support for Native students through programming, expanding Native studies disciplines, and working with local tribes would do even more. Certainly, they would make land acknowledgments something other than empty gestures.

Native American and Indigenous studies offer non-Western epistemologies that can only strengthen the academy. There is ample opportunity to introduce Indigenous knowledge systems across disciplines in ways that benefit students, the populations they might serve, and their relationships to the lands they inhabit. As illustrated in the case of the University of California, Riverside, land acknowledgments can become an excellent launching point for addressing these broader issues. They can lead to the centering of Indigenous intellectual theory and praxis and utilize local histories to incorporate Indigenous knowledges. They can build conversations around how Native people have always cared for the land—a point on which the non-Native population has much to learn.

Merging land recognition into the classroom curriculum, in short, is a great way to explore Native sovereignty and legacies, educational ways of knowing, and environmental stewardship. Hopefully, the current trend in land acknowledgments will facilitate future collaboration between Natives and non-Natives—both inside and outside of the classroom.

NOTES

1. For more on this concept, see the chapter in this volume by Donald L. Fixico.

2. For more on Indigenous environmental issues, see the chapter in this volume by Paul Kelton and James Rice.

3. For more on this point, see the chapter in this volume by Brady DeSanti.

4. Patrick Wolfe, "Settler Colonialism and the Elimination of the Native," *Journal of Genocide Research* 8, no. 4 (2006): 387–409.

5. Stephen May, "Critical Multiculturalism and Cultural Difference: Avoiding Essentialism," in *Critical Multiculturalism: Rethinking Multiculturalist and Anti-Racist Education*, ed. Stephen May (New York: Routledge, 1999), 11–41.

6. George J. Seifa Dei, "Knowledge and Politics of Social Change: The Implication of Anti-Racism," *British Journal of Sociology of Education* 20, no. 3 (1999): 395–40.

7. Nancy Lesko and Leslie Bloom, "Close Encounters: Truth, Experience and Interpretation in Multicultural Teacher Education," *Journal of Curriculum Studies* 30, no. 4 (1998): 375–95.

8. George J. Sefa Dei, "Mapping the Terrain of a New Politics of Resistance," in *Anti-Colonialism and Education: The Politics of Resistance*, ed. George J. Sefa Dei and Arlo Kempf (Leiden: Brill, 2006), 1–23.

9. Eve Tuck and K. Wayne Yang, "Decolonization Is Not a Metaphor," *Decolonization: Indigeneity, Education & Society* 1, no. 1 (2012): 1–40.

10. Benjamin Reese, "Diversity and Inclusion Are Not Enough," *Inside Higher Ed* (2020), https://www.insidehighered.com/views/2020/06/18/colleges -shouldnt-simply-focus-diversity-and-inclusion-also-attack-systemic-racism.

11. Gurminder K. Bhambra, "Sociology and Postcolonialism: Another 'Missing' Revolution?" *Sociology* 41, no. 5 (2007): 871–84; Reese, "Diversity and Inclusion Are Not Enough"; Tuck and Yang, "Decolonization Is Not a Metaphor."

12. Tuck and Yang, "Decolonization Is Not a Metaphor."

13. Marta Araújo, "Racismo.pt," in *Somos Diferentes, Somos Iguais: Diversidade, Cidadania, e Educação*, ed. Teresa Cunha and Sandra Silvestre (Santa Maria da Feira, Portugal: Acção para a Justiça e Paz, 2008), 25–49.

14. Tuck and Yang, "Decolonization Is Not a Metaphor."

15. Megan Red Shirt Shaw, "Beyond the Land Acknowledgement: College 'LAND BACK' or Free Tuition for Native Students," 2020, https://hackthe gates.org/wp-content/uploads/2020/08/Redshirt-Shaw_Landback_HTGreport .pdf.

16. Michael W. Apple, *Ideology and Curriculum*, 4th ed. (New York: Routledge, 2018).

17. Vine Deloria Jr. and Daniel R. Wildcat, *Power and Place: Indian Education in America* (Golden, CO: Fulcrum, 2001).

18. Ramón Grosfoguel, "The Dilemmas of Ethnic Studies in the United States: Between Liberal Multiculturalism, Identity Politics, Disciplinary Colonization, and Decolonial Epistemologies," *Human Architect: The Journal of the Sociology of Self-Knowledge* 10, no. 1 (2012): 81–90.

19. For more on Native student perspectives, see the chapter in this volume by Taylor Hummel.

PART THREE

Reflections on Teaching Native American History

How I Learned to Teach Indian History

A Memoir

THEDA PERDUE

I never took a course in American Indian history. In fact, I do not recall Indians being mentioned in any of the United States history courses I took. Nevertheless, for thirty-five years in five different universities, I taught Indian history courses that ranged from freshman surveys to graduate seminars. I realize that not everyone who wants or needs to teach a course in Native history will have the opportunities that I have had, but my experiences might be helpful to some. Most non-Indians of my generation who came to teach Native history had little training and few resources. That has changed. But teaching Indian history as a non-Indian, I think, still requires a kind of knowledge that is experiential.

I grew up in southern Georgia, and the only things I learned about Indigenous people as a child came from family vacations to Cherokee, North Carolina, where we dutifully attended the outdoor drama *Unto These Hills*, and from the Sunday night ritual of watching *Bonanza* on television. (The mother of Little Joe, my favorite character, supposedly had Native ancestry.) I was surrounded by evidence of Indigenous people, including the Ocmulgee Mounds in Macon, where I went to college, but I do not think I ever associated ancient sites with modern Indians. I am not sure I even thought about Native people as part of the contemporary world.

What I did discover in college was a new approach to thinking, studying, and writing about race. I had been a racial "liberal" since high school, when I shocked my teacher in my all-White high school by doing a report on Martin Luther King's "Letter from Birmingham Jail" (1963). But I did not think deeply about race as anything other than an unjust political and economic system. Then I heard a series of lectures by George Tindall, a professor of history at the University of North Carolina, that introduced me to the idea that race is socially, historically, and culturally constructed. I decided to go to graduate school in history.

The summer before I entered graduate school at the University of Georgia I spent some time in the mountains of north Georgia, where I happened upon the Chief Vann house. Built in 1803–4 by a Cherokee named James Vann, the three-story brick house challenged the little I knew about Native people. James Vann and his son Joseph were wealthy businessmen and planters, and by the 1830s the younger Vann held over a hundred African Americans in bondage. How could this be? The Vanns were not themselves White, nor were the other wealthy Cherokees who by 1835 held a total of 1,592 slaves. My visit to this historic site provided me with a research topic. My assigned graduate adviser was Charles Crowe, a social and intellectual historian who taught the only African American history course in the department. There was no Indigenous history course. When he learned about my interest in Cherokee slaveholding Professor Crowe sent me to the anthropology department, where I enrolled in Charles Hudson's course on southeastern Indians. It was the only course on Indians I ever took. Between the two Charlies, however, I found the direction and encouragement I needed to pursue my master's and then dissertation topic.

Connect with the Field

I probably would have become simply a southern historian with a scholarly interest in race had it not been for a job advertisement that appeared in December 1974. Western Carolina University was searching for a Cherokee historian. Although I had not yet taken my qualifying exams, the hurdle one must clear before writing a dissertation, I applied. Almost no one wrote Cherokee history in those days, so I got the job. While I worked on developing a course in Cherokee history I began teaching the first half of world history in January 1975. I took exams at UGA that spring.

I had just started teaching at WCU when I attended my first professional meeting, the Southern Anthropological Society, and presented a paper drawn from my master's thesis. I was terrified. When I rose to deliver my paper I grasped the lectern, which was covered with a cloth, only to discover that it was a cardboard box turned upside down. I recovered and read the paper. I think it was well received but I really don't remember. I do remember the people I met and the papers I heard. Lively discussions often followed formal papers, and several publishers had book exhibits. I met the editor who ultimately published my first book.[1]

Ever since that first professional meeting I have attended historical and interdisciplinary conferences regularly. Among others, I joined the Southern Historical Association, the American Society for Ethnohistory, and the Organization of American Historians, all of which publish scholarly journals. Through these and other organizations I have gotten to know some of the most distinguished historians in the country and keep up with their work. I have met young historians presenting new ideas and research, and I have had the opportunity to talk with prospective graduate students. The most memorable conference I have attended was the inaugural meeting of the Native American and Indigenous Studies Association. This was my first academic conference in which non-Native scholars like me were in the minority. Most of the attendees were young, and their enthusiasm was contagious. These Native voices have enriched the field in ways I could not have imagined when I attended that first SAS conference.

In addition to academic association conferences, local libraries, historical societies, and colleges sometimes hold conferences that bring scholars together to make public presentations. I have attended, organized, and participated in such events. As an attendee, I have had an opportunity to hear people who are working in the field and engage them in conversation. As an organizer or participant, I have been able to spend time with people whose work I admire. For example, I organized a small conference at Western Carolina in the late 1970s and invited anthropologists Robert K. Thomas and Raymond Fogelson, who had participated in a cross-cultural research project with the North Carolina Cherokees in the 1950s, to speak. We spent several days together and had long conversations about how the Eastern Band Cherokee Reservation, Qualla Boundary, had changed. If I had not invited them, I would have missed priceless conversations, anecdotes, and insights.

Listen and Learn

The summer after I went to Western Carolina, I conducted research in Oklahoma and elsewhere and began writing my dissertation on slavery among the Cherokees. Soon I faced a real challenge. My department chair had asked me to teach an evening course on Cherokee history at Qualla Boundary, where the university was setting up a branch. About thirty students, most of them older than I was, enrolled in the class. I introduced myself and told them a bit about where I came from and how I ended up standing before them. I then asked each class member to tell me who they were and why they had signed up for the class. When I got to a man in the back row, who looked to be about forty, he stood up and demanded to know why I thought I knew anything about Cherokees. I tried to answer by telling the class about my research and preparation but nothing satisfied him. He found fault with the syllabus I passed out, the assigned readings, class policies, and so forth. Finally he sat down and I proceeded with introducing the course.

Midway through the three-hour class we took a break. I was tempted to flee, but two of the older people in the class approached the lectern. One was a highly respected teacher and the other was a member of tribal council. Softly, the teacher said, "I am so sorry. He is not one of us." The council member continued, "He is an Oklahoma Cherokee, but he was not raised there. He grew up in Miami. He does not know how to behave." Then the teacher assured me, "We are very glad you are here, and we look forward to learning what you can tell us about our history." The "outsider" did not return. As it turned out, I learned more than I taught.

Not surprisingly, my students knew different things than I did. I had learned Cherokee history from scholarly books and archives, and I could fit their tribal history into the contours of American history. In terms of the written past, my students were aware of James Mooney's fieldwork in the 1880s and his historical introduction to *Myths of the Cherokee*, but they had little knowledge about more recent scholarship.[2] In terms of historical events, they knew about removal (but their version reflected "Unto These Hills"), the Civil War, and the tribal constitution. They knew far less about late nineteenth- and especially twentieth-century Cherokee events.

But they did know the toll that the boarding schools had taken on their parents, grandparents, and great-grandparents. They understood what the Great Depression had been like on Qualla Boundary. They had served in World War II or knew people who had. The past followed them into the present. They still faced discrimination. They continued to deal with the Bureau of Indian Affairs. They participated in an economy largely based on tourism, which promoted stereotypes of Indians. They lived in tight-knit communities where it was difficult to make a living but, usually, even more difficult to leave. Many of my students spoke or understood the Cherokee language and, despite attending church on Sundays, held to a set of beliefs unique to their people. I listened and I learned.

So, what is the takeaway from my early experience teaching Cherokee history? Few readers of this autobiographical essay will ever have the opportunity I had in my eight years at WCU, where I taught Cherokee students, made Cherokee friends, took a Cherokee cooking class (yes, I know how to make bean bread), drove an elderly Cherokee couple when they wanted to go somewhere at night, and knew the people who got the Museum of the Cherokee Indian and the *Journal of Cherokee Studies* off the ground. These experiences were unique to the time, place, and circumstances.

Develop Common Themes and Highlight Diversity

After eight years at WCU I moved to Clemson University in South Carolina, two hours from Qualla Boundary. At Clemson I held a position in southern history, and I taught a range of courses in that field. I had not been there long when I got a call from a person at the North Carolina Department of Cultural Resources who asked me to write a little book on the state's Indians. At that point, I only really knew about Cherokees—the Indian history I taught at WCU was strictly Cherokee history—but I agreed. Cultural Resources then put me in touch with the North Carolina Commission of Indian Affairs, the state agency that dealt primarily with three urban Indian associations and the tribes North Carolina (as opposed to the federal government) had recognized. The Eastern Band of Cherokees held a seat on the commission, but since the EBCI had federal recognition the commission could offer them relatively little. At that point the state-recognized tribes were the Coharie, Haliwa-Saponi, Indians of Person County (now Saponni), Lumbee, and Waccamaw-Siouan. By 2017 the Meherrin and Occaneechi Band of the

Saponi Nation had joined them, and the number of urban associations had grown to four.

My liaison with the commission was Danny Bell, who is Coharie and Lumbee. Danny introduced me to a whole new world of Indians. These tribes shared some things—racial discrimination, substantial acculturation, and the creation of Native churches and schools, for example—but each tribe also had a unique history. Exploring those histories and getting to know people from these tribes led me to an appreciation of Native diversity even among Indian tribes *within a single state!* Intellectually, I was perfectly cognizant of the fact that Cherokees were not like Navajos and Navajos were not like Sioux, but now I was confronted with weaving more subtle but equally real differences into a single narrative.[3]

Writing this book coincided with my development of a course on southern Indians, which further expanded the number of tribes I had to learn about in depth. From the Seminoles in Florida to the Alabama Coushattas in Texas to the Pamunkeys in Virginia, I needed to capture the diversity of the Native South and still construct a coherent course with a beginning, middle, and end. Southern history provided a template. Southeastern Indians depended heavily on agriculture for their subsistence, but the South's mild climate, fertile soils, and racism led to a colonial culture that dispossessed Native people.

For the five large Native nations dispossession meant forced relocation west of the Mississippi River although remnants remained in the South. Most of those remnants achieved federal recognition. For smaller tribes, especially those who had no history of treaties with the United States, dispossession meant reclassification as "mulatto" or "colored." Some melded into White or African American communities. Others separated themselves from both Black and White and maintained a tribal identity even though few outside their group recognized it. All endured hostility and discrimination. They remained "colored" in the eyes of most Whites, although they new they were Indians. Integration in the 1960s brought new challenges, especially for tribes that had their own segregated Indian schools that institutionalized their identity.[4]

Writing about North Carolina Indians and developing a course on southern Indians prepared me for yet another challenge. While I was at Clemson I presented a paper at a meeting of the Australia–New Zealand American Studies Association, which took place in New Zealand. I met two members of the history department at the University of Auckland. When one of them decided to accept a position in the United

States he recommended that I take his place for a semester while the department looked for a permanent replacement. Always ready for an adventure, I went down under in 1987. I taught two survey courses, one on US history and one on Native American History. The first course I had taught several times; the second not at all.

To teach this Native American history survey I had to construct a narrative that made sense of the disparate histories of hundreds of different peoples. Furthermore, I had to do so in New Zealand with limited resources. Library holdings on Native people were minimal, textbooks were prohibitively expensive, and the internet did not exist. Students knew little about American Indians, but they did know about tribes. The Maoris, the Indigenous people of New Zealand, politically organize themselves in tribes, and those tribes, like some federally recognized tribes in the United States, had signed treaties with the British colonizers of New Zealand. Treaties are made only between sovereign entities, and sovereignty means that a polity has the right to govern itself. At the time I was in New Zealand the Waitangi Tribunal, established to hear Maori claims for violations of sovereignty, had just had its authority extended back to the Treaty of Waitangi (1840). Maoris were contesting land rights, fisheries, and even access to radio frequencies.[5]

In some ways there are substantial differences between Maoris and American Indians—Maoris, for example, constitute 15 percent of New Zealand's population while American Indians and Alaska Natives make up between 1 and 2 percent of the US population. Rather than a single document like the Treaty of Waitangi, which all Maori tribes signed, each Native American nation has its own set of treaties (or none) and therefore a different struggle with the United States over the terms of those treaties. Nevertheless, British colonization and sovereignty gave me themes that my students understood. I simply helped them explore these themes among peoples other than Maoris.[6]

Identifying themes with which the instructor is comfortable and that provide space for adequate exploration is the key to teaching an American Indian history survey. History is more than one damn thing after another. It is a way of examining the past so that we can understand the relationship between cause and effect. In order to achieve that objective we have to make sense out of chaos. We must have organizing themes that tie the episodes of the past together. Indigenous history is no different. Over the years, I have used a variety of themes—race, sovereignty, gender, colonialism—to explore difference. By difference, I do not mean just the dichotomy between Europeans and Indians but among tribes as well. Themes do not mean a single narrative but a framework through which students can learn to appreciate the richness of Native America.

Living in the Present

Since I am a historian I teach the past, but Indians, of course, live in the present as well. Therefore, I think that it is unconscionable to teach Native American history without acknowledging the present. I always brought my history courses up to the present, but the connection between past and present for Native people became particularly significant for me after I moved to the University of Kentucky in 1988. The previous year, a landowner in western Kentucky sold the "right" to excavate an Indigenous site on his land to a group of private individuals who used a tractor to unearth seven villages and a mound. Native people had occupied the Slack Farm Site from 1400 to 1650 and they left behind houses, storage pits, and burials. The looters kept pottery, stonework, and other saleable items but tossed aside human remains. Native people around the country were outraged, as were archaeologists, scholars in other disciplines, and many in the general public.

Among the national Indian leaders who came to Kentucky to protest this desecration was Dennis Banks, one of the founders of the American Indian Movement. For several years Banks made his home in northern Kentucky. I was among several faculty members who invited him to speak at the University of Kentucky. He lectured to a largely, maybe exclusively, non-Indian audience about Native rights and efforts to empower Native people to demand their rights, especially the right of Natives to their past. Banks and others lobbied the state legislature until it passed one of the nation's toughest laws protecting human remains. In 1990, influenced in part by the Slack Farm desecration, Congress passed the Native American Graves Protection and Repatriation Act (NAGPRA), which further protected sacred sites. This very indirect brush with Indian activism made me determined to connect my courses more clearly to current issues and to make a greater effort to ensure that Indigenous people had a voice in the academy.

In 1995 the University of North Carolina invited my husband, Mike Green, and me to visit for a semester. Native students at UNC had become increasingly insistent on having Indian studies courses. UNC's interest in Indians was centered in the anthropology department, which had sponsored the study of Cherokee, North Carolina, in the 1950s. By the 1990s there was little interest in Native American cultural anthropology, but the department did have a cohort of first-rate archaeologists, an archaeology lab with an active research program, and an impressive collection of artifacts. Indians and archaeologists often opposed each other, but the director of the lab had generated considerable good will as a supporter of NAGPRA. Beyond archaeology the history department had a course on the books in Indian history, but adjuncts, some more successful than others, taught it. Native students did not find that arrangement acceptable and began pressuring the administration and the chair of the history department to do something. When UNC invited us to visit, everyone understood that this was an audition.

One of the things we were able to do was bring together North Carolina Indians and both Native and non-Native academics from around the state. Danny Bell, my old friend from the N.C. Commission on Indian Affairs, now worked at UNC in the study abroad office, and he helped us identify participants for a daylong conference open to the public. Funding from the North Carolina Humanities Council made the event possible. In a series of formal presentations, tribal members told academics about their people, and academics shared their research projects. Each session also included ample time for questions and discussions. The new head of the state Indian commission spoke at a luncheon. The turnout astonished us. It was the first time many of the attendees had ever been on the UNC campus; it was the first time they had been invited. The students as well as the Indian community welcomed us, and at the end of the semester they were sorry to see us go. But in 1998 we returned as tenured professors with a charge from the dean to build an American Indian Studies Program. In the ten years before the economic recession of 2008 and the subsequent shift of North Carolina politics to the right, we had the academic and financial support to do just that. But building a program meant demonstrating a demand. That meant teaching lots of students in lots of classes.

A Native Voice

For the first time in my career I taught Indian history almost exclusively—a freshman survey on North American Indians;

upper-level undergraduate courses on southeastern Indians, Cherokee history, and Native women's history; an honors course on North Carolina Indians; a senior seminar on Indian removal; and graduate seminars on Native history. At the University of Kentucky I had directed dissertations in Indian history and had graduated very fine PhD students. I continued to train graduate students at UNC as well.[7] The real challenge was the freshman survey in Native history, which enrolled between 180 and 220 students, depending on the lecture hall capacity. I lectured two days a week and supervised graduate students who held small discussion sections on a third day.

The textbook I used was Colin Calloway's *First Peoples*.[8] I never abandoned it for newer textbooks as they became available. There were four reasons. First of all, the narrative text was relatively brief, which meant that I could assign additional readings without lots of student complaints. It also gave me room to elaborate in lecture on particular issues without repeating the text. Second, there were unusually perceptive questions that guided my teaching assistants in their discussion sections. Third, each chapter included a selection of primary sources produced by Indians. And fourth, carefully constructed bibliographies helped me prepare myself to teach this course. In addition to Calloway's text I assigned novels by Indigenous authors. This was another way I could introduce a Native voice. My favorites were Louise Erdrich's *Love Medicine*, Susan Power's *Grass Dancer*, LeAnne Howe's *Miko Kings: An Indian Baseball Story*, and N. Scott Momaday's *House Made of Dawn*. I think they worked in part because they had strong characters who were about the age of my students.

The internet presented further opportunities. Mike and I both used *Indian Country Today* in class. Three or four times during the semester I posted a contemporary news story on the class website and lectured about the historical context or asked my teaching assistants to discuss the article in their sections. I also did mini-lectures (five minutes at the beginning of class) on intriguing events, personal anecdotes, and even interesting Native figures who died in the course of the semester. One of my favorites was on Henry Lambert, who had dressed up in polyester feathers for decades to entertain tourists in Cherokee, North Carolina. He began his spiel by telling his audience how inauthentic the feathers were and then taught his listeners about real Cherokees. With the tips he made Lambert sent his children to college; one of them became a lawyer and chief at Qualla Boundary. The week of the World

Series I did a mini-lecture on the 1911 Series in which Philadelphia Athletics pitcher "Chief" Bender (Ojibwe) faced off against New York Giants catcher "Chief" Meyers (Cauhilla). In these mini-lectures I tried to make the Natives whom the students read about more real.

In 2006 UNC established the American Indian Center to serve Native students, foster relationships with Native communities, and promote research on American Indians. One of the first programs developed by the AIC was Elder in Residence. Each year the AIC invites a prominent Native leader to spend several days on our campus. They meet with faculty and students, speak to classes, and deliver a public lecture. This program has brought to UNC remarkable people including LaDonna Harris and Ada Deer.

Get Out and About

After we moved to North Carolina Mike and I drove across the South visiting Native communities. In some of these we had an "in." In Alabama the grandparents of a Poarch Creek student invited us to lunch with the chief and council, and in Texas we spent an afternoon with a Coushatta woman from whom I had bought baskets for years. But we did not know anyone in most of these tribes. We wrote to each of them before we left home, explained that this was a "get acquainted" trip not a research trip (no note pad, computer, or tape recorder), and we made appointments with whomever the tribal offices thought I should meet. Sometimes it was a public affairs officer, sometimes the chief, and sometimes a museum director or archivist. In one case, the chief, council, and tribal attorney met with us; the tribe was involved in litigation and taking no chances. The welcomes were warm, even the attorney's, and the knowledge we acquired was substantial. In Louisiana the Jena Choctaw chief loaded us into the tribal van and took us to the plantation on which her people had worked as sharecroppers. In the same state the Houmas arranged for us to meet two former chiefs at the tribal headquarters, which had been the segregated school for Houma children. This road trip had a major impact on how I taught Native history.

There are Indian communities scattered across the United States, and they present priceless opportunities for learning. For anyone who decides on a road trip or Saturday foray, my advice is to read whatever you can about the community, including the tribal newspaper or website, before you visit. Contact the public information office, tribal office, or whatever entity deals with visitors. Make clear that you are not a tourist but an educator who is deeply interested in the community. Ask to visit a school, a community center, or a library. Make an appointment with the director of a museum or cultural center. And go to learn. Don't pass up Indian casinos (unless you have a gambling problem). I am not a gambler but I always stop and walk through casinos. I eat in the restaurant and I browse the gift shop, which sometimes carries books about the tribe. Casinos also often have displays of tribal history, which can be very revealing.

Native communities are usually amenable to field trips by students. Mike and I took college professors participating in a National Endowment for the Humanities Summer Seminar on field trips to visit the Eastern Band of Cherokees, the Catwabas, and the Lumbees. We took undergraduate honors students at UNC to Qualla Boundary and to Pembroke, where Lumbees are centered. I accompanied a UNC bus tour for new faculty to Cherokee. One summer we organized a Cherokee Study Abroad Program in which Tol Foster, a Creek citizen and an English professor, took a group of UNC undergraduates to the Cherokee Reservation in Oklahoma for six weeks. Nothing really replaces face-to-face engagement.

Reflections

I retired from teaching in 2011. In my career I probably taught Native history to three thousand students. My graduate students have ended up in four different countries, where most of them teach Native American history. I hope all my students remember everything I taught them, but I am willing to settle for an awareness that American Indians have a history both interwoven with and independent of United States history. Today Native people live on reservations, in cities, on farms, and in small towns. They are teachers and accountants, farmers and ranchers, doctors and lawyers, truck drivers and factory workers, unemployed and impoverished. They are Americans. But they are also citizens of their own nations, and they value their own cultural traditions, history, and sovereignty. My husband, Mike Green, always ended his twentieth-century Indian history class by reminding his students that Indigenous people are a very small minority in this country. Most non-Indians ignore the needs, concerns, and rights of

Native people because they know nothing about them. Then he pointed out to the students that they no longer had that excuse. With knowledge comes responsibility. May our students leave our classes with a clear sense of their responsibility to respect Native people and to support them when their rights are threatened.

NOTES

1. Theda Perdue, *Slavery and the Evolution of Cherokee Society, 1540–1866* (Knoxville: University of Tennessee Press, 1979).

2. James Mooney, *Myths of the Cherokee* (Washington, DC: Government Printing Office, 1902).

3. Theda Perdue, *Native Carolinians: The Indians of North Carolina* (Raleigh: North Carolina Department of Cultural Resources Division of Archives and History, 1985; revised edition with Christopher Arris Oakley, 2010).

4. For more on these issues, see the chapter in this volume by Marvin M. Richardson.

5. For more on treaties and sovereignty issues, see the chapter in this volume by Margaret Huettl.

6. For more on comparative approaches to Native history, see the chapter in this volume by Ann McGrath.

7. For my approach to directing graduate students, see Greg O'Brien, "An Interview with Theda Perdue and Michael D. Green," in *The Native South: New Histories and Enduring Legacies,* ed. Tim Alan Garrison and Greg O'Brien (Lincoln: University of Nebraska Press, 2017), 1–32.

8. Colin Calloway, ed., *First Peoples: A Documentary Survey of American Indian History,* 5th ed. (New York: Bedford/St. Martin's, 2015).

Teaching American Indian History Using the Medicine Way

DONALD L. FIXICO

In February 1984 a young Euchee man with Down Syndrome called Richard Brown lived outside the town of Kellyville, Oklahoma. Every day Richard would walk west along Highway 33 before turning onto a road to his grandmother's house. This particular February afternoon the temperature became bitingly cold, and Richard did not have his heavy coat as snowflakes began to fall. According to the February 10 edition of the *Sapulpa Herald,* Brown decided to get to his grandmother's house by cutting across a field with shrub oak trees and high grass, at which point he became lost. The evidence indicated that as the afternoon darkened he seemed to have become confused and changed directions multiple times. According to the paper, confusion, the dropping temperature, and improper clothing combined to cause fatal hypothermia. The empirical facts alone make Richard Brown's death tragic, and it was made even more so when details emerged that non-Native people long had bullied him for his health condition.[1]

The above report provides an entirely Western explanation for what happened to Richard Brown. In the Euchee worldview reality combines the physical and the metaphysical. Ghosts, dreams, and visions are part of this way of life, and Euchees (like several other tribes as well as more than a dozen other cultures around the world) believe in Little People. They provide a clear, *Native* framework for this story. No doubt Richard was shivering and confused as the night darkened and snow fell, but he nevertheless clutched his arms, folded them, and kept walking.

In the wind he heard someone calling his name. He walked toward the voice. He heard his name called again and turned to walk in the direction it had come from. Then another voice called his name, and he changed directions yet again. In the Euchee Way, on that winter day in 1984 the Little People took Richard's spirit with them. Knowing that he was the object of derision, one of the Little People called his name, then another, then another, until he became lost. Metaphorically, he had completed the Circle of Life, and the Little People took him to the Other Side of Life.[2] Skeptics of this version of events should perhaps consider it within the context of prevailing Western, Judeo-Christian traditions. A particularly curious story from long ago, for example, describes a man in a desert talking to a burning bush claiming to be Yahweh. No proof exists that this encounter ever actually happened—only that someone wrote it down. Those willing to consider the "truth" of Moses might also consider the "truth" of Euchee lifeways.

At the very least, the Euchee explanation of Richard Brown's life and death should force audiences to consider the non-Western realities at the core of the American Indian world. It also illuminates a crucial point for history teachers: to be most effective, Indigenous history requires a holistic inquiry into both human and nonhuman realities. It is an organic form that I identify as the *Medicine Way*, and it consists of Indigenous worldviews—a Cheyenne perspective, a Mohawk logic, a Navajo ethos, or a Seminole view—expressed through a combination of physical and metaphysical realities. The Medicine Way historical lens interprets the world through tribal traditions as well as relationships between humans and animals, plants, spirits, and sacred landscapes. It is diametrically opposed to the post-Enlightenment Western, linear way of thinking, where only empirical evidence matters. Embedded subconsciously within Native people who grew up traditionally, it is a significant factor in teaching and learning. Unfortunately, it remains a largely unknown tool to many teachers at all levels. Acknowledging the Medicine Way is a crucial starting point for exploring American Indians and their collective histories.

The Medicine Way and the Complexities of Teaching Indigenous History

Before proceeding it would be good to define the label "American Indian history." Academically, it is the professional interpretation of the Indigenous past. It could mean a strict disciplinary approach, but in recent decades it also has come to include multidisciplinary programs typically labeled American Indian studies (AIS) or Native American studies (NAS). AIS ranges far beyond history as traditionally practiced. A good example of the distinction between the two approaches draws from the moment when Columbus sailed into the Caribbean and mistakenly called the Arawak people "Indians." Historians traditionally have researched and analyzed the empirical facts involved in this episode, meaning that they have addressed who, what, where, when, and why. The result is a depiction of a human-to-human encounter, and on some level it approximates history as investigative journalism. AIS, by contrast, is more rooted in the Medicine Way. It takes into consideration the culture and lifeways of the Arawaks as well as Columbus's culture and worldview. The Medicine Way depicts a human-to-human encounter, but it includes animals, plants, the nonliving, and metaphysical experiences.

Indian history certainly has come a long way since the 1970s, when classes generally consisted of "myth of the vanished Indian" oversimplifications and glorified descriptions of how the American military defeated tribes in battle. Even as the "New Western" historiography inspired a "New Indian" historiography in the 1980s and 1990s, it still was not uncommon for "teaching Indian history" to mean using stilted facts conveyed upon VHS tapes, slides, or filmstrips as visual backups. Today, by contrast, it is not uncommon to see courses covering the boarding school experience, Indigenous activism during the Red Power era, the ambiguities of Indians serving in the American military, and even the complexities of miscegenation. The New Indian history provided a tremendous service in this regard by centering Indigenous people, seeking out Native points of view, and delving more deeply into tribal communities. Yet regardless of their sophistication, most modern classes remain limited by the fact that they focus primarily upon Indian-White relations and are linear in fashion. An unfortunate but all too common consequence is that students receive very little *exclusively* Indigenous history, an imbalance of interpretation that continues to favor mainstream generalizations.

In the Medicine Way different understandings of history prevail over Western linearity. In this genre Indians control the discourse, so interested non-Indians must lower their mainstream guard if they want to learn what Indians were really like and how and why their cultures and histories matter. An example from my own experience illustrates the point quite well. Many years ago when I was an assistant professor, I taught the second half of the US history survey. For most of the students it was a required course, and I must confess I did not particularly enjoy teaching some of the subjects on my syllabus. One lecture involved Calvin Coolidge, not particularly one of our more dynamic presidents. I proceeded to write his name in the middle of the blackboard. Thereafter I wrote "laissez-faire capitalism" in the corner and drew a line to his name. I continued to do this with other facts, connecting them with chalk to his name, like spokes on a wheel with Coolidge at the center. One non-Indigenous student eventually raised her hand and asked, "Professor Fixico, why don't you put your notes on the board in the upper left-hand corner, and write the next line below it?" I was stunned. It never occurred to me to teach in such linear fashion. My logic was that by putting Calvin Coolidge at the dead center of the blackboard, with various one- to three-word facts associated with him, there could be no confusion about the point of that day's class. Needless to say, I did not receive the greatest teaching evaluations that semester.

That experience and my growing up as a traditional Mvskoke-Seminole in Oklahoma inspired me to write *The American Indian Mind in a Linear World*.[3] I had always wondered why scholars consistently failed to explain how Indigenous elders employ their own logic, specific to their own cultural ways of knowing. But in Western-oriented classes students read, write, or type notes left to right in a rectangular classroom while the earth is rotating in a cycle as it has done for millions of years. My point: people who are cyclical by nature and more visual will be challenged in linear classrooms, which decrease their creativity and inhibit their willingness to speak up in class. More fundamentally, linearity can limit the acquisition of knowledge. The Medicine Way offers an alternative approach.

Learning about a People Not Like Me

So how does the Medicine Way translate into actual teaching and learning? After all, well-meaning teachers already must overcome significant challenges. It is fair to generalize, for example, that the majority of twenty-first-century students are not interested in studying history. Enrolling in a survey course often means little more than fulfilling a core requirement, while STEM-focused state standards place ever greater pressure on humanities and social science disciplines to "make it relevant" to the modern world.

Directly related is the challenge of overcoming the preconceived notions held by most non-Indians. Although they will not admit it, White and African American students typically find it difficult to relate to Indians—who do not look like them and who come from vastly different cultures with different logics and worldviews. To close this cultural gap it is important to find "common ground" for points of classroom discussions. A good place to begin is to confront thirty-four particularly pervasive (and pejorative) stereotypes, all of which are rooted in the 1,642 wars, battles, attacks, and skirmishes authorized by the United States government against Indian nations between 1776 and 1900.[4] Put another way, American history as it has been taught for generations draws from a multi-century mainstream whitewashing that has "subalterned" and marginalized Indians—at best. Teachers must first and foremost confront this non-attitude. To teach the subject successfully an instructor must be aware of the stereotypes stuck in the heads of students sitting (or snoring!) in the classroom. Although a bit dated, Robert Berkhofer Jr.'s 1978 book *The White Man's Indian* directly addresses the reality that Indians are an image(s) in non-Indian minds.[5]

From that point, an excellent way to pursue a more interconnected interpretation of American history is to examine specific themes in deeper detail. I push my students to identify thematic developments in everything they do—reading assignments, lectures, class discussions, even exams. One semester at Arizona State University on the first day of class, I explained my approach and asked the students to bring five themes to the next session. One student remarked, "Professor Fixico, I see themes everywhere that I had never seen before." It was a way of waking students' minds and providing them with a tool to learn about life. The thematic approach has the added benefit of introducing students to a number of perspectives.

Given their complexity, two historical examples serve to illustrate the usefulness of the thematic approach: the Battle of the Little Bighorn of 1876 and the Wounded Knee Massacre of 1890. Both are well-known events in Indian and American western history. The only point on which there is no dispute regarding the Little Bighorn affair (or the Battle of Greasy Grass, as the Lakota call it) is that George Armstrong Custer led 215 soldiers of the Seventh Cavalry into a slaughter. Military historians cannot agree on exactly what that means. Some insist Custer acted heroically. Others have called him a reckless fool. Either way, thousands of pages have been written about it since the event transpired—from Custer's rather defensive wife to author T. J. Stiles, who won the 2016 Pulitzer Prize for History for his *Custer's Trials: A Life on the Frontier of a New America.*[6]

Indians have profoundly different perspectives of what happened on June 25–26, 1876, but they are not uniform. The Oglala Holy Man Black Elk described the event in his autobiography *Black Elk Speaks*, for example, but to Lakota allies the Northern Cheyenne the confrontation looks slightly different.[7] One Cheyenne view draws from Wooden Leg, a warrior who fought against Custer. Another comes from the Cheyenne elder John Stands in Timber, who used tools of memory and oral tradition to describe what his grandmother remembered about the battle.[8] Still other perspectives come from Hidatsas, who helped supply Lakotas, and from the Crow people who served as scouts for Custer's Seventh Cavalry. Thomas LeForge provides one Crow view of Greasy Grass, but his interpretation is complicated by the fact that he was a White man who had assimilated into the Crow. Although he was accepted and "passed" as a Crow warrior, he was a cultural navigator, a person going back and forth between cultures with ease.[9]

The infamous Wounded Knee Massacre of 1890 is no less complex. In this incident there is the military version of events: that Ghost Dancers were dangerous and in need of disarming. On the other side, Lakotas rightly explain that women, children, and the elderly overwhelmingly were the victims of the massacre. This affair is especially interesting because in addition to the Lakota version, there is Charles Eastman's view. His perspective is Indian because he was Dakota (Santee Sioux), but he was also boarding school–educated and trained as a medical doctor at Boston Medical School. So, his Indigenous perspective is complicated. On the one hand, he was raised in the Dakota Way into his teen years and retained knowledge of it throughout his life. On the other hand, after becoming a physician he settled into the White world of New England.[10]

Linear historical narratives obliterate these nuances, thereby limiting the learning process. A question naturally arises: How can a modern student (or scholar) get a better sense of what happened at Greasy Grass or at Wounded Knee? The thematic, holistic Medicine Way helps to disentangle these moments with enough detail that students can begin to understand the problematic nature of the American historical narrative. And that in turn helps them locate Indigenous polities more firmly as central characters in the story of the continent.[11]

Another effective teaching approach is to pose a problem to a class. Modern educators call this tool "active learning"—everyone must vote, take a side, and make a decision. One example from my own experience: On the eve of the 1832 Black Hawk War in Wisconsin the Sauk leader Black Hawk called for warriors from the Sauk and Fox to join him and take back their homeland from White settlers. A rival leader, Keokuk, was a mixed-blood Fox. He was a shrewd negotiator, and people did not always trust him. I present the class with context regarding both the leaders and the situation. Students then vote either to follow Black Hawk into battle (knowing they are likely to die) or to follow Keokuk's leadership in signing more treaties (knowing it will force them to move away from their homeland, but that it would ensure a path to survival). A final question then emerges: Who was the true patriot, Black Hawk or Keokuk? The majority of my classes over the years have proven willing to strike the red war pole in the village and risk their life in battle. The point, however, is that this problem-solving situation encourages the class to get involved and to think about the Black Hawk War from an Indigenous perspective. And that in turn encourages them to rethink the simplicity of the American historical narrative.

Given the general modern indifference to history, connecting with current events provides yet another way to teach Indian histories using the Medicine Way. The recent struggle against the Dakota Access Pipeline in 2016–17 is a perfect example. As with problem solving, students are a lot more likely to learn from an active model. In this particular case, the central point would be to try to understand the myriad perspectives driving the crisis: that of the water protectors, the pipeline owners, law enforcement, environmentalists, the tribal chairman of the Standing Rock Sioux Tribe, and even the president of the United States.

Studying pipelines the Medicine Way further yields insight into issues of sovereignty, treaty rights, and federal Indian law. Complexities once again abound, so much so that one's head might begin to spin: 374 ratified US-Indian treaties exist, along with unrecognized treaties, confederate Indian treaties, European treaties with Indian tribes, and US-Indian agreements that were not called treaties (many of these occurred after the treaty-making process stopped in 1871). Furthermore, there are roughly 275 major federal laws between the earliest trade and intercourse acts of the late 1700s and 2020—and the number only continues to increase. Directly connected to statutory regulation are associated major court cases. A firm number depends on how one defines a "major Indian court case," but it is safe to say that there easily are over a hundred.

Exploring the pipeline debate using the Medicine Way offers a direct path for making sense of these issues. It also covers themes such as power, Mother Earth, water, capitalism, colonialism, and politics. Other current issues for classroom discussions might include Indian leadership, protecting sacred sites, race and ethnicity, Indian gaming, Indian health, Indian labor history, and Indians in borderlands.

Final Thoughts

At the end of the day, the most important objective of any teacher is to help teach students think critically and analytically. They need to be challenged intellectually and in a positive forum so that they realize the relationship between concepts, themes, and ideas. Instructing at this level moves beyond mere familiarity with the material to focus upon the relationships between historical events, research data, ideas, and concepts. With that in mind, it is crucial to maintain clear goals for the classroom. I also believe that there is an intellectual difference between teaching and lecturing, and I have come to learn that the former is much easier and more productive than the latter. In order to inspire students, it is my mission to present different perspectives by engaging in a process of active learning to the highest degree possible.

Careful preparation for each class also is crucial for establishing an intellectual dialogue with students. Teach each class like it is your last one. Help students "find their voice" in discussions and in their writing. Mainstream society is competitive and articulate, and students need to learn how to express their point of view as well as they can. Lastly, a respected professor is a "people" person who will take the time to listen and advise students and wisely balance time between instructing and research.

One final thought. Teaching Indian history requires allowing your students to know how passionate you are about your craft. Think about what you want students to "take away" from your class. I tell mine that they will forget most of the information that we cover, but that my objective is to make them "think deeply." Many things I teach in class are about life in general. But in an Indian reality, in the Medicine Way, thinking about the processual nature of life is crucial. All things are connected. So, I put a lot of thought into teaching Indian history. I flip the switch mentally before entering the classroom—even if I had a flat tire driving to campus—to do the best that I possibly can. When I return to my office and collapse in my chair, I am exhausted, feeling the amount of energy and passion spent teaching. In my office are certain meaningful things that are powerful to me, and they restore positive energy needed for the rest of the day.

NOTES

1. Mendy Mayberry, "Body Found in Woods," *Sapulpa Herald* 71, no. 127 (February 10, 1984).

2. Donald L. Fixico, *Call for Change: The Medicine Way of American Indian History, Ethos & Reality* (Lincoln: University of Nebraska Press, 2013), 41–42.

3. Donald L. Fixico, *The American Indian Mind in a Linear World: American Indian Studies and Traditional Knowledge* (New York: Routledge, 2003), 125–26.

4. Another six stereotypes are positive, while another six fall into the category of "neutral." Donald L. Fixico, "Interviews and Conversations: Roundtable on Massacre at Mountain Meadows," *Dialogue: A Journal of Mormon Thought* 42, no. 1 (Spring 2009): 128–29.

5. See Robert F. Berkhofer Jr., *The White Man's Indian: Images of the American Indian from Columbus to the Present* (New York: Alfred A. Knopf, 1978). Preconceived notions are part of the "othering" process coming from Edward Said's intellectual discourse on the "exotic" in his seminal work *Orientalism* (New York: Vintage Books, 1978).

6. Elizabeth B. Custer, *Boots and Saddles; or, Life in Dakota with General Custer* (1885; Big Byte Books, 2018); Elizabeth B. Custer, *Tenting on the Plains; or, General Custer in Kansas and Texas* (1887; Franklin Classics, 2018); Elizabeth B. Custer, *Following the Guidon* (1890; Madison & Adams, 2020); T. J. Stiles, *Custer's Trials: A Life on the Frontier of a New America* (New York: Vintage Books, 2015). See also Michael A. Elliott, *Custerology: The Enduring Legacy of the Indian Wars and George Armstrong Custer* (Chicago: University of Chicago Press, 2007).

7. John Neihardt, *Black Elk Speaks: Being the Life Story of a Holy Man of the Oglala Sioux* (1932; Lincoln: University of Nebraska Press, 1979), 105–30.

8. Thomas B. Marquis, interpreter, *Wooden Leg: A Warrior Who Fought Custer,* 2nd ed. (1931; Lincoln: University of Nebraska Press, 2003); John Stands In Timber and Margot Liberty, *Cheyenne Memories* (1967; Lincoln: University of Nebraska Press, 1972), 191–211. For more on military issues, see the chapter in this volume by Mark van de Logt.

9. Thomas B. Marquis, *Memories of a White Crow Indian (Thomas H. Leforge)* (1928; Lincoln: University of Nebraska Press, 1974), 205–78. Older examples include Manteo and Wanchese at Roanoke in 1585–1586, and John Sassamon in the English colony of Plymouth circa 1675. The latter's death provided the spark for what has become known as King Phillip's War.

10. Between 1902 and 1918 Dr. Charles Eastman wrote thirteen books, starting with *Memories of an Indian Boyhood* (1902; Mint Editions, 2021).

11. I have taught at eleven different universities, and over the years I have learned to accept that I am a storyteller. Stories are excellent pedagogical devices, not just because they entertain or capture student interest but also because they offer insight into multiple perspectives. They reveal understandings from within the tribal world and show that leaders made decisions based on logic derived from their ethos and reality.

Transnational History and Deep Time

Reflections on Teaching Indigenous History from Australia

ANN MCGRATH

This chapter explores two concepts that can inform the teaching of Indigenous history in American class-rooms: transnational and deep history. *Transnational approaches* unsettle accustomed ways of thinking about historical issues too often constrained by the parameters of nation, tribe, or region. *Deep history approaches* move beyond modernity's time frames to explore the longue durée of Indigenous histories. Of the two, the former is perhaps more widely known. Transnational approaches are well tested in the United States and Australia, with a small but growing comparative literature now available. Though colonized at different moments (the British first arrived in Australia with convict labor in 1788, two centuries after the English invasions of North America at Roanoke, Jamestown, and Plymouth), their national histories, which also commenced at different times, are more interconnected than we might imagine. For example, the first convict cargo to Australia included eleven African Americans who were freed slaves. More significantly, these colonies and nations exchanged and implemented common European ideas, policies, and practices relating to race, gender, and colonialism — and the practice of history itself.[1]

The deep history approach is not as well known and developed as transnational approaches now are. Its crucial importance lies in the fact that "history" is a problematic concept for Indigenous people.[2] After all, prevailing chronologies, periodizations, and narratives derive from Western concepts and generally have been written by the colonizer classes. In the Indigenous world, "time" and "history" maintain decidedly non-Western definitions. Indians and Aborigines engage in rich modes of historical interpretation and certainly develop new modes of practice, including in the filmic and digital space. They may not, however, wish to stand under the umbrella of history as practiced in Western academe. More fundamentally, both Indigenous Americans and Aboriginal Australians maintain knowledge of deep landed connections, having lived on their respective continents for millennia prior to the European invasions. Anthropologists generally agree that the Americas were first settled 12,000–15,000 years ago and Australia 60,000 years ago, although new archaeological research leads to ever-shifting "earliest dates."

Ancient arrival should not imply uniformity of culture, of course. Indigenous peoples have myriad (and contrasting) traditions, lifeways, economies, and social structures in the Americas and in Australia. Today these nations hold onto cherished values, drawing pride and strength from cultural continuity. Indigenous polities have demonstrated remarkable resilience amid the uneven weight of colonizing power relations. Many have embraced modernity. Amidst multiple colonizing dispossessions, dramatic disruption, and social change, they continue to assert their long-held sovereignty. "Deep history" considers this sovereignty over longer time periods outside European chronologies.[3] Introducing the longue durée widens the temporal scope of inquiry, thereby enabling us to start thinking more "historically" about experiences not defined by European action. It need not start with writing, for there are many other kinds of material and oral evidence upon which to draw. By expanding temporality beyond the modern, and beyond epochs of literacy, we might be able to rethink what history is, when it starts, and who is in it.

By using the interdisciplinary methods of transnational and deep history, teachers can expand their students' insight into individual human action and agency.

Transnational History

As a generalization, "transnational history" is a call to think beyond national boundaries — that is, the modern borders of large nation-states such as the United States and Australia. Histories of both countries still tend to be written within national frameworks and primarily for local audiences.[4] Accounting for the experiences of other polities, other "nations," changes both points of reference and the persuasiveness of historical arguments.[5] As historian Kat Ellinghaus has explained, both nations would profit "from the realization that their origins lie in a global process of colonization by Europeans." Crossing national boundaries can change the way both "Australians and Americans view their own histories."[6] In my view, the term "transnational" does not only apply to colonizer nation-states and to relationships between them or comparisons across them, but also to the *"colonized" transnational*. This label is appropriate for Indigenous polities in the geographic spaces defined as Australia or North America—they were people dealing not only with the newly arrived colonizing powers but also with each other's nations.

The scale of undertaking the transnational approach is admittedly daunting, but a quick survey of realities reveals its utility. Both the United States and Australia comprise many distinctive Indigenous tribes and sovereignties with contrasting experiences. Australia, for example, has approximately 250 distinctive language groups. Aboriginal organizational structures do not fit neatly into the definition of "tribe." Leadership is complex and not based upon a chief system. Aboriginal people frequently use "language groups" and "clans" as definitional terms, while their use of "country" indicates a sense of nationhood associated with discrete tracts of land. They describe themselves as "traditional custodians" rather than "owners" in the proprietorial sense of Western law.[7] As with American Indians, Australian Aboriginals experienced frontier violence, forced removals, forced land sales, segregation, underpayment, intrusions by the colonizer legal system, loss of economic opportunity, land entitlements, and explicit political exclusion. And as in North America, there is a complex history of Indigenous Australian action and reaction to such invasions, including economic, material, political, cultural, and spiritual initiatives, as well as technical and social innovation.[8]

Considering nations alongside each other, in other words, helps teachers and scholars challenge old presumptions, expectations, and conclusions.[9] An excellent specific example is the dilemma of interracial courtship and marriage. In North America there was great anxiety about White women intermixing with dark-skinned people—what I call "the marital middle ground." In Australia, racial anxieties were sparked when White and Asian men intermixed with Aboriginal women, prompting segregation policies.[10] At the same time, courtship, marriage, and love could defy colonialism's edicts.

In a powerful example, in 1826 a young White woman from Cornwall, Connecticut, called Harriett Gold courted a Cherokee student, Elias Boudinot, and their engagement sparked intense controversy. Boudinot was threatened with lynching, and both were burned in effigy, while their engagement ripped apart her family. Yet they married, and under guard the newlyweds traveled from Cherokee Country in western North Carolina and Georgia to Connecticut, and ultimately to the Indian Territory (now Oklahoma). Boudinot became the renowned editor of the first Indigenous newspaper, the *Cherokee Phoenix*. Another interesting and teachable courtship is that of Mary Brian Stapler and the Cherokee chief John Ross or Kooweskoowe. The two were well aware of the subversive nature of their relationship, which makes their flirtatious letters incisive, humorous, and illuminating.

Moving to Australia's Queensland frontier, the White missionaries and government men who obsessed about intermarriage themselves broke the strict regulations they advocated by carrying on secret love affairs with Aboriginal women. Through actively negotiating and regulating intermarriage, Australian Aboriginal women and men asserted and enforced their own governance structures and strict marital law. In the longer term, where possible, they harnessed intermarriage in order to facilitate the transmission of Indigenous sovereignty. In so doing, they expanded their familial networks beyond racial categories and outside the colonizer power structures that limited Indigenous agency.

Teachers might consider the comparative similarities between American adoptions of Indigenous children and the Australian problem of "stolen children." In 2008 the Australian prime minister Kevin Rudd made a public apology in the national parliament to the "stolen generations," a long-awaited moment that brought the nation to a halt. Rudd's speech is readily accessible on YouTube. Poignant songs such as Archie Roach's "Took the Children Away" tell the story with the emotion it deserves. *Rabbit-Proof Fence*, the movie based on the removal of the Australian Aboriginal girl Doris Pilkington, is a moving, beautifully told epic.[11] As with American Indigenous adoptions, the post-generational trauma and impact on Aboriginal families has been profound.

Deep Time History

Like many disciplines in the Western academy, history has evolved to serve the nation-state. An unfortunate side effect has been that Indigenous polities have become largely irrelevant to the preferred grand narratives.[12] Given the presumptive power of colonizer nations and of Western traditions, "discovery dates" and "landing dates" have become the pivotal points of historical periodization. For discoveries, think 1492 broadly, or more specifically 1620 and the modern American commemoration of Thanksgiving. (It was actually Congressman Elias Boudinot, the Cherokee editor's namesake, who revived celebration of the day.)[13] For Australians, the moment of discovery considered worth "celebrating" is Governor Phillip's landing with the first fleet of convicts at Port Jackson in 1788.[14] These European discoveries of other places, of course, are imagined from the perspective of "Old World" Europe. In effect, "discoverers" have arbitrarily and ahistorically become special, as their "landings" and their supposed "first gaze" of others' lands have been used in historical and legal narratives to justify empires taking possession of *vacuum domicilium*.[15] It is an important reminder: such history tellings not only provide problematic frameworks for national identity, but they also underpin triumphalist myths and legends that readily break down under scrutiny.[16] Listening to diverse voices and taking account of cross-cultural perspectives are vital.[17]

The concept of "deep time" attempts to deconstruct the framing of history as "before or after European arrival." Historians may not know exact dates for Indigenous occupation in North America or Australia, but we know that they predate European occupation by many thousands, maybe tens of thousands of years. Some scholars have taken it even further. Medievalist Daniel Smail and anthropologist Andrew Shyrock contend that scholars and teachers need to work closely with biological and other scientists to understand the long history of hominids.[18] Dipesh Chakrabarty argues for an expanded framework that takes geological time into account—a necessary shift to understand the modern era of human-induced climate change.[19] Many humanities scholars, including environmental historians, increasingly promote an analysis that considers animals, plants, and things as "actants" in history—a position that challenges the assumed centrality of human action.[20] Insights from several other disciplines are required to inform a study of deep history. Studies by geologists, climate scientists, geographers, geomorphologists, astrophysicists, and other scientists provide relevant insights into vast climatic and ecological change and astrological events that affected human history. Archaeologists, who regularly work with earth scientists, geneticists, and dating experts, focus attention upon ancient human environments, surviving manufactures, rock and cave art, and various other kinds of material evidence.

Deep time methods need to acknowledge Indigenous ontologies—what historian Donald Fixico has called the *Medicine Way* of knowing.[21] Genuine research collaborations with Native representatives and communities are vital to such academic projects.[22] Indigenous accounts—those previously written, recorded by others, and continuing in living oral traditions—contain knowledge of scientific and historical significance, including information about astrological events, sea rise during the Pleistocene era, the formation of rivers and bays, the eruption of volcanoes, and other events relating to climatic change.[23] Indigenous techniques provide insight into the deep human past that predate literacy and literate traditions.

Epic narratives transmitted over many generations by Native peoples can offer particular illumination of Indigenous ways of knowing about deep time. Many of these accounts have been recorded in the archives by non-Indigenous literary scholars, anthropologists, and linguists. Although generally classed as legends, creation or dreaming stories, myths, or folklore, these narratives, which I call "ancient memory," offer an important means by which to explore the longue durée. Deeply associated with land, culture, and heritage, these epic narratives are repositories of knowledge. They may not "look" like traditional historical evidence because of their origins in oral tradition, but they offer enriching perspectives. They serve different narrative functions, with stories of superheroes, ancient creation ancestors, humans morphing into animals, and geographical features that defy the usual definition of "history." "Ancient" in its vital threads, such Medicine Ways continue as living, interpretative, and dynamic practices.[24] Although much more careful research is needed, such transcribed Indigenous histories provide powerful ways to teach Native histories.

"Deep histories" remind us that Indigenous histories are told as a multisensory experience. They were not designed as texts. Their many performative mediums include song, dance, rock art, ochre, acrylic, oil, sculpture, and performance. The National Museum of the American Indian showcases a range of presentation techniques. Museums and keeping places increasingly present Indigenous histories via direct story-telling in film, audio, and video, along with craft, artistic interpreta-tions, digital storytelling, and landscape-based performative practices. Many Indigenous communities use multimedia to explore their deep pasts, developing exhibitions, films, and television programs. Digital history projects such as "Deepening Histories of Place" have developed audio and video stories choreographed by Aboriginals from around Australia.[25] Regionally based projects such as the Ara Irititja Project recorded "stories from a long time ago" of the Anangu people of central Australia in a purpose-built digital archive.[26] Via a visual storytelling practice known as "cultural mapping," Aboriginal people at places such as Lake Gregory and the Willandra Lakes/Lake Mungo region are mapping their relationships to land, mobility, and their life stories.[27]

The traditions of rock art and other art forms in Australia and North America deserve careful attention, for they are an invaluable archive for the study of deep history and they also record the history of colonial-ism. Indigenous historians tell their history through weaving, through dying and crafting various objects of familial and sacred significance, through travel and exchange, through oral narratives that involve per-formances, and rituals that include dance and song. *Songlines: Tracking the Seven Sisters*, an exhibition at the National Museum of Australia, re-counted landscape-based stories with richly painted and animated visu-als, the stories linking different Indigenous groups across vast tracks of inland Australia.[28] Epic narratives were told through travel and artistic representation in dance, body paint, sand and bark paintings, tree and rock engravings, and many other visual arts.

A note on archaeology, human remains, and genomics is in order. Although DNA research offers important insights into the deep human past, its long association with racist discourses has rendered it highly controversial. Indigenous peoples have suffered a shocking history of colonial tomb raiding, the stealing and selling of human remains. With no regard for community beliefs about respecting their dead, the remains of recently deceased members of communities and those of people who lived thousands of years ago were long displayed or stored away in imperial and national museums far from Indigenous lands.[29] In 1990, the US Congress passed the Native American Graves Protection and Repatriation Act (NAGPRA) to restore control and custodianship to the relevant Indigenous people, when they can be located.[30] Similar policies apply in Australia. Given the unethical practices of the past, many Indigenous people are understandably skeptical about research on human remains. They share a concern that the disturbance of ancient graves will cause damaging effects among the living. Until those remains are repatriated, Indigenous peoples suffer the strain of fulfilling a deeply felt moral obligation to right this injustice.

An example from Australia illuminates the dilemma quite well. In 1969 and in the early 1970s cremated human remains appeared on the erosive dunes of a now dry ancient salt lake at Lake Mungo, in New South Wales. They were found to date back at least forty thousand years, overturning contemporary views that Aboriginal people occupied Australia for only half or a quarter of that time. Local representatives were not consulted about their exhumation or their removal to a distant university for examination. Despite persistent protests by Aboriginals, "Mungo Lady" did not finally return to her burial place until 1992. It took another twenty-five years to return "Mungo Man," along with the remains of more than one hundred other individuals.

Local Aboriginals see these people as relatives and ancestors, not as mere "scientific discoveries." Their remains offer crucial insights into the ancient Indigenous past for physical anthropologists, geoscientists, and other dating experts. Yet the intrusive and destructive techniques used by many scholars disturbed the local Indigenous land custodians— the Mutthi, Nyaampa, and Barkindji. Many believe that these remains have been amply researched and too long interfered with.[31] Many other human remains continue to surface, but elders discourage research or excavation on them.[32] Yet future generations may wish to know more and every year, genetic, isotopic, and other scientific techniques advance to potentially reveal yet more significant information about the lives these individuals lived in deep time. About where they travelled to and from, what they ate, how they treated disease and injuries, their rituals and possibly even aspects of their beliefs. More Indigenous scholars and experts are practicing in these fields, but all working in such a sensitive field need to respect local Indigenous protocols. Working closely with Indigenous knowledge custodians adds value for everyone in this field.

In the academy, transnational and deep history approaches are still in early stages of development, but potentially they might redress the thematic and temporal gaps created by national history telling—where Indigenous peoples remain "history's outsiders." Teachers are skilled in using many different kinds of evidence, but to pay adequate attention to Indigenous histories, new methodologies and new skills are urgently required. For one thing, in order to research deep time, historians of all backgrounds need to work with local Indigenous knowledge custodians. In order to develop a fully collaborative practice, Indigenous historians—whether they consider themselves scholarly or community historians—need to be in charge or in positions of parity. This way, teams can integrate ancient memory narratives alongside other forms of knowledge. If we can do this in our teaching, we will advance historical awareness in productive new directions that will expand, enhance, and transform the discipline of history.

NOTES

1. Cassandra Pybus, *Black Founders: The Unknown Story of Australia's First Black Settlers* (Sydney: UNSW Press, 2006). One notable distinction between Australia and the United States lay in the recognition of Indigenous polities at the earliest stages of colonization. Unlike in North America, British authorities did not negotiate treaties with Australian Aboriginal people. With limited exceptions where earlier governors declared martial law, Aborigines were classed as subjects of the Crown and in principle fell under the criminal law. Unlike the well-known American Indian and Maori wars, Australian colonists engaged in undeclared warfare. As a result, legacies of historical denial endure to the present.

2. Ann McGrath and M. Jebb, ed., *Long History, Deep Time: Deepening Histories of Place* (Canberra: ANU Press, 2015).

3. Key categories such as "prehistory" have tended to reinforce European primacy—as if history had to start with White people, literacy, and their notions of modernity. Americanists often dub this Indigenous epoch as "pre-Columbian time"; Australians use "precontact" or pre-British arrival. Key dates pivot around the arrival of European discoverers such as Columbus, Captain Cook, and the earliest colonists. Although their arrival may mark a key turning point, it certainly did not mark the beginning of human history on these lands. For Australian histories that "start" with the coming of White colonists, see for example Patricia Grimshaw, Marilyn Lake, Ann McGrath, and Marian Quartly, *Creating a Nation, 1788–1990* (Ringwood, Vic: McPhee Gribble, 1994); Ann McGrath, "Lady Mungo and the New and Old Discovery Narrative," in *Unmasking Ideology in Imperial and Colonial Archaeology: Vocabulary, Symbols, and Legacy*, ed. Bonnie Effros and Lai Guolong (Los Angeles: Cotsen, 2018); Ann McGrath, "On the Sacred Clay of Botany Bay: Landings, National Memorialization, and Multiple Sovereignties," *New Diversities* (December 2017); Ann McGrath, L. Rademaker, and B. Silverstein, "Deep History and Deep Listening: Indigenous

Knowledges and the Narration of Deep Pasts," *Rethinking History* 25, no. 3 (2021). For more on how to teach archeological issues, see the chapter in this volume by Maureen Meyers.

4. Historian Ian Tyrrell called for transnational histories as a means of shaking free the profound influence of "American exceptionalism." Ian Tyrrell, "American Exceptionalism in an Age of International History," *American Historical Review* 96, no. 4 (October 1991): 1031–55; Ian R. Tyrrell, "Reflections on the Transnational Turn in United States History: Theory and Practice," *Journal of Global History* 4, no. 3 (2009): 453–74; and Gary B. Nash, "The Hidden History of Mestizo America," *Journal of American History* 82, no. 3 (December 1995): 941–64.

5. Until the 1970s in Australia, historians shied away from writing about even the nineteenth and twentieth centuries of Aboriginal Australia, leaving most of the work to anthropologists and linguists. As Aboriginal activists declared in the bicentenary protests of 1988: "Australia has a Black History." There has been a great flowering of Indigenous history since then, including numerous autobiographies and excellent historical texts by Indigenous authors. Frances Peters-Little, Ann Curthoys, and John Docker, *Passionate Histories: Myth, Memory and Indigenous Australia* (Canberra: ANU Press, and Aboriginal History, 2010). Aboriginal Studies Press, Fremantle Arts Centre Press, and Magabala Books have been important players in this regard.

6. Kat Ellinghaus, *Taking Assimilation to Heart: Marriages of White Women and Indigenous Men in the United States and Australia, 1887–1937* (Lincoln: University of Nebraska Press, 2006), 220.

7. Over the twentieth century, a lively activist exchange was sought between Native Americans and Indigenous Australians, who have also engaged with Black rights movements. Perhaps due to globalizing Indigenous movements, including United Nations Indigenous initiatives, some Australian Aboriginal people refer to their landed and political entities as "tribes" and, increasingly, as "nations." John Maynard, *Fight for Liberty and Freedom: The Origins of Australian Aboriginal Activism* (Canberra: Aboriginal Studies Press, 2007).

8. I have provided a longer summary of Australian policy in "A National Story," in *Contested Ground: Australian Aborigines under the British Crown*, ed. Ann McGrath (Sydney: Allen & Unwin, 1995), 359–97. One can find a comparative US-Australia approach in Ann McGrath, "Introduction: A Perfect Marriage?," in *Illicit Love: Interracial Sex and Marriage in the United States and Australia* (Lincoln: University of Nebraska Press, 2015).

9. McGrath, "Introduction: A Perfect Marriage?"

10. See McGrath, *Illicit Love*, 2; Martha Hodes, ed., *Sex, Love, Race: Crossing Boundaries in North American History* (New York: New York University Press, 1999); Martha Hodes, *White Women, Black Men: Illicit Sex in the Nineteenth-Century South* (New Haven: Yale University Press, 1997).

11. Phillip Noyce, *Rabbit-Proof Fence* (2002); "Sorry, Kevin Rudd's Apology to the 'Stolen Generation,'" https://www.youtube.com/watch?v=b3TZOG pG6cM; Ann McGrath, "Taking Charge of the Offspring of Mixed Frontier Unions," in *Antipodean Childhoods: Growing Up in Australia and New Zealand*, ed. Helga Ramsey-Kurze and Ulla Ratheiser (Cambridge: Cambridge Scholars Publishing, 2010); Margaret D. Jacobs, *White Mother to a Dark Race: Settler Colonialism, Maternalism, and the Removal of Indigenous Children in the American West and Australia, 1880–1940* (Lincoln: University of Nebraska Press, 2009).

12. In many ways Indigenous nations become "people without history." Ann McGrath, "Deep Histories in Time, or Crossing the Great Divide," in *Long History, Deep Time: Deepening Histories of Place*, ed. Ann McGrath and Mary Anne Jebb (Canberra: ANU Press, 2015), 1–32; Ann McGrath, "People of the Footprints: Rediscovery, Indigenous Historicities, and the Science of Deep Time," *Interventions* 24, no. 2 (2021): 181–207.

13. McGrath, *Illicit Love*, 63.

14. For example, see Gary B. Nash, *First City: Philadelphia and the Forgiving of Historical Memory* (Philadelphia: University of Pennsylvania Press, 2006); see also Colin G. Calloway, *Crown and Calumet: British-Indian Relations, 1783–1815* (Norman: University of Oklahoma Press, 1987).

15. *Vaccuum domicilium*: vacant land. Historian Jean O'Brien uses New England to elucidate the colonizer obsession with White "firsting," which she has paired with a sentimental approach to "the last Indian" or Indigenous "lasting." Jean M. O'Brien, *Firsting and Lasting: Writing Indians Out of Existence in New England* (Minneapolis: University of Minnesota Press, 2010).

16. For more on this point in the American context, see the chapter in this volume by Mark van de Logt. The Australian example is discussed at more length in McGrath, "Lady Mungo."

17. McGrath, Rademaker, and Silverstein, "Deep History and Deep Listening."

18. Andrew Shyrock and Daniel Lord Smail, *Deep History: The Architecture of Past and Present* (Berkeley: University of California Press, 2011).

19. Dipesh Chakrabarty, "The Climate of History: Four Theses," *Critical Inquiry* 35, no. 3 (2009): 197–222.

20. Bruno Latour, *An Inquiry into Modes of Existence* (Cambridge: Harvard University Press, 2013). For earlier Australian-based discussions, see Deborah Bird Rose, *Country of the Heart: An Indigenous Australian Homeland* (Canberra: Aboriginal Studies Press for AIATSIS, 2002); Deborah Bird Rose, *Dingo Makes Us Human: Life and Land in an Australian Aboriginal Culture* (Oakleigh, Vic.: Cambridge University Press, 2000).

21. Donald Fixico, *Call for Change: The Medicine Way of American Indian History* (Lincoln: University of Nebraska Press, 2013). See also the chapter in this volume by Donald L. Fixico.

22. Robert W. Preucel, "Indigenous Archaeology and the Science Question," *Archaeological Review from Cambridge* 27, no. 1 (2012): 121–41; Robert W. Preucel and Stephen A Mrozowski, *Contemporary Archaeology in Theory: The New Pragmatism* (Chichester, UK: John Wiley & Sons, 2010).

23. Duane Hamacher, "Meteoritics and Cosmology among the Aboriginal Cultures of Central Australia," *Journal of Cosmology* 13 (2011): 3743–53; Patrick D. Nunn and Nicholas J. Reid, "Aboriginal Memories of Inundation of the Australian Coast Dating from More than 7000 Years Ago," *Australian Geographer* 47, no. 1 (2016): 11–47. See also Ann McGrath and Lynette Russell, "History's Outsiders," and Chris Ballard, "Transmission's End? Cataclysm and Chronology in Indigenous Oral Tradition," both in *The Routledge Companion to Global Indigenous History*, ed. A. McGrath and L. Russell (London: Routledge, 2021).

24. In northern Australia, Rob Paton shows how, in order for a community thrown out of kilter by tragedy to become healthy again, one Indigenous community's history worked to realign and readjust their historical narratives. Rob Paton, "The Mutability of Time and Space as a Means of Healing History in an Australian Aboriginal Community," in McGrath and Jebb, *Long History, Deep Time*, 67–82. See also Fixico, *Call for Change*; Ann McGrath, "Is History Good Medicine?" *Journal of Australian Studies* 38, no. 4 (2014): 396–414; Christopher B. Teuton, *Cherokee Stories of the Turtle Island Liars' Club* (Chapel Hill: University of North Carolina Press, 2012); Peter Nabokov, *A Forest of Time: American Indian Ways of History* (New York: Cambridge University Press, 2002); Minoru Hokari, *Gurindji Journey: A Japanese Historian in the Outback* (Honolulu: University of Hawaii Press, 2011).

25. The following site contains several downloadable histories that our team for "Deepening Histories of Place: Sites of National and International Significance" created with Indigenous communities; see various sites and products at www.deepeninghistories.anu.edu.au.

26. Ara Irititja Project; http://www.irititja.com.

27. Kim Mahood, *Position Doubtful: Mapping Landscapes and Memories* (Brunswick, Vic.: Scribe, 2016). See also "A 'Treasure Map' of Indigenous History in Australia," https://re.anu.edu.au/a-treasure-map-of-indigenous-history-in-australia.

28. Margo Neale, ed., *Songlines: Tracking the Seven Sisters* (Canberra: National Museum of Australia Press, 2017).

29. Cressida Fforde, Jane Hubert, and Paul Turnbull, eds., *The Dead and Their Possessions: Repatriation in Principle, Policy and Practice* (London: Routledge, 2002); and Chip Colwell, *Plundered Skulls and Stolen Spirits: Inside the Fight to Reclaim Native America's Culture* (Chicago: University of Chicago Press, 2017).

30. Chip Colwell, "The Sacred and the Museum: Repatriation and the Trajectories of Inalienable Possessions," *Museum Worlds* 2, no. 1 (2014): 10–24; Chip Colwell-Chanthaphonh, T. J. Ferguson, Dorothy Lippert, Randall H. McGuire,

George P. Nicholas, Joe E. Watkins, and Larry J. Zimmerman, "The Premise and Promise of Indigenous Archaeology," *American Antiquity* 75, no. 2 (2010): 228–38; and Chip Colwell-Chanthaphonh, *Living Histories: Native Americans and Southwestern Archaeology* (Lanham: Altamira 2010).

31. Ann McGrath and Malcolm Allbrook, "Collaborative Histories of the Willandra Lakes," in *Long History, Deep Time*, 241–52; Ann McGrath and Andrew Pike, director/producer, *Message from Mungo*, documentary film (Canberra: Ronin Films, 2014, DVD. 70 mins); Rosanne Kennedy, Leane Jeanine, Ann McGrath, Nicole Moore, and Maria Nugent, "Roundtable: *Message from Mungo* and the Scales of Memory," *Australian Humanities Review* 59 (April/May 2016), 247–58.

32. At the same time, Indigenous Australians and Americans both appreciate what they have learned from less-intrusive types of archaeological research, especially if the process has been a collaborative one with community representatives. More young Indigenous people are training in related fields. Some people are now becoming very interested in using contemporary (as opposed to ancient) DNA research to understand lost family links and connections and for the purpose of historical reconciliation. For more on this point, see Keith Wailoo, Alondra Nelson, and Catherine Lee, eds., *Genetics and the Unsettled Past: The Collision of DNA, Race, and History* (New Brunswick, NJ: Rutgers University Press, 2012); and Ann McGrath, "Deep Histories in Time." See also the chapter in this volume by Maureen Meyers.

FOR FURTHER READING

Ballantyne, Tony, and Antoinette M. Burton. *Bodies in Contact: Rethinking Colonial Encounters in World History*. Durham, NC: Duke University Press, 2005.

Ballantyne, Tony, and Antoinette M. Burton. *Moving Subjects: Gender, Mobility, and Intimacy in an Age of Global Empire*. Urbana: University of Illinois Press, 2009.

Brooks, James F., ed. *Captives and Cousins: Slavery, Kinship, and Community in the Southwest Borderlands*. Chapel Hill: University of North Carolina Press, 2002.

Cole, Anna, Victoria Haskins, and Fiona Paisley. *Uncommon Ground: White Women in Aboriginal History*. Canberra: Aboriginal Studies Press for AIATSIS, 2005.

Edmonds, Penelope. *Urbanizing Frontiers: Indigenous People and Settlers in 19th-Century Pacific Rim Cities*. Vancouver: UBC Press, 2010.

Ellinghaus, Kat. *Taking Assimilation to Heart: Marriages of White Women and Indigenous Men in Australia and the United States, 1887–1937*. Lincoln: University of Nebraska Press, 2006.

Ford, Lisa. *Settler Sovereignty: Jurisdiction and Indigenous People in Australia and the United States, 1788–1836*. Cambridge, MA: Harvard University Press, 2010.

Grimshaw, Patricia. "Interracial Marriages and Colonial Regimes in Victoria and Aotearoa/New Zealand." *Frontiers: A Journal of Women's Studies* 23, no. 3 (2002): 12–28.

Grimshaw, Patricia. *Paths of Duty: American Missionary Wives in Nineteenth-Century Hawaii*. Honolulu: University of Hawaii Press, 1989.

Haskins, Victoria. *Matrons and Maids: Regulating Indian Domestic Service in Tucson, 1914–1934*. Tucson: University of Arizona Press, 2012.

Jacobs, Margaret D. *White Mother to a Dark Race: Settler Colonialism, Maternalism, and the Removal of Indigenous Children in the American West and Australia, 1880–1940*. Lincoln: University of Nebraska Press, 2009.

Lake, Marilyn, and Henry Reynolds. *Drawing the Global Color Line: White Men's Countries and the Question of Racial Equality*. Carlton: Melbourne University Press, 2008.

Maynard, John. *Fight for Liberty and Freedom: The Origins of Australian Aboriginal Activism*. Canberra: Aboriginal Studies Press, 2007.

McGrath, A. "On the Sacred Clay of Botany Bay: Landings, National Memorialization, and Multiple Sovereignties." *New Diversities* 19, no. 2 (2017): 85–102.

McGrath, A. "People of the Footprints: Rediscovery, Indigenous Historicities, and the Science of Deep Time." *Interventions* 24, no. 2 (2021): 181–207.

McGrath, A., L. Rademaker, B. Silverstein. "Deep History and Deep Listening: Indigenous Knowledges and the Narration of Deep Pasts." *Rethinking History* 25, no. 3 (2021): 307–26.

McGrath, A., and L. Russell, eds. *The Routledge Companion to Global Indigenous History*. London: Routledge, 2021.

Salesa, Damon. *Racial Crossings: Race, Intermarriage, and the Victorian British Empire*. Oxford: Oxford University Press, 2011.

Smithers, Greg. *Science, Sexuality, and Race in the United States and Australia, 1780–1940*. London: Routledge, 2009.

Stoler, Ann L. *Along the Archival Grain: Epistemic Anxieties and Colonial Common Sense*. Princeton, NJ: Princeton University Press, 2009.

Van Toorn, Penny. *Writing Never Arrives Naked: Early Aboriginal Cultures of Writing in Australia*. Canberra: Aboriginal Studies Press, 2006.

Veracini, Lorenzo. *Settler Colonialism: A Theoretical Overview*. New York: Palgrave Macmillan, 2010.

Wanhalla, Angela. *In/Visible Sight: The Mixed-Descent Families of Southern New Zealand*. Wellington: Bridget Williams Books, 2009.

Wanhalla, Angela. *Matters of the Heart: A History of Interracial Marriage in New Zealand*. Auckland: Auckland University Press, 2013.

Wolfe, Patrick. "Corpus Nullius: The Exception of Indians and Other Aliens in U.S. Constitutional Discourse." *Postcolonial Studies* 10, no. 2 (2007): 127–51.

Wolfe, Patrick. "Land, Labor, and Difference: Elementary Structures of Race." *American Historical Review* 106, no. 3 (June 2001): 866–905.

Wolfe, Patrick. "Nation and MiscegeNation: Discursive Continuity in the Post-Mabo Era." *Social Analysis* 34 (October 1994): 94–152.

Being There

Experiential Learning by
Living Native American History

BERNARD C. PERLEY

A crucial element of teaching and understanding American Indian history is the reconciliation of the colonial/settler narrative with the traumatic experiences of Indigenous communities. This chapter describes an interdisciplinary and collaborative project that emphasized experiential learning as a means by which to construct a shared, respectful, and celebratory space for learning the tense realities of their mutual histories. The installation project, titled *Experiencing Native North America*, is configured to celebrate Indigenous languages, religions, and landscapes in the interior of the display while capturing the tensions and traumas of colonial history on the exterior. It is interdisciplinary, representing contributions from the fields of English, history, education, and anthropology. It allows participants to walk through and around the historical/sacred space in order to *live* Native American history.

A collaboration of faculty from the University of Wisconsin–Milwaukee and the language teachers and administrative staff at Milwaukee's Indian Community School of Franklin, Wisconsin, the installation is designed to provoke conversations with constituencies across all institutions and communities. It initially was shared with the Milwaukee Indian Community School, the Educators Network for Social Justice, the Wisconsin Indian Educators Association, the Native American Literature Symposium, and several other Milwaukee community venues. The multiple venues reflected the value of the installation as a learning environment for all ages. The coauthors/participants recognized the pedagogical potential for the installation to serve as an exportable learning environment easily adaptable to other Native American experiences and locales. This chapter outlines the development of the installation as a critical reflection on American history. It also explores ways for participatory repurposing of the installation, as well as how such activities provide a crucial contribution to knowledge and constituency building in the service of Indigenous education.

Journey into Native American History

The original installation project was developed during a year-long seminar on capitalism at the University of Wisconsin–Milwaukee. Titled Coyote's First World Casino, the seminar had the critical participatory components that eventually would evolve into the installation piece. This shared learning experience was instrumental in fulfilling the participants' goal of learning as social action. I conceived of the visual/experiential exploration of Native American economic development to allow other scholars and participants to intellectually engage theories of American history and its impact on Native American economies. It allowed others to experience the traumas associated with colonial history that influence the decisions Native communities made (and continue to make) to assure their survival in colonial worlds. The research emphasized the tensions between American history and Native American efforts to revitalize community traditions (language and cultural revitalization, economic self-determination, health and well-being). The requisite scholarly component required peer-reviewed publications and public/academic presentations.

The presentations all had a common constraint: the linear temporal structure of reading and listening. My academic paper, "Gaming the System: Imperial Discomfort and the Emergence of Coyote Capitalism," emphasized the importance of recognizing the role of colonial history in appreciating emergent Native American strategies of survival against coercive force. I organized the traumatic historical periodization around the themes of empire, manifest destiny, termination, and globalization. These themes provide the background for arguing for "the historically informed American Indian participation in global markets characterized by culturally grounded practices of economic development, cultural revitalization, and global cosmopolitanism."[1] While completing the scholarly components, however, I realized that academic rhetoric did not present Native American trauma adequately—it contains a predilection to impart an abstract understanding rather than a visceral knowledge of distress. To remedy this distance aspect of abstraction, I decided to find a way to allow audiences and participants to experience the trauma themselves. The result was the creation of the Coyote's First World Casino art installation piece, which was displayed in the *Visualizing Sovereignty* exhibit at the University of Wisconsin–Milwaukee Student Union Gallery in November and December 2014.

The installation is configured to juxtapose two worlds. The interior is a configuration of the sacred space of Native North America while the exterior represents colonial/settler history. The interior was a reproduction of a map of the Effigy Mound Culture archaeological/historical site at Lizard Mound State Park, just north of Milwaukee, Wisconsin. That site was chosen both to acknowledge the Indigenous ancestors of the Milwaukee area and to serve as the axis mundi for the sacred space. The background of the map is divided into three horizontal sections. The top delineates a series of chevrons representing the upper world in acknowledgment of the Oneota tradition. The middle section delineates horizontal lines representing the underworld (again, acknowledging the Oneota tradition). Finally, the bottom third delineates double-curve motifs representing the Maliseet tradition. The background provides both the structural organization for the interior and the ancestral organizing principle of the Indigenous communities of the Great Lakes Nations and the Wabanaki of the Northeast. The map of Lizard Mound State Park is reproduced corresponding to the cardinal directions and reflects the view of the mounds as if the viewer were standing in the center of the mounds. Superimposed on the map was the Maliseet prayer of thanksgiving, a collaborative project that was completed years earlier at Tobique First Nation, New Brunswick, Canada. Both the prayer and the landscape provide the deep roots of ancestral knowledge that are conveyed through Native American language, religion, culture, and landscape.

The exterior represented four historical periods of colonial history—empire, manifest destiny, termination, and globalization. I chose these themes to outline the "colonial capital cataclysms" endured by Native Americans as part of the long process of dispossession of lands, cultures, religions, and languages. The themes also highlighted the ironies of colonial ideologies of discovery, American nationalism, modernity in the United States, and the rhetoric of beneficent globalization. Specifically, *empire* was accompanied by images of Spanish atrocities against the Native peoples of present-day Caribbean and Mexico. *Manifest destiny* was accompanied by images of the 1890 massacre of Sioux women, children, and men at Wounded Knee to highlight the hypocrisy of America's claimed moral mandate to "overspread the land." *Termination* was selected to highlight the willingness of the United States government unilaterally to break treaty obligations to sovereign Indigenous communities. Termination was especially relevant to Wisconsin, as the Menominee Nation was one of the first to be "terminated." Finally, *globalization* was selected to challenge the neoliberal assertion that global development would "lift all boats," instead suggesting that it extended capitalist overreach at the expense of disempowered populations. The images accompanying globalization included the mascots of the Washington professional football team and the Cleveland professional baseball club. The "mascot" images correspond to the market for American naturalized racism disguised as fun and games.

The physical dimensions of the installation space measured 20 feet by 20 feet. Each "side" of the pictorial space was 6 feet wide by 5 feet high and composed of three 2-foot-wide by 4-foot-high lower panels. These panels in turn supported 2-foot-wide by 1-foot-high smaller panels for the interior and exterior sides. Altogether, for all four sides there were twenty-four 2×4 panels and twenty-four 1×2 panels. The total height of the installation measures 7 feet, 6 inches.

Toward Experiential Learning

There are many ways to experience the installation. Each "side" is a triptych corresponding to the cardinal directions. The interior prayer panels are designed to acknowledge the different elements of significant relations in Native American worlds. If the viewer/participant recites the prayer in proper sequence, they must begin in the interior and approach the east-facing panels. The first line gives thanks to the sun and therefore requires the viewer/participant to face east to begin (as per the Maliseet prayer). The viewer/participant then turns to the right to face southward to continue the prayer. By the end, the viewer/participant has turned 360 degrees and has faced the four cardinal

View of the *Experiencing Native North America* installation at the Milwaukee Indian Community School, Franklin, Wisconsin. Photo by Bernard Perley.

directions. The exterior faces reflect the four cataclysms of colonial/settler history as experienced by Native Americans (as described above). *Empire* is on the obverse face of the east-facing lines of the prayer. *Manifest destiny* is on the obverse face of the south-facing lines. *Termination* is on the obverse face of the west-facing lines. *Globalization* is on the obverse face of the north-facing lines. The center panels of the exterior faces are representations of slot machines that symbolically distribute the "riches" derived from colonialism. Those riches include the names of tribes eradicated by colonial powers, the treaties broken by the US government, the nations terminated by the US government, and the mascot names and images still used by professional sports teams, high schools, and universities. The viewer/participant can walk in and out of the installation, viewing the exterior panels first before viewing the interior panels, or vice versa.

The intent was to juxtapose the strength and calm of Native sacred space (the core of survival and perseverance) with the ongoing trauma revealed by the exterior history of colonization. The viewer/participant cannot help but be immersed in the colonial/settler historical narrative assumed to be impartial. When the exhibit opened, attendee responses were very positive. Many commented that they experienced distress while looking at and reading the exterior panels but felt calm and relief while reading and viewing the interior panels. Those comments confirmed the potential for the installation piece to serve as a teaching and learning tool—not only did the participants abstractly *learn* about these issues, they *experienced* the trauma and well-being themselves.

During the opening reception, Native American faculty members started a conversation to brainstorm about the potential for a collaborative project inviting diverse populations to learn and experience Indigenous history in a mutually respectful setting. The challenge was to take the Coyote's First World Casino installation and transform it into a broader experiential learning tool. This new installation project eventually brought together scholars from the University of Wisconsin–Milwaukee English, history, education, and anthropology departments. The heart and soul of the installation was a collaborative translation of a thanksgiving prayer by the Milwaukee Indian Community School

View of Coyote's First World Casino installation. Photo by Bernard Perley.

Menominee and Oneida language teachers, together with the Anishi-naabemowin instructor at UW–Milwaukee. The Maliseet text had been translated years before and served as the model for the prayer/sacred space portion of the project. The result of these collaborative engage-ments was a new installation, *Experiencing Native North America.*

From Art Installation to Experiential Pedagogy

The success of the Coyote installation inspired UW–Milwaukee faculty to conceptualize how research and advocacy can transcend disciplinary boundaries. The resulting effort underscored the value of the installation for collaborative pedagogy and the trans-portability of the experiential learning environment. The installation would continue to adapt to the context and concomitant constituency at the time of public presentation. One additional benefit of the experi-ential learning environment was the ability of the components to take on lives of their own. The remainder of this chapter discusses the ways these pedagogical benefits were developed and shared across contexts and constituencies.

The key reasons for coming together were to challenge academic and experiential boundaries and to emphasize the participants' common experiences as members of their respective Native American commu-nities. They were aware that their experiences do not neatly fit into academic categories. The goal for interdisciplinary collaboration was to share common experiences, knowledge, and concerns to encourage greater understanding of the Native American experience in the United States. Dr. Cary Miller provided historical contextualization as well as lists of recommended reading for exploring historical traumas. Dr. Margaret Noodin coordinated the translation of the Maliseet prayer of giving thanks into Anishinaabemowin and coordinated with the lan-guage teachers at the Milwaukee Indian Community School translations of the Maliseet prayer into Oneida and Menominee. Drake Sommer coordinated the pedagogical sessions for the workshop during the Wis-consin Indian Educators Association (WIEA) conference and the Edu-cators Network for Social Justice (ENSJ) conferences. I revised the "casino" panels to reflect the new teaching and learning goal of the installation and changed the interior prayer panels to reflect the prayer translations into Anishinaabemowin, Oneida, and Menominee. The com-pleted transformation of the installation was set up at the Milwaukee

Indian Community School then hosting the Educators Network for Social Justice conferences (April 25, 2015, 2016).[2]

Welcome to Native North America

The central pedagogical idea of the installation was to celebrate Milwaukee, Wisconsin, as ancestral sacred land. Milwaukee lies at the heart of the Effigy Mound Culture, which is why I selected Lizard Mound State Park for the axis mundi as Native American sacred space for the installation. All participants in the collaboration reinforced the central organizing principle by contributing local historical knowledge and languages (emphasizing, for example, that "Milwaukee" and "Wisconsin" are derived from Indian words). During the public presentations speakers celebrated the Indigenous ancestral and historical presence by welcoming the audience/participants to *Native* North America. This is a key conceptual anchor because colonial/settler society has erased the Indigenous presence but kept Native place-names—the effect of which is that they have become semiotic tombstones inappropriately reflecting absence. Deliberately acknowledging Milwaukee, Wisconsin, as Indigenous land was not meant to serve a similarly exclusionary purpose. Rather, the coauthors/participants explicitly called for greater inclusiveness by explaining that American history does not start at 1492. Place-names are not semantic abstractions severed from history and experience. The coauthors/participants invited all constituencies, viewers, and participants to share in the deep-time history of Native North America.

Coauthors/participants received very positive feedback from ENSJ participants. Among the comments were requests to bring the installation back to the conference the following year. The benefit of the component structure of the installation, meanwhile, made it feasible to transport it to other venues. The next stop was the WIEA conference in Madison, Wisconsin. The installation itself did not change from earlier iterations, but the participants and the venue were different enough to require a reconsideration of the presentation. The next stop was the 2017 Native American Literature Symposium (NALS) at Mystic Lake Casino, Prior Lake, Minnesota. The theme of the symposium was "Our Land and Water." The interior panels of the installation were perfect representations of the integrated theme of landscape with Indigenous religious/spiritual beliefs. The installation was displayed in the book exhibit throughout the symposium to allow symposium participants to interact with the installation. The goal of the presentation was to re-inforce the NALS mission to focus on Native American stories as living traditions that are expressed through "art, prose, poetry, film, history, politics, music, philosophy, and science—from our worldview."[3] The in-stallation was a material representation of how Native American stories are best understood as integrated experiences by community members rather than the purview of a single academic domain. The installation was the physical manifestation of history, religion, geography, linguistics, art, poetry, political science, philosophy, and education. Though the installation was static, it required viewers/participants to walk through and around the space to be able to fully appreciate the interconnected-ness of all those academic domains of knowledge.

Conclusion: Life in Native North America

The installation would continue to find additional venues for display in the Milwaukee area and beyond. It no doubt stimulated conversations among diverse constituencies beyond the awareness of the coauthors/participants and offered fresh avenues through which to understand Native worlds in colonial contexts. One of the most beau-tiful outcomes of the installation, for example, was a coloring book based on prayer card images and text downloaded from the project's website. With the support of the Reservation Business Committee, the Fond du Lac Band of Lake Superior Chippewa decided to print and assemble the prayer cards into 8 ½ x 11 inch pages to form a coloring book. The completed books were then distributed to children on the reservation as part of their Halloween treat.[4] The experiential aspect of the coloring pages may not be a face-to-face interactional experience, but the collaboration and conversations that generated its pages con-tinue to provide experiential learning by *being there*.

Although it has been dismantled and stored until the next invitation for display and interaction, the installation has its own trajectory and vitality. It was designed to generate conversations with multiple constit-uencies in education across all institutions and communities. The multi-ple venues in which the installation drew audience participation reflected the value of the installation as a learning environment for all ages. The coauthors/participants recognized the potential for the installation-as-pedagogy to be an exportable learning environment easily adaptable to other Indigenous experiences and locales. This chapter outlines the development of the installation as a critical reflection on American history, to the participatory repurposing of the installation, and the crucial contribution toward knowledge and constituency building in the service of Native American education.

The participatory aspect of the installation as a learning environment is crucial for recognizing how the multiple voices, stakeholders, and constituencies come together to experience Native North America. Colonial history cannot be separated from Native American worldviews and experiences. Collaboration grew organically and changed according to context and constituencies. The installation was a focal point and catalyst for sharing knowledge and experience. In each iteration and instance, the installation brought students, teachers, parents, college professors, community activists and advocates, and interested parties together to exchange knowledge, ideas, and experiences. The installation was and is a living document in that it continued to change from its antecedent Maliseet prayer to the core of the Coyote's First World Casino seminar, to *Experiencing Native North America*, to broad distribution of the Anishinaabemowin version of the prayer for giving thanks.

As a material construction the installation itself is in and of itself inert. Its real contributions to teaching and learning are the conversations and experiences that it catalyzes. A similar installation exercise need not be on such a large scale. Our coauthors/participants suggested during a workshop session that it would be easy to replicate the prayer environment with easels in a classroom, with poster board images and texts for support. The prayer can be translated into any Indigenous language. The background imagery could correspond to any sacred landscape. The flexibility of the lessons between the inside of the installation and its outside elements can be adapted to any context. Finally, the conversations and the learning opportunities that arose from the installation-as-pedagogy are the most exciting participatory benefits of *Being There* to learn about Native American experience. That is where the *life* of Native North America resides.

NOTES

1. Bernard Perley, "Gaming the System: Imperial Discomfort and the Emergence of Coyote Capitalism," in *After Capitalism: Horizons of Finance, Culture, and Citizenship*, ed. Kennan Ferguson and Patrice Petro (New Brunswick, NJ: Rutgers University Press, 2016), 216.

2. *Critical Collaboration: Repatriating Indigenous Knowledge Systems*, Bernard Perley, Margaret Noodin, Gary Miller, Sommer Drake.

3. Native American Literature Symposium website, http://www.mnsu.edu/nativelit/aboutnals.html (accessed January 26, 2018).

4. Personal communication with Dr. Margaret Ann Noodin, December 2017. The images in their outline form even prompted many adults to want to color the images!

čwé·ʔn neyękwaʔnawè·rih

Reflections on Teaching Indigenous
History from a Native Student

TAYLOR HUMMEL

O n March 23, 2013, I gathered with other citizens of
the Tuscarora Nation at the site of Neyuherú·kęʔ
located near Snow Hill, North Carolina. It was here that, three centuries
earlier, our ancestors had fought to repel English aggressors in what colonists came to call the "Tuscarora War." Our delegation—large enough
to fill three coach buses—drove through the night from our territory
in New York to attend a conference at East Carolina University (ECU)
commemorating the fall of Fort Neyuherú·kęʔ. Elders, youth, and all
the ages in between were represented on our journey south, some seeing our ancestral territory for the first time. The experience was a sober-
ing reminder of the artificial nature of American historical narratives.

I remember walking through the Greene County History Museum
only a few miles from Neyuherú·kęʔ. The museum had put together an
exhibit showcasing the artifacts excavated from the site. Over and over
again the exhibit labels and descriptions emphasized how the war "devastated" the Tuscarora. Only one sentence—at the end of the exhibit—
mentioned that twenty-first-century citizens of the Tuscarora Nation
live on reservations in New York and Ontario. If someone without
knowledge of our nation's current territories walked through the small
museum, I doubt they would leave with the impression the Skarù·ręʔ
are still alive and that Skaruręʔkyéha·ʔ continues on. Though the room
was full of Tuscarora people, the museum all but considered us dead.

At the conclusion of the conference the buses left me and five others behind to travel back to New York on foot from Fort Neyuherú·kę?. Our purpose: to honor the journey our ancestors made three centuries earlier. So far from a narrative of defeat and destruction, the 2013 Tuscarora Migration Project illuminated one of survival and reunion with our Haudenosaunee brothers to the north. The project took seventy days and crossed 1,300 miles along the approximate route our ancestors traveled northward to our current territories. Rather than dwell on tragedy and devastation, we celebrated the strength and tenacity of our ancestors and recognized that because of the difficult decisions our ancestors made to leave their homelands, we are still able to call ourselves Skarù·rę? today.

Both the Tuscarora Migration Project and the Greene County History Museum's exhibit illuminate how far general audiences need to go to restore Native Americans to a central position in the continent's historical narrative and to recognize the vital role Indigenous polities continue to play in the United States. They further stand as excellent avenues for exploring the complexities of the Indigenous experience in the classroom. As a Native student, American history has always been a strange subject to me. I have had to actively insert my ancestors into the dominant narrative because the textbooks left them out. I have found myself unexpectedly thrust into the role of an expert on all things Indigenous, correcting assumptions that exist because of the stilted narrative. I have needed to educate both fellow students and faculty members on Native issues.

Growing up on the Tuscarora Nation territory, I never had to answer questions that seemed to me to have obvious answers. I never needed to explain that I live in a house rather than a tipi, that most tribes and nations do not have casinos, or that Native American cultures differ from one another in the same way that European cultures differ from one another. Perhaps most crucially, back home I never had to remind people that Tuscaroras have not vanished. Such ignorant assumptions exist because of the inherently artificial nature of the discourse of American history. The master narrative of the birth, growth, and ascension of the United States requires our absence. It perpetuates damaging assumptions about Native people that too often stand uncontested.[1] On the rare occasions when Indians do make it into modern curricula, the focus is on trauma and victimization rather than agency and autonomy. The reason seems clear to me: although no doubt well intentioned, teachers who rely uncritically upon historical documents and archaeo-logical data unwittingly use material that lacks explicit Native voices.

As a (Native) scholar I certainly try to correct errors and faulty assumptions when I can. I highlight Indigenous strength and agency and how they shape Indian Country today. I tell people about Tuscarora athlete Frank Mt. Pleasant and his role in the development of football's forward pass.[2] I tell them about how Tuscaroras fought the construction of the Lewiston Reservoir with such vigor and success that it ended up only half the size the New York Power Authority originally intended.[3] I tell people čwé·ʔn neyękwaʔnawè·rih: "We are still moving about." Tus-caroras were not pushed aside as easily and definitively as the Greene County History Museum would have its visitors believe. We are not "past tense," as the Tuscarora Migration Project makes clear. Our ances-tors fought, acted strategically, and made decisions that ensured that Tuscarora people would continue to move about three hundred years later.

This chapter explores the erroneous nature of the American histo-rical narrative through the intertwined themes illuminated at the ECU conference. It focuses specifically upon my educational experiences. Al-though I am a Tuscarora woman, I think my insights speak to concerns across Indian Country today.

Going Off-Rez

If history is the story we tell ourselves about the past, then we must be mindful of who tells the story. Growing up, I attended the Tuscarora Indian Elementary School on the reservation. The Tusca-rora School complies with the standard curriculum of the state of New York, but it is unique in that it also incorporates a language program—started in 1970—and a culture and history program that began in 1990. In culture class our teacher told us about the great city of Tenochtitlan and the technological marvels of the Aztec empire. At a young age we knew Columbus was not a hero and that the real story of Thanks-giving is far more complicated than the standard narrative. We learned about how our ancestors organized themselves, and how the Tusca-rora, Onondaga, and Tonawanda Seneca Nations continue to use tradi-tional forms of government.[4] History was taught in a way that made it relevant to us. We were never absent from the narrative. Our teachers empowered us with the knowledge that Native history is ancient on this continent, beginning long before Columbus's arrival on the shores of Taino territory.

Things changed when I left the Tuscarora School to go to "off-rez" middle and high schools. At that time nothing similar to the above language and culture classes were offered, although we did have a Native American Club.[5] In social studies classes Indigenous peoples came up only briefly and tended to serve as foils—to Columbus and his "discovery" in the fifteenth century, for example, or to Americans committed to "manifest destiny" in the nineteenth century. Our textbooks treated Indigenous peoples as only tangentially related to the formation of the United States. They used words such as "primitive" to describe the tools and governments used by my ancestors. Such a gulf between this narrative and the one offered at the Tuscarora School confused me. After all, I had learned that our ancestors were quite innovative with their materials and organization. Today, my youthful confusion offers an important lesson: "primitive" is a subjective term rooted in the biases of Western cultural assumptions.

My university experience was as different from my middle and high schools as those were from the Tuscarora School. Although I entered Dartmouth College with several scholarships and a lot of financial aid, I continued to face financial troubles and had to work most of my time there. I could not afford flights back home and did not want to burden my family, who were also facing trouble financially. Money issues were accompanied by serious culture shock. I consistently felt compelled to prove my Nativeness to White peers who had never met an Indigenous person before. I had to address a multitude of strange assumptions about Natives, as well as the recurrent question, "How much Indian are you?" On several occasions I met students who suggested that my ethnic background was the only reason I got into Dartmouth. I believed them. I struggled with my first-year courses, which were faster-paced than anything I had experienced. That everyone seemed to be ten steps ahead of me only fueled my sense of inadequacy and convinced me that I did not actually belong at such a prestigious institution. I had to remind myself continually that I was taking and passing the same classes as my peers.

Despite these uncomfortable personal interactions, I eventually found a place within the Native community on campus. I decided to take Native American studies courses and found the experience enriching. I was surprised by the number of Native faculty, which included a

Tuscarora professor. My professors were wonderfully supportive and genuinely interested in correcting the narrative of the United States within their respective fields. I eventually followed my interest in archaeology and majored in both anthropology and Native American studies. The courses were amazing. One, for example, upended notions of a "primitive" precontact America by taking an in-depth look at the Mississippian city of Cahokia. Another included a section that thoroughly dismantled myths that Native people did not build large mound structures. This was the history I recognized and wanted to learn more about.

Oral Tradition, Cultural Tradition, and the Challenges of Archaeology

There remained a major limitation, however. When teaching Native American history, modern scholars tend to rely primarily on archaeological excavations conducted without Native input and uncritically utilizing written records from non-Native sources. Moreover, archaeologists and historians have had a maddening tendency to refer to the time prior to European arrival as "prehistory." This is not acceptable, and use of the term—which continues to appear in archaeological reports and history textbooks—has insidiously reinforced stilted narratives by implying that American history begins with the advent of European colonization, which is simply not true. It represents the way Western scholars understand history and flows naturally from their privileging of written records over the oral traditions of Indigenous peoples. Western scholars often dismiss Indigenous oral traditions as legend or myth. This is problematic, considering the expert role archaeologists and other researchers play in Native histories today.

The Native American Graves Protection and Repatriation Act (NAGPRA) is a law providing guidelines for the identification and repatriation of Native American human remains, funerary objects, sacred objects, or objects of cultural patrimony that are "(i) In Federal possession or control; or (ii) In the possession or control of any institution or State or local government receiving Federal funds; or (iii) Excavated intentionally or discovered inadvertently on Federal or tribal lands."[6] Prior to the passing of NAGPRA, Native American human remains and grave sites on federal and tribal lands were considered property of the United States government rather than descendant communities.

While the law is well intentioned, NAGPRA puts the power of identifying cultural affiliation primarily in the hands of archaeologists, while it is up to tribes to provide the "proof." This is a problem for reasons described by the late Mohawk scholar Salli M. Kawennotakie Benedict: "Archaeological principles and definitions are presently not harmonized with the cultures that are being studied. .... Arbitrary archaeological definitions for cultural affiliation currently separate Aboriginal peoples from their ancestors and are among several of the hurdles that are thrown up as obstacles to recovery."[7] Archaeological ideas of cultural affiliation separate modern tribes from the remains of those we consider our ancestors, those who cared for the land before us, and those whose bodies nourished the soil we depend on today.

As an archaeologist, I have found many of my colleagues subscribe to the myth that some cultures before or after European colonization "disappeared" mysteriously when certain pottery designs or point types no longer appear in the archaeological record, thus limiting opportunities to discuss possible cultural affiliation with modern tribes. However, our stories tell us differently. For purposes of identifying cultural affiliation, NAGPRA requires that multiple lines of evidence are consulted including oral tradition. In addition to being a source of cultural values and moral principles, traditional stories are also a vehicle for historical documentation and can provide insight into the supposed cultural "disappearances" seen in the archaeological record.

Western archaeological interpretations of non-Western cultures are deeply rooted. They grow out of the complex origins of the modern field of archaeology. As it did across the world, American archaeology began as a nation-building tool. In the nineteenth century the United States labored to construct an origins story, and as they did so they systematically excluded Native peoples. And from their first digs archaeologists provided the "hard" evidence to support this Indian-free narrative. Indeed, as Euro-Americans moved west following the American Revolution, they were awed by the mound sites dotting the landscape. In 1847 Ephraim Squier and Edwin Davis conducted a particularly influential examination of a mound site in the Mississippi Valley.[8] They brought into the excavation the assumption that "Indians were hunters averse to labor, and not known to have constructed any works approaching [these mounds] in skillfulness of design or in magnitude." By definition they could not have built the mounds, then, because their evidence positively revealed "that the mound-builders were an agricultural people, considerably advanced in arts . . . and consolidated government."[9] For these two archaeologists, the mound builders were comparable to ancient Egypt's pyramid builders and other "great" civilizations. They also were an "extinct race," a characterization that recast contemporary Indigenous nations as newcomers to North America.[10]

Squier and Davis's interpretations relied exclusively on narrative traditions from their Western European background. Even so, their excavation strongly influenced the beginnings of the discipline of archaeology within the United States. It became a crucial part of the nineteenth-century discourse surrounding Indigenous peoples in North America. With a few strokes of the pen Squier and Davis erased Indians from millennia of continental history, regardless of oral traditions connecting the mounds with the burials of their ancestors. Their conclusions lent scientific legitimacy to the continuation of the genocidal logic of manifest destiny.

In short, my undergraduate experience brought a two-edged reality. On the one hand, I found a historical narrative that dismantled the poor logic and cultural biases of the New York educational system. On the other hand, because of its own contradictions my chosen major did not go far enough to "move the needle" in terms of public awareness of the Indigenous place in the American narrative. Indians still seemed to have vanished.

Reaching Out to the Local

Another contradiction of my undergraduate experience lay in Dartmouth College itself. On the one hand, its 1769 charter explicitly states that educating Indigenous people is a priority. Clearly, what the college's founders had in mind was ethnocentric in the extreme, but in 1972 Dartmouth decided to take this mandate seriously. Since then it has developed a Native American Program that in many ways is the model for all other programs across the country. On the other hand, Dartmouth rests on Abenaki land, and their village sites dot the entire Connecticut Valley. Despite this fact, I rarely heard anyone mention it outside of my Native American studies courses. Understanding who lived in the area previously is important, and I recommend educators conduct self-location exercises in their own courses. Not acknowledging the Indigenous people whose land you stand on lends credence to the narrative that Indians have vanished.

I feel I should provide merely one example from an environmental studies class I took. In one writing assignment I shared part of the Haudenosaunee creation story, and the professor sent me an email afterward asking if I would share it with the class. I never responded, and the professor never mentioned it again in person. The request made me uncomfortable because—in addition to not knowing the creation story perfectly—I felt like the professor was better served approaching one of the several nearby Abenaki communities to provide their creation story. The college sits, after all, on their land. The professor's request made me feel used, too, like it was my job to supplement the class with the "Native Perspective." Indigenous polities are as myriad and complex as their European counterparts, however, which means I can no more "speak for Indians" than a Romanian can "speak for Europeans." It is better to acknowledge and form relationships with local Indigenous communities than to ask Native students from outside the region for perspectives that might not be relevant. As an alternative, try working with tribal nations to set up a field trip to their current territory. If you find that no Native communities are easily accessible, try visiting cultural centers, museums, or national heritage sites that focus on Native history.

As with the Greene County History Museum, however, it is imperative not to forget to analyze critically the narratives presented. Although they have made headway in recent years, museums and national heritage sites often lack the voices of the Native people whose history they are telling. The omission stems from a century of stilted federal policy. In 1906, President Theodore Roosevelt convinced Congress to pass the American Antiquities Act. It was designed to preserve the national heritage of the United States by penalizing unauthorized collection or excavation of ruins or monuments on federal land. It further protected objects collected from sites in a museum and established a permit system for studying archaeological resources. Finally, under the secretary of the interior's guidelines the act made clear that only "qualified" people and projects could conduct archaeological investigations on federal land.[11] While this latter point certainly reduces grave robbing and looting, in practice it also has excluded traditional knowledge holders from the process. As a consequence, the American Antiquities Act gave legal legitimacy to archaeological narratives rooted in Western biases. The delegitimization of Native voices became worse in 1966, when thousands of years of Native history were subsumed into the national heritage of the United States through the passage of the National Heritage Protection Act.[12]

I provide this discussion as a way to shed light on the problematic nature of relying solely on archaeology and documents written by non-Native people. I ask that you contextualize all sources of information. Remember that even primary sources contain inherent biases, and that non-Native accounts of Native communities often lack the cultural context to understand the intricacies of events. It can be easy to focus on how Native people were victimized and ignore acts of agency.[13] Avoid that trap. Look for written oral histories or traditions. Better yet, invite a guest speaker to class. And when on a field trip to a historic site, think about the people who lived there and where they are now. Acknowledging the continued presence of Indigenous communities will help end the destructive cycle of distancing Native people from the continent's shared past, present, and future.

There and Back Again: A Skarù·ęʔ Tale

The Grapevine Story—a Tuscarora oral tradition first written down by Tuscarora soldier and painter David Cusick in 1825—is the story of how the ancestral Haudenosaunee became separate nations and how the Tuscarora people came to occupy the inner coastal plain region of southeastern Virginia and northeastern North Carolina.[14] In part because of this shared history, the Tuscarora Nation became the sixth nation of the Haudenosaunee Confederacy by 1722, whereas other nations that migrated to live with the Haudenosaunee were absorbed. After returning north to ancient homelands, the Tuscarora quickly became involved in Haudenosaunee politics. This relationship had profound effects on American history and continues to be a powerful force today.

The conference at ECU and the exhibit at the Greene County History Museum focused on a brief but significant moment in Tuscarora history. However, not only does our history predate the first time a European took out a quill to write about us—as the Grapevine Story shows—our story also continues beyond our supposed "expiration date" of March 23, 1713, just as the Tuscarora Migration Project celebrated. The tragic narrative of the "vanishing Indian" is an inaccurate retelling of the course of American history.

The Tuscarora Historical Society—a group of Tuscarora people interested in Tuscarora history—has proven to be a powerful mechanism for exploring our narrative and its relationship to broader historical forces in the United States. The society began as a small group of people who met around a dining room table to read and discuss material written about our nation. We have since grown to about fifteen to twenty people who meet weekly. As we read through material usually written about us by non-Native authors—much less Tuscarora authors—we are taking the mainstream tragic narrative of our history, correcting it, and adding to it as we do so.

In March 2017—instead of going to other conferences—the Tuscarora Historical Society put on one of our own with all Tuscarora presenters and all Tuscarora-run display tables.[15] When we put on the conference, we focused on including people from our community with different areas of expertise. We had people who talked about lacrosse, genealogy, the history of our beadwork, our language, and so many other aspects of Skarureʔkyéha·ʔ—our life and history. The event was open to all because we wanted people to learn our history our way, not from a museum that tells us the Tuscarora are dead, but from the people who are very much alive. Utilizing a multitude of sources, we were able to develop a deeper understanding of our history that might not be possible otherwise.

American history—especially Native American history—is incomplete when taught in isolation from modern Native communities. This leads to the perpetuation of an inaccurate narrative of tragedy and victimization in classrooms across the country. One of the most crucial things you can do is know on whose land you and your institution are located. Understand the context surrounding your sources for Indigenous history. Include readings and guest lectures by Native scholars and community members. Stay accountable to the communities you work with. Acknowledge the diversity of Native American history and contextualize that history with modern communities. Consider how these historical issues are also linked to present-day social justice issues that tribal nations continue to face. What is the point of history if not to situate and contextualize ourselves today? With this essay, I hope I have made the case for utilizing archaeological and historical sources more critically and for including the discussion of modern Native communities in your courses because—despite what the neocolonial narrative of the United States suggests—we are still moving about.

NOTES

1. Merely one example: in New York it is not uncommon to hear that Europeans settled on virgin land in the Adirondacks because the mountains were too cold for Native people to live there year-round—despite oral traditions and archaeological evidence powerfully suggesting otherwise. See Curt Stager, "Hidden Heritage," *Adirondack Life*, June 2017, 55–66.

2. In *The Real All Americans* (New York: Doubleday, 2007) Sally Jenkins provides excellent insight into how modern football developed out of Carlisle Indian School.

3. Bryan Printup and Neil V. Patterson Jr., *Tuscarora Nation* (Mount Pleasant, SC: Arcadia, 2007).

4. Culture classes extended beyond just historical lessons. At times community members came to share stories. Once, for example, my father came in to describe his experience as a "skywalker," or ironworker, working in New York City building skyscrapers.

5. The middle and high school currently have a Tuscarora history class and a Tuscarora language course that students can take for college credit. Three years ago, Native American Club students petitioned the school board to change Columbus Day to Indigenous People's Day. The school board voted unanimously in favor of renaming it Indigenous People's Day.

6. Native American Graves and Repatriation Regulations, 43 C.F.R. § 10.1– 10.17. https://www.ecfr.gov/current/title-43/subtitle-A/part-10.

7. Salli M. Kawennotakie Benedict, "Made in Akwesasne," in *A Passion for the Past: Papers in Honour of James F. Pendergast,* ed. James V. Wright and Jean-Luc Pilon (Ottawa: Canadian Museum of Nature, 2004), 435–54.

8. Ephraim G. Squier and Edwin H. Davis, *Ancient Monuments of the Mississippi Valley* (1848; Washington, DC: Smithsonian Institution Press, 1998).

9. Squier and Davis, *Ancient Monuments,* 45.

10. Squier and Davis, *Ancient Monuments,* 306

11. Darby C. Stapp and Michael S. Burney, *Tribal Cultural Resources Management: The Full Circle to Stewardship* (New York: Altamira Press, 2002), 45–46.

12. Ojibwe archaeologist Sonya Atalay argues that archaeological preservation of national heritage "advance[s] the colonialist agenda by legally taking the care and management of culturally significant sites important to living communities today away from communities and putting it in the hands of archaeologists." Even though these laws give sites certain protections and the resources to enforce them, the "care and management" specified is generally determined by professional archaeologists whose priorities might not be in line with those of local Native communities. Sonya Atalay, *Community-Based Archaeology: Research with, by, and for Indigenous and Local Communities* (Berkeley: University of California Press, 2012), 93.

13. Compare, for example, Anthony Wallace's grim portrayal of the Seneca in *The Death and Rebirth of the Seneca* (New York: Knopf, 1970) to Kurt A. Jordan's *The Seneca Restoration, 1715–1754: An Iroquois Local Political Economy* (Gainesville: University Press of Florida, 2008).

14. David Cusick, *David Cusick's Sketches of Ancient History of the Six Nations: Comprising First — a Tale of the Foundation of the Great Island, (now North America,) the Two Infants Born, and the Creation of the Universe. Second — a Real Account of the Early Settlers of North America, and Their Dissensions. Third — origin of the Kingdom of the Five Nations, which was Called a Long House: the Wars, Fierce Animals, &c.* (Turner & McCollum, 1848).

15. The Tuscarora History Conference is now an annual event and remains open to the public.

Contributors

DENISE I. BOSSY is an associate professor of history at the University of North Florida, where she teaches courses on American Indians, early America, comparative slaveries, local history, and gender and race. She is the editor of *The Yamasee Indians: From Florida to South Carolina* (2018) and the author of articles and book chapters on the Native and colonial South. Her current book projects include a monograph on the Yamasees and an Indigenous history of Northeast Florida, which she is cowriting with archaeologist Keith Ashley.

JOHN P. BOWES is a professor of history at Eastern Kentucky University. He is the author of *Land Too Good for Indians: Northern Indian Removal* (2016) and *Exiles and Pioneers: Eastern Indians in the Trans-Mississippi West* (2007). His current manuscript project, "Indian Removal: A History in Several Acts," is currently under contract.

BRADY DESANTI (Lac Courte Oreilles Ojibwe) is the director of the Native American studies program and an associate professor of religious studies at the University of Nebraska at Omaha. His work focuses on North American Indigenous history, religious traditions, and popular culture.

N. BRUCE DUTHU (Houma) is Samson Occom Professor and Chair of Native American and Indigenous Studies at Dartmouth College. He is the author of *American Indians and the Law* (2009) and *Shadow Nations: Tribal Sovereignty and the Limits of Legal Pluralism* (2013), as well as multiple book chapters and journal articles.

TAI S. EDWARDS is an associate professor of history at Johnson County Community College, where she teaches US and Indigenous peoples history and is the director of the Kansas Studies Institute. She is the author of *Osage Women and Empire: Gender and Power* (2018). Her teaching and research focus on colonialism, Indigenous peoples, gender, and disease.

DONALD L. FIXICO (Shawnee, Sac and Fox, Mvskoke and Seminole) is Regents' and Distinguished Foundation Professor of History and Distinguished Scholar of Sustainability in the Global Institute of Sustainability at Arizona State University. Trained in ethnohistory and as a policy historian, his work focuses on American Indian history and the West. He has written and edited fifteen books, has taught on faculty at four universities, and has been a visiting professor at seven universities.

ANDREW K. FRANK is the Allen Morris Professor of History at Florida State University. He specializes in the history of the Native South. His publications include *Before the Pioneers: Indians, Settlers, Slaves, and the Founding of Miami* (2017) and *Creeks and Southerners: Biculturalism on the Early American Frontier* (2005). He is currently writing a history of the Florida Seminoles from their origins to the present.

MARGARET HUETTL is an assistant professor in history and ethnic studies at the University of Nebraska–Lincoln. She earned her PhD in history from the University of Nevada, Las Vegas, her MA in Native American history from the University of Oklahoma, and her BA from the University of Rochester. Her research examines Ojibwe or Anishinaabe sovereignty and settler colonialism in a transnational context, centering on Anishinaabe ways of knowing.

TAYLOR HUMMEL (Skarù·ręˀ/Tuscarora) earned her BA in anthropology and Native American studies from Dartmouth College and is a graduate student in the archaeology program at Cornell University. She resides on the Tuscarora Nation territory in New York, where she works as a curriculum development assistant for the Nęyękwawętaˀθkwáhshek Tuscarora Language Program. She is also a member of the Tuscarora Historical Society, which promotes the sharing and preservation of Tuscarora history and knowledge for their community.

PAUL KELTON is the Robert David Lion Gardiner Chair of American History at the State University of New York at Stony Brook. He examined the biological processes involved in the European takeover of the

Americas in two books: *Epidemics and Enslavement: Biological Catastrophe in the Native Southeast, 1492–1715* (2007) and *Cherokee Medicine, Colonial Germs: An Indigenous Nation's Fight against Smallpox, 1518–1824* (2015). By placing local struggles with epidemics within the large-scale context of colonialism's social disruption, structural violence, and political upheaval, his research has contemporary relevance to debates over global health disparities and emerging infectious diseases.

JOSHUA THUNDER LITTLE (Oglala Lakota) is a PhD student in history at the University of California, Riverside. His research focuses on Oceti Sakowin resistance, sovereignty, and the protection of water. The project applies Lakota knowledge systems to demonstrate how Lakota people have always protected water as a relative.

ANN MCGRATH is the WK Hancock Distinguished Professor in the School of History at the Australian National University, where she is the director of the Research Centre for Deep History and holds the 2017–22 ARC Kathleen Fitzpatrick Laureate Fellowship. Her publications include *Illicit Love: Interracial Sex and Marriage in the United States and Australia* (2015), which was awarded the NSW Premier's History Prize, and *Long History, Deep Time* (with Mary-Anne Jebb, 2015). Most recently, with Lynette Russell, she edited *The Routledge Companion to Global Indigenous History* (2021).

MAUREEN MEYERS is a senior archaeologist at New South Associates, Inc. in Stone Mountain, Georgia. Her research interests include frontiers of the Mississippian world and Native craft production, specifically fibers and shell beads. She has conducted extensive excavations at two Mississippian mound sites in southwestern Virginia. In addition, she is actively engaged in research about the Westos, a mid-seventeenth-century Indian slaving group in the Southeast. She also studies field safety in archaeology, particularly sexual harassment.

DEVON A. MIHESUAH (enrolled citizen of the Choctaw Nation of Oklahoma) is the Cora Lee Beers Price Professor in the Humanities Program at the University of Kansas (KU). She is the author of numerous award-winning books on Indigenous history and current issues, including *Recovering Our Ancestors' Gardens: Indigenous Recipes and Guide to*

Diet and Fitness (2020). She is former editor of the *American Indian Quarterly* and oversees the American Indian Health and Diet Project at KU.

Nancy Marie Mithlo (Chiricahua Apache) is a professor of gender studies, art history, and visual arts at the University of California at Los Angeles. She also is a core faculty member of the American Indian Studies Interdepartmental Program. She earned her PhD in cultural anthropology from Stanford University in 1993. She has taught at the University of New Mexico, the Institute of American Indian Arts, Santa Fe Community College, Smith College, California Institute of the Arts, and the University of Wisconsin–Madison.

Theda Perdue is Atlanta Distinguished Professor Emerita of Southern Culture at the University of North Carolina at Chapel Hill. She is the author or coauthor of ten books, including *Cherokee Women: Gender and Culture Change, 1700–1835* (1998), which won the Julia Cherry Spruill Award for the best book in southern women's history and the James Mooney Prize for the best book in the anthropology of the South. She is the editor or coeditor of six books, including *Sifters: Native American Women's Lives* (2001). She has served as president of the Southern Association for Women Historians, the American Society for Ethnohistory, and the Southern Historical Association. She is also a member of the executive board of the Organization of American Historians.

Bernard C. Perley (Maliseet, Tobique First Nation) is an associate professor in critical Indigenous studies at the University of British Columbia. His research explores the causes of language and culture loss in Native American communities and advocates innovative revitalization strategies for Native American communities. He is the author of *Defying Maliseet Language Death* (2011). His recent publications and installation pieces are collaborative projects with other Native scholars and community members designed to promote experiential learning of Indigenous cultures, histories, and knowledge systems.

Kristofer Ray teaches history at the University of North Carolina Wilmington. He is a student of the early modern American Indian experience broadly, Native-European interaction in trans-Appalachia specifically, and the European construction of Indigenous slave law. In addition to several book chapters, edited volumes, and journal articles, he is the author of *Cherokees, Europeans, and Empire in the Trans-Appalachian West, 1670–1774* (forthcoming) and *Middle Tennessee, 1775–1825: Progress and Popular Democracy on the Southwestern Frontier* (2007).

JAMES D. RICE is the Walter S. Dickson Chair of English and American History at Tufts University. The author of *Nature and History in the Potomac Country: From Hunter Gatherers to the Age of Jefferson* (2009), he is currently writing a synthesis of Native American environmental history from Oaxaca to the Arctic and from the first human habitation of North America to the present.

MARVIN M. RICHARDSON (Haliwa-Saponi) received his PhD in 2016 from the University of North Carolina at Chapel Hill and is an independent scholar. He is currently revising his manuscript "Racial Choices: The Emergence of the Haliwa-Saponi Indian Tribe, 1835–1971" in preparation for publication.

ROSE STREMLAU is an associate professor of history and gender and sexuality studies at Davidson College. Her book *Sustaining the Cherokee Family: Kinship and the Allotment of an Indigenous Nation* (2011) won the 2012 Willie Lee Rose Prize from the Southern Association of Women's Historians. She has published half a dozen scholarly articles and essays and has won multiple grants and fellowships, including from the National Endowment for the Humanities.

MIYE NADYA TOM (Walker River Paiute) is a lecturer at the University of Nebraska at Omaha. A postcolonial scholar, she has researched, published, and lectured on race/ethnicity in education both nationally and internationally. In 2019 she was guest editor of the "Indigenous knowledges as vital contributions to sustainability" issue of UNESCO's *International Review of Education*, which brought together Indigenous scholars from North America, Latin America, the Pacific Islands, and Africa. She is currently concluding her MFA in creative nonfiction at the Institute of American Indian Arts in Santa Fe, New Mexico

MARK VAN DE LOGT is an associate professor of history at Texas A&M University at Qatar. He is the author of *War Party in Blue: Pawnee Scouts in the U.S. Army* (2010) and *Monsters of Contact: Historical Trauma in Caddoan Oral Traditions* (2018). His forthcoming book, *Between the Floods: A History of the Arikaras,* is based primarily on Arikara oral traditions and oral histories.

GRAY H. WHALEY is an associate professor of history at Southern Illinois University, where he teaches courses on Native American history, environmentalism, and the American West. He is the author of *Oregon and the Collapse of Illahee: U.S. Empire and the Transformation of an Indigenous World, 1792–1859* (2010).

Index

Abenaki people, 315
Aboriginal people. *See* Australia; New Zealand
activities for classrooms: allotment and, 97–98, 103–4, 106–9; American Indian Chicago Conference (AICC) and, 194; American Revolution and, 67–68, 69; archaeology and, 18, 19, 21, 25; art installations and, 307; cartography and, 65–66; child welfare and, 165–66; colonialism and, 98–99; creation stories and, 212nn11–12; Dakota Access Pipeline (DAPL) and, 280–81; food and foodways and, 223–24; local history and, 26–27; origin stories and, 146; peoplehood and, 192–93; pre-Columbian history and, 17; religion and ceremony and, 200–201; sacred sites and, 209–10; thematic approach and, 278–81; tribal rolls and, 101–2; types of slavery and, 50; warfare and, 61–62, 70, 71
adaptation, 187–90, 285, 299–300, 312
Adena culture, 15
agriculture: civilization and, 214; dams and irrigation and, 155–56; development of corn and, 218; environmental effects of, 151–52;

gender and, 153, 220; gradual introduction of, 151; hunting and fishing and, 217; Indigenous knowledge and, 219, 221, 222; Mississippian Period and, 15–16; regional differences in, 147–48; removal policies and, 154; residential schools and, 221; Three Sisters and, 147, 148; Woodland Period and, 14, 15
ahtone, heather, 229, 234
AIA. *See* American Institute of Archaeology (AIA)
AICC. *See* American Indian Chicago Conference (AICC)
AIM. *See* American Indian Movement (AIM)
AISES. *See* American Indian Science and Engineering Society (AISES)
Alaska Native Claims Settlement Act, 128
Alaska v. Native Village of Venetie Tribal Government, 128
Alcatraz Island occupation, 130, 138
Alchon, Suzanne, 38
Alexie, Sherman, 127
Algonquian people, 4, 148, 150
allotment: activities for classrooms and, 97–98, 103–4, 106–7, 108–9; assimilation and, 94, 95, 97; blood quantum and, 105; citizenship and,

allotment (*continued*)
99; contested claims and, 103–4; cultural persistence and, 5–6; families and family structures and, 95–98, 100; gender and, 99; land improvements and, 102, 103; land loss and, 104–5, 106, 154; mapping and, 102–3, 109n6; meaning of, 93, 94–95; natural resources and, 99–100, 104, 154, 155; reservations and, 93, 137; resistance to, 93, 102–3, 107–9; resources for teachers and, 97; results of, 102–7; tribal rolls and, 100–102, 140; in typical classroom presentations, 4–5, 93. *See also* land loss and retention; termination

Alvord, Lori Arviso, 206

American Antiquities Act, 23, 316

American Board of Commissioners for Foreign Missions, 80

American Indian Chicago Conference (AICC), 193–94

American Indian Movement (AIM), 130, 173, 179, 181, 268

American Indians. *See* Native Americans

American Indian Science and Engineering Society (AISES), 239–40

American Indian studies. *See* Indigenous studies

American Institute of Archaeology (AIA), 26

American Revolution, 4, 68–69

Amherst, Jeffrey (Lord), 162

Anangu people, 290

Ani-kituwah people, 7. *See also* Cherokee people

Anishinaabe people, 7, 158, 205. *See also* Chippewa people; Odawa people; Ojibwe people; Potawatomi people

Anishinaabemowin people, 304, 307. *See also* Anishinaabe people

anthropology, 199–200, 228, 263, 269

Apache people, 4, 53, 178, 208, 232–35, 233, 241

Apalachee people, 32, 33

Apapos, Juana, 239, 241

Apess, William, 115, 116, 117–19, 122

Ara Irititja Project, 290

Araújo, Marta, 250

Arawak people, 276. *See also* Taino people

Archaeological Conservancy, 25

Archaeological Resources Protection Act (1979), 24–25

archaeology: American Antiquities Act and, 316; as American nation-building tool, 314; band societies and, 13; certification programs for amateurs in, 26; collaborative research and, 291–92, 296n32; cultural resource management and, 23; dating artifacts and sites and, 20–21; deep history and, 289; DNA research and, 290, 296n32; excavation methods and, 18–20; laws and legal decisions and, 22–25, 319n12; mistreatment of Native remains and, 24; Native input and, 313–14, 315; pre-Columbian history and, 17–18; provenience and, 18–20; tomb raiding and, 290–91, 316; Vanishing Indian myth and, 314–15; virgin soil thesis and, 34; volunteer opportunities in, 25

Arikara people, 72, 155, 157. *See also* Sahnish people

Arikara War, 73

Arkansas Archaeology Survey, 26

artifacts, 15, 20–21, 23–25, 60–61, 316

arts and art history: activities for the classroom and, 307; American Indian Curatorial Practice and, 229–30, 236, 237, 242–43; art installation as pedagogy and, 304–5, 306–7; basketry and, 239–41; best practices and, 231–32; deep history and, 290; Indigenous goals in, 232, 234, 236; interpretation and, 232–42; miscategorization of Native arts and, 228, 243n1; Native voices and, 229, 230; noninterference and, 239–40, 241–42; portraiture and, 236, 237–39, 238; pottery and, 14–15, 21; prayer cards and, 306; refusal to share knowledge and, 234–35; resources for teachers and, 230, 239–41; traditional and modern as descriptors and, 231; Visual Thinking Strategies (VTS) and, 233–34, 235. See also specific works and installations

assimilation: allotment and, 94, 95, 97; bans on Native religion and, 202; cultural genocide and, 167n4; erasure and, 163; family structure and, 97; food and foodways and, 218–19; multicultural education and, 250; presence of federal officials and, 99; residential schools and, 137; tribal criminal authority and, 125; of Whites into Indigenous communities, 279

Atalay, Conya, 319n12

Australia, 284–88, 290–92, 292n1, 292–93n3, 293n5, 293n7, 295n24

authenticity, 176, 192–93, 231, 270

Autochtone people, 7

Autry Museum of the American West, 235, 239, 241

Aztec people, 51, 311. See also Mexica people

Bad River Reservation, 138–39

Ball, Martin, 212–13n16

Banks, Dennis, 268

Bannock War, 71

Barkindji people, 291

Basso, Keith, 208, 212–13n16

Battle of Fallen Timbers, 63, 70

Battle of Greasy Grass, 4, 63, 71, 278–80

Battle of Horseshoe Bend, 63

Battle of Little Bighorn. See Battle of Greasy Grass

Battle of Tippecanoe, 63, 70, 71

Bear River Massacre, 62

Bear Shield, 88

Bell, Danny, 269

Bender, "Chief," 271

Benedict, Salli M. Kawennotakie, 314

Benevenuto, Jeff, 164

Bering Strait, 12

Berkhofer, Robert, Jr., 278

Berlin, Ira, 51, 52

Berry site (North Carolina), 16

Bettincort, Clyde, 181

Billie, James E., 173, 174, 178, 179–80, 181

Blackbird, John, 138

Black Elk, 61, 279

Blackfeet people, 72

Black Hawk, 61, 62, 280

Black Hawk War, 70, 71, 280

Black Lake Killas (film), 158–59

blood quantum, 100–101, 105, 106–7, 312

Blue Jacket, 69–70

boarding schools. See residential schools

Boldt, George Hugo, 139

Boldt decision, 139

Bone, Joseph P., 164

Boudinot, Elias, 78, 81, 287, 288

Bowden, Bobby, 177

Boy Scouts of America, 155
Braddock, Edward, 62, 63
Brant, Joseph, 68
Brave, John, 202–3
Brilliant, Richard, 238–39
Brinkley, William, 187
Brown, Richard, 274
Brown v. Board of Education, 193
bureaucracy, 93, 98–103, 104
Bureau of Indian Affairs, 155, 157, 265
Burning Man festival, 14
Burns, Ken, 88

Cactus Hill (Virginia), 13
Cahokia, 16, 152, 313
Cahuilla people, 239, 254
Calloway, Colin, 166, 167n4, 270
Cameron, Catherine, 33, 34
Camp Grant Massacre, 62
Canadian Truth and Reconciliation Commission, 164, 165, 248
Canary Effect, The (film), 165–66
Canby, Edward R. S., 72
Carlisle Indian Industrial School, 137
Carter, Kent, 109n6
cartography, 65–66, 102–3, 109n6
casinos, 132, 272
Catawba people, 66, 150, 272
Catlin, George, 179
CCC. *See* Civilian Conservation Corps (CCC)
CDC. *See* Centers for Disease Control and Prevention (CDC)
Census Office, 100, 109n4
Centers for Disease Control and Prevention (CDC), 207
ceremonies. *See* religion and ceremony
CERT. *See* Council of Energy Resource Tribes (CERT)
Chakrabarty, Dipesh, 288

Chavis, Ben, 186
Cherokee Nation v. Georgia, 78, 80–81, 82
Cherokee people: arts and, 230, 231; assimilation and, 218–19; Cherokee Constitution and, 81–82, 85; Cherokee history courses, 262, 264–65; Cherokee language and, 265; *Cherokee Phoenix* and, 81, 287; demonstrating civilization and, 187; eastern versus western Cherokees and, 264; epidemic disease and, 36; Five Civilized Tribes and, 17, 185; gender and, 220; humans and nature and, 150; learning from, 272; nomenclature and, 7; removal policies and, 78–79; reservations and, 263, 264–65; slaveholding and, 218, 264; Thanksgiving and, 288; tribal sovereignty and, 81–83, 88; in typical classroom presentation, 79–80; *Unto These Hills* (drama) and, 261, 264; white advocates of, 118; Wilma Mankiller and, 179. *See also* Ani-kituwah people; Qualla Boundary (reservation)
Cheyenne people, 61, 72, 148, 157, 279
Cheyfitz, Eric, 114
Chickamauga people, 69
Chickasaw people, 17, 36, 66, 70, 83, 185, 218
Chief Joseph, 64
child welfare. *See also* residential schools
child welfare and adoption, 52, 165–66, 199, 287
Chippewa people, 7, 120
Choctaw people: agriculture and, 271; American Indian Chicago Conference (AICC) and, 194; archaeology and, 24; assimilation and, 218–19; Battle of Fallen

Timbers and, 70; epidemic disease and, 36; Five Civilized Tribes and, 17, 185; Indian Child Welfare Act and, 127; removal policies and, 83

Chucalissa (Tennessee), 16

citizenship, 99

Civilian Conservation Corps (CCC), 24

civil rights. *See* Native civil rights movement

Clark, George Rogers, 68

Clausewitz, Carl von, 73

climate change, 32, 36, 158–59, 215, 221, 240. *See also* environment

Coharie people, 265, 266

colonialism and imperialism: activities for classrooms and, 98–99; arts and, 242; Australia and, 284; bureaucracy and, 93, 98–99; capital cataclysms and, 300–301, 302–3; Christian colonial ideology and, 114; decolonization and, 236, 249–50; deep history and, 290; epidemic disease and, 38–39; food and foodways and, 215; guilt over, 235–36; health and, 220; historical periodization and, 288; Indigenous slavery and, 54–55; Indigenous spiritual practices and, 147; multicultural education and, 253; poverty and, 159; race and racism and, 251; shattering effects of, 53, 57; structural violence and, 39–40, 49; trading colonies versus settler colonialism and, 35; transnational history and, 286; in typical school presentations, 3; unifying Indigenous themes and, 267–68; White firsting and, 294n15

Columbian exchange, 3

Columbus, Christopher: Arawak people and, 276; Black Legend and, 161; Columbus Day and, 319n5; genocide and, 160, 161; historical periodization and, 292–93n3, 305; Indigenous education and, 311–12, 319n5; slavery and the slave trade and, 48; solar eclipse of 1504 and, 160; in typical school presentations, 11

Comanche people, 34, 53, 72, 217

Conestoga people, 69

Cook, James, 292–93n3

Coolidge, Calvin, 277

Copper Treaty, 135

Cortés, Hernán, 31

Council of Energy Resource Tribes (CERT), 157

Coushatta people, 271

Coyote's First World Casino installation, 299, 303, 304, 307

Creek people: allotment and, 109n6; epidemic disease and, 36; Five Civilized Tribes and, 17, 185; Indigenous literature and, 113–14; removal policies and, 83; slavery and the slave trade and, 53; warfare and, 4, 71. *See also* Creek people

Cree people, 149

crime and criminal justice, 122–25, 127n19, 138. *See also* laws and legal decisions

Crosby, Alfred, 152–53

Crowe, Charles, 262

Crow people, 72, 148, 279

cultural appropriation, 174–76, 182

Curtis Act, 109n6, 187

Cusick, David, 317

Custer, George Armstrong, 63, 71, 72, 278–79

Dakota Access Pipeline (DAPL), 158–59, 248, 256, 280

Dakota people, 279
D'Alemberte, Talbot "Sandy," 173–74, 180, 181
Dances with Wolves (film), 99
DAPL. *See* Dakota Access Pipeline (DAPL)
Dartmouth College, 312, 315
Darwin, Charles, and Darwinism, 38
Davis, Edwin, 314–15
Davis, Jefferson, 71
Dawes Act, 94, 95, 109n2, 154, 187
Debo, Angie, 104
Declaration of Independence, 68, 87
Declaration of Indian Purpose, 193–94
Deer, Ada, 271
Dei, George Sefa, 250
Delaware people, 66, 86. *See also* Lenape people
Deloria, Vine, Jr., 199, 208–9, 229, 253
demographic collapse: birthrates and, 32, 34; climate change and, 32; culpability for, 161–62; dying race thesis and, 115–16; epidemic disease and, 35–37, 49; genocide debate and, 29, 37–38, 40; God's will and, 38; labor exploitation and, 32; malnutrition and, 32, 34, 35; migration and, 34, 35–36; population and, 31, 36–37; slavery and the slave trade and, 33–34, 45, 49; structural violence and, 33, 49, 242; virgin soil thesis and, 29–32, 34, 36, 39–40, 49, 152, 161, 288, 294n15; warfare and, 60
Denetdale, Jennifer Nez, 131
de Soto, Hernando, 16, 31
Diamond, Jared, 152
Diné people, 7, 72, 131, 146, 155–57, 206. *See also* Navajo people
disability, 274–75
discovery doctrine, 115, 116, 123, 132, 301

disease epidemics. *See* epidemic disease
"Dish with One Spoon" treaty, 133
diversity, equity, and inclusion. *See* multicultural education
Duro v. Reina, 127n19

East Carolina University, 309, 311, 317
Eastman, Charles, 279
education: American Indian Centers and, 271; collaborative pedagogy and, 303–4; cost of, 312; Elders in Residence and, 271; environmental knowledge and, 154; experiential pedagogy, 304–5; Indian schools and, 298, 302; indigenized, 253, 256; Indigenous language and culture and, 311–12, 319nn4–5; Indigenous programming and, 252–53; Indigenous schools and, 266, 271; Indigenous students and, 311–13, 315; Indigenous voices and, 254; multicultural, 249, 250–51, 252, 253, 257; on versus off reservation, 311–13
Educators Network for Social Justice (ENSJ), 298, 304–5
Effigy Mound Culture, 300, 305
Ellinghaus, Kat, 286
Emerald Mounds (Mississippi), 16
enrollment. *See* tribal rolls
ENSJ. *See* Educators Network for Social Justice (ENSJ)
environment: activities for classrooms and, 146; agriculture's effects on, 151–52; allotment and, 107, 154; complexity of Indigenous relationship to, 148–50; dams and irrigation and, 155–56, 203; deep history and, 288–89; fire for land management and, 151; food and

foodways and, 147–48, 215, 221; health and, 220, 221; historic preservation and, 240; Indigenous knowledge and, 219, 239, 255, 257; origin stories and, 146–47; personhood in the natural world and, 201–2, 203–6, 207, 210, 211–12n6; reciprocity and, 256; removal policies and, 153–54; resources for teachers and, 158–59, 239–41; stereotypes about Indigenous people and, 145, 159. *See also* climate change; natural resources

epidemic disease: captive-taking and, 52; contextualization of, 30–32, 34–35, 37, 39–40, 49, 161–62; in typical school presentations, 3; Indigenous resilience and, 49–50; Indigenous response to, 36–39; "Navajo Plague" and, 206; resources for teachers and, 206–7; shatter zone and, 16–17; slavery and slave trade and, 34, 45, 47, 49; smallpox and, 31, 32, 34, 35, 121. *See also* demographic collapse; health and medicine

erasure: demographic collapse and, 37; food and foodways and, 219–20; genocide and, 163, 164; language suppression and, 220, 230; museum exhibits and, 309, 310, 311; Native place-names and, 305; portraiture and, 239–40; racial classification systems and, 185–86, 190–92; reservations and, 136; residential schools and, 220–21, 230; stereotypes about Indigenous people and, 192, 278; universality and, 233; Vanishing Indian trope and, 145–46, 163, 228, 276, 294n15, 309–11, 314–15, 317–18; vanishing

policy and, 190; virgin soil thesis and, 39

Erdrich, Louise, 115–16, 119–25, 127, 270

Erie people, 53

ethnocentrism. *See* race and racism

ethnogenesis, 32

Etowah (Georgia), 16

Euchee people, 274

Evarts, Jeremiah, 78, 80

Everett, Edward, 83, 119

Experiencing Native North America installation, 298–307, 302

FAM. *See* First Americans Museum (FAM)

families and family structures: access to resources and, 98, 149; allotment and, 93, 95–98, 100; band versus tribal society and, 14; Census definition of, 100, 109n4; marriage practices and, 51–52, 53, 149, 189, 286–87; matrilineal descent and, 96; people and the land and, 255–56; resources for teachers and, 97; traditional Native patterns of, 96–97; tribal rolls and, 100–101. *See also* child welfare and adoption

Ferdinand (King of Spain), 48

Fetterman Fight, 63

First Americans Museum (FAM), 229

First Nations, 7

Five Civilized Tribes, 17, 185, 187

Five/Six Nations people, 7, 67–68. *See also* Haudenosaunee people; Iroquois people

Fixico, Donald, 289

Florida Public Archaeology Network, 26

Florida State University, 171–82

Fogelson, Raymond, 263
Folsom (New Mexico), 13
food and foodways: activities for classrooms and, 223–24; bison and, 71, 72, 154, 214; ceremony and, 215; counterinsurgency tactics and, 70; dying race thesis and, 116; environment and, 215, 221; erasure of Indigenous identity and, 219–20; fishing, hunting, and gathering rights and, 129–30, 131, 137–41; food choices and, 217–18; health and medicine and, 218–19, 222; homogenization of, 32; hunter/gatherer versus agricultural societies and, 115; in typical classroom instruction, 214; maize and, 151, 152; malnutrition and, 32, 34, 35; pottery and, 14–15; refugee migration and, 35–36; regional foodways and, 147–48, 149; removal policies and, 154; residential schools and, 220–21; resources for teachers, 225n3, 225n6; societal organization and, 148; Three Sisters and, 151; tradition and, 216–17; in typical classroom instruction, 214. *See also* agriculture
forced labor systems. *See also* labor exploitation; slavery and the slave trade
Ford Foundation, 229
Fort Berthold Reservation, 89
Fort Laramie Treaty, 71
Fort Necessity, 4
Fort Oswego, 69
Fort William Henry, 69
Fosburgh Lumber Company, 190
Foster, Tol, 272
Fox people, 62, 280
fracking, 4–5
Friends of the Indian, 107

Garden Creek site (North Carolina), 15
Garrison Dam, 89
Gates, Merrill, 96–97, 98, 107
gender and gender roles: agriculture and, 14, 153, 220; allotment and, 99; Australia and, 284; family structure and, 96–97; female deities and, 219; foodways and, 219–20; sexual violence and, 122–23, 124–25; slavery and slave trade and, 33, 46, 51; US government policy and, 153; virgin soil thesis and, 39. *See also* sex and sexuality
genealogy, 186, 189
General Allotment Act of 1887. *See* Dawes Act
genocide: biological versus cultural, 164, 166, 167n4, 242; as contested term, 160–61; definitions of, 161, 162–63, 164, 166, 167n5; as difficult concept, 73–74n1; epidemic disease and, 161–62; erasure and, 163, 164; ethnocide and, 166; Holocaust and, 160, 162–63; manifest destiny and, 315; multicultural education and, 250; in "peacetime," 72; residential schools and, 165; scientific legitimation of, 315; UNDRIP and, 163, 167n6; UNGC and, 162–63; warfare and, 60. *See also* demographic collapse
George III (England), 68
Geronimo, 61
Ghost Dancers, 70
Gichi-Waabizheshi, 135–36
Giishkitawag (Joe White), 138
Glacier National Park, 88
globalization, 301, 302
Gnadenhütten Massacre, 62, 69
Gold, Harriet, 287
Gone, Joseph P., 164, 166

Gordon, Philip, 139
grave sites, 23–25, 268–69, 290–91,
    313–14
Great Lakes Indian Fish and Wildlife
    Commission, 141
Great Lakes Nations, 300
Green, Mike, 81, 268, 270, 271, 272
Greene County History Museum,
    309, 310, 311, 316, 317
Green Party, 158
Greenpeace, 158
Grosfoguel, Ramón, 253
Gros Ventre people, 164
Guale people, 32, 33
Gurnoe, Richard "Dick," 138–39
Gurnoe case. See Wisconsin v.
    Gurnoe

Haliwa people, 186–95, 265
Haney, Michael, 173, 174
Harjo, Joy, 113–14
Harmar, Josiah, 69–70
Harney, William S., 71
Harris, LaDonna, 271
Harrison, William Henry, 70, 71
Haudenosaunee people: alliances
    and, 133; American Revolution
    and, 68; captive-taking and, 52, 53;
    creation stories and, 203–4, 316;
    humans and nature and, 150;
    nations of, 317; nomenclature and,
    7; origin stories and, 146; Tuscarora
    Migration project and, 310. See also
    Five/Six Nations people; Iroquois
    people
Head-Smashed-In Buffalo Jump
    (Alberta, Canada), 14
health and medicine: addiction
    and, 222; healing history and,
    295n24; health disparities and, 39;
    Indigenous knowledge and, 154,
    218–19, 220–21, 274–75; religion

and ceremony and, 199, 206–7, 222.
    See also epidemic disease
Hedgepeth, John Conrad, 192
Hensley, William Iggiagruk, 128
Hidatsa people, 148, 155, 157, 279
Hillyard, George W., 188
Hinton, Alexander Laban, 164
historiography: American exception-
    alism and, 293n4; canon of, 80;
    colonial historians and, 39–40;
    deep history and, 284–85, 288–92;
    genocide and, 40, 163–64; geology
    and archaeology and, 289, 290,
    291; Indigenous historians and,
    84–85, 86; Indigenous slavery and,
    54; New Indian history and, 276;
    oral and material evidence and,
    188–89, 285, 289–90, 313, 317,
    319n1; paternalism and, 38; period-
    ization and, 288, 292–93n3, 299,
    305, 313; slavery and the slave
    trade and, 44, 47; stilted American
    narratives and, 309–11, 313, 315–16,
    318; virgin soil thesis and, 30–32,
    36–40, 152; Western versus Indige-
    nous conception of history and,
    284–85
Hobbes, Thomas, 69
Ho-Chunk people, 2, 236, 237–38,
    238. See also Winnebago people
Hockings, Nick, 137
Hogan, Linda, 128
Holm, Tom, 186, 190
Holocaust, 160, 162–63
Holy Elk, Ray, 193
Hopewell culture, 15
Hopi people, 147, 209
Houma people, 271
Housen, Abigail, 234
Houser, Allan, 228, 232–35, 233, 236,
    243n1
Howe, LeAnne, 270

Hudson, Charles, 262
Hull, Kathleen, 36–37, 39
human trafficking, 47
hunting and fishing: agriculture and, 217; Archaic Period and, 14; bison and, 154, 202–3; dams and irrigation and, 155, 158; fire for land management and, 151; fishing, hunting, and gathering rights and, 129–30, 131, 137–41; Indigenous knowledge and, 219; Pleistocene-Holocene transition and, 150–51; regional differences in, 147–48; residential schools and, 220–21; tribal sovereignty and, 157–58; US government policies and, 153; Woodland Period and, 15
Huron people, 148; *See also* Wendat people; Wyandot people

imperialism. *See* colonialism and imperialism
Indian Child Welfare Act (1978), 127, 165
Indian Civil Rights Act (1968), 123, 127
Indian Country Today (digital news platform), 270
Indian Health Service, 222
Indian Knoll (Kentucky), 14
Indian law. *See* laws and legal decisions; treaties
Indian Removal Act, 78, 80, 87
Indian Service, 94–95, 98, 104
Indian Territory, 87–88
Indian Trade and Intercourse Acts, 69
Indian Wars, 69–72
Indigenous Americans. *See* Native Americans
Indigenous history: in Australia, 293n5; Christian ideology and, 117–21; collaborative learning and, 303–4; community healing and, 295n24; contestations over tribal homelands and, 114–15, 116; contradictions with received US history and, 5, 7; crime and criminal justice and, 122–25; deep history and, 284–85, 305; definition of, 275–76; demand for courses in, 269, 270; early periods of, 12–17, 22, 150–51; environmental history and, 145–46, 150–58; experiential learning and, 261, 298–307, 302, 303; genocide as organizing theme in, 161, 162; Indigenous elementary schools and, 311–12; Indigenous knowledge and, 263–65, 269–71, 292; Indigenous political narratives and, 112–13; Indigenous voices in policy making and, 121; installation as pedagogy and, 304–5, 306–7; interdisciplinary work and, 263, 304; local history and, 26–27; local Native communities and, 315–17, 318; longue durée of, 284, 285; Medicine Way and, 275–77, 280–82, 289; multisensory presentation and, 289–90; Native diversity and, 266–67; Native students and, 310; oral tradition and storytelling and, 283n11, 289, 315; past and present connections and, 268–69; people without history and, 294n12; race and racism and, 118, 119; thematic approaches and, 267–68, 278–79, 299; transnational approaches and, 284, 285–87; tribal sovereignty and, 113–14, 125; in typical school presentations, 3–4, 11; value of in the classroom, 6–7, 125; victimization versus agency and, 310, 318; Western linearity and, 276–77. *See also*

Indigenous studies; *specific authors and works*

Indigenous languages, 220, 230, 265, 311

Indigenous literature, 124, 270, 298, 305–6

Indigenous People's Day, 319n5

Indigenous studies: Florida State University and, 179; Indigenous knowledge and, 254–55, 257; Indigenous students and, 312–13, 315; interdisciplinary work and, 304–5; Medicine Way and, 276, 280–82, 289; responsibilities of learners and, 272–73; study abroad programs and, 272

Industrial Revolution, 154–55

In the Light of Reverence (film), 209

Ironstrack, George, 85

Iroquois people, 7, 52, 65, 68, 133, 146, 220. *See also* Five/Six Nations people; Haudenosaunee people

Isabella (Queen of Spain), 46–47, 48–49

Jackson, Andrew, 4, 70–71, 78, 80, 82, 39, 153

James, George Wharton, 241

Jefferson, Thomas, 68, 75n14

Jemison, Mary, 61

Jim Crow, 6

Joara (village), 16

Johnson, Chiitaanibah, 29, 40

Johnson v. McIntosh, 78, 114–20, 122–23, 132

Jones, David, 30, 38, 39

Jones, Tom, 236–38, *238*, 242

Jumonville's Glen, 4

Kalk, Curt, 137–38

Keen, Norman L., 191

Kelly, Fanny, 61

Kelton, Paul, 34, 36, 37–38, 39

Kennewick Man, 24

Keokuk, 62, 280

Kickapoo people, 64, 86

Kidder, T. R., 13–14

King, C. Richard, 173

King, Martin Luther, Jr., 262

King Philip's War, 4, 47, 65, 283n9

Kiowa people, 72

Knox, Henry, 134

Kooweskoowe. *See* Ross, John

Kuckkahn, Tina, 140

labor exploitation, 32, 49, 56, 57. *See also* slavery and the slave trade

Lac Courte Oreilles reservation, 138, 139–40, 199

Lac du Flambeau reservation, 137, 140

Ladd, Ed, 229

LaDuke, Winona, 158

Lake George Mounds (Mississippi), 16

Lakota people: anthropology and, 199; autobiographical accounts and, 61; battles and wars and, 64, 72, 278–79; ceremony and, 211n3; foodways and, 148; Great Sioux Reservation and, 87; oil pipelines and, 158–59; people and the land and, 255–56; personhood in the natural world and, 204–5; sacred pipe and, 213n18; sacred sites and, 208, 209; schools and, 193; treaty rights and, 130

Lambert, Henry, 270

land acknowledgments, 247–57, 315–16

land loss and retention: arts and, 240–41; community disruption and, 248; contestations over tribal homelands and, 114–17; continued

land loss and retention (*continued*)
relationship to land and, 254;
cultural persistence and, 6; health
problems and, 219, 220; improvements and, 102, 103; "Indian
Country" and, 128; Indigenous
vocabulary of, 286; *Johnson v.
McIntosh* and, 118, 122; land alienation and, 105; land cessions and,
87, 99; land quality and, 95; land
repatriation and, 250, 251; removal
policies and, 84–85, 86; societal
organization and, 149–50; unconstitutional takings and, 127; unremoved people and, 187–88, 195.
See also allotment; removal policies
Larsen, Clark Spencer, 32–33, 39–40
laws and legal decisions: discovery
doctrine and, 115, 116–17, 127–28;
archaeology and, 22–25; Dakota
Access Pipeline (DAPL) and, 280–
81; Indigenous literature and, 113.
See also crime and criminal justice;
specific laws and decisions
LeForge, Thomas, 279
Lemkin, Rafael, 162–63, 166, 167n6
Lenape people, 66. *See also* Delaware
people
Lewiston Reservoir, 311
Lick, Dale W., 177
Lincoln, Abraham, 71
literature. *See* Indigenous literature
Little Turtle, 69–70
livestock raising, 155, 218, 222
Lizard Mound State Park, 300, 305
Lonetree, Amy, 242
Lone Wolf v. Hitchcock, 127
Lord, Erica, 242
Luban, David, 126n1
Luiseño people, 240, 254
Lumbee people, 192–94, 265–66, 272
Lumpkin, Wilson, 82

Lynch, Inez, 191
Lynch, T. P., 191
*Lyng v. Northwest Cemetery Protective
Association*, 127

MacDonald, David, 165
Madley, Benjamin, 242
Magegawbaw, 135
Makah people, 158
Maliseet people, 300, 301, 304, 307
Mandan people, 148, 155, 157, 202–3
manifest destiny, 301, 302, 312, 315
Mankiller, Wilma, 179
Manteo, 283n9
Maori people, 267, 292n1
maps. *See* cartography
Marias River Massacre, 62, 73
Marshall, John, 4, 78, 82, 132
Marshall Trilogy, 132, 137
mascots. *See* team mascots
Mato Tipila (Lodge of the Bear), 208,
209
Maynor, Lacy, 194
McCoy, Isaac, 80
McCrae, Jane, 68, 69
McDonnell, Michael, 65
Meadowcroft Rockshelter (Pennsyl-
vania), 13
medicine. *See* health and medicine
Medicine Way, 275–77, 280–82, 289
Meehccikilita, 85
Menominee people, 301, 304
Meredith, America, 231
Meriam Report, 193
Merrell, James H., 39–40
Mesquakie people, 62
Mexican War, 71
Mexica people, 51. *See also* Aztec
people
Meyers, "Chief," 271
Miami people, 66, 83–86
Miami University (Ohio), 84–85

migration, 12–14, 16–17, 22, 32–37, 64, 71. *See also* removal policies

Mille Lacs reservation, 138, 140

Mille Lacs v. Minnesota, 140

Miller, Cary, 304

Milwaukee Indian Community School, 298, 302, 303–5

Mississippian culture, 15–16, 64

Mississippi Band of Choctaw Indians v. Holyfield, 127

Mitchell, Anna Belle Sixkiller, 230

Mitsitam Native Foods Café, 217

Modoc War, 71–72

Mohawk people, 66, 68, 314

Mole Lake reservation, 140

Momaday, N. Scott, 127, 270

Monk's Mound, 152

Mooney, James, 264

Morris, Thomas, 66

Moulton, Gary, 81

mound builders, 13–15, 313–15. *See also specific sites*

Moundville (Alabama), 16

Mount Rushmore occupation, 130

Mt. Pleasant, Frank, 311

multicultural education, 249, 250–51, 252, 253, 257

Muneta, Ben, 206–7

Mungo Lady and Mungo Man, 291

Museum of the Cherokee Indian, 265

museums, 228, 230, 243n1, 265, 309–11, 316–18. *See also specific museums*

Mushkegowuk people, 149

Mutthi people, 291

Mvskoke people, 113–14, 277. *See also* Creek people

Myaamia Center, 84–85

NAGPRA. *See* Native American Graves Protection and Repatriation Act (NAGPRA)

NALS. *See* Native American Literature Symposium (NALS)

National Congress of American Indians, 194

National Endowment for the Arts, 233

National Endowment for the Humanities, 272

National Forest Service, 24, 25

National Historic Preservation Act (NHPA), 22–23, 316, 319n12

National Museum of Australia, 290

National Museum of the American Indian, 25, 230

National Park Service, 24, 25

National Register of Historic Places (NRHP), 23, 25, 240

Native American and Indigenous Studies Association, 263

Native American Graves Protection and Repatriation Act (NAGPRA), 23–25, 268–69, 290, 313–14

Native American history. *See* Indigenous history

Native American Literature Symposium (NALS), 298, 305–6

Native American studies. *See* Indigenous studies

Native Americans: arrival of in Americas, 12; as athletes, 270–71, 311; as Black under law, 6, 185–97; continued presence of Indigenous communities and, 317; as distinct polities versus singular group, 52–53; diversity among, 266–67; as dying race, 115–16; first settlement by, 285; in higher education, 251–52; legal identities of, 186, 188; lost world of, 155; as minority population, 272; nomenclature and, 7; in popular media, 4; as primitive, 17,

Native Americans (*continued*)
312, 313; as savages, 115, 116, 200; stereotypes about, 175–77, 198, 265, 278. *See also* Indigenous history; Indigenous studies

Native civil rights movement: actions of, 130; Alcatraz Island occupation and, 138; cultural persistence and, 6; education and, 252–53; fish-ins and, 139; globalizing Indigenous movements and, 293n7; Haliwa Indian Club and, 193; Indian Civil Rights Act and, 123; Red Power and, 194, 208, 249, 252–53; termination and, 156; in typical school presentations, 4–5

Natonabah, Andy, 206

natural resources: access to, 164–65; allotment and, 99–100, 102, 104, 107, 155; dams and irrigation and, 155–56, 158, 203; fishing, hunting, and gathering rights and, 137–38; food and foodways and, 217; fossil fuel industry and, 158–59; historic preservation and, 240; Indigenous knowledge and, 149, 219; lumber industry and, 190; mining and, 164–65; Native resistance and, 311; oil pipelines and, 158–59; pairings of literary and legal texts and, 128; sacred sites and, 209; societal organization and, 149–50; treaties and, 129–31, 135, 222; tribal sovereignty and, 131, 156–57. *See also* climate change; environment

Navajo people, 4, 7, 72, 146, 155–56, 206, 218. *See also* Diné people

NCAA, 172–73, 180, 181–82

Nesper, Larry, 137

New Deal, 24

New Zealand, 267

Nez Perce people, 64

Nez Perce War, 71

NHPA. *See* National Historic Preservation Act (NHPA)

NoDAPL movement. *See* Dakota Access Pipeline (DAPL)

Noodin, Margaret, 304

Northwest Ordinance, 69, 75n17

NRHP. *See* National Register of Historic Places (NRHP)

Nyaampa people, 291

Oakes, Richard, 6

Obama, Barack, 163

O'Brien, Jean, 294n15

Ocmulgee Mounds, 16, 261

O'Connell, Barry, 119

Odawa people, 7, 66, 133

Office of Indian Affairs, 73, 103

Oglala people, 279

Ojibwe people: archaeology and, 319n12; creation stories and, 212nn11–12; fur traders and, 134–35; interrelatedness and, 212n13; Indigenous literature and, 115, 116, 119; nomenclature and, 7; removal policies and, 135–36; reservations and, 136, 142n15; Three Fires Confederacy and, 133; treaties and, 129–31, 134–41; beliefs of, 199, 204–6, 212n13. *See also* Chippewa people

Oliphant v. Suquamish Indian Tribe, 122–25

Omaha people, 152

Oneida people, 304

Oneota people, 300

Onondaga people, 311

Ortiz, Simon, 113

Osage people, 35–36, 152, 156–57

Osburn, Katherine M. B., 108

Osceola, 70, 171–73, 177–79, 181

Osceola, Max B., Jr., 180–81

Pardo, Juan, 16
Paredes, Anthony, 178, 179
Paton, Rob, 295n24
Pawnee people, 72
Paxtonites, 69
peace pipe, 134
Pearson, J. Diane, 186
Peinado, J. Carlos, 89
Penn, William. *See* Evarts, Jeremiah
peoplehood, 186–87, 190–93, 195n2
Pequot people, 115, 116
Pequot War, 63, 65
Perdue, Theda, 81
Phillip, Arthur, 288
Pick-Sloan Plan, 89
Pike, Zebulon, 35
Pilkington, Doris, 287
Pine Tree Treaty, 135
pipelines, 4–5, 6, 221. *See also* Dakota
    Access Pipeline (DAPL)
Plains Wars, 72
Poarch Creek people, 271
Polis, Jared, 251
political status of Indigenous people:
    citizenship and, 97; federal and
    state recognition and, 194, 195, 265,
    266; in US versus Australia, 286,
    292n1, 293n7; unremoved tribes
    and, 266; voting rights and, 188,
    196n8, 232
Ponca people, 87–88
Pontiac's War, 66
Potawatomi people, 7, 86, 133
poverty. *See* wealth and income
Poverty Point (Louisiana), 13–14
Power, Susan, 270
Powhatan, 4, 148
Pratt, Richard, 137
Price, Pendalton, 237, *238*
Proclamation Line of 1763, 67,
    74–75n10
Prophetstown movement, 63, 70

Pueblo people, 31, 1113, 27, 147
Pueblo Rebellion, 72
Puritans, 4

Qualla Boundary (reservation), 263,
    264–65, 270, 272
Quapaw people, 152
Quebec Act (1774), 67
Quetone, Joe, 178

Rabbit-Proof Fence (film), 287
race and racism: allotment and, 94,
    97; anti-treaty protests and, 129,
    140; Australia and, 284; Black/
    White binary and, 4, 6, 55, 185–86,
    189, 191–94, 266; blood quantum
    and, 105; discovery doctrine and,
    115; DNA research and, 290,
    296n32; essentialism and, 145; food
    and foodways and, 215, 221; Indig-
    enous literature and, 118, 119;
    invention and codification of race
    and, 51, 55; learning about, 262;
    marriage and, 51–52, 286–87; mul-
    ticultural education and, 250–51,
    253; passing and, 279; paternalism
    and, 70–71; photography and, 239;
    racial classification and, 185–86,
    190–92, 195, 249, 266; racial insensi-
    tivity in the classroom and, 50;
    racialization of Indian country
    and, 57; redface and, 171, 175,
    177, 179, 181; reverse racism and,
    140; team mascots and, 177, 301;
    unremoved people and, 189, 193,
    266; White supremacy and, 186,
    190
railroads, 154
Railway Enabling Act, 4
Rangel, John Paul, 231
Ray, Kristofer, 67
Red Cloud's War, 73

Red Shirt Shaw, Megan, 251

Reese, Benjamin, 250

refugees, 45

religion and ceremony: activities for classrooms and, 146, 200–201, 209–10, 212nn11–12; belief and practice and, 265; bison and, 202–3; ceremonial objects and, 229; Christian ideology and, 38, 114, 117–21; Christian missionaries and, 32–33, 35, 81, 94, 98–100, 153, 220, 287; collaborative learning and, 303–4; conversion and, 46, 53; creation stories and, 14, 147, 201–4, 206, 211n5, 212n11, 219, 289, 316; cultural sensitivity and, 210, 211n2; dance and, 232–35, 233; death and, 274–75; definitions of religion and, 211n3; diversity of traditions and, 198, 199; early historical periods and, 13–15; experiential learning and, 301–2; fishing, hunting, and gathering rights and, 137; food and foodways and, 215; Ghost Dancers and, 279; harmony and balance and, 146–47, 205, 206, 210; health and medicine and, 206–7, 222, 274–75; humans and nature and, 147, 149; Indigenous churches and, 189–92, 193, 266; interrelatedness and, 203, 204–7, 210, 212n13; landscape and, 305, 307; Mormons and, 71; personhood in the natural world and, 201–7, 210, 211–12n6; powwows and, 195; prayer cards and, 306, 307; refugee migration and, 35–36; removal policies and, 153–54; resources for teachers and, 208, 209, 212n13; sacred pipe and, 208, 213n18; sacred sites and, 127, 207–10, 212–13n16, 268; sacred space and, 4–5, 302–3; scholarly misappraisals of, 198–201; shamanism and, 211n1; tomb raiding and, 291; trade and, 16; treaty ceremonies and, 134; tricksters and, 147, 205, 212n11; windigo and, 205–6, 212n13

removal policies: adaptation prior to, 17; Cherokee people and, 78–83; chronological extent of, 87–89; common language of, 79–80; environment and, 153–54; ethnic cleansing and, 78; health problems and, 219; in typical school presentations, 5; Indian Wars and, 71–72; opposition to, 80–83, 85–86; racial categorization and, 249; resources for teachers and, 80–81, 83–86, 88, 89, 91n27; sacred sites and, 209; self-removal and, 188–89; slavery and the slave trade and, 56; Trail of Tears and, 4, 79–83, 209; treaties and, 135–36, 280; tribal sovereignty and, 81–83, 85–86, 88; unremoved people and, 187–88; *Unto These Hills* (drama) and, 264. *See also* land loss and retention; reservations

reservations: allotment and, 93, 137; Christianity and, 120; dam construction and, 87, 89; education and, 253; erasure and, 136; Indigenous perspectives on, 142n15; misappropriation of lands on, 87; Native American history courses and, 263, 264–65; natural resource exploitation and, 155, 156; resistance to, 71; resources for teachers and, 127–28; treaties and, 136–37; tribal criminal authority and, 122, 124–25

residential schools: "kill the Indian to save the man" and, 137, 165; Boarding School Syndrome and,

221; erasure of Indigenous identity and, 220–21; forced labor and, 57; genocide and, 165; Indigenous knowledge and, 264; Indigenous leaders and, 156; land acknowledgments and, 248; language and culture loss and, 230; pan-Indian identity and, 165; in typical school presentations, 4–5

resources for teachers: allotment and, 97; archaeology and, 25–26, 27; arts and, 230, 239–41; dam construction and, 89; documentary collections and, 166; environment and, 158–59, 239–41; epidemic disease and, 206–7; families and family structures and, 97; food and foodways and, 225n3, 225n6; Indigenous people as, 264–65, 271–72, 317; interdisciplinary conferences and, 263; interrelatedness and, 212n13; justifications for dispossession of Native Americans and, 116; newspapers and, 270, 271–72; oral history and, 188–89; pairings of literary and legal texts and, 127–28; primary sources and, 60–61; removal policies and, 80, 83–86, 88–89, 91n27; sacred sites and, 208, 209; slavery and the slave trade and, 46; textbooks and, 270; treaties and, 142n4; tribes' and nations' websites and, 26

Restrictions Bill (1908), 105

Revolutionary War. *See* American Revolution

Richardson, Alfred, Jr., 188, 189

Richardson, B. B., 192

Richardson, John, 187

Richardson, P. A., 188–89

Richardson, Reese, 189–90

Richardson, W. R., 192, 194

Richardville, Jean Baptist, 85

Ridge, John, 78

Roach, Archie, 287

Rogue River War, 71

Roosevelt, Franklin, 24

Roosevelt, Theodore, 316

Ross, John, 78, 80, 81, 187, 287

Rowlandson, Mary, 61

Royal Ontario Museum, 133

SAA. *See* Society for American Archeology (SAA)

Sacramento State University, 29–30, 40

Sahnish people, 155. *See also* Arikara people

Sand Creek Massacre, 61, 62, 73, 161

Santa Clara Pueblo v. Martinez, 127

Saponi people, 186–93, 195, 265–66

Sassamon, John, 283n9

Sauk people, 62, 280

Section 106 of the NHPA. *See* National Historic Preservation Act (NHPA, 1966)

Section 110 of the NHPA. *See* National Historic Preservation Act (NHPA, 1966)

segregation and integration, 85–86, 93, 134–35, 189–93, 266

Seminole people, 17, 83, 128, 171–82, 185, 277

Seminole Wars, 70, 71

Seneca people, 155, 311

Serpent Mound (Ohio), 15

Serrano people, 254

Seven Years' War, 4, 65, 66

Sevier, John, 69

sex and sexuality, 5–6, 39, 53, 57. *See also* gender and gender roles

Shawnee people, 66, 70, 86

Sherman, Aleksandra, 233

Shoah. *See* Holocaust

Shore, Jim, 181

SHPOs. *See* State Historic Preservation Offices (SHPOs)

Shrock, Andrew, 288

Simpson, Audra, 235

Sinclair, Murray, 164

Siouan people, 177, 194, 265

Sioux people, 4, 71, 87, 127, 279–80. *See also* Dakota people; Lakota people; Oglala people

Sisolak, Steve, 252

Sisquoc, Lorene, 241

Sitting Bull, 64

Six Nations people. *See* Five/Six Nations people

Slack Farm Site, 268

slavery and the slave trade: abolition and, 56; adoption of captives and, 52; alternative forms of enslavement and, 47, 50–53; Australia and, 284; Black/White binary and, 189; Columbus and, 48; epidemic disease and, 34, 45, 47, 49, 52; erasure and, 34, 55, 57; fugitives and, 187; gender and, 34, 46, 51; in typical school presentations, 4, 45; Indigenous slaveowners and traders and, 17, 52–54, 57, 64, 218, 262, 264; Indigenous slave trade and, 33, 48–49, 53–56; medicine and, 218; myths about, 44–56; of Native versus African people, 5; racialization and, 51, 55–56; removal policies and, 56, 188; resistance to, 46, 56–57; resources for teachers and, 46; sex and sexuality and, 53; shatter zone and, 16–17; trade patterns and, 33–34, 35, 54; warfare and, 64; westward expansion and, 119. *See also* labor exploitation

Smail, Daniel, 288

smallpox. *See* demographic collapse; epidemic disease

Smith, Jaune Quick-to-See, 231–32

Smith, Theresa, 212n13

Smithsonian Institution. *See also* National Museum of the American Indian

Soboba people, 240, 241–42

Soboba Reservation, 239, 240, 241

societal organization, 12–16, 64, 115, 148–50

Society for American Archaeology (SAA), 25

Sommer, Drake, 304

Spence, Mark David, 88

Spencer, Beverley, 174

Springwood, Charles, 173

Squier, Ephraim, 314–15

Standing Bear, 88

Standing Bear v. Crook, 88

Standing Rock Reservation, 158–59, 248, 256

Stands in Timber, John, 279

Stapler, Mary Brian, 287

State Historic Preservation Offices (SHPOs), 23, 25, 26

St. Clair, Arthur, 62, 63, 69–70

St. Croix reservation, 140

Stiles, T. J., 279

St. Laurent, Bryan, 173–74

Stuart, Robert, 136

Sumner, Charles, 56

Suquamish people, 122–23, 124–25

Susquehannock people, 148

Swedlund, Alan, 38

Table Rock Reservation, 164

Taino people, 160, 161, 312. *See also* Arawak people

Tax, Sol, 193

taxation, 105, 106, 132

Taylor, Zachary, 71, 136

team mascots, 171–82, 301, 302
Tecumseh, 62, 70
TEK. *See* Traditional Ecological Knowledge (TEK)
Tending the Wild (film), 239
Tenskwatawa, 70
termination, 4–5, 156, 301, 302. *See also* allotment
Texas Rangers, 73
Thanksgiving, 4, 214, 288, 311
Third World Liberation Front, 252
Thirteenth Amendment, 56
Thomas, Robert K., 263
Three Affiliated Tribes, 89, 156–57, 203; *See also* Arikara people; Hidatsa people; Mandan people
Three Fires Confederacy, 133. *See also* Odawa people; Ojibwe people; Potawatomi people
Tiger Jumper, Betty Mae, 179
Timucua people, 32, 33
Tindall, George, 262
Tobique First Nation, 300. *See also* Maliseet people
Tommie, Howard, 176–77
Tongva people, 254
tourism, 176, 265, 270
trade, 14, 16–17, 33–35, 74–75n10, 99, 134–35. *See also* slavery and the slave trade
Traditional Ecological Knowledge (TEK), 239
Trail of Tears. *See* removal policies
Transformers (film), 99
treaties: annuities and, 134, 136; anti-treaty protests and, 129, 140; congressional ratification of, 99; Dakota Access Pipeline (DAPL) and, 280; dispossession and, 130, 133–34; as enduring statements of rights, 130, 131; food and foodways and, 215, 221–22; Indigenous versus non-Indigenous understandings of, 74n2; *Lone Wolf v. Hitchcock* and, 127; natural resources and, 129–31, 22; New Zealand and, 267; peace pipe and, 134; persistence of treaty rights and, 136, 139–41, 157–58; removal policies and, 87, 135–41, 280; reservations and, 71, 136–37; resources for teachers and, 127–28, 142n4; termination and, 301, 302; treaty negotiations and, 132–34, 141; tribal sovereignty and, 130, 136, 141, 222; tribes without treaties and, 266; wampum exchange and, 133; written documents versus spoken words and, 133–34, 135. *See also specific treaties*
Treaty of Fort Laramie, 130
Treaty of La Pointe, 136
Treaty of New Echota, 82–83
Treaty of Paris (1763), 66
Treaty of Waitangi, 267
tribal rolls, 100–104, 127, 156
tribal sovereignty: allotment and, 94, 100; American Indian Chicago Conference (AICC) and, 194; arts and, 240–41; bureaucracy and, 98, 102; cultural persistence and, 6; Dakota Access Pipeline (DAPL) and, 280; deep history and, 285; fishing, hunting, and gathering rights and, 129–32, 137–41, 157–58; food and foodways and, 221–22; fossil fuel industry and, 158–59; Indigenous literature and, 113–14, 125; Indigenous political narratives and, 112–13; laws and legal decisions and, 116; natural resources and, 156–59; *Oliphant v. Suquamish Indian Tribe* and, 123, 124–25; removal policies and, 81–82, 85, 88;

tribal sovereignty (*continued*)
strategies to preserve, 187; team
mascots and, 171–75, 177–82;
treaties and, 130–31, 136, 141, 222;
tribal criminal authority and,
127n19; in typical school presentations, 4–5; unremoved people and,
194, 195; US Constitution and, 113,
114, 131–32; US Supreme Court
and, 124, 132; *Worcester v. Georgia*
and, 82–83
Tribble, Fred, 139–40
Tribble, Mike, 139–40, 141
Trudell, John, 6
Tuck, Eve, 235–36, 250
Turtle Island, 131
Tuscarora Historical Society, 318
Tuscarora History Conference,
320n15
Tuscarora Migration Project, 310, 311,
317
Tuscarora people, 309–13, 317–18
Tuscarora War, 309
"Two Row Wampum" treaty, 133,
142n4
Tyrrell, Ian, 293n4

UNDRIP. *See* United Nations Decla-
ration of Rights for Indigenous
Peoples (UNDRIP)
UNESCO World Heritage sites, 14.
See also specific sites
UNGC. *See* United Nations Genocide
Convention (UNGC)
United Indian Nations Repatriation
Committee, 173
United Nations Declaration of Rights
for Indigenous Peoples (UNDRIP),
163, 167n6
United Nations Genocide Conven-
tion (UNGC), 162–63, 165, 166,
167n5

United States Geological Survey, 102
*United States v. Sioux Nation of Indi-
ans,* 127
United States v. Washington. See Boldt
decision
United States v. Wheeler, 113, 114
University of California–Riverside,
254, 257
University of Mississippi, 24, 26–27
University of Wisconsin–Milwaukee,
298, 299, 303–4
urban associations, 265–66
US Civil War, 4, 86
US Constitution, 113, 114, 131–32
US Supreme Court, 56, 124, 132. *See
also* laws and legal decisions;
specific cases
US v. Billie, 128
US v. Michigan, 140

Vanderlyn, John, 68
Vann, James, 262
Vann (Cherokee chief), 17
violence, structural, 33–36, 242
Violence Against Women Act, 125
virgin soil thesis. *See* demographic
collapse
Visualizing Sovereignty exhibit, 301
Voigt decision, 140–41

Wabanaki people, 300
Waccamaw people, 194, 265
Wahunsenecawh (Powhatan). *See*
Powhatan
Walleye War, 130, 140–41
Wanchese, 283n9
warfare: activities for classrooms
and, 61–62, 70–71, 278–80; asymmetrical, 63, 65, 74n4; bow and
arrow and, 15; buffer zones
between territories and, 150;
climate change and, 32; colonial,

64–66; genocide and, 60, 164–65, 242; germ warfare and, 162; guerilla tactics and, 63, 70; Indigenous versus European norms and, 63, 64, 65; "just wars" and, 49; land use changes and, 152, 153; Native victories and, 62–63; policy shifts and, 73; refugee migration and, 35; removal policies and, 87; savagery and, 60, 68, 116; shatter zone and, 16–17; slavery and the slave trade and, 33–34, 64; in typical classroom presentations, 65; as violent political confrontation, 75n17. *See also specific conflicts*
War Jack, LaNada, 6
War of 1812, 71
Washington, George, 69, 70, 73, 134
Washita Massacre, 62
Waterbuster (film), 89
water rights, 4–5
wealth and income: activities for classrooms and, 106–7; allotment and, 102, 106–7; colonial capital cataclysms and, 300–301, 302; cost of education and, 312; economic development and, 299–300; food and foodways and, 215, 221; US government policy and, 159
Webster, Daniel, 118
Wendat people, 148, 150. *See also* Huron people; Wyandot people
Westo people, 33, 53
westward expansion, 29–71, 75n14. *See also* manifest destiny
White, Joe (Giishkitawag), 138
White, Richard, 149

White Bull, 61
White Pine Treaty, 135
Wildcat, Daniel R., 253
Williams, Eunice, 61
Winnebago people, 7. *See also* Ho-Chunk people
Winnemem Wintu people, 209
Winterville Mounds (Mississippi), 16
Wirt, William, 118
Wisconsin Indian Educators Association, 298, 304
Wisconsin v. Gurnoe, 138–39
Wiseman, Maury, 29–30, 40
Wolfe, Patrick, 249
Wooden Leg, 61, 279
Wool, John, 165
Woolford, Andrew, 164
Worcester, Samuel, 78
Worcester v. Georgia, 78, 82, 132
Works Progress Administration (WPA), 24
World War II, 4
Wounded Knee, 4, 62, 70, 161, 208, 279–80, 301
WPA. *See* Works Progress Administration (WPA)
Wyandot people, 86. *See also* Huron people; Wendat people

Yakima War, 71
Yamasee people, 53
Yang, K. Wayne, 235–36, 250
Yellowstone National Park, 88
Yosemite National Park, 88

Zuni people, 229

The Harvey Goldberg Series
for Understanding and Teaching History

Understanding and Teaching the Modern Middle East
Edited by Omnia El Shakry

Understanding and Teaching the Holocaust
Edited by Laura J. Hilton and Avinoam Patt

Understanding and Teaching American Slavery
Edited by Bethany Jay and Cynthia Lynn Lyerly

Understanding and Teaching the Civil Rights Movement
Edited by Hasan Kwame Jeffries

Understanding and Teaching the Age of Revolutions
Edited by Ben Marsh and Mike Rapport

Understanding and Teaching the Cold War
Edited by Matthew Masur

Understanding and Teaching Native American History
Edited by Kristofer Ray and Brady DeSanti

*Understanding and Teaching U.S. Lesbian, Gay, Bisexual,
and Transgender History, second edition*
Edited by Leila J. Rupp and Susan K. Freeman

Understanding and Teaching the Vietnam War
Edited by John Day Tully, Matthew Masur, and Brad Austin